Wellbeing in Developing Countries

In a world where many experience unprecedented levels of wellbeing, chronic poverty remains a major concern for many developing countries and the international community. Conventional frameworks for understanding development and poverty have focused on money, commodities and economic growth. This book challenges these conventional approaches and contributes to a new paradigm for development centred on human wellbeing. Poor people are not defined solely by their poverty, and a wellbeing approach provides a better means of understanding how people become and stay poor. It examines three perspectives: ideas of human functioning, capabilities and needs; the analysis of livelihoods and resource use; and research on subjective wellbeing and happiness. A range of international experts from the fields of psychology, economics, anthropology, sociology, political science and development evaluate the state of the art in understanding wellbeing from these perspectives. This book establishes a new strategy and methodology for researching wellbeing that can influence policy.

IAN GOUGH is Professor of Social Policy and Deputy Director of the ESRC Research Group on Wellbeing in Developing Countries at the University of Bath. He is the co-author of *Insecurity and Welfare Regimes in Asia, Africa and Latin America* (Cambridge, 2004) and *A Theory of Human Need* (1991) which was the winner of both the Deutscher and the Myrdal Prize.

ALLISTER MCGREGOR is an economic anthropologist and lectures in development policy analysis at the University of Bath. He is Director of the ESRC Research Group on Wellbeing in Developing Countries and is the author of numerous articles on development policy and practice. He has worked with a wide range of international development agencies and has extensive primary fieldwork experience in South and Southeast Asia.

Wellbeing in Developing Countries

From Theory to Research

Edited by

Ian Gough and J. Allister McGregor

CAMBRIDGE
UNIVERSITY PRESS

CAMBRIDGE UNIVERSITY PRESS
Cambridge, New York, Melbourne, Madrid, Cape Town, Singapore, São Paulo

Cambridge University Press
The Edinburgh Building, Cambridge CB2 8RU, UK

Published in the United States of America by Cambridge University Press,
New York

www.cambridge.org
Information on this title: www.cambridge.org/9780521857512

First published 2007

Printed in the United Kingdom at the University Press, Cambridge

A catalogue record for this book is available from the British Library

Library of Congress Cataloguing in Publication data

Wellbeing in developing countries: from theory to research/edited by Ian Gough
and J. Allister McGregor. – 1st ed.
p.   cm.
Includes bibliographical references and index.

ISBN 978-0-521-85751-2 (hardback)

1. Basic needs–Developing countries.   2. Well-being.   3. Quality of
life–Developing countries.   4. Quality of life–Research.   I. Gough, Ian.
II. McGregor, J. Allister.   III. Title: Wellbeing in developing countries.
IV. Title.

HC59.72.B38W45 2006
306.09172´4–dc22   2006032430

ISBN 978-0-521-85751-2 hardback

Allister McGregor would like to acknowledge the contribution that Louise, Eoin, Ailsa and Jamie make to his wellbeing.

Ian Gough would like to acknowledge the contribution to his wellbeing of Amy, George, Oliver, Ted, Esther and William.

Contents

Figures   *page ix*
Tables   *x*
Notes on contributors   *xii*
Acronyms   *xviii*
Preface   *xxi*

Introduction   1

1 Theorising wellbeing in international development
   IAN GOUGH, J. ALLISTER MCGREGOR AND
   LAURA CAMFIELD   3

Part I Human needs and human wellbeing   45

2 Conceptualising human needs and wellbeing
   DES GASPER   47

3 Basic psychological needs: a self-determination theory
   perspective on the promotion of wellness across
   development and cultures
   RICHARD M. RYAN AND AISLINN R. SAPP   71

4 Measuring freedoms alongside wellbeing
   SABINA ALKIRE   93

5 Using security to indicate wellbeing
   GEOF WOOD   109

6 Towards a measure of non-economic wellbeing
   achievement
   MARK MCGILLIVRAY   133

Part II Resources, agency and meaning   155

7   Wellbeing, livelihoods and resources in social practice
    SARAH WHITE AND MARK ELLISON   157

8   Livelihoods and resource accessing in the Andes:
    desencuentros in theory and practice
    ANTHONY BEBBINGTON, LEONITH HINOJOSA-VALENCIA,
    DIEGO MUÑOZ AND RAFAEL ENRIQUE ROJAS LIZARAZÚ   176

9   Poverty and exclusion, resources and relationships:
    theorising the links between economic and social
    development
    JAMES COPESTAKE   199

Part III Quality of life and subjective wellbeing   217

10 Cross-cultural quality of life assessment approaches
    and experiences from the health care field
    SILKE SCHMIDT AND MONIKA BULLINGER   219

11 Researching quality of life in a developing country:
    lessons from the South African case
    VALERIE MØLLER   242

12 The complexity of wellbeing: a life-satisfaction conception
    and a domains-of-life approach
    MARIANO ROJAS   259

Conclusion: researching wellbeing   281

13 Researching wellbeing across the disciplines: some key
    intellectual problems and ways forward
    PHILIPPA BEVAN   283

14 Researching wellbeing: from concepts to methodology
    J. ALLISTER MCGREGOR   316

References   351
Index   387

Figures

2.1   Venn diagram of the three modal usages of 'needs'   65

6.1   Scatter plot of wellbeing index and income per capita   138

8.1   A livelihoods framework. From Bebbington 2004a.
Reproduced by permission of Edward Arnold   181

8.2   Map of Peru and Bolivia   184

9.1   The Figueroa *sigma* model   202

9.2   A reflexive framework for appraisal of development
interventions   214

10.1   Results of measuring the same structure for eight items
of the EUROHIS-QoL eight-item index with one latent
variable QoL, overall and for each country in the
EUROHIS study ($n = 4$, 849)   236

10.2   Structural model of WHOQoL-old (the WHOQoL
adaptation for older adults) and universal fit statistics   237

11.1   South African Quality of Life Trends: percentages of
South Africans happy, satisfied with life, and seeing life as
getting better or worse   247

11.2   South African Quality of Life Trends: percentages
satisfied with life-as-a-whole   248

14.1   A wellbeing framework   337

Tables

2.1 A modal analysis of the five types of 'need'   56
2.2 A comparison of the modes employed in definitions of need   56
2.3 The scope for confusion in usage of 'subjective/objective wellbeing'   60
2.4 Relating concepts of wellbeing to the stages in Sen's enriched narrative of consumer choice, consumption and functioning   62
5.1 Linkage between regime type and forms of security/insecurity   114
5.2 Autonomy and security trade-off   116
6.1 Zero-order (Pearson) correlation coefficients between commonly used wellbeing indicators ($n = 173$)   137
6.2 Rank-order (Spearman) correlation coefficients between commonly used wellbeing indicators ($n = 173$)   137
6.3 Correlation coefficients between wellbeing indicators   138
6.4 Correlations between μ_i and wellbeing indicators   139
6.5 Wellbeing data: selected countries   140
6.6 Correlation coefficients between estimates of μ_i and wellbeing indicators   143
6A.1 Principal components analysis results   149
9.1 Stakeholder analysis of options for reducing economic exclusion   204
10.1 Types of equivalence tested in publication reviewed and adapted from Bowden and Fox-Rushby (2003) across nine measures of QoL (in %)   232
12.1 Life satisfaction and satisfaction in domains of life: descriptive statistics   268
12.2 Life satisfaction and domains of life satisfaction: CES specification   270
12.3 Differences in satisfaction across gender: mean values   272
12.4 Differences in satisfaction across age groups: mean values   273

12.5   Differences in satisfaction across education groups:
       mean values   274
12.6   Differences in satisfaction across income group: mean
       values   275
12.7   Satisfaction in domains of life and socioeconomic and
       demographic variables – linear specification: regression
       analysis   277
13.1   An ideal-type depiction of some of the research models
       with which the WeD team is negotiating   294

Notes on contributors

SABINA ALKIRE   is an economist interested in the ongoing development of the capability approach initiated by Amartya Sen. Her
publications include *Valuing Freedoms: Sen's Capability Approach and
Poverty Reduction*, as well as articles in philosophy and economics.
Research interests include value judgements in economic decision-
making, the conceptualisation and measurement of individual
agency freedoms (empowerment) particularly in South Asia, and
further development of the capability approach by the academic,
policy and activist communities. Previously she has worked for the
Commission on Human Security, coordinated the culture–poverty
learning and research initiative at the World Bank, and developed
participatory impact assessment methodologies with Oxfam and the
Asia Foundation in Pakistan. She has a DPhil. in Economics, an
MSc in Economics for Development and an MPhil. in Christian
political ethics from Magdalen College, Oxford, and is currently a
Research Associate at the Global Equity Initiative, Harvard
University.

ANTHONY BEBBINGTON   is Professor of Nature, Society and Development in the Institute of Development Policy and Management at
the University of Manchester. A geographer by training, he was
previously Associate Professor at the University of Colorado at
Boulder and has worked at the World Bank, International Institute
for Environment and Development, Overseas Development Institute and University of Cambridge. His work in Latin America
addresses: the relationships among civil society, livelihoods and
development; social movements, NGOs and rural development;
and extractive industries and environmental movements. Books
include *Los Actores de Una Decada Ganada* (Quito: Abya Yala,
1992, with G. Ramon and others), *EI Capital Social en los Andes*
(Quito: Abya Yala, 2001, with V.H. Torres), *NGOs and the State in
Latin America* (London and New York: Routledge, 1993, with

G. Thiele) and *The Search for Empowerment: Social Capital as Idea and Practice at the World Bank* (West Hartford: Kumarian, 2006, with M. Woolcock and others).

PHILIPPA BEVAN   is a researcher in the sociology of development who, until recently, was a member of the ESRC research group Wellbeing in Developing Countries (WeD) based at the University of Bath. Her main role was as Country Coordinator of the Ethiopia WeD programme and she is a co-author of a forthcoming WeD country study of the social and cultural construction of quality of life in Ethiopia. In her research activities she uses relevant theoretical and methodological developments in sociology to advance the empirical study of quality of life, social inequality, and social and cultural reproduction and change in poor countries. Recent publications include 'Conceptualising in/security regimes' and 'The dynamics of Africa's in/security regimes', chapters 3 and 6 in *Insecurity and Welfare Regimes in Asia, Africa and Latin America* (I. Gough, G. Wood *et al.*, Cambridge: Cambridge University Press, 2004).

MONIKA BULLINGER   studied Psychology and Sociology at the Universities of Konstanz and Saarbrücken, Germany, as well as Psychology and Anthropology at Yale University USA. After completing her MA and Ph.D. degrees, she took up a scientific assistantship at the Institute for Medical Psychology at Munich University (LMU) in Germany and was an invited Guest Worker at the National Institutes of Health (NIH) Bethesda, USA. She has been involved in Quality of Life research since 1986 and is a former President of the International Society for Quality of Life Research (ISOQoL). She has been Professor of Medical Psychology at Hamburg University Medical School since 1996.

LAURA CAMFIELD   is the Research Officer responsible for Subjective Quality of Life within WeD and also coordinates WeD research in Thailand. Her research interests include: quality of life and subjective wellbeing, specifically how people characterise living well or a 'good life'; qualitative and quantitative methodologies, including creation and use of measures, and participatory research; and chronic illness, disability and HIV/AIDS. She has contributed chapters to a number of volumes, including 'QoL in Developing Nations' in K. C. Land (ed.), *Encyclopedia of Social Indicators and QoL Research, Vol. 3* (New York: Springer Publishing Company, 2006) and 'Subjective measures of well-being for developing countries' in W. Glatzer, S. Von Below and M. Stoffregen (eds.), *Challenges for the Quality of Life in Contemporary Societies* (London: Kluwer Academic, 2004) and co-authored 'Resilience and wellbeing in developing countries' with J. Allister McGregor in M. Ungar (ed.), *Handbook for Working with Children and Youth: Pathways to Resilience across Cultures and Contexts* (Thousand Oaks, CA: Sage Publications, 2005).

JAMES COPESTAKE is a senior lecturer in economics and international development at the University of Bath. His research interests include poverty and wellbeing, agrarian change, microfinance and aid management. He has worked in the UK, Bolivia, Peru, India, Zambia and Malawi.

MARK ELLISON is a former member of the Wellbeing in Developing Countries (WeD) research group at the University of Bath. His interests are in project management and the incorporation of values into 'rational' models. He has run introductory project management training programmes for fieldworkers.

DES GASPER has worked as an Associate Professor at the Institute of Social Studies, The Hague since working in Botswana and Zimbabwe through the 1980s. He is currently also affiliated as Visiting Professor to the University of Bath. His publications include *Arguing Development Policy* with Raymond Apthorpe London: Cass, 1996) and *The Ethics of Development* (Edinburgh: Edinburgh University Press, 2004, and New Delhi: Sage India, 2005).

IAN GOUGH was educated in economics at Cambridge before researching and teaching social policy at Manchester University. During this period he published *The Political Economy of the Welfare State* (London: Macmillan, 1979, translated into six languages, including Chinese, Japanese and Korean) and, with Len Doyal, *A Theory of Human Need* (London: Macmillan, 1991), winner of both the Deutscher and the Myrdal prizes. In 1995 he moved to become Professor of Social Policy at the University of Bath where he is now Deputy Director of the five-year ESRC-funded Research Group on Wellbeing in Developing Countries (WeD). His recent books include *Insecurity and Welfare Regimes in Asia, Africa and Latin America*, co-authored with Geof Wood and other colleagues at Bath. Some of his essays are published in *Global Capital, Human Needs and Social Policies: Selected Essays 1993–99* (Basingstoke: Palgrave, 2002). He is Honorary Editor of the *Journal of European Social Policy*, and a member of the Academy of Social Sciences.

LEONITH HINOJOSA-VALENCIA is a Peruvian researcher and teacher at the Institute of Development Policy and Management at the University of Manchester. She gained a BA and MA in Economics from the Universidad Nacional San Antonio Abad del Cusco and the Université Catholique de Louvain, and a Ph.D from the University of Manchester. Her research interests are local and regional economics and social development, impact assessment, and NGOs. Her current research revolves around market formation and the relationships between institutions and livelihoods in the Andes. She is also involved in consultancy work with development interventions.

MARK MCGILLIVRAY   is a senior Research Fellow at the World Institute for Development Economics Research of the United Nations University in Helsinki, Finland and an Inaugural Fellow of the Human Development and Capabilities Association. His recent publications include the edited volumes *Human Well-being: Concept and Measurement* and *Inequality, Poverty and Well-being*, both published by Palgrave Macmillan.

J. ALLISTER MCGREGOR   is Director of the five-year ESRC-funded Research Group on Wellbeing in Developing Countries (WeD) and a Senior Lecturer in International Development at the University of Bath. He has a disciplinary background in economics and social anthropology and has extensive experience of primary fieldwork in South and Southeast Asia. He has published many journal articles on the development policy and processes in Bangladesh and Thailand, as well as more generally on the role and functioning of development agencies.

VALERIE MØLLER   is professor and director of the Institute for Social and Economic Research, Rhodes University, South Africa. Over the past thirty years she has conducted research on a wide range of South African quality-of-life concerns. She leads the South African Quality of Life Trends Project that produces regular updates on the subjective wellbeing of South Africans.

DIEGO MUÑOZ   studied agricultural engineering at Texas A&M University, and environmental management and planning at the Latin American Environmental Sciences faculty in La Plata, Argentina. He is currently affiliated with DfID in La Paz, Bolivia and works mainly as an advisor and consultant on rural development issues with the Bolivian Government, international organisations that work in Bolivia, and different national and international institutions that have rural development projects in Bolivia and other Andean countries. His previous publications include *Small Farmers, Economic Organizations and Public Policies: A Comparative Study* (IIED, PIEB, DfID and Plural

Editores, 2004) and *Public Policies and Processes in the Bolivian Andes* (IIED, 2001)

MARIANO ROJAS holds a masters degree in economics from the Universidad de Costa Rica and a Ph.D in Economics from Ohio State University, and is based at the Universidad de las Américas, Puebla, Mexico. His main areas of research are Subjective Wellbeing and Quality of Life, and Economic and Political Development.

RAFAEL ENRIQUE ROJAS LIZARAZÚ is an economist based at the Centro de Estudios and Proyectos s.r.l, Bolivia. Engaged in consultancy since 1990, he specialises in the planning and evaluation of rural development projects.

RICHARD M. RYAN is a clinical psychologist who has been on the faculty of the University of Rochester since 1981, and is currently Professor of Psychology, Psychiatry and Education. He is a specialist in adult psychotherapy and human motivation, and he regularly consults with schools, organizations and teams on issues regarding motivation, performance and wellness. With Edward Deci he has been a principal developer of self-determination theory, which is being researched and applied internationally. Ryan has been a visiting scientist at the Max Planck Institute, and an award-winning teacher and researcher. He has also co-authored two books and more than two hundred published articles in the areas of human personality, culture, motivation and wellness.

AISLINN R. SAPP is a graduate student currently working on her doctoral degree at the University of Rochester Department of Clinical and Social Psychology.

SILKE SCHMIDT gained her doctoral degree at the University Hospital of Jean in 2000, and since 2001 has been based at the Institute for Medical Psychology, University of Hamburg, Germany. Her research interests include cross-cultural analyses of health-related quality of life, cross-cultural aspects of determinants of health, and analysing international data on health indicators using analytical epidemiology. She is a WHO collaborator in the EUROHIS project, and previous publications include *The DISABKIDS Handbook* with S. Schmidt, C. Petersen, M. Bullinger, and The DISABKIDS Group (Lengerich: Pabst Scientific Publishers, 2005), and 'Current issues in cross-cultural quality of life instrument development' with M. Bullinger (*Archives of Physical Medicine and Rehabilitation*, 8429–33, 2003).

SARAH WHITE   is a lecturer in sociology and international development and Director of the Centre for Development Studies at the University of Bath. Her research interests include gender, childhood and race; culture, religion and wellbeing; participation, rights and the politics of development intervention. Her main research location is Bangladesh.

GEOF WOOD   is Professor of International Development, and Dean of the Faculty of Humanities and Social Sciences, at the University of Bath. After early fieldwork in Africa he conducted extensive research in North India, Bangladesh and Pakistan over three decades, with additional work in Nepal, Afghanistan, Thailand, Venezuela and Peru. He is involved in policy analysis and action-research with governments, NGOs and international agencies. Previous research themes: rural development and class formation; irrigation; social development and empowerment; microfinance; urban livelihoods; and public institutional performance. He is currently focused upon insecurity, welfare regimes, wellbeing and strategies of de-clientelisation.

Acronyms

ACLO	Acción Cultural Loyola
AEA	American Economic Association
AIDS	Acquired Immune Deficiency Syndrome
AKRSP	Aga Khan Rural Support Programme
APDH	Anatomy / Physiology / Dynamics / History
ASCA	Accumulating Savings and Credit Association
CCAIJO	Centro de Capacitación Agro-Industrial Jesús Obrero (Jesús Obrero centre of agro-industrial training)
CEP	Centro de Estudios y Proyectos (Centre for studies and projects)
CFA	Co-Financing Agency
CIPCA	Centro de Investigación y Promoción del Campesinado (Centre for peasant research and promotion)
CONACYT	Consejo Nacional de Ciencia y Tecnologia (National Council of Science and Technology, Mexico)
COOP	Dartmouth COOP Dartmouth Primary Care Cooperative Information Project
DfID	Department for International Development
DSM	Diagnostic and Statistical Manual of disorders
EGQLHM	European Group for Quality of Life and Health Management
EORTC	European Organization for Research and Treatment of Cancer
ESRC	Economics and Social Research Council
EUROHIS	European Health Interview Survey
EuroQoL	European Quality of Life Project Group
FACT	Functional Assessment of Cancer Treatment
FLIC	Functional Living Index Cancer
FoKF	Foundations of Knowledge Framework
GDI	Gender-related Development Index
GDP	Gross Domestic Product

GEM	Gender Empowerment Measure
GHQ	General Health Questionnaire
GNP	Gross National Product
HDI	Human Development Index
HIV	Human Immunodeficiency Virus
HPI	Human Poverty Index
HRQoL	Health Related Quality of Life
HD	Human Development
HS	Human Security
HUI	Health Utilities Index
IAA-Canas	Instituto de Apoyo Agrario Canas (Canas Institute for agricultural support)
ICD	International Classification of Diseases
ICF	International Classification of Functioning
IDPM	Institute for Development Policy and Management
IFI	International Finance Institutions
IIED	International Institute for Environment and Development
ILO	International Labour Organization
IPTK	Instituto Politécnico Tomás Katari (Tomás Katari Polytechnic Institute)
IQMSC	Integrated Questionnaire for the Measurement of Social Capital
IQOLA	International Quality of Life Assessment Project Group
ISOQOL	International Society for Quality of Life Research
ISQOLS	International Society for Quality of Life Studies
LSMS	Living Standard Measurement Survey
MDG	Millennium Development Goals
NGO	non-governmental organisation
NHP	Nottingham Health Profile
OLS	Ordinary Least Squares
OWB	Objective Wellbeing
PIEB	Programa de Investigación Estratégica en Bolivia (Programme of Strategic Research in Bolivia)
PPA	Participatory Poverty Assessment
PPP	Purchasing Power Parity
PQLI	Physical Quality of Life Index
PRA	Participatory Rural Appraisal
PRSP	Poverty Reduction Strategy Paper
Qhana	Qhana Centro de Educación Popular (Qhana centre of popular education)
QoL	Quality of Life

QWB	Quality of Well-Being Scale
RAE	Research Assessment Exercise
RANQ	Resources And Needs Questionnaire
RDP	Reconstruction and Development Programme
ROSCA	Rotating Savings and Credit Association
RPF	Resource Profiles Framework
RRA	Rapid Rural Appraisal
SDT	Self-Determination Theory
SEIQOL	Schedule for the Evaluation of Individual Quality of Life
SIP	Sickness Impact Profile
StatsSA	Statistics South Africa
SWB	Subjective Wellbeing
THN	Theory of Human Need
UK	United Kingdom
UN	United Nations
UNDP	United Nations Development Programme
US	United States
VMPPFM	Vice Ministry for Citizen Participation and Municipal Strengthening (Bolivia)
WB	Wellbeing
WeD	Wellbeing in Developing Countries research group
WHO	World Health Organization
WHOQOL	World Health Organization Quality of Life Group
WONCA	World Organization of National Colleges, Academies, and Academic Associations of General Practices/Family Physicians

Preface

Wellbeing is a term much in vogue. It is to be found in many diverse places: from the lifestyle pages of newspaper supplements; to health food and spiritual healing shops; to government policy documents. For some it is a broad and attractive term, for others it is messy, imprecise and conceptually dangerous. The arguments contained in this book suggest that 'love it or hate it' the social sciences globally must confront the challenges it poses. Wellbeing is now commonly used by governments and politicians in developed countries as the policy documents and legislation of the UK, Europe and North America indicate. In England, the Local Government Act of 2000 charges local authorities with the responsibility of 'promoting well-being', while in Scotland the Local Government Act of 2003 grants local authorities new power to 'advance well-being'. The term features less commonly in our thinking and policy in relation to developing countries. For some it may appear that wellbeing is a luxury that developing countries, and particularly the poor men, women and children who live in them, could do without. We argue not.

Experiences of living and working with people in a wide range of developing countries tell us that they have as vivid and valid notions of wellbeing as do people in wealthier countries, where it appears more possible to buy one's way to wellbeing. The things that bring different people wellbeing in many different societies around the globe can take many shapes and forms, but many of them are familiar across a wide range of quite different cultures: the love of friends and family, of music and verse, of dancing, of food, of a good joke. The list could go on.

Our challenge, however, is to reconcile this everyday observation with a professional concern for understanding why poverty persists and for the design of policies to eradicate it. In this respect it was felicitous that our attention was drawn to a call from the UK Economic and Social Research Council for research into 'poverty, inequality and quality of life in developing countries'. These themes had been the focus of work by members of the Centre for Development Studies at Bath for a number of years. They had also been the topic of discussion in a forum of debate between colleagues from different research traditions and disciplines. It was this cross-disciplinary exchange which provided the basis for the proposal to the ESRC for the establishment of the 'Wellbeing in Developing Countries' (WeD) Research Group at the University of Bath. The Group was granted funding to run for a five-year period from 2002 to 2007. This is the first volume output of the WeD group and the members of the group would like particularly to acknowledge not only the generous funding that the ESRC has provided but also their enthusiasm and support for the work of the group.

WeD seeks to develop a more holistic vision of wellbeing to inform our understanding of social change and international development. The principal goal of WeD is *to develop a conceptual and methodological framework for understanding the social and cultural construction of wellbeing in developing countries*. While stated primarily in academic and conceptual terms, the intention is for the research to be policy relevant and for it to highlight the practical value of the knowledge that such a framework and methodology can produce. To do this WeD is applying this framework in detailed empirical studies of twenty-six communities in four developing countries: Bangladesh, Ethiopia, Peru and Thailand.

The programme of work has been divided broadly into three stages: conceptual and methodological development, fieldwork, and analysis. This volume reports on the first of these phases. It is about conceptualising development through the novel lens of human wellbeing and about proposing new research agendas to study it, improve our understanding and guide policy. Its aims are to synthesise perspectives from the key social science disciplines and also to bring notions from diverse and non-development literatures into engagement with viewpoints and experiences from developing countries.

This volume took shape at an international workshop held at the Hanse Wissenschaftskolleg in Delmenhorst, near Bremen, Germany, in July 2004. There members of the WeD research team from Bath and the four research countries were joined by international experts from all continents except Australasia. The three days of lively exchanges were crucial in exposing our emerging ideas to a jury of peers, and in learning about state-of-the-art developments across a range of disciplines. This book reflects that origin in combining chapters by WeD members and outside scholars. We are grateful to the Hanse Institute for generously hosting and co-funding the workshop. We would like to thank those participants at the Hanse workshop who contributed to discussion but who are not authors here. Thanks to: Zulfiqar Ali, Teo Altimirano, Ashebir Desalegn, Joe Devine, Marion Glaser, Wolfgang Glatzer,

Charles Gore, Monica Guillen-Royo, Dennis Huschka, Awac Masae, Andy McKay, Fara Mee-Udon, Heinz-Herbert Noll, Alula Pankhurst, Becky Schaaf, Hetan Shah, Virginia Williamson and Katie Wright. Particular thanks go to Des Gasper not only for his valuable contributions to the workshop, but also for his detailed and helpful comments on subsequent chapter drafts.

Not all members of the WeD research team were present at the Hanse meeting and we recognise the contributions that both past and present members of the team have made to the development of ideas within the group. Occasional visitors to WeD have also provided stimulus and provoked discussion, so thanks are due to Raymond Apthorpe, Janet Billson, Hartley Dean, Danny Ruta, Nasrin Sultana, Feleke Tadele and Solomon Tesfaye for their visits during the first two years of WeD. In Bath, the WeD administrative support team of Jane French, Diana Duckling, Mark Ellison and Becky Lockley all made valuable contributions to the success of the Hanse meeting. In producing this volume Tom Lavers and latterly Emer Brangan have expertly marshalled the drafts, converted them into a unified text and guided the whole volume through to publication. We are immensely grateful to them for their dedicated work.

Lastly, we reserve special thanks for two groups: the WeD field research teams in all four study countries who have worked hard to meaningfully ground the research methodology that we discuss here; and also the people of the communities in which the research has been carried out. Despite the challenges of their own daily lives they have engaged patiently with our time-consuming schedule of enquiries.

Every effort has been made to trace the copyright holders for permission to reproduce the extract from *The Chosen Place, The Timeless People* by Paule Marshall but we would be pleased to make the necessary acknowledgements at the first opportunity.

Introduction

1 Theorising wellbeing in international development

Ian Gough, J. Allister McGregor and Laura Camfield

1.1 Development and wellbeing

At first sight it appears incongruous to discuss wellbeing in relation to developing countries. Most often, and properly, our attention and concern is for the many people who experience suffering as a consequence of their poverty. However, there are a number of reasons why it is important to confront this apparent incongruity. The first is to acknowledge the fully rounded humanity of poor men, women and children in developing countries; recognising that they are not completely defined by their poverty, nor can they be fully understood in its terms alone. Poor people in developing countries strive to achieve wellbeing for themselves and their children. For the poorest, and in the worst instances, this will largely be a struggle to limit the extent of their illbeing and suffering. But even alongside deprivations, poor men, women and children are able to achieve some elements of what they conceive of as wellbeing, as Biswas-Diener and Diener (2001) demonstrate; without this, we would argue, their lives would be unbearable. Furthermore, it is striking that the non-poor in developing countries can often experience what appear to be high levels of life satisfaction. Wellbeing is far from an irrelevant concept in the study of international development.

From this perspective the notion of poverty (or rather poverties) has a number of limitations and the literature around it is becoming increasingly complex and to some extent muddled. There are discussions and debates over many different types of poverty; from consumption to income poverty; to poverty defined in terms of the human development index or by social exclusion. Poverty can be relative or it can be absolute. The argument that will be advanced in this volume is that 'wellbeing' (including its inevitable obverse of illbeing) is a wider concept that can usefully encompass and connect these debates over different types of poverty. The volume does not argue that we abandon concepts of poverty; they all have their different analytical and policy uses, but that we locate them in a wider discourse about wellbeing.

Current efforts to champion notions of multidimensional poverty reflect wider shifts in thinking about international development. Over time the global community has in effect been moving towards conceiving 'development' as the organised pursuit of human wellbeing. This has involved broadening the notion of development from a narrow economic conception, to encompass human development and wider ideals such as participation and freedom. At its broadest and most utopian, the objective of international development could be described as the creation of conditions where all people in the world are able to achieve wellbeing. Thus the purpose of development policies and the *raison d'être* of governments and the agencies that generate and implement the specific policies and programmes, is to work to establish those preconditions in different societies. The Millennium Goals Declaration can be seen as motivated by a minimal version of such a radical goal.

Of course, this all begs the question: what do we mean by wellbeing? The older English term 'welfare' can be traced back to at least the fourteenth century, when it meant to journey well and could indicate both happiness and prosperity (Williams 1983). In the twentieth century it gradually came to be associated with the assessment of and provision for needs in the welfare state, and acquired an increasingly objective, external interpretation. But in the latter decades of the century new discourses on agency, participation, and multidimensional views of poverty paved the way for a reinvention of the older notion of wellbeing, which can be traced back to Aristotle and the Buddha. Perhaps unsurprisingly, the nature of wellbeing is by no means agreed. The new edition of the usually concise and parsimonious *Oxford Companion to Philosophy* (Honderich 2005) has difficulty in defining its meaning: 'Variously interpreted as "living and faring well" or "flourishing", the notion of wellbeing is intricately bound up with our ideas about what constitutes human happiness and the sort of life it is good to lead'.

This suggests that wellbeing is an umbrella concept, embracing at least 'objective wellbeing' and 'subjective wellbeing' (SWB), although as we shall see later in the volume this very distinction is contentious and potentially problematic. Gasper in Chapter 2 defines the former as 'externally approved, and thereby normatively endorsed, non-feeling features of a person's life, matters such as mobility or morbidity'; and

SWB as 'feelings of the person whose wellbeing is being estimated'. He goes on to make finer distinctions between seven categories and eleven subcategories of wellbeing, including 'wellbeing as activity' (Bruton 1997). The conclusion of his and our mapping work is to accept plurality; wellbeing is still a novel category in applied social science, such that no settled consensus on its meaning has yet emerged.[1] It is, however, a useful term, beneath which a variety of related ideas and concepts can shelter.

We will argue here for a conception of wellbeing that takes account of the objective circumstances of the person and their subjective evaluation of these. But both the objective circumstances and perceptions of them are located in society and also in the frames of meaning with which we live. Thus wellbeing is also and necessarily both a relational and a dynamic concept. States of wellbeing/illbeing are continually produced in the interplay within the social, political, economic and cultural processes of human social being. It cannot be conceived just as an outcome, but must be understood also as a process.

Across the social science disciplines there are many diverse contributions to contemporary debates over wellbeing. At the same time the term has a potentially important communicative function to play for both the social sciences and for policy discourses. The intention of this book is to provide a space for some of this interdisciplinary debate about what we mean by wellbeing and what its relevance is for both academic study and policy.

Inasmuch as it evokes competing visions about what it might mean to live well, wellbeing must be considered in relation to wider conceptions of *development* as 'good change' (cf. Chambers 1997). But understandings of and prescriptions for development depend on and change with dominant conceptions of wellbeing. The dominant conception in the modern, post-war development era has been an economic one – wellbeing comprises the material resources people control and can utilise and dispose of, measured by income and at aggregate levels by national income per head. But as we have indicated, over the last two decades this has been challenged at the level of conceptual argument and, equally important, measures and indicators. This book is structured around three particular challenges and seeks to relate them to each other and build from them.

---

[1] Amartya Sen uses 'wellbeing' in a distinct way to refer to 'a person's being seen from the perspective of her own personal welfare', as contrasted with 'agency goals', which can include other goals such as pursuing the welfare of others (Sen 1993: 35–6). This usage does not appear to be a common one and we shall not follow it here.

From money poverty to human development

First, the idea of development has been extended from economic to human development. This has long been a theme of heterodox writers, critics and activists from Gandhi through Dudley Seers, ul Haq and others, but undoubtedly it was the welfare economist and Nobel prize-winner Amartya Sen who played a notable role in placing such ideas on the global agenda in the last quarter of the last century. Sen disputed that command over commodities or income could provide an adequate space within which to assess wellbeing or poverty. This was to confuse a means with more basic ends, and to grasp the latter, new concepts were required. Sen initially identified the ends of human life as human capabilities and functionings – what people are notionally able to do and to be, and what they have actually been able to do and to be. At the most general level we should thus evaluate the extent of people's freedom to live the kind of life which they have reason to value (see Robeyns 2005 for a clear introduction to his approach).

The philosopher Martha Nussbaum (2000) has taken the idea further to embrace numerous non-economic aspects of life such as the expression of imagination and emotions, affiliation and play. In 1991, Doyal and Gough contributed an alternative theory of basic human needs and identified health and autonomy as universal prerequisites for wellbeing, whatever is our more substantive notion of wellbeing. Both they and Nussbaum espouse a universal list of basic needs/capabilities, which is open to variable expression in different contexts. The last decade of the last century saw a renewed interest in these ideas. Since 1990, the annual Human Development Reports have monitored international progress in meeting a range of basic needs and extending basic capabilities. In 2004 the new international Human Development and Capability Association was formed to foster this perspective.

From money poverty to resources and agency

Second, the 1990s saw the emergence of a range of different 'livelihoods frameworks' (Rakodi 1999). These took account of the ways people make use of a wider range of 'assets' and strategies than had previously been absorbed in formal micro-economic models. The frameworks had some common points of departure, in particular Sen's publications in the early 1980s on entitlement, and work on vulnerability by a range of authors, and championed by Chambers. Sen's interpretation of modern famines as due to the decline of entitlements with which people acquire food stimulated a broader notion of vulnerability (Sen 1981a). This broader framework encompasses not just economic, but social and political vulnerability and prompts a richer analysis of the resources people utilise to mitigate their vulnerability. These extend beyond monetised commodities and certain public services to include human capital, natural capital and later on social capital.

Placing greater emphasis on the social and cultural dimensions of the exercise of agency in the struggle for livelihoods, researchers at the University of Bath developed the Resource Profiles Framework (RPF) to generate a bottom-up perspective for comprehending what different people actually do in the round of their lives, in order to secure not only a livelihood, but also a meaningful and bearable form of life for themselves. This differed by using the concept of resources rather than capitals or assets, where resources are understood as socially and culturally negotiable.[2] Anticipating the discussions of wellbeing here, the resource profiles framework recognised that a far wider range of things, such as relationships (including adverse relationships like clientelism) and cultural status, can be both means and ends. It also provides a more realistic framework for handling people's reactions to rapid change in today's world. It can be argued that the present globalising world differs from earlier stages of modernisation in the sheer rate and complexity of change that it presents – and most notably for poor countries and peoples. This presents a challenge to development thinking, and highlights the need for approaches that will help us comprehend how different people cope with rapid change – change which often goes to the core of their very identity (Lawson, McGregor and Saltmarshe 2000).

From money poverty to subjective wellbeing and quality of life

The third, more recently ascendant challenge has returned to the individual subject, to question substantially the ends of development and how we conceive and measure them. The related ideas of 'Subjective Wellbeing', 'Life Satisfaction', 'Quality of Life' and 'Happiness' have brought subjective evaluations centre-stage and propose to measure these directly rather than via proxies such as resources or human development. This perspective has been developed in different disciplinary bases, notably health services research into health-related quality of life, the psychology of hedonic balance and life satisfaction, and the economics of happiness. By the start of the millennium some of these strands were fusing and cross-fertilising in interdisciplinary arenas such as the International Society for Quality of Life Studies (ISQOLS)

---

[2] Five categories of resources are identified – material, human, social, cultural and natural (or environmental).

and the *Journal of Happiness Studies*. Though the vast bulk of such work has been disconnected from development issues, there is a close but as yet little explored affinity between this research and the literature on participation in development. The merger between these streams is forming the third fundamental challenge to narrow economism in thinking about wellbeing and development.

This book is the first to set out, discuss and relate all three of these critical approaches to conceptualising and explaining wellbeing in developing countries. Initiated by the ESRC research group on Wellbeing in Developing Countries (WeD) at the University of Bath it provides an overview of its first phase in which concepts, theories and methodologies for the study of wellbeing were reviewed. The volume builds on a small international workshop held at the Hanse Wissenschaftskolleg in Germany, where we were privileged to hear leading researchers report on and evaluate the state of the art in understanding wellbeing from different disciplinary perspectives. The book brings together papers by key contributors to the three movements described above alongside contributions from WeD researchers. It is organised around the three themes of Human Needs, Resources, and Quality of Life. In each section there are papers whose primary focus is conceptual and others where it is methodological, though the dividing line is a rough-and-ready one.

An important feature of the WeD research and of this volume is its interdisciplinary range. The following chapters come from anthropology, economics, political theory, psychology and sociology. Moreover, the disciplines do not reside in separate compartments. Thus we find psychologists writing on basic needs (Ryan and Sapp), sociologists writing about resources (White and Ellison) and an economist writing on subjective life satisfaction (Rojas). The book is built on the premise that cross-disciplinary communication and understanding is necessary to conceptualise human wellbeing; to research it; and to debate the policy implications of it.

In the remainder of this chapter we review the three bodies of literature which were the starting points for this study of wellbeing, explain the rationale for the structure of the book and preview the contributing chapters. In the final chapter of the book we reflect on the points of convergence and the challenges that confront a wellbeing research agenda and outline the methodology developed for the WeD empirical research programme. This methodology provides further insight into the ways that the three organising themes of needs, resources and quality of life cohere in a unified research programme on human wellbeing.

1.2   Human needs and capabilities

The concept of human needs has long been a cornerstone of development thinking. The idea that there is a core set of basic needs which must be satisfied if we are to consider development to have taken place stretches back to colonial government policy. It has long underpinned national strategies for development in major developing countries such as China and India. But the idea did not gain notable momentum in international development policy until 1976, when the International Labour Organization adopted a Declaration of Principles and Programme of Action for a Basic Needs Strategy of Development and in 1978 when the World Bank initiated work on basic needs. These initiatives marked some of the first global institutional responses to the inadequacies of Gross Domestic Product (GDP) and economic growth as measures of either development or human welfare. As a measure of development GDP is limited because of the restricted conception of resources which it uses. As a measure of welfare the problems of per capita GDP are legion: it takes no account of the composition of output between need satisfiers and luxuries (nor between those elements of consumption which are 'good' or 'bad'); nor of the distribution of welfare between groups and within families; nor of the direct impact of production on human wellbeing; nor of the side-effects of production on the environment and the biosphere and hence of the sustainability of future production and welfare. A critical and imaginative response to these omissions was long overdue. Yet by the mid 1980s the basic needs movement was starting to founder.[3] Why?

At one level it fell victim to the resurgent neoliberal wave that had been building through the post-war years and gained ascendancy in the early 1980s. The ability of states to define authoritatively what it was that people needed was heavily questioned; needs were only legitimately expressed as the preferences of individuals in markets. But it was also criticised from very different ideological perspectives. Critics from developing countries regarded the basic needs idea with suspicion, seeing it as a further example of post-imperial patronisation and cultural imperialism. Illich (1992: 88) wrote: ' "Basic needs" may be the most insidious legacy left behind by development' (quoted by Gasper 2004: 153). Others saw the needs agenda as a means of blunting their demand

---

[3] This is not to deny the range and quality of writings on the topic that appeared in the 1980s; both conceptual, including Braybrooke (1987), the important collection edited by Lederer (1980), Plant *et al.* (1980), Springborg (1981); and those relating needs to development, including Max-Neef (1989), Stewart (1985), Streeten (1984), and Wisner (1988). Furthermore many countries and NGOs continued to inhabit and develop the needs discourse; but it disappeared for a time as a global discourse.

for a New International Economic Order. The *dependista* thinking which was prominent at the time instead stressed structural considerations and the prior necessity for developing countries to reduce their economic dependence on the West.

The basic needs thinking of the time appeared particularly vulnerable to two sets of critiques from quite different sources: from economists' criticisms of needs as opposed to wants met through markets, and from growing post-modern currents critiquing its so-called arbitrary postulates about human nature from a relativist perspective (Doyal and Gough 1991: chs 1, 8). In sum, as Des Gasper writes in Chapter 2, the fall of basic needs theory reflected its lack of conceptual depth, technical refinement, and an appealing political language suited to its time.

Now basic human needs are back on the political map. The UN Summit on Social Development in Copenhagen in 1995 agreed on a set of targets for tackling world poverty over the next twenty years, and five years later the Millennium Declaration was adopted by the General Assembly of the United Nations in September 2000. The accompanying Millennium Development Goals (MDGs) go on to set targets and identify indicators for many basic needs, for example survival (e.g. infant mortality), health (e.g. prevalence of HIV/AIDS and malaria), hunger, access to safe water, and education (literacy and primary school enrolment).

The revitalisation of the basic needs movement at this time requires some explanation. Perhaps most obvious is the accumulating evidence on the persistence of extreme poverty among many people around the world. Despite years of experimenting and spending on development programmes, the stark reality is that in many countries, and especially those in Sub-Saharan Africa, there has been at best modest growth coupled with increasing poverty. In some other countries whose economies have enjoyed growth the impact on poverty has been disappointing. At another level, the end of communism and the Cold War has ushered in a quite novel form of global order, one where new inequalities threaten the stability of capitalism yet without the alternative vision provided by state socialism. In these circumstances ideological opposition to basic needs and social rights becomes otiose or even counter-productive.

A final explanation for the rebirth of interest in basic needs has been new conceptual thinking, most influentially in the work of Amartya Sen. In a series of publications and lectures (beginning with the *Tanner Lectures* at Stanford University (1979b)), Sen has presented the case for viewing wellbeing, alongside poverty and suffering, in terms of human functionings and capabilities. This approach breaks with traditional economics, which typically conflates wellbeing with either utility (happiness, satisfaction, desire fulfilment) or with resources (income, wealth, commodity command). In effect, he inserts a chain of new concepts to bridge the gap between these two poles as follows:

Commodities $\rightarrow$ *Commodity Characteristics* $\rightarrow$ *Capability to Function* $\rightarrow$ *Functioning* $\rightarrow$ Utility

Drawing on Lancaster's work (1966) he distinguishes between a commodity and its set of characteristics or desirable properties (see also Max-Neef 1989). A meal, for example, may have the properties of satisfying hunger, establishing social contacts or providing a focus for household life. Conversely, a number of distinct commodities will often share one or more characteristics, as when all (or most) foodstuffs have the characteristic of satisfying hunger. More significantly, he introduces the important new concepts of functioning and capability. A *'functioning'* is 'an achievement of a person: what she or he manages to do or to be' (Sen 1985a: 12). Sen's initial claim was that a person's wellbeing should be viewed in terms of the totality of 'beings' and 'doings' she or he actually achieves. Going further, a person's *capability* set represents the vector of all the different functionings she or he is able to achieve. It is distinct from functioning (bare achievement) in that it reflects a person's real opportunities or positive freedom of choice between possible lifestyles. This immediately opens up two distinct and important spaces for thinking about wellbeing.

While income and commodities undoubtedly contribute to wellbeing, there is no obvious or straightforward link between material things and the ability to function for various reasons. Notably people typically differ in their capacity to convert a given bundle of commodities into valuable functionings (*ceteris paribus*, a rickshaw cyclist requires a higher intake of calories than those he pulls who have a more sedentary lifestyle). Similarly, the other pole of welfare or utility ultimately reduces wellbeing to mental states such as pleasure or proxies for mental states, namely desire fulfilment or the fact of choice. Other valuable achievements, particularly in the physical, social or political sphere of life (such as avoiding malnutrition, being able to move around, achieving self-respect, having civil liberties, etc.) only matter insofar as they influence utility levels. The crucial problem here is that utility 'can be easily swayed by mental conditioning or adaptive expectations' (Sen 1999: 62). The ability of people to adapt to harsh environments and unforgiving situations means that expressed satisfactions may be a poor guide to objective life situations. Sen (1984) cites evidence from a post-famine health survey in India, which suggests significant disparities between the externally observed health of destitute widows and their own subjective impressions of their physical state, in comparison with the levels of wellbeing reported by widowers in the same situation. Widowers experienced less morbidity than widows yet reported lower subjective wellbeing. If our concern is with anything other than subjective well-being, we are pushed in the direction of capabilities or functionings.

However, as Alkire illustrates in Chapter 4, it is no easy task to operationalise, measure and track capabilities. The capability-set of a person includes 'not only the opportunities that people had actually chosen … but also the counterfactual opportunities that had been open to them that they had not chosen'. Alkire surveys and suggests some ways to capture this elusive notion, but in the 1980s it seemed beyond reach.[4] Thus the main focus narrowed down to a person's chosen functionings, or what a person succeeds in doing with the commodities and commodity characteristics at her disposal, given her personal characteristics and environment. But this too is an extremely broad notion. Valuable functionings may include the ability to play the sax-ophone, to act generously towards friends or to feel good about oneself. There is no self-evident way to evaluate these and compare them across persons or groups of people. The capabilities approach lacks 'a meth-odological side-car', writes Alkire in Chapter 4.

Agreement is more likely on a list of *basic* functionings. However, though Sen has always recognised in practice and in a series of famous works on famine, for example, that common and egregious threats to wellbeing do exist, he has repeatedly refused to endorse a list of such threats. His work underpins the well-known Human Development Index, which prioritises longevity, literacy and schooling, alongside (the logarithm of) per capita GDP. Nevertheless, agreement on common human needs beyond this minimum will remain elusive in the absence of a theoretically informed conception and 'list' of basic needs.

Martha Nussbaum has developed such an alternative – a 'thick' notion of human capabilities which both parallels and differs from Sen (Nussbaum 2000). She extols a broad vision of human flourishing and is prepared to identify a lengthy cross-cultural list of human 'functional capabilities': life, bodily health, bodily integrity, sense/imagination/ thought, emotions, practical reason, affiliation, concern for other

---

[4] Arneson (1989: 28) wrote: 'I doubt that the full set of my functioning capability [matters] for the assessment of my position. Whether or not my capabilities include the capability to trek to the South Pole, eat a meal at the most expensive restaurant in Omsk … matters not one bit to me, because I neither have, nor have the slightest reason to anticipate I ever will have, any desire to do any of these and myriad other things'. Quoted in Ruta et al. forthcoming.

species, play, and control over environment. Initially derived from an Aristotelian framework, it is 'informed by an intuitive idea of a life that is worthy of the dignity of the human being' (Nussbaum 2006: 70). In recent years, she has presented these capabilities as the source of political principles for a liberal, pluralistic society; she also asserts that they form the content of 'an overlapping consensus among people who otherwise have very different comprehensive conceptions of the good' (2006: 70).[5] Reflecting her disciplinary backgrounds in philosophy, law and ethics, Nussbaum advances a richer picture of human life than Sen, yet is willing to countenance that there are universal capabilities applicable to all peoples everywhere. However, the foundations of her approach are arguably controversial and its potential for securing cross-cultural consensus is thus far unproven (Clark 2002; Menon 2002).

In the past two decades there have been many attempts to develop theorisations and lists of basic needs, functionings, and related concepts. Alkire (2002a) summarises thirty-nine of these and analyses nine in detail. However, these are very diverse lists embracing very different things. In the WeD research framework we have drawn explicitly on Doyal and Gough's *Theory of Human Need* (1991). The theory of human need (THN)[6] seeks to provide a 'fully universalisable' conception of needs/capabilities, an explicit critique of cultural relativism, and a moral grounding for strong right-claims to their satisfaction (Gough 2003). THN identifies a conceptual space of universal human need; recognises cultural variety in meeting needs; but aims to avoid subordinating the identification of needs to such cultural contexts. The argument is explicitly 'hierarchical'[7] and moves in the following stages (Doyal and Gough 1991: chs 4, 8; Gasper 1996; Gough 2003, 2004).

First, THN distinguishes between two types of goals: *needs*, which are believed to be universalisable or potentially applicable to all people, and *wants*, which are not necessarily so and indeed will tend to reflect particular cultural environments. The universality of need rests upon the belief that if needs are not satisfied then serious *harm* of some objective kind will result. THN defines serious harm as fundamental disablement in the pursuit of one's vision of the good, whatever the nature of that

---

[5] But her earlier emphasis on reflexivity and awareness of others as the core of human nature means that she continues to regard practical reason and affiliation as 'architectonic capabilities', as the 'core of the core' (Gasper 2004: 183).

[6] Hereafter we will refer to the theory of human need as THN.

[7] However, it must be stressed that this has nothing in common with Maslow's (1970) hierarchical theory of needs as motivations. As THN argues (1991: ch. 3) and as Gasper demonstrates in Chapter 2, there is no necessary correspondence between drives and motivations and 'normative priority goals'.

vision.[8] This is not necessarily the same as subjective feelings like anxiety or unhappiness. Another way of describing such harm is as an impediment to successful social participation. THN argues that we build a self-conception of our own capabilities through interacting with and learning from others. It follows that participation in some form of life without serious arbitrary limitations is a fundamental goal of all peoples.

Second, *basic needs* are then defined as those universal preconditions that enable such participation in one's form of life. These are identified as *physical health* and *autonomy*. Survival, and beyond that a modicum of physical health, is essential to be able to act and participate. Humans also exhibit autonomy of agency – the capacity to make informed choices about what should be done and how to go about doing it. This is impaired, they argue, by three things: severe mental illness, poor cognitive skills, and by blocked opportunities to engage in social participation. At a higher level, they identify critical participation – the capacity to situate the form of life one grows up in, to criticise it and, if necessary, to act to change it. This more dynamic type of participation requires a second-order level of *critical autonomy*. Without critical autonomy, the ability of human societies to adapt to changes in their environment would be gravely weakened. It is an essential prerequisite for innovation and creative adaptation, especially in times of transformation and upheaval.

Third, accepting that these common human needs can be met in a multitude of different ways by an almost infinite variety of specific 'satisfiers', THN goes on to identify those characteristics of need satisfiers that everywhere contribute to improved physical health and autonomy. These 'universal satisfier characteristics', or *intermediate needs* for short, are grouped into eleven categories: adequate nutritional food and water, adequate protective housing, non-hazardous work and physical environments, appropriate health care, security in childhood, significant primary relationships, physical and economic security, safe birth control and childbearing, and appropriate basic and cross-cultural education.[9] All eleven are essential to protect the health and autonomy

[8] We qualify this in the final chapter when discussing the relation between the individual and social order, and recognise that we must debate whether all visions of the good can be regarded as equally socially acceptable.

[9] This list, like all taxonomies, is in one sense arbitrary (Doyal and Gough 1991: 159). The groups are 'verbal wrappings' or 'labels' designed to demarcate one collection of characteristics from another. Moreover, the word-labels used will be ambiguous – they will 'not contain or exhaust the meaning of the need identified'. Ambiguity can be reduced by increasing the numbers of characteristics or 'need categories'. Yet the larger the set, the greater the problems in comprehending the totality of human needs.

of people and thus to enable them to participate to the maximum extent in their social form of life. These intermediate needs are based on the codified knowledge of the natural and social sciences. This knowledge changes and typically expands – today often at dizzying speeds – through time.[10] Thus the concept of human need is historically open to such continual improvements in understanding.

However, fourth, a quite distinct method is required to identify specific *need satisfiers* in particular contexts. Across the world and throughout history, cultural repertoires of beliefs and practices have been developed by communities in relationship to the particular natural and social environments they inhabit. These generate meanings for people within that community and provide durable solutions to the recurrent problems that those individuals and collectivities face. These default solutions provide and justify the numerous concrete need satisfiers which enable people to meet their needs. However, cultural identities are multiple and 'solutions' are contested, notably in mobile and migrant populations within the peripheral zones of capitalism (Altamirano *et al.* 2004). To adapt need satisfiers to a rapidly changing environment, THN argues, a 'dual strategy' is required. Any rational and effective attempt to resolve disputes over needs and improve practices to meet needs 'must bring to bear both the codified knowledge of experts and the experiential knowledge of those whose basic needs and daily life world are under consideration. This requires a *dual strategy of social policy formation* which values compromise, provided that it does not extend to the general character of basic human needs and rights' (Doyal and Gough 1991: 141). The universal can guide but never dictate the local vision of what must be done to achieve wellbeing in specific contexts.

Yet, fifth and last, THN recognises certain common dilemmas in all collectivities which set bounds on their variation. Four societal preconditions – production, reproduction, cultural transmission and political authority – must be satisfied by all social forms of life if they are to survive and flourish over long periods of time (1991: 80–90). The hypothesis is advanced that 'the degree to which individual needs are capable of being satisfied in principle will depend in practice on the degree of such societal success'. Similarly, 'the success of social forms of life will in turn be predicated on the health and autonomy of its members' (1991: 89). Several chapters in this book further explore this mutual dependence of

---

[10] Doyal and Gough are comfortable to acknowledge that humans as a species have made and continue to make progress in their capacity to understand and satisfy their needs (1991: 111).

social and individual development. Yet, though individual needs can never be *satisfied* independently of the social environment, and though need satisfiers are context-specific, THN insists that basic needs must be *conceptualised* independently of any specific social environment.

Much other rich thinking about human need is explored by the contributors in Part I of this volume, which modifies THN in various ways, for example the dividing line that it draws between the objective, externally observable and the subjective. Though THN recognises the constraints placed on a person's autonomy by severe mental illness, recent research points to the further importance of subjective attributes such as self-confidence, dignity and absence of shame in the exercise of autonomy. In recent years the work of Richard Ryan and Edward Deci and their collaborators within psychology has done much to augment and give content to these ideas on autonomy and practical reason (e.g. Brown and Ryan 2003; Ryan and Deci 2001). Building on previous work on the relationship between types of motivation, pursuit of goals, and psychological wellbeing, they develop an alternative philosophy and psychology of wellbeing, 'eudaimonism', which considers wellbeing as fulfilling or realising one's *daimon* or true nature through the actualisation of human potentials (Ryan and Deci 2001: 143).[11] They demonstrate the centrality of autonomy alongside competence and relatedness as a universal psychological need, interpreting autonomy as the experience of willingly originating and endorsing one's actions. However they recognise that this forms a continuum, ranging from actions undertaken purely to obtain a reward or escape punishment or to avoid feelings of guilt, to more positive endorsement of one's action (Chirkov *et al.* 2003; Ryan and Deci 2000b). This illustrates how one strand of psychological theory and research enriches the approaches to human need and objective wellbeing outlined above.

The work of Sen, ul Haq, Nussbaum, Doyal and Gough, Ryan and Deci, and others lend support to common criteria and indeed some common measures of objective wellbeing. They underpin at various removes most of the Millennium Development Goals and more ambitious indicators of empowerment and autonomy. There is now a solid conceptual and empirical foundation for a notion of objective wellbeing, which does not necessarily correspond with individual subjective perceptions, or aggregate measures of income and control over commodities. Different perspectives within this approach are elaborated and explored in Part I of this volume.

---

[11] Eudaimonic wellbeing represents an alternative to both psychology's traditional focus on clinical pathology, and subjective wellbeing or 'hedonic psychology' (Diener 1984; Kahneman *et al.* 1999).

1.3   Resources, livelihoods and wellbeing

During the 1980s and 1990s there were a number of notable advances in research frameworks and methodologies for understanding the actual lives that people in developing countries live. The term 'actual lives' refers to the desire to research people's actual choices and actions in relation to possible opportunities (see Alkire, Chapter 4); it also signals a departure from discussions of poor people that abstract them almost completely out of the picture. A substantial body of work in development studies has moved from narrowly conceived income 'poverty' analyses to understanding how 'livelihoods' are constructed; and then on to still wider notions of 'resource strategies', which seek to take better account of the social and cultural structures within which these are located. These approaches can make a useful contribution to the emerging discussion on a concept of wellbeing and they provide the focus for the second part of this volume.

One thing that is striking when one spends any amount of time with men, women and children who are living day to day in poverty is their resourcefulness. Where many of us from much more privileged backgrounds would be defeated by such hardship, and find it difficult to see ways of living in these conditions, those who do display remarkable resilience and innovation, and through hard work, survive. This is not romanticism or an attempt to idealise poverty and the poor – it is an observable fact. As the currently popular statistics tell us, millions of people around the world live on less than one dollar a day and are apparently without obvious means of meeting their daily needs of food and shelter. While many succumb, especially children, most survive. The puzzle for those involved in research and practice at the frontline of development has been to understand how they do this.

Amartya Sen's development of an entitlement approach to understanding famines in the early 1980s provided one important stimulus for new thinking in this area of study. While there were important predecessor studies in economic and social anthropology and in the development administration literature, the entitlement approach provided a well-organised way of thinking through the detail of the dynamics of famines and why some people die while others do not. The difference, argued Sen, was explained by people's ability to translate – or not – endowments into entitlements in respect of food. Thus, according to Sen's analysis in the Ethiopian famine of 1973, pastoralists were particularly badly affected not only by their animals dying from a lack of food and water but the interplay of this with a relative decline in the market value of their livestock in respect of other foodstuffs. In the

Bengal famine of 1943, fishing households were particularly affected as the value of their entitlements declined in relation to the price of grain and rice. The notion of entitlement encompassed what people were able to produce, what they were able to exchange and what they were able to claim in other ways. This type of approach shifted analysis beyond a narrow focus on income and the material resources people owned, towards the investigation of how they secured access to what they need. In doing so it extended our imagination about the types of resources that might be deployed and the strategies that might be adopted to realise entitlements.

This analysis fitted well with another tradition of study of agricultural systems focusing on the vulnerability of the poor, notably Robert Chambers's *Rural Development: Putting the Last First* (1983). Its idea of 'poverty ratchets' (the progressive loss of entitlements over time) highlighted both the notion of vulnerability and the dynamics of poverty. *Vulnerability* was a concept that particularly drew on studies of food insecurity, but Chambers' analysis took account not just of seasonal or natural disasters but also of social and political dimensions of the poverty processes. It argued the need to take account of the role of indigenous knowledge – the understanding that poor people themselves have of their poverty and vulnerability. In his work on pastoralist communities in Sub-Saharan Africa, Jeremy Swift (1989) elaborated an entitlement approach by focusing on the strategies that households employed to manage different types of assets and claims in the face of vulnerability and food insecurity. This was complemented by further work seeking to explain morbidity in famines by De Waal (1989).

These contributions stimulated a number of parallel researches into the ways in which people in developing countries secured their livelihoods. Bebbington, Hinojosa-Valencia, Muñoz and Lizarazú in Chapter 8 of this volume review a distinction between two strands of the 'livelihoods frameworks': between those that emphasise 'what people *think and do*', and 'what they *have and control*'. While both stress the agency and coping ability of poor people, each develops a different discourse and arguably take different ontological paths with consequently different connections to wellbeing.[12]

---

[12] Aside from these two paths of intellectual development, a third route from the essay on entitlement led to further engagement with development ethics and philosophy and to debating the 'capabilities and functionings' concepts subsequently advanced by Sen. These have been discussed in the preceding section, but much of this discussion has a tendency to become detached from the empirical study of development and has had more to do with debating lists and levels of abstraction rather than the actual lives of poor people.

The 'having and controlling' form of livelihoods framework focuses on notions of 'capitals and assets'. From a food security perspective and with strong roots in natural resources research traditions, authors such as Longhurst, Conway, Scoones and others established the basis for what has become known as the Sustainable Rural Livelihoods framework. Working closely with the Natural Resources Division of the UK Department for International Development this found its fullest elaboration in a 1998 publication by Carney. This sets out the model of five categories of 'capital assets': natural, human, financial, physical and social. Caroline Moser, working with the World Bank, developed her Asset Vulnerability Framework particularly to bring this type of analysis to bear on urban populations and also incorporated some of her prior gender concerns (Moser 1998). The assets identified by that framework were: labour, human capital, housing and infrastructure, household relations, and social capital.

There were strong synergies here with the emerging work of Robert Putnam (1993) on social capital. The equation of social capital with economic success and societal progress supported and legitimated the language of capitals and was exactly the kind of meta-development story which development agencies could work with. It fitted well with grander discourses of governance and complemented the thin agenda on markets and competition by attending to the social domain. At a more operational level, the 'capitals and assets' approaches gave development agencies a simple framework for identifying and formulating more strategic and sophisticated poverty-focused interventions (Rakodi 1999). These could include supplementing the 'capital' holdings of individuals and households as well as building social capital and 'civil society' as a form of support for the poor.

The second, 'thinking and doing' livelihoods framework has been more sociological or anthropological in its orientation and purpose. Here the work of Norman Long on the development 'interface'[13] during the early 1990s was important (Long and Long 1992), as was the influence of authors such as James C. Scott on the moral economy (1985), and Pierre Bourdieu on symbolic capital (1997). A specific form of this type of livelihoods approach, as introduced in section 1.1 of the chapter, was developed by a group working at the University of Bath and was labelled the Resource Profiles Approach or Framework (see Lewis *et al.* 1991; Lewis and McGregor 1992; Saltmarshe 2002). An important and ontologically significant difference between the RPF and 'capitals/assets'

---

[13] The point of interaction and encounter between the client and bureaucrat in development interventions.

thinking is that the value of resources in pursuit of goals or objectives is contingent on the goals and also on the context and the circumstances within which the livelihood and broader wellbeing outcomes are being negotiated (see Chapter 7). Beginning with the study of means rather than ends, the RPF approach implicitly accommodated the long-standing recognition within the basic needs and capabilities approaches that something like good health is simultaneously both.

The RPF emerged from a number of empirical, ethnographic studies in rural Bangladesh conducted during the 1980s. Bangladesh, despite being so uniformly flat and wet, exhibits considerable regional variation, and within localities there is a bewildering array of endeavours and experiences among rural people as they pursue their 'livelihood'. One of the challenges confronting village level studies in Bangladesh has been to escape from the 'naturalist' or 'neo-Malthusian' view that poverty is primarily due to scarcity of 'resources' in relation to the large number of people. Rather, these village studies recognised that the competition for scarce resources was a profoundly social phenomenon.[14] As Stephen Gudeman put it, in reference to the study of rural life in a different continent, 'the process of gaining a livelihood is culturally constructed in diverse ways' (1986: 28).

The RPF conceives of individuals and households constructing livelihoods using a range of social and cultural resources alongside the familiar material, human and environmental resources. *Social* resources are those relationships people invest in to try to secure entitlements; *cultural* resources refer to symbols of status or markers of identity that can be deployed in negotiations over the value of endowments. This approach draws on a wide-ranging set of debates in economic anthropology, but the work of Laurence Rosen is particularly relevant. Following the work of Geertz (1973, 1979, 1983), Rosen's study of market behaviour in Morocco explores the ways in which individual identity is negotiated in transactions in the bazaar, using a range of cultural symbols and referents, and then how this identity is significant for the treatment one receives in the bazaar (Rosen 1984). This idea resonated in the study of rural Bangladesh, where notions of malleable identity abound and where the treatment of individuals in the market or in relation to the state is highly dependent on the identity one is able to

---

[14] Generally see Sahlins 1974, and for Bangladesh see Chowdury 1978 and Jahangir 1982. Erik Jansen's adoption of a Barthian framework in his 1986 publication *Rural Bangladesh: Competition for Scarce Resources* is a good example of this, and similar ideas were embodied in Willem van Schendel's notion of 'self-rescue' (W. Van Schendel, 'Self-rescue and survival: The rural poor in Bangladesh', paper to ASA Australia Conference (mimeo), 1986).

establish. The notion of Muslim caste vividly illustrates the interplay between material and cultural resources in the Bengali context (Arefeen 1982; van Schendel 1981). As a common Bangla proverb puts it: 'last year I was a Johola, this year I am a Shekh; and next year if prices rise I will be a Said'.[15]

The proverb captures the notion that the acquisition of material resources permits the renegotiation of cultural and religious identity, which in turn can result in material benefits. From this perspective, the social and cultural dimensions of societal structures play a significant role in enabling or constraining different individuals and households in their struggles for 'livelihoods'. It is this engagement with culture and its inclusion as one category of resource with which 'livelihoods' and (if we extend that notion) wellbeing are pursued that marks the RPF as a framework distinct from the 'capitals/assets' model. The RPF is built on the anthropological tradition of assuming that what people do has meaning for them and that it reflects what they value, both in terms of outcomes they are striving for and the processes they engage in to try to achieve those outcomes. It recognises that people may not always suc-ceed in achieving their objectives, and that they may be dissatisfied with both outcomes and processes, but in general they are not defeated and continue to have aspirations which they strive to meet.[16]

The RPF also posits that as people engage in these processes they are participating in the reproduction of structures within their society. The term structure here encompasses the values that are embedded in the processes they engage in, as well as the institutions and organisations which are, on the face of it, accorded relevance and legitimacy by repeated engagement with them. The institution of dowry provides a controversial example here. Although understood by many as a major cause of destitution and gendered disadvantage for poor families with daughters as well as a mechanism for the entrapment of young women, its persistence in South Asia reflects a view that it remains an accepted institution for social and moral bonding in communities across the subcontinent (see Khan and Seeley 2005).

Tony Beck's impressive empirical study of life in rural West Bengal (1994) is another path-breaking example of the 'thinking and doing'

---

[15] The name or title of Johola refers to a low Muslim caste associated with weaving, while the names Shekh and Said denote middling and then higher-caste labels, with implicit claims to traceable lineages to the middle east, redolent with elite and religious status. See Jack (1927).

[16] The term 'defeated' is used here intimating the sense of 'homeostatic defeat' as proposed by the psychologist Robert Cummins (2002a) and discussed later. This involves not just physical but also psychological collapse. See below for further discussion, and also Camfield and McGregor 2005.

approach to livelihoods, when he explores the struggles of poor people not just for resources, but also for respect. A series of articles by McGregor on credit and debt in rural Bangladesh also employs this perspective to understand the evolution of policy debates and the emergence of microfinance NGOs in that country (1989a, 1989b, 1994, 1998[17]). The work of Bebbington (1999), Zimmerer (1996) and Zoomers (1999) on the importance of identity in livelihoods in the Andes represents another tradition in development studies which emphasises the significance of struggles for identity.

Livelihoods frameworks have attracted their fair share of criticism, but most have not distinguished between these two variants. One criticism contends that livelihoods frameworks have been crudely instrumentalist, concerned primarily with means rather than ends. However, this is less the case for the 'thinking and doing' strand, which is built on recognition of the importance of understanding the relationship between means and ends. It highlights some of the sterility of the means/ends discussion, recognising that resources, especially when understood as more than just material, can be and are most often both means and ends. This point is emphasised by Alkire in Chapter 4 here and is set out by Sen in relation to the notion of freedom. In integrating the RPF with the Theory of Human Need, the WeD research recognises that resources are inextricably bound up with needs and in some cases can be understood as the flip-side of them. The satisfaction of needs constitutes the resources with which individuals and households pursue their next round of ends. Satisfying needs for food one day ensures that the human resource, the body, is better prepared for work the following day. Further, the needs that people aspire to satisfy can often be taken as indication of the resources, or means, that they perceive they require to live a good life in their particular community and context.

A different criticism that potentially applies to both types of livelihoods framework is that they over-emphasise the agency of the poor and so obscure the role of structure in constraining the poor. This impression reflects broader shifts in the sociology of development. In the early 1990s the sociology of development gave itself a tentative pat on the back for emerging from its theoretical 'impasse' of the 1970s and 1980s – a preoccupation with structuralist explanations of social processes (Booth 1994: 298). The new approaches, advanced by European sociologists and anthropologists, reasserted the importance of individual

[17] J. A. McGregor, 'A poverty of agency: Resource management amongst the poor in Bangladesh', paper presented at the Fifth Workshop of the European Network of Bangladesh Studies, 18–20 April 1998.

agency in the face of social structure. The work of Norman Long and the Wageningen School's actor-oriented approach particularly illustrates this approach. This drew on a range of other influences, not least the work of Bernard Schaffer (Schaffer and Lamb 1974) on 'access' and James C. Scott's work on moral economy (1985). Long's (1989) interface approach explored negotiations between clients and bureaucrats in development interventions, in order to provide an ethnographic explanation of the differential outcomes observed. The emphasis on negotiation was crucial in as much as outcomes are not seen as predetermined, but as the result of complex interactions affected (but not entirely determined by) wider structures.

However, there is fine line between an 'actor-oriented' approach painting a rosy picture of the peasant with power and agency (albeit subordinate), and underestimating the significance of the societal structures within which they live. Brass (1996) provides a stinging critique of what he regards as the common failure of the new approaches to explain the resilient patterning of relationships between rich and poor. James C. Scott's various publications using a moral economy approach illustrate this problem well (e.g. *Weapons of the Weak* 1985, *Domination and the Arts of Resistance* 1990). His avoidance of concepts of class or an overt examination of the role of the distribution of wealth and power in society obscures the ways that structure systematically constrains not only the social room for manoeuvre of the poor, but also their ability to conceive of realistic alternatives; or, to put it another way, the way that structure contributes to the reproduction of their poverty of agency.[18]

A final criticism that can be levelled particularly at the 'capital/assets' type of livelihood approach is that they threaten to mystify differences between households. This problem is inherent in an uncritical acceptance of the notion of 'capitals' and the relatively simplistic view of what people *have* as the main explanation of their poverty. As we have argued and as Sen has pointed out, it is not just about what people have but what their goals and aspirations are; what they are trying to do with what they have, and about what choices they make in trying to achieve these goals. Moreover, in adopting the language of 'capitals', these frameworks tend to reify social constructions whose meaning and reality is constantly being negotiated.

The term social capital is particularly misleading in that it suggests that relationships are 'owned' and ever-present. Rather, the relationships in which people invest must be understood as claims on reciprocity

---

[18] *Ibid.*

appealed to when they are needed. Some of these appeals to relationships may be strengthened and made more predictable by contract and law, or by broader notions of 'rights', but in many cases the appeals are more circumstantial. This underpins our understanding of the vulnerability of poor people in developing countries[19] (Wood 2003). By concentrating on the 'having' and ignoring the less tangible resources which individuals and households deploy, the 'capitals/assets' approach fails to distinguish between those who can benefit from 'social capital' and those who cannot, let alone those who may be clearly harmed by it (Putzel 1997). They thus obscure not only the diversity of strategies that different households adopt in their pursuit of livelihoods and wellbeing, but also reduce insight into the processes that reproduce their poverty. It is this level of detail and attention to process which tends to be missing from the new generation of official development procedures and documents, such as Poverty Reduction Strategy Papers (PRSPs); as such they are likely to fail to reduce poverty sustainably (Booth 2005).

The emphasis on the role of social and cultural resources in the Resource Profiles Framework distinguishes it from the 'capital/assets' type of approach to the analysis of livelihoods and poverty. Both the World Bank 'Asset Vulnerability Framework' and the British Department for International Development (DfID) supported 'Livelihoods' approach conflate the social and cultural into a category of 'social capital'. In doing so both hide the significance of the role of culture, values and norms in constructing and legitimating the identities necessary for the pursuit of livelihoods and wellbeing. The RPF differentiates better between different individuals and households in different contexts. It also challenges development practice to engage with issues with which it has historically been uncomfortable: peoples' values, goals and cultures. From the RPF perspective, the persistence of poverty has as much to do with the reproduction of meaning in societies, as it has to do with what people have and do not have. As we argue later, this suggests that we should separate the terms 'doing' and 'being' which Sen has brought together in his definition of functioning. It is systems of meaning, negotiated through relationships within society that shape what different people can and cannot do with what they have. And, by giving sense to a person's doing, meaning translates the 'having' and 'doing' into 'being'.

[19] J. A. McGregor, 'Poverty and patronage: A study of credit, development and change in rural Bangladesh', Ph.D thesis submitted to the University of Bath, 1991.

1.4   Subjective quality of life: happiness and satisfaction with life as a whole

The third component in the conceptual movement from poverty to wellbeing in development thinking goes by various labels including quality of life, subjective wellbeing, life satisfaction, and happiness. All bring subjective feelings and evaluations centre-stage and propose to conceive and measure these directly rather than via other proxies. Different disciplines and perspectives have contributed to this stream of research, but three have been of special importance and are surveyed here: subjective quality of life research by health psychologists and clinicians (see Chapter 10), the psychology of affect balance and life satisfaction, and the economics of happiness.[20] Although these streams mainly originated in rich countries and reflect their concerns, they are expanding into the developing world.[21] Their relevance to understanding poverty and wellbeing has only recently been appreciated within development studies, but they have a clear antecedent in the concern with 'participation' and participatory research, with which we begin.

The participatory perspective in development coalesced in the late 1980s and 1990s at the confluence of several distinct streams. At one extreme, Rapid Rural Appraisal (RRA) was devised for development consultants seeking quicker and more cost-effective techniques to assess people's material conditions and social networks in the field. At the other, participatory research was developed as a means to empower disadvantaged people by giving them tools of analysis and awareness, for example, by community organisers influenced by Paolo Freire's ideas of conscientisation (Bennett and Roberts 2004; Freire 1970). Criticism of the quality of preparatory research and planning from both academics and the supposed 'beneficiaries' (for example, members of the African liberation movements whose slogan was 'nothing about us, without us'), combined with the sheer weight of experience, supported the perspective that people living within a situation had a better understanding of

---

[20] This omits the earlier 'social indicators' movement, which brought together researchers from sociology and social policy, psychology and economics in the third quarter of the last century. Andrews and Withey (1976) and Campbell, Converse and Rodgers (1976) can be seen as founders of this approach, which typically defines and measures quality of life as a combination of subjective and objective dimensions. It has fostered the construction of subjective datasets from the 1970s onwards (e.g. Easterlin 2003).

[21] For example, the World Health Organization's sponsorship of cross-cultural quality of life measures (WHOQOL Group 1995), the extension of the EuroBarometer surveys of social and political attitudes to Africa, Latin America, and East Asia, and the work of happiness economists reviewed in Guillen-Royo and Velazco 2006.

the many issues facing them than outside experts 'bussed in' for a few days or weeks (Chambers 1992).

Out of this emerged the Participatory Rural Appraisal (PRA) approaches developed by Robert Chambers and others in the late 1980s and early 1990s. The ambitious World Bank's 'Voices of the Poor' study perhaps represents its apogee,[22] although the quality of different components of the project was variable, and it has stimulated much critical reflection among practitioners (e.g. Cooke and Kothari 2001; Cornwall and Pratt 2003). The key promise of participatory methodologies is that they are 'experience-near' in terms of their participant/respondents: they are able to reflect more closely the knowledge and worldview of people themselves than more formal, abstract, or 'scientific' approaches.

The desire to create both a space for people to reflect on and share their experiences, and conduct research that generates valuable outcomes for participants, policy-makers, and practitioners, is what, we contend, links participatory and 'quality of life' research (White and Pettit 2004). Examples of mutually beneficial engagements are the use of participatory methodologies by individualised quality of life measures such as the *Person Generated Index*,[23] and the combination of participatory research and measurement in the *Participatory Numbers Network* (Holland and Abeyasekera forthcoming). However, most quality of life research has been undertaken in rich Western countries and reflects their concerns. We begin our survey of this literature with research by health psychologists and clinicians.

Research into *health-related quality of life* was developed in the mid 1970s by health scientists and psychologists to track people's perception of their health status (for example the Sickness Impact Profile, Bergner *et al.* 1976). This was mainly in response to the need for more sensitive measures to compare treatments for chronic illness and to identify the most cost-effective of these. Health-related QoL has measured people's perceptions of their health status through both subjective questions about satisfaction and emotions (Nord *et al.* 2001), and 'self-report'

---

[22] The study was published in three volumes: volume I, *Can Anyone Hear Us?*, synthesising eighty-one Participatory Poverty Assessments conducted by the World Bank in fifty countries (Narayan 2000); volume II, *Crying Out for Change*, drawing on participatory fieldwork conducted in 1999 in twenty-three countries (Narayan and Chambers 2000); and volume III, *From Many Lands*, offering regional patterns and country case-studies (Narayan and Petsch 2002). It was supplemented by Brock's (1999) review of participatory research on criteria for poverty, illbeing, or vulnerability, which took place outside the PPA framework and was consequently considered to be more challenging.

[23] Ruta 1998; for an example of its adaptation and use in rural Ethiopia, see P. Bevan, B. Kebede and A. Pankhurst, 'A report on a very informal pilot of the Person Generated Index of Quality of Life in Ethiopia', unpublished work, WeD, University of Bath, 2003.

objective questions about symptoms and functional status.[24] The use of measures outside their countries of origin (for example, the SF-36, which has now been used in over sixty countries (Ware and Sherbourne 1992) prompted cross-national comparative research, and the establishment of international bodies to 'quality control' the translation and validation process (see Chapter 10). This process was accelerated by their increasing use in international clinical trials (Spilker 1990, 1996). As the net of countries widened, a range of new issues and problems became apparent. For example, while people in different cultures experience common diseases, they may attach different meanings to them, or indeed not recognise some prevalent conditions as diseases at all. For many anthropologists this rules out cross-cultural studies of people's health status or health-related quality of life across cultures. But some applied anthropologists and medical sociologists have attempted to use quality of life research to bridge the gap between universal medical classifications of diseases and the representation of culturally variant meanings and experiences (for example, Guarnaccia 1995; Lambert and McKevitt 2002).

Perhaps the most successful and influential cross-national research programme has been the World Health Organization Quality of Life Group (WHOQOL), established in 1991, which formed one of the initial planks of the WeD research. It defines quality of life as 'an individual's perceptions of their position in life in the context of the culture and value systems in which they live, and in relation to their goals, expectations, standards and concerns' (WHOQOL Group 1995). WHOQOL developed a common international protocol to construct generic QoL profile measures. For example, all fifteen of the original WHOQOL centres contributed to the definition of the facets that comprised the six domains of Quality of Life.[25] Questions were drafted by population focus groups, which generated ideas within each centre as to the best way to ask locally appropriate questions about people's quality of life. The programme has shown that although country populations show different levels of QoL across domains, the overall structure has a high cross-cultural validity for all domains, suggesting a

---

[24] While Nord maintains that 'the term "quality of life data" should be used ... only in connection with data about people's subjective feelings about life' (Nord et al. 2001: p. 3), he acknowledges that the majority of health-related quality of life measures combine both forms of data. This is also true of the way 'general' quality of life is operationalised, despite a historical disconnect between the two areas (Cummins et al. 2004; Michalos 2004), represented by their two membership organisations ISQOLS and ISOQOL.

[25] Physical, Psychological, Social, Environmental, Economic and Spiritual (the last two domains are not included in the more commonly used WHOQOL-BREF).

high degree of universality (Skevington *et al.* 2004). However, it faces several problems: the WHOQOL is about health-related quality of life and does not directly address the issue of autonomy; moreover, although many of the original field centres were in developing countries or transition economies, arguably the agenda had already been set by the 'expert review' which established the six domain structure and there was little modification to this after item development and piloting.

The second stream of research into SWB has been conducted exclusively within the discipline of psychology. Psychologists have long been interested in life satisfaction and happiness (e.g. Bradburn 1969; Cantril 1965; Maslow 1970); however, the topic only entered mainstream psychology in the mid 1980s. This was facilitated by the development of valid measures of these concepts such as the Satisfaction With Life Scale (Diener *et al.* 1985), which has been used in over sixty-one nations (e.g. Suh *et al.* 1998). In 1999 Daniel Kahneman and his colleagues published *Well-Being: The Foundations of Hedonic Psychology*, 'to announce the existence of a new field of psychology ... Hedonic psychology ... is the study of what makes experiences and life pleasant or unpleasant' (Kahneman *et al.* 1999: ix). This synthesises over a decade of work and demonstrates that positive affect and negative affect can be operationalised and measured, albeit they are orthogonal and not opposite ends of a single continuum as was previously supposed.

Hedonic psychology also incorporates research on life satisfaction, associated with the work of Ed Diener and others. This typically asks people to rate their satisfaction with their 'life as a whole', and claims that this data converges well with other types of measures, such as the views of friends and anthropogenic markers such as extent of smiling. Compared with momentary balance of affect, this entails a cognitive and evaluative element, however brief. More typically subjective wellbeing is ascertained by combining measures of affect balance with life satisfaction, following Diener's earlier work (Diener 1984; Diener and Griffin 1984). In addition, there is flourishing research into domain-specific satisfactions, such as satisfaction with one's work, family, housing, etc., as investigated by Rojas in Chapter 12. The variety of different measures raises the interesting philosophical question of which form of happiness is the 'real' one[26] (Diener *et al.* 2000), which links to the debate over

[26] This will in part depend on what the researcher wants to achieve by assessing someone's subjective wellbeing; while domain-specific or even objective assessments would give the most accurate evaluation of the person's current state, if the researcher wanted to know the person's basis for decision-making or planning (e.g. 'shall I join this new credit and savings group?'), they might be better off using the global assessment.

'top-down' and 'bottom-up' theories of happiness, recently extended to developing countries.[27]

This research has generated a mass of solid findings on the determinants of SWB. They include personality factors, such as extraversion versus neuroticism (Deneve 1999; Vitterso and Nilsen 2002), good-quality relationships (Myers 1999), and working towards goals and achieving them (Emmons 1996; Oishi 2000). The relationship between income and wealth and SWB is non-linear across income groups and countries: greater income improves wellbeing among the poor, but above a certain point where basic needs are met it yields drastically diminishing returns.[28] On the other hand, low income and few material goods in comparison with others within your society is usually a negative predictor of wellbeing (Eggers, Gaddy, and Graham 2004; Frank 2004). So too is materialism, the pursuit of money for its own sake (Kasser 2002).

There is growing evidence also on the reverse effect of SWB on life achievements and objective conditions. A person's subjective happiness and life satisfaction impacts strongly and positively on success in the major domains of life, notably love, work and health. For example, Lyubomirsky et al. (2005) find that happiness is associated with an extra seven years of life expectancy, ceteris paribus. Thus in addition to its intrinsic, experiential value, SWB plausibly contributes to human development. This includes the 'worthwhile ends' of happiness, enjoyment, rest and relaxation (Clark 2002), and the acquisition of a range of useful resources, discussed in the previous sections.

The third disciplinary strand in this movement is the economics of happiness. This refers to the move by some economists from exclusive use of 'revealed preferences' to self-reported accounts of satisfaction with life or happiness (Frey and Stutzer 2002). It combines techniques used by economists and psychologists to assess wellbeing, and explores areas where revealed preferences provide limited information (for example, the effect on wellbeing of inequality or unemployment). Happiness economics marks a return to the idea, and more importantly the measurement, of utility, as practitioners argue that asking people to report their SWB provides a 'satisfactory empirical approximation to

[27] See Headey et al. 1991; Møller and Saris 2001; Saris and Andreenkova 2001; and Chapters 11 and 12 in this volume.

[28] Richard Layard sets the current threshold at $20,000, using data from the World Values Survey (Layard 2005). There are outliers: negative ones in the Former Soviet Union and Eastern Europe, and positive ones predominantly in Latin America. For example, Worcester's analysis (1998) of the 1995 World Values Survey data placed Venezuela tenth and the Philippines twelfth for happiness, despite per capita GDP of $8,090 and $2,762 respectively, and HDI scores of 0.86 and 0.67 (1998).

individual utility' (Di Tella *et al.* 1997; Frey and Stutzer 2002: 403; Graham forthcoming). Richard Layard's (2005) recent work takes this further, contending that happiness provides both an overall motivating device akin to Bentham's balance of pleasure and pain, and a unifying principle to guide policy (see also Collard 2003). Two centuries on, utility has been reshaped as a respectable concept in economics.[29]

Despite this accumulating understanding, there are persistent problems in researching happiness and subjective quality of life, which are multiplied when our attention turns to developing countries. First, there is the pervasive propensity of people to *adapt* to changes in their life circumstances: the related phenomena of 'adaptive preferences', 'hedonic adaptation', 'the hedonic treadmill', or 'response shift' (Cummins and Nistico 2002; Frederick and Loewenstein 1999; Parducci 1995; Schwartz and Sprangers 1999). This involves the unconscious process of adjusting expectations to reality, through either a recalibration of one's internal standards or a reprioritisation of one's values. This ability to adapt would appear to be a ubiquitous feature of the human condition and applies to individual losses (physical disablement) and gains (winning the lottery) (Brickman *et al.* 1978), and to collective misfortunes (natural disasters) and improvements (economic growth and prosperity). All confound any simple reliance on subjective quality of life scores when making intrapersonal comparisons or comparisons over time.

A more ambitious model of adaptation is provided by Cummins' 'homeostatic theory of SWB' which proposes an evolutionary mechanism for the predominantly positive life evaluations which most people display. Essentially a 'dispositional brain system' keeps individual life satisfaction in a narrow, positive range, partly through a 'conscious "buffering system"' of 'positive cognitive biases' like self-esteem, perceived control, and optimism (Cummins 2002a). Cummins proposes a linear pathway to SWB from environment ('mild extrinsic conditions'), to successful adaptation, to perceptions of need satisfaction (Cummins,

---

[29] Happiness economists have been active in developing countries; for example, Graham and Pettinato (2002) on Latin-America and Russia; Fafchamps and Shilpi on Nepal (2004) (see also M. Fafchamps, and F. Shilpi, 'Subjective well-being, isolation and rivalry' (mimeo), CSAE, Department of Economics, University of Oxford, (2003); Knight and Song on rural China (J. Knight and L. Song, 'Subjective wellbeing and its determinants in rural China' (mimeo, 2004); Gandhi Kingdon and Knight on South Africa (G. Gandhi Kingdom and J. Knight, 'Community comparisons and subjective wellbeing in a divided society', paper presented at Northeast Universities Development Consortium Conference, Montreal, 1–3 October 2004); and the recent work of Guillen-Royo and Velazco on Thailand (2006) and on Ethiopia ('Exploring the determinants of happiness: Evidence from rural Thailand and Ethiopia', paper presented at the Social Policy Association Conference in Bath, June 2005). See also Rojas in Chapter 12.

Gullone and Lau 2002). The stability of life satisfaction in this model might seem to be a problem; however, Cummins maintains that 'the fact that it is generally predictable and stable enhances its usefulness ... because the values for subjective QoL can be referenced to a normative range [which] is homeostatically maintained' (Cummins 2002b: 264). This provides the best way of identifying an 'aversive environment' (264). However, further empirical research shows that adaptation does not apply to all life events and that some people do not return to their previous level of SWB.[30] Nevertheless, the universal human capability to adapt raises difficult questions concerning the interpretation and comparison of measures of SWB.

A second, related problem is the role of 'social comparison'. When making a coherent response to an abstract question about subjective wellbeing, people typically utilise 'frames' (Kahneman and Tversky 1984), including the performance of others (Buunk and Gibbons 2000; Parducci 1995), in order to manage stress or anxiety, or increase self-esteem and motivation. If we assume that people like to maintain a positive self-view, they can reinforce this by their choice of reference group or area for comparison.[31] For example Michalos' study of over 18,000 students in 39 countries found that the 'comparison gap' was the strongest correlate of life satisfaction, happiness, and people's satisfaction with their health, far stronger, in fact, than their objective health status (1991).

When researching SWB in developing countries, further problems are encountered, or old ones exacerbated. One concerns issues of cultural bias and preferences, illustrated by the small but growing corpus of cross-cultural empirical research. Diener and Suh (1999) report a strong positive correlation across countries between national values of individualism and reported subjective wellbeing (though this is confounded by another correlation between individualism and income per head). One crucial problem is that 'SWB appears to be a more salient concept for individualists'. Another issue is that 'individualists tend to weight their emotional experiences heavily whereas collectivists emphasise interpersonal factors when they construct life satisfaction judgments' (Diener and Suh 1999: 442). Christopher (1999) identifies a greater emphasis on other-centred emotions, and a 'modesty bias' in evaluating SWB in East Asian cultures (such as Chinese, Japanese and Korean), the opposite to the 'global positivity bias' found in North America (Strack et al. 1990).

---

[30] See studies of divorce (Lucas et al. 2003), bereavement (Stroebe et al. 1996), and unemployment (Clark et al. 2004).

[31] Flexibility in the choice of areas for evaluation is characterised as 'conceptual-referent' theory within economics (Rojas 2005) and 'selective evaluation' within psychology (Taylor et al. 1983).

These findings lend support to theoretical concerns about cultural bias. The very concept of SWB and the research designs to tap it appears to generate higher levels of SWB in more western, individualist cultures.

Lastly, there is the impact of harsh or 'aversive' environments on the suitability and cogency of 'happiness' as a general indicator of wellbeing. Peterson (1999: 289–90) stresses that theories of personal control are 'transactional, spanning the individual and the environment and being concerned in particular with the interplay between the two ... Personal control is both a cause and a consequence of the way people respond to their environment'. Increasing people's self-efficacy, a common aim of social development interventions, can therefore give the erroneous and dangerous impression that 'powerless people can always control their lives if they wish, [placing] the blame for continued oppression on the dysfunctional thinking of the oppressed' (Franzblau and Moore 2000: 93–4). Happiness or perceived self-efficacy may not necessarily be helpful in hostile environments. The literature on 'depressive realism' finds that people exhibiting depression may exhibit greater realism in assessing the challenges they face: they are 'sadder but wiser' (Alloy and Ackerman 1988). 'To paraphrase a famous aphorism, hedonic adaptation "provides the serenity to accept the things one cannot change, the courage to change the things one can, and wisdom to know the difference"' (Frederick and Loewenstein 1999: 303). If a person's life-goals are not 'congruent' with either themselves or their environment, both SWB and psychological need fulfilment may suffer (Ryan et al. 1996; Sheldon et al. 2004).

On the other hand, much research upholds the universal importance of *hope* to subjective wellbeing. 'A large body of research points clearly to the fact that feeling competent and confident with respect to valued goals is associated with enhanced wellbeing. Furthermore, it is clear that goal progress, on average, predicts enhanced wellbeing, particularly goals that are rated as important' (Ryan and Deci 2001: 156). This echoes the emphasis in THN on self-confidence as a component of autonomy (Doyal and Gough 1991: 63). Furthermore, *critical* autonomy is essential in navigating through life and in making such judgements. This is especially so when environments change rapidly, as in the present era for many in the developing world, and when existing cultural repertoires cannot keep pace. Such enduring dilemmas cannot be resolved simply by researching 'happiness' – something more akin to eudaimonic wellbeing is called for.[32]

---

[32] See Chapter 3. This is recognised by the Positive Psychology movement within psychology, which not only promotes 'positive [emotional] experiences' but also 'seeks to understand and build the strengths and virtues that enable individuals and communities to thrive' <http://www.positivepsychology.org/executivesummary.htm>.

At present, the overwhelming proportion of individual-level research into SWB or subjective quality of life uses samples of people from the rich countries – indeed, predominantly psychology students at American universities! The applicability of many of these findings to the poor, the insecure, the trapped and the exploited is, to say the least, unproven. This returns us to the participatory poverty research in development studies discussed above and its relation to SWB research. The WeD group are exploring their congruence and mutual support, especially in defining (i.e. generating content for) measures of subjective QoL and wellbeing. However, as White and Pettit (2004) point out, this work makes a sharp distinction between the *relational* approach, researching people's knowledge and worldviews within specific cultural frames of reference, and the *subjective* approach, measuring individual SWB in a more quantitative way. The former is more typical of some of the resource profiles approaches discussed in section 1.3 and must be distinguished from research into QoL and SWB. The relationship between the two is explored further in Chapter 14.

1.5   Plan of the book

Human needs and human wellbeing

Des Gasper (Chapter 2) opens Part I by exploring the relationships between ideas of human needs and human wellbeing. He argues that both terms require conceptual clarification if they are to fulfil their academic and policy promise. Clarification of the concepts is not an idle pastime but an essential precondition in domains of social policy and development where the reduction in muddled terminology can smooth communication between and within scientific communities, and inform and influence communication in wider arenas. The return of the Basic Needs thinking in the 1990s has, he suggests, been built on stronger conceptual foundations and an attractive operationalisation in the Human Development Index and the work of the UNDP. Building on Doyal and Gough, David Braybrooke, Manfred Max-Neef and David Wiggins, he develops a fuller 'grammar' of need which distinguishes three modes of use of the term: needs as drives or motivations (mode A needs); needs as means to any end (mode B); and needs as normative priority goals (mode C). He goes on to show how the disciplines of economics, sociology, psychology, politics and philosophy differ in their focus and how seldom these analytical distinctions are consistently respected.

Turning to wellbeing Gasper argues that this is a still more complex term. Even if we restrict ourselves to material wellbeing, it can embrace economic opulence, 'objective' needs and a variety of psychological states. But combining these concepts with the earlier modes of needs discourse reveals interesting conflicts as well as overlaps. For example, some mode A drives are non-functional or dangerous (such as addictions), whereas some mode C ethical priority goals 'lack a behavioural motor behind them'.[33] He concludes that needs theory remains an important conceptual tool in the struggle for an improved conception of human wellbeing. However, to fix it in contemporary discourses requires both a better explanatory theory of need satisfactions and a more sophisticated measurement and communicative device than the Human Development Index. We need 'need' if moves towards 'good change' are to be developed and deepened. It is to this theoretical and measurement task that the remaining chapters turn.

In an important contribution from the discipline of psychology, Richard Ryan and Aislinn Sapp identify innate, evolved, universal and objectively verifiable psychological needs and propose cross-cultural ways of measuring their satisfaction (Chapter 3). Just as all organisms have certain prerequisites without which they will suffer degraded growth and impaired integrity, so all humans require that their basic psychological needs be met in order to experience wellbeing. Three psychological needs are critical here: autonomy, competence and relatedness. Autonomy is the capacity to experience one's actions as self-regulated, volitional and integrated; competence is the experience of opportunities to exercise and expand one's capacities; relatedness concerns feeling socially connected, in both a general sense of social integration and a specific sense of feeling cared for and significant to others. The coincidence with the central elements of THN is evident in all this, though the two streams of work have evolved in independent disciplines.[34]

The hypothesis that these needs are universal then permits a cross-cultural investigation of the extent to which different social contexts are beneficial or harmful to psychological need satisfaction. Again a distinction is drawn between the basic needs and their manifestation or expression in different societies. Assimilation of the ambient values of

---

[33] It is notable that 'learning' or 'education' finds a place on almost all universal lists of components of objective wellbeing (OWB) yet there is little evidence from Voices of the Poor and other investigations of local values that knowledge is considered as a good-in-itself, as opposed to an instrumental benefit (Gough 2004: 302).

[34] No doubt reflecting shared influences, from humanist psychology back to the early Marx.

one's culture normally enhances one's competence and relatedness; yet social values do not determine human nature and not all cultural values and practices are equally beneficial for meeting basic psychological needs. Cultures are not the 'absolute sculptor of human behaviour'. Thus empirical cross-cultural research can be conducted to establish which practices and social and cultural environments help or harm wellbeing. The task in the future is to extend this research to the majority of the peoples of the world in developing countries to test the general applicability of the notion of basic psychological needs and to identify the social contexts where these are harmed or can flourish.

In Chapter 4 Sabina Alkire turns to a related family of ideas: Amartya Sen's concepts of individual capabilities and his more recent reinterpretations of this in *Development as Freedom* and elsewhere. She notes that new ideas influence thinking and action more easily if they 'drive up with a novel methodological side-car attached'. Thus the idea of human development came to prominence with the methodological tool of the Human Development Index or HDI. While the relationship between the idea and the method is often publicly uneasy, the fact that such pairings are both common and fruitful can hardly pass notice. Yet Sen's capability approach as a way of framing wellbeing and agency has proved hard to operationalise – a convincing measuring rod is lacking even to measure the expansion or contraction of basic capabilities. To begin rectifying this, Alkire investigates two ways forward originating from different disciplines.

The first considers a measure of empowerment comprising two factors, agency and 'opportunity structures', which together relate to the idea of 'autonomy' in THN. Degrees of empowerment can then be measured according to both the existence of opportunities to make a choice and actual use of these opportunities. Thus: 'if a woman in Benin wants to send her daughter to school, is there a school for the daughter to go to? If yes, does the woman actually make the decision to send her daughter to school? If yes, does the daughter actually attend school?' Developing a variety of indicators, it is claimed that these can identify and compare the opportunity structures open to different individuals in different settings. The second approach builds on Richard Ryan's work on cross-cultural autonomy, specifically his scale of choices from integrated internalisation (maximum autonomy) to external imposition or pressures (heteronomy). But rather than pursuing a single measure Alkire advocates developing specific measures of the autonomy a person experiences in different domains of her life, such as health, education, friendships and collective decision-making. In both approaches these measures of empowerment, agency and opportunities would need to be compared with the actual functionings of people, in order to identify those who don't have certain choices, and those who do but choose not to exercise them. It should enable research to distinguish those who are 'starving' from those who are 'fasting'.

Both basic need and capability approaches recognise the crucial importance of a basic level of security in human wellbeing, but in Chapter 5 Geof Wood argues strongly for giving it greater prominence. Security and predictability express a primordial instinct to seek safety for oneself and valued others, and to avoid fear of uncertainty. Security can represent the exercise and the enhancement of personal control and autonomy over events and processes affecting one's wellbeing over time. However, Wood wants to inject a note of realism by focusing on the informal conditions that influence predictability and on behaviours 'which are, or could be, in the control of ordinary people in poor situations, given modest policy support'. Here he draws on recent and contributory work on insecurity and welfare regimes in the developing world that distinguishes three meta-regimes: insecurity regimes, informal security regimes and welfare state regimes (Gough and Wood *et al.* 2004). The first, Bevan (2004b) argues, is characteristic of many of the failing states of Sub-Saharan Africa. These lack any predictable settings for individuals, households and communities and are distinguished by widespread conditions of gross insecurity. But more common across developing countries it is argued are informal welfare regimes which are founded on a notion of 'dependent security', wherein poor people trade some measure of informal protection and predictability in return for dependence on patrons and longer-term insecurity and where these relations of patronage constitute the foundations of the state (McGregor 1989b).

But how are we to operationalise 'dependent security' and thus render it useful to a wellbeing research agenda? Is this another case of a missing methodological sidecar? In the last section Wood identifies seven principles for improving security within informal regimes: altering time preference behaviour; enhancing capacities to prepare for hazards; formalising rights; 'de-clientelisation'; enlarging choice via pooling risks; improving the predictability of institutional performance; and strengthening membership of well-functioning collective institutions. In each case he proposes indicators to track these posited preconditions. Consideration of these dimensions, he argues, provides a way in which socio-economic security can be integrated into future analysis of wellbeing.

Issues of measurement and methodology are the central concern of Chapter 6 by Mark McGillivray, but he returns to macro-measures of human development. Starting from the well-known Human Development Index (HDI), he notes that country scores are highly correlated with national income per capita, the most accepted measure of economic wellbeing achievement. This suggests that HDI does not capture the rich essence or vitality of the wellbeing concept. But rather than rejecting it as redundant, he notes that some countries perform better in the HDI than predicted by per capita income and some countries perform worse. Building on this he develops a measure *Mu* (μI) to capture that part of wellbeing achieved independently of income. The chapter then looks at correlations between this measure and other wellbeing-related indicators. He finds that measures of youth education status and gender empowerment perform best, although best of all is the widely used indicator of adult literacy. Though this is purely a measurement exercise, these findings throw fresh light on the theory and operationalisation of human need: wider notions of health and still more of personal *autonomy* require new and distinct research approaches.

Resources, agency and meaning

The three chapters in Part II all explore the linkages between concepts of resources, social relationships and development practice and how these three then relate to a concept of wellbeing. Sarah White and Mark Ellison begin in Chapter 7 by detailing the contributions a concept of 'resources' can make to our understanding of wellbeing. Their major argument is that resources do not have a fixed meaning but are constituted through social practice – their meaning is contingent on both the intention of their use and the negotiation of their meaning with others. This argument has implications for how we research wellbeing and for development practice. While we may construct 'resource profiles' to record material, human, social, cultural and natural resources, their significance for wellbeing will depend on understandings about how these resources can and cannot be used and the value that can be achieved from them in particular contexts. Importantly they note that all forms of resources have material, relational and symbolic dimensions. For example, while land can be conventionally categorised as a material resource, in many specific contexts and in particular instances we cannot overlook its relational and symbolic dimensions. As such we should avoid repeating the errors of other frameworks that reify categories of capitals or assets and analytically trap them in one dimension or the other.

This analysis helps to expose 'the conceit', whereby development agencies assume that because they are familiar with 'a resource' they understand what would constitute its appropriate or 'rational' use in a different social, political and cultural context. The chapter concludes with a plea for a degree of balance between a universal framework and one sensitive to local understandings. In researching wellbeing they argue, 'the need is for a model which is sufficiently open and dynamic that it can be used in a variety of contexts in order to expose the specificity of each'.

Chapter 8 by Bebbington, Hinojosa-Valencia, Muñoz and Lizarazu is drawn from a more detailed engagement with development agencies and practice. Based on a study of NGO interventions in the highlands of Bolivia and Peru, the chapter highlights a number of *desencuentros* – discontinuities or disconnects – between the understanding and intentions of the agencies and the rural people they were working with. The chapter provides a brief and critical review of the conceptual background and development of livelihoods approaches, differentiating between those that focus on what people 'think and do', and those that are more concerned with what people 'have and control'. Leaning more towards the 'think and do' type of approach, the chapter moves on to discuss a range of different *desencuentros*. The common factor linking these, they argue, is that interventions are driven more by organisational momentum and inertia than by close engagement with the realities and aspirations of the populations. Thus, there is an apparent misconception that the livelihood strategies of rural people are more static, spatially fixed and agriculturally focused than is the case. Rather the authors emphasise the importance of taking account of time: while the livelihoods of rural households in the present were focused on the use of material and natural resources, and this then was the focus of intervention, their aspirations for the future were more concerned with investment in human resources, to enable future generations to escape from agriculture.

A further and crucial area of *desencuentro* is around the notion of collective action, a major topic of academic and political debate in the countries of the Andes. The authors note that much intervention has been focused on promoting collective action for the management of natural resources, in the belief that this was building on the traditions of *comunero* systems, but they argue that this misperceives the organisation of production within the communities. While the community has played a strong role in governing resource management, it has not had the same role in respect of production. In adopting too sweeping a view of the role of collective action the interventions underestimate differentiation within communities and dissatisfaction among *comuneros* regarding the inequality of benefits from collective arrangements. This, they argue, is an important explanation of the rise of more privately oriented strategies.

James Copestake in Chapter 9 is similarly concerned with understanding the nature of wellbeing in Latin America and the 'intrinsic [and] instrumental worth of material, cultural and political relations'. Focusing on Peru he connects the study of wellbeing with Latin American scholarship on inclusion and exclusion. He argues that we need to explore the ways in which inventories of resources relate to inclusionary and exclusionary processes in Peruvian society. In order to do this he reviews the formal economic model developed by Adolfo Figueroa to explain the persistence of dualism, inequality and poverty in developing societies such as Peru. The chapter explains the *sigma society* model and proposes a stronger dialogue between this type of formal economic modelling and the insights offered by other social sciences. What is novel for economics about the model is that it provides an endogenous explanation of the persistence of exclusionary processes in terms of structured interlinkages between the economy, polity and cultural systems. Like the Resource Profiles Framework, it considers the ways in which elite groups in societies such as Peru invest in status differences and cultural barriers to defend unequal power relations.

In the final section of the chapter, Copestake considers the implications for the role of development agencies and intervention in such societies. The model, he argues, warns against a false optimism that economic growth can resolve the structural dynamics that reproduce exclusion, poverty and dualism. Like White and Ellison, he argues that if development agencies are to adopt a more realistic approach they must focus on the negotiation of relationships rather than fixed notions of resources. They must also be more reflexive in their analyses of development contexts; placing themselves, their relationships and their values within these analyses.

Quality of life and subjective wellbeing

Silke Schmidt and Monika Bullinger open Part III with a survey of subjective quality of life (QoL) research in the medical and healthcare fields, where approaches to the assessment of individual health-related QoL (HRQoL) have burgeoned over the last two decades (Chapter 10). Measures that reflect the values and concerns of healthcare professionals, policy-makers, 'clients' and taxpayers in rich countries can encounter problems when applied to the developing world; hence they review recent cross-cultural research and illustrate both its complexity and the advances in understanding that have been achieved. The common challenges include identifying the important components of QoL (whether in the field of health or more broadly) and ensuring that all nations, cultural groups, and a representative selection of people from those groups are involved in the research from the start. Other challenges include that of accurate translation between different languages and the need for comprehensive psychometric and field-testing to ensure conceptual, measurement and scalar equivalence. Schmidt and Bullinger consider that the World Health Organization Quality of Life measure (WHOQOL) is a leading instrument, due to its rigorous development process involving simultaneous work in fifteen centres, seven of which were located in developing countries or 'transition' economies.

The authors conclude that quality of life data can be compared in a meaningful way across nations and cultural groups. Furthermore, the WHOQOL study suggests that the components of HRQoL constructed by different cultures are similar, lending strong support to the notion that the concept of QoL is a 'cross-cultural universal', at least in relation to health.[35] However, Schmidt and Bullinger conclude that extending quality of life studies to very different cultures requires a readiness to accept new and different assessment tools and outcome indicators in both research and practice.

One developing country that has undertaken a consistent enquiry into quality of life for more than a quarter of a century is South Africa, and in Chapter 11 Valerie Møller summarises its findings and methodological lessons. Though South Africa is classified as a middle-income country, it exhibits huge inequalities in income and infrastructure, plus social and cultural diversity, which make it a useful 'social laboratory' for such research. The core task of the South African QoL Trends project was 'to define the essence of the good life in South Africa and to develop the method that would tell us to what extent real life matched the good life'. This was driven by a desire to 'lend a voice to the invisible people', especially the black and coloured populations, and to demonstrate that illiterate people could participate meaningfully in such surveys. Discovering early on that the correlation between subjective assessments and objective living conditions in South African samples was unusually strong, they decided to focus on the former, which had previously been neglected. The questions were phrased in terms of personal QoL as the researchers wanted people to describe and evaluate their own lives, but this proved limiting due to the strong role of collectivism in South African society and people's desire to take social quality of life into account.

---

[35] L. Camfield and S. Skevington 'Quality of life and wellbeing', paper presented at the inaugural workshop of the ESRC research group on Wellbeing in Developing Countries, University of Bath, 13–17 January 2003 have also found considerable overlap between the common domains and facets developed within the WHOQOL group and the basic and intermediate needs of THN, with the exception of critical autonomy.

Since the survey has traversed the ending of Apartheid and the coming of democracy in South Africa, it offers a unique perspective on the impact of rapid and deep political and structural change on personal QoL. Moller reports that immediately after the first open elections in South Africa both domain-specific and global life satisfaction rose to the levels found in western nations and became equalised across groups, only to fall back a year later when it appeared that the promised changes were failing to occur. The big picture given by the numbers was enhanced by case studies with particular population groups, for example, 'time use' studies of young and elderly people. When the group asked, 'what would make ordinary South Africans happy?' this split along economic lines, with poor South Africans requesting improvements to their living conditions (for example access to jobs, utilities and education), and richer respondents focusing on safety, security and a strong economy.

Finally Mariano Rojas in Chapter 12 reports a study of life satisfaction in another middle-income developing country, Mexico. He takes an inferential or 'bottom-up' approach to the data and expresses his commitment to studying a 'person of flesh and blood in her circumstance'. He characterises the researcher's role as understanding, not assessing, since the person surveyed must be the authority on their condition. Rather than ask about satisfaction with life 'as a whole', he investigates satisfaction with concrete areas of being, such as work, health and family life. On the basis of information from the Mexican survey, the investigation uses factor-analysis techniques to define seven 'domains of life' (health, economic, job, family, friendship, personal and community) and to construct indicators of satisfaction in these domains. Interestingly, six of the seven domains derived by Rojas's principal components analysis parallel those derived from Cummins's (1995, 1996) meta-analyses of measures of QoL and life satisfaction.

Rojas reports that satisfaction in the family domain (satisfaction with spouse, children and rest of family) is crucial for life satisfaction, together with the health, personal and job domains. Education seems to be intrinsically valuable as its effect spreads across all domains, particularly those most important for life satisfaction. However, the overall fit between satisfaction with all domains-of-life and overall life satisfaction is low. Moreover, the non-poor were only 6 per cent more satisfied with their lives as a whole than the poor were, which raises interesting questions around the relationship between global and domain-specific life satisfaction, and the reliability of global questions (Diener et al. 2000). Rojas concludes that wellbeing, understood as life satisfaction, and approached from a 'domains of life' perspective, is a complex phenomenon. There are intricate interrelations between the domains of life, and their relationship to global life satisfaction is non-linear. Therefore, policies to improve wellbeing should focus not only on those domains that are very important, but also on those domains where satisfaction is relatively low.

Conclusion: researching wellbeing

The final part of the book addresses the question of how the concept of wellbeing might be translated into an effective research programme that can yield valuable insights both for academia and for policy. In the penultimate chapter Philippa Bevan identifies five sets of barriers to the type of multidisciplinary research that a wellbeing agenda requires. While the other four are not be underestimated, she focuses her chapter on the intellectual and disciplinary barriers and develops a framework for reflecting upon these. Based on an independent research project which included the WeD programme and other attempts at multi-disciplinary poverty research as its subjects, she develops what she calls the Foundations of Knowledge Framework (FoKF).

The FoKF identifies nine foundational elements of conceptual thinking in the social sciences as they attempt to study poverty: the domain or research question; the value or normative standpoint; the ontology or underlying assumptions about the nature of the world; the epistemology or ways of knowing about the world; the central theories and models; the associated methodologies and modes of analysis, the nature of the empirical findings; the rhetorical language in which the results are couched; and the implications for policy and practice. These, she argues, generate the intellectual barriers to successful multi- or interdisciplinary communication and work. All nine must be considered when academics from different disciplinary or sub-disciplinary backgrounds come together in efforts to collaborate effectively. The Framework is essentially a means of making explicit what assumptions, presumptions or blind spots are present in particular disciplinary contributions to the study of poverty or wellbeing. In the final part of the chapter she builds on the framework to advocate a number of positions with respect to the nine elements which she regards as necessary for the success of future studies of wellbeing.

Following on from this, Chapter 14 concludes the volume with a description of the transition from conceptual framework to an operational methodology for studying the social and cultural wellbeing in developing countries. In order to do this the chapter explores what the major themes of convergence and challenge are that have arisen out of the contributions to the volume. It notes a strong willingness for interdisciplinary communication and is optimistic about the emergence of a transdisciplinary agenda for researching wellbeing that can be both academically valuable and of relevance to policy thinking. The chapter uses the points of convergence to reconsider the bridges that exist between the needs, resources and QoL frameworks and seeks to highlight where further challenges both to conceptual thinking, empirical research and policy lie.

Part I

Human needs and human wellbeing

2 Conceptualising human needs and wellbeing

Des Gasper

2.1 Needs and wellbeing: issues and themes

What are the relationships between human needs and human wellbeing? I will address the question by considering the conceptual linkages between these two umbrella categories. This requires investigation of the nature of each of them as a family of concepts. That is attempted in sections 2.3 and 2.4 of this chapter. I briefly point to the further topic of their empirical connections in section 2.5. Bracketing these discussions, the opening and closing parts of the chapter consider and compare human needs and human wellbeing as research programmes. How far is the wellbeing programme a continuation or successor to the tradition of thinking and investigation on human needs, and what lessons may arise from the somewhat troubled history of research on needs?

The rise of wellbeing as an important, if not yet major, research focus in development studies and policy and more widely is extremely welcome and long overdue. As recently as 1994, Routledge's *The Social Science Encyclopaedia* (Kuper and Kuper 1994) could appear without an entry on wellbeing or quality of life or happiness. Even in two excellent late 1980s textbooks on the emergent field of economic psychology (Furnham and Lewis 1986; Lea, Tarpy and Webley 1987) wellbeing remained a minor theme. Lea *et al.* in over 500 pages did not discuss it as a separate topic; Furnham and Lewis devoted just four pages to the relationship between wealth and happiness. Often wellbeing was considered no topic for science; or income and wealth remained largely taken for granted as the synthetic concerns which would reflect or provide opportunity for every other value.

Quality of Life research has, it is true, been active since the 1960s, but it has been a delimited specialist interest, largely confined to and within rich countries. The attention in the 1970s to the Physical Quality of Life Index (PQLI) did not have much impact or endure. Only during the

I would like to thank Ian Gough for very helpful advice.

1990s with the Human Development school of thought centred in the United Nations Development Programme (UNDP) can we say that a broader quality-of-life focus became common in studies of low-income countries. Importantly, UNDP's work has treated both income-poor and income-rich countries in the same frame.

Subjective Wellbeing (SWB) research too has been a partly separate, specialist interest of some psychologists, largely limited, again, to and within rich countries. Only with the large-scale entry of participatory methods of investigation into development studies in the 1990s has attention to SWB become substantial worldwide, sometimes even challenging the dominance of income measures.

While applauding the rise of wellbeing research, and its present appearance in development studies, we should remember that this is overall still rather little, rather late. We should diagnose old and new resistances that this research stream may face, and its internal limitations and problem areas, in order to avoid or at least mitigate a subsequent phase of decline and even rejection such as occurred for work on *basic human needs*. The substantial 1970s wave of work on needs, the PQLI etc., was strongly criticised, opposed and to a large extent set aside in the 1980s and early 1990s. The opposition came from multiple sources, including, for example, radical Greens such as Ivan Illich (1978), not only from true believers in markets and economic growth. What warnings and lessons for tactics and strategy can we draw from the rise and fall of basic human needs research and policy in the 1960s to 1980s?

The starting point for this chapter is the hypothesis that conceptual clarification in these areas, wherever possible, is essential and not a luxury pastime. The needs movement foundered for long in a mire of messy conceptualisation. The work on wellbeing has a basic armoury of concepts from psychology, ethics and welfare economics (seen in the work of, for example, Ed Diener, Derek Parfit and Amartya Sen), but may require more standardisation of a shared, integrative and tested set of terms. While no set of terms can be more than an imperfect set of working simplifications, not all sets are equally adequate. Better terminology can smooth communication between and within scientific communities, and influence and educate communication in wider arenas. Simplified concepts are an inevitable requirement in domains of social policy where research must interface with politics, politicians, planning, planners, public debate and debating publics. The difficulty is that each area of research and each forum of public debate tends to establish its own set of working simplifications to match its context-specific concerns. Even if internally adequate, the set may fail to match the sets of terms created in other contexts. Continuing with inconsistent and often unconsidered usages has a price. Careful attention is required then to which simplified schema or linked set of schemas will be relevant and workable, rather than risk that the wellbeing programme sinks into the mire or becomes pushed into a denigration zone as 'old politics', 'old thinking', like needs approaches were. Is such a conceptual framework attainable?

The chapter's main focus is on concepts, as a basis for refining models of wellbeing and needs and their relations. We will address the following misconceptualisations:

- First, that 'needs' is a single category; instead we must distinguish at least descriptive, instrumental and normative modes, and several different levels within each;
- Second, that 'Wellbeing' (WB) is a single unified category or just SWB (itself presumed to be unitary), or just either 'Objective Wellbeing' (OWB) or SWB; instead we must distinguish again between several levels and related categories.

More refined conceptualisation serves to establish needs approaches and wellbeing research as methodologies or frameworks in investigation, sets of questions rather than just packages of answers – in other words as research programmes.

The WeD project, with its multidisciplinary base and use of Doyal and Gough's complex theory of need, has a good start in conceptualisation. This chapter looks for complementary insights. It does not attempt to cover all the important aspects of needs discourse and focuses instead on the possible interrelations with wellbeing discourse.

2.2   The fall and rise of needs theory

In 1989, *The Economic Journal*, journal of the UK Royal Economic Society, published a ninety-page commissioned survey of development economics by Nick Stern, later the Chief Economist and Senior Vice President of the World Bank (2000–2003) and subsequently head of the Government Economic Service in the UK Treasury. The World Bank of the 1970s had espoused and to some degree pursued a policy priority to basic needs, largely interpreted as basic material needs that were to be conceptualised and specified by government planners, often economists. The approach was familiar from much earlier planning, for example in wartime, in state socialist countries and the Government of India, and in provision for refugees. Stern, the commissioned voice of late 1980s establishment development economics, expressed that mainstream's rejection and expulsion of what was now an alien conceptual body:

the basic needs ideas [of 'the so-called "basic needs" approach'; Stern 1989: 644] have real problems. What needs are basic and more worryingly what levels are held to be essential minima? What if these levels are infeasible ... ? Who decides which needs are basic and the appropriate level? In what sense are they basic if people who can afford to attain them do not choose to do so? ... [The questions] are not easy to answer in a satisfactory way and one is left with a certain scepticism about the approach. (Stern 1989: 645)

Ironically, during his later tenure as World Bank Chief Economist and then as a Permanent Secretary in the UK Treasury, Stern inherited and formally endorsed the late 1990s commitments to the Millennium Development Goals, a programme of priority to basic needs fulfilment (even if only slow and partial) that represented proposed answers to his late 1980s questions. Some needs, such as for life of a reasonable duration, freedom from easily controlled diseases, literacy and numeracy, freedom from physical violence, are specifiable in ways that can satisfy the demands of 'a certain scepticism', as was apparent in 1989 to those who were ready to see. However, setting criteria of perfection for other approaches serves to eliminate them from consideration before one then proceeds with one's own thoroughly imperfect approach.

How did the basic needs approach fall from favour? In addition to political economy and political circumstance, the following weaknesses contributed: first, lack of clarity in the approach on its diverse sources and their distinct and sometimes competing characters; second, lack of a technical language that was both sufficiently refined and systematised yet sufficiently vivid, memorable and thus usable; and third, lack of a political language that was sufficiently flexible and appealing.

How did the basic needs approach revive and evolve into more robust forms or successors after the attacks and denigration in the late 1970s and 1980s? First, I suggest, by better distinguishing between diverse modes of needs theorising; second, by much stronger conceptualisation; and third, by engaging more savvily in the politics of ideas.

In distinguishing modes, normative needs theorising and instrumental needs theorising were explicitly distanced from fixed commitments in psychological theory, as we will see in section 2.3. In conceptualisation, relevant distinctions were introduced or standardised:

- between needs (as priority functionings) and satisfiers (things which could allow those functionings); satisfiers vary enormously whereas the needs they serve can be shared and stable; we can thus distinguish levels of generality and distinguish stages in causal sequences;

- between attaining/attainment and being able to attain (or in other words between functioning and capability); and between guaranteeing attainments and strengthening capabilities;
- between orders of priority: for example, education and health and physical security are often given highest priority, above even employment and housing; and
- between various types of policy-relevant activity: setting a policy framework for discussing ends, versus prioritising, versus setting targets, versus attempted public sector delivery.

The systematising work along these lines by Johan Galtung, Carlos Mallmann and others in the late 1970s (e.g. Lederer 1980) was too late and incomplete to save the basic needs approach from the antagonistic forces that arrived in power. The subsequent period out of favour was used by some determined and creative theorists of needs (or, in Sen's case, of a next generation of concepts), such as Penz, Braybrooke, Max-Neef and Sen, to systematise various conceptual and theoretical insights. Len Doyal and Ian Gough took over this improved toolbox, and integrated a wealth of relevant work from the diverse sciences of wellbeing.

Peter Penz, in a book (1986) that influenced Doyal and Gough, had patiently deconstructed the mainstream economics principle of consumer sovereignty, which holds that our criterion of assessment should simply be what consumers choose or would choose. The principle proves to be massively under-defined, since preferences are in part endogenous and for several other reasons. It is only defensibly operationalisable through large-scale supplementation by normative principles of a quite different character that grow out of thinking about the substance of human interests. Penz was led back first to happiness as a criterion, abandoned far earlier by economists but much more measurable today; but that criterion too is weakened by endogeneity and by many of the same problems that face preference fulfilment. He concluded instead in favour of basic needs, understood as the requirements of physical and mental health and other basic human interests (a modicum of security and social inclusion, etc.), as giving a conception that could rationally command the support of diverse political viewpoints by ensuring the conditions needed for each of their diverse principles to acquire relevance (Penz 1991).

Thus besides better conceptualisation, needs approaches became more effectively located in wider intellectual and political space. More appealing and more ethically charged labels were found – 'human development' and 'human security' (e.g. Gasper 2005a; St. Clair 2004, 2006) – and then connected to the powerfully focusing and motivating theme of human rights. Attention-catching, thought-provoking indices were devised: the Human Development Index (HDI) and its siblings. And an insulated, influential organisational niche was created in 1989: the UN's Human Development Report Office was created with intellectual independence yet public access and influence. In all three respects – labels, indices and niche – Mahbub ul Haq's contribution was vital.

The next two sections concentrate on the clarification of modes and the systematisation of concepts, first for needs and then for wellbeing and the connections. We return in the final section to the politics of ideas and consider possible implications for the strategy of the present-day research programme on wellbeing.

2.3   Conceptualising human needs

Despite considerable criticism, including in forms more hostile than Stern's (e.g. Springborg 1981), the term 'need' continued and continues in massive, daily use in many fields of social policy (see e.g. Brazelton and Greenspan 2000; Witkin and Altschuld 1995), management, and marketing (see Jackson, Jager and Stagl 2004), including in the international social policy areas of the Millennium Development Goals and humanitarian aid. Needs language caters to extremely widespread functional requirements – to make analyses of motivation thicker and more realistic, and to indicate instrumental roles, typically towards priority objectives; but it is hard to order, precisely because of how widespread and varied such roles are.

Meanings and obscurities

A recent study of needs assessment in humanitarian emergencies reported that the term 'need' has become a source of confusion there, given, it proposed, at least three substantially different meanings in the humanitarian context.

1 Basic human needs ('food is a basic human need')
2 A lack of basic human needs ('these people need food')
3 A need for relief assistance or some other humanitarian intervention ('these people need food aid') (Darcy and Hofmann 2003: 16).

The first meaning is need as a noun, something that is needed; the second is need as a verb, about the needing of the noun. Darcy and Hofmann warn that a noun-language of need is sometimes misleading. 'discussion of the *need* for protection tends to "commodify" a concept that cannot be reduced to these terms' (2003: 17). The more important distinction is between the first two meanings and the third, which refers to a particular method or satisfier (e.g. food aid) for fulfilling the more general need (food). '[N]eeds assessment is often conflated with the formulation of responses, in ways that can lead to resource-led intervention and close down other (perhaps more appropriate) forms of intervention' (2003: 16), for example monetary aid or employment provision rather than relief food supply.[1]

Darcy and Hofmann propose to drop the term 'need' and replace it by other terms, including 'risk', particularly 'acute risk'. In addition to the ubiquity and endlessness of chains of implied requirements (or, to use a less ambiguous term, requisites), and the noun-verb ambiguity, they hold that use of the term 'risk' is less likely to lead to the conflation of problem assessment and response formulation. In contrast to the word 'need', the word 'risk' will not be applied to response formulation too. Yet, after these remarks, and like the rest of us, Darcy and Hofmann's report continues using the concepts of need and needs intensively.

So, although needs language can be a source of confusion at present in humanitarian assistance, the appropriate route may be to upgrade rather than avoid it. We can go far further in clarification than do Darcy and Hofmann. It is sobering to consider that long-standing clarifications remain little known.

Modes of needs discourse

Philosophers such as Brian Barry (1990), Paul Taylor (1959) and David Wiggins (1985) consolidated a number of important insights about needs language. Several of them are captured in a 'relational formula': A needs S, if S is a necessary condition for A to achieve N, and N is either directly an approved priority or is a necessary condition for achievement of the accepted approved priority P. Policy-oriented scholars took further steps, adding knowledge drawn from the complexities of practical use and policy debate. David Braybrooke's *Meeting Needs* (1987) and Doyal and Gough's *A Theory of Human Need* (1991), in particular,

---

[1] The study later implicitly adds perhaps other meanings of need: (4) what is required for reducing the non-fulfilment of basic human needs, and (5) what is required for providing relief assistance or whatever other policy response. Each of these requisites will then have its own requirements.

highlighted that the chains of instrumental linkage can be long. Since they definitely do not have to contain only two or three links, a more complex vocabulary or usage is required. They also insist that the discourse of instrumental linkages towards priority objectives must be distinguished from the discourse of species-wide behavioural potentials and propensities. This distinction had been obscured by optimistic evolutionary ideology, from both the political left and right. Doyal and Gough's chapter 'The Grammar of "Need"' distinguished thus between:

1 'a drive or some inner state that initiates a drive ... Here "need" refers to a *motivational force* instigated by a state of disequilibrium or tension set up in an organism because of a particular lack (Thompson [*sic*], 1987, p. 13)' (Doyal and Gough 1991: 35); and
2 'a particular category of goals which are believed to be universalisable' (1991: 39) because they are necessary conditions for avoidance of serious harm.

This distinction is not consistently respected even in social science usage. I became more aware of this during a 1993–95 UK ESRC research project on human needs and wants, part of a multi-project programme on social science analyses and interpretations of global climate change sponsored by the Battelle Foundation. The programme led to a four-volume study, edited by Steve Rayner and Elizabeth Malone (1998), which included an extensive chapter on needs and wants (Douglas, Gasper, Ney and Thompson 1998). During a workshop in the needs-wants project it became evident that the participants – psychologists, economists, philosophers, sociologists, anthropologists – held to no consistent usage of 'need', as individuals, not only across disciplines. Yet most of us had read and thought about needs since the 1960s or 1970s. We jumped between different usages almost from one sentence to the next: between the variants identified by Darcy and Hofmann – more basic needs versus satisfiers; and verbs versus nouns – and also between needs as explanatory forces and factors, needs as (pre) requisites, and needs as particular sorts of moral priority claims.

Investigation in a range of literature confirmed that pervasively inconsistent usage existed not simply between different disciplines but was ingrained in the usages within disciplines. Sometimes need was referred to as an inbuilt (whether inborn or inculcated) drive, sometimes as the implied requirement of a given objective, sometimes as a normative priority, sometimes as presumptively all three at once – rarely with any explication or apparent awareness of this complex and fluctuating usage. By distinguishing modes, we can identify when jumps occur, consciously examine proposed linkages and jumps, and assess when they are acceptable and when not.

The prevalence of not only multiple usages but unannounced and even undetected mid-paragraph jumps between meanings suggested that a more emphatic and elaborate statement of grammar was required than in Braybrooke or Doyal and Gough. I proposed a fuller grammar for the field in the chapter which emerged for the Battelle study (Douglas *et al.* 1998) and more thoroughly in an earlier paper (Gasper 1996). The main ideas appear in an updated version in Gasper 2004, chapter 6. Here I will outline part of that framework, and then in section 2.4 relate it to ideas concerning wellbeing.

We can usefully distinguish three modes. In mode A, 'need' is a term used in evaluatively neutral description or explanation: to refer to a want or a drive or a potential. In mode B, a 'need' is a requisite for achieving an objective. Thus the requisite's normative necessity depends on the status of the objective, and on how essential it is for reaching that objective. In mode C a 'need' establishes a strong normative claim since the objective is a normative priority and the requisite is indeed essential. In all modes there is an ambiguity inasmuch as 'need' is sometimes applied to the objective and sometimes to the implied requisite. Further, whereas in mode A 'need' typically figures as a noun, a presence, in mode B it can often appear as a verb, a lack.[2]

What are the relationships of the modes? First, mode C, concerning priority objectives and requisites, is of course a subset of mode B which concerns any objectives and requisites. But we might sometimes encounter references to an instrumental mode as containing only the instrumental usages which are not in mode C. Second, mode A often overlaps with the other two, when fulfilment of some mode A need, some want or drive or potential, is seen as necessary for achievement of a specified objective (mode B), which may be a normative priority (mode C). Table 2.1 illustrates these interrelations, showing five possible cases. The five cases are: purely in mode A (type 1); purely in mode B (types 4 and 5); in both modes (types 2 and 3). If in mode B, a need can be either also in mode C or only of mode B. We will examine these cases further in section 2.4.

---

[2] Within these modes, there are dozens of different specific concepts of need (as indicated in Gasper 1996, 2004). Some are worth grouping further and keeping separate from others. For example, in mode A, needs which are expected to explain wants might be contrasted with needs that are expected to explain satisfactions; likewise, inborn needs against inculcated needs.

Table 2.1 *A modal analysis of the five types of 'need'*

| | NOT MODE B | MODE B | |
		MODE B ONLY	MODE C ALSO
MODE A	Type 1	Type 2	Type 3
NOT MODE A	–	Type 5	Type 4

Table 2.2 *A comparison of the modes employed in definitions of need*

	ECONOMICS DICTIONARY	SOCIOLOGY DICTIONARY	PSYCHOLOGY DICTIONARY	POLITICS DICTIONARY	PHILOSOPHY COMPANION	DOYAL & GOUGH
MODE A	–	X	X			X
MODE B	–	X		X	X	
MODE C	–	–	(X)	(X)	(X)	X

The threefold division of modes is an extension and generalisation of Doyal and Gough's contrast between a motivational force and an universalisable value or goal. Mode A covers more types of descriptive entity than only types of motivational force and covers more motivational forces than only drives; mode C could cover more types of normative claimant than universalisable goals; and we have, in addition, highlighted mode B.

Distinguishing mode B too is important: it is widespread in social science and everyday usage; it is correspondingly highlighted in Taylor's (1959) classic semantic dissection; and, vitally, recognising it helps us to understand why and how the common conceptual slippage between modes A and C occurs.

If we check our framework against some dictionary definitions of need we find all modes in use, but no discipline appears to refer regularly to all three (see Table 2.2). One – the social science discipline with the greatest resources and political influence, economics – has often tried to abandon the term altogether. Fortunately it remains the exception.

The Penguin Dictionary of Economics (Bannock, Baxter and Davis 1992) ignores the term 'need' (and 'basic need'). This is not an outlier case. Mainstream economics has systematically shunned needs-theorising, partly due to a confusion between modes. (Vivid examples of both shunning and confusion, over several decades, are collected in Jackson *et al.* 2004.) Resistance to engaging in mode C discourse on ethically/ publicly reasoned priorities as opposed to reliance on individual preferences alone, and objection further to claims that the State should then provide such priority items, has contributed irrationally to rejection of mode A and mode B discourses too, as if the three were inseparable. Much of economics remains primitive or completely deficient in explanation of wants, as if this would impugn the sovereign consumer, and in investigation of human requisites, which can become politically embarrassing for the privileged. For study of human requisites Dasgupta (1993) is a noble exception; he endorses the N-word.

The Penguin Dictionary of Sociology (Abercrombie, Hill and Turner 1994) records two meanings: first, a need as a factor that motivates individuals – this fits our mode A; and second, need as a functional prerequisite – this fits mode B.

The Penguin Dictionary of Psychology (Reber and Reber 2001) records what it considers are two main meanings and some subsidiary (more problematic or less common) ones. (1) 'Some thing or state of affairs which, if present would improve the wellbeing of an organism.' This seems to fit mode C, if we take wellbeing as a normative category, as is implied by the name. However, the lack of specification of which type of organism (a bacterium?) leaves the ethical status of the needs in doubt. (2) 'The internal state of an organism that is in need of such a thing or state of affairs' – this concerns a lack, as compared to the first meaning, which concerned what would remedy a lack. In addition: (3a) a need as a drive – a mode A meaning, which the dictionary correctly warns often does not apply for mode C needs; and (3b) a need as a motive or incentive, wish, desire or craving – in other words, other mode A meanings.

The Oxford Dictionary of Politics (McLean and McMillan 2003) adopts mode B: 'what is required in order to do something or achieve some state of being'. It continues: ' "Human needs", for example, have been taken to describe requirements which must be satisfied if harm to an agent is to be avoided'. If we deem 'harm' a morally charged term, then the supportive definition perhaps moves into mode C; likewise when, later in the entry, purported needs are the proposed 'requirements of human flourishing'. However, the language here is evaluative, indicating what is desirable, rather than prescriptive, indicating what is proposed for action in the light of all relevant factors.

The Oxford Companion to Philosophy (Honderich 1995) sits in the same way near the border of modes B and C but perhaps within mode B: 'what an organism requires to live the normal life of its kind', with 'normal' promptly clarified as 'flourishing rather than merely surviving'. Absence of the need (or, to be precise, a need-satisfier) causes harm. But the definition speaks of any organism, not specifically human beings, which weakens any presumption that the flourishing involved (of say a mosquito) carries normative significance in a moral universe of humans.

Doyal and Gough's theory of need highlights the distinction between modes A and C (1991: ch. 3). It investigates the content of needs that derive from the requirements of being a competent member of one's society and of avoiding fundamental harm. It does not highlight and define mode B in addition to modes A and C.

Definition of only modes A and C leaves the two apparently quite different and evokes too little modal caution. The incoherent pattern of usage across disciplines can be better understood and remedied by delineation of mode B in addition. We can then see how mode B usage and mode A usage are too easily slid into each other, since both are positive: normatively neutral. And we can see also how mode B and mode C usages are too easily fused, since both use an instrumental logic and there is ambiguity often over whose are the objectives referred to (e.g. 'the organisation's objectives', 'the policy's objectives', 'society's objectives'). Overall, usage across the whole field, from mode A through to C, can slide thus into an often incoherent, undifferentiated mire.

Elements of normative needs discourse

Within mode C discourse a number of further elements must be distinguished. One could similarly elaborate within mode A, as psychologists and phenomenologists do; but here we focus on normative needs discourse, as prelude to a discussion of *wellbeing*. Braybrooke (1987) identified the following constituent elements in normative needs discourse:

1 implicitly, a decision-making group deciding for a particular target population within a particular political community (the three can be identical but are often not);
2 a criterion / target objective which one uses to determine need – for example, health or autonomy or a conception of human flourishing;
3 a set of types of need, derived as proposed necessary implications of that criterion;
4 a set of levels, such as illustrated later in the middle column of Table 2.4 below, at each of which we specify satisfiers contributing towards the chosen criterion;
5 at each level, for each of the types of need (where relevant), a specified indicator and a specified provision target.

For our present purposes a few points merit highlighting. First, concerning the instrumental linkages between levels: a satisfier can contribute to fulfilling several needs; a need/lack can often be met by many alternative satisfiers; and not all proposed satisfiers are effective. Second, within mode C (normative) needs discourse, each possible criterion of priority generates a particular specification of implied requisites, normatively fundamental needs. The criteria found in use range from as little as survival (to a normal human lifespan) to as much as 'human flourishing' (Gasper 1996, 2004). Thus, third, from an understanding of mode C needs as the requisites for wellbeing, we see that different conceptions of wellbeing lead to different specifications of needs. And fourth, each particular level chosen as the focus in needs discourse matches a particular sort of conception of wellbeing, as section 2.4 will now show.

2.4   Concepts of wellbeing and their interrelations with concepts of need

Conceptual confusion is widespread within the field of wellbeing too. One factor has been that mainstream economics, shielded and satisfied by its doctrine of people's wants/preferences as the central and sometimes even only acceptable normative criterion, long avoided the empirical and conceptual investigation of wellbeing, abandoning it to other disciplines.

We should again distinguish several variants and several levels. The various concepts of wellbeing in use will be seen to correspond primarily to different levels. A contrast between modes is less important here, for wellbeing is more consistently a normative concept than is need. Perhaps ironically, this normative concept of wellbeing includes a major branch known as 'objective wellbeing', in contrast to so-called 'subjective wellbeing'. OWB centrally considers externally assessed and approved, and thereby normatively endorsed, non-feeling features of a person's life, for example matters such as mobility and (low) morbidity. SWB centrally refers to feelings and/or judgements of the person whose wellbeing is estimated.

If the approver is the person herself, and if feeling good is an approved feature, indeed, even the overriding approved feature, then we would have a case where the OWB and SWB categories overlap. In general, however, the approved features concern non-feelings aspects: such as health, longevity, autonomy and access to desired or approved opportunities. Insofar as health covers mental health, then the categories can overlap there, for example with reference to depression or its absence. Further, the more that feelings are based on systematic and deep reflection the more might SWB overlap in character with OWB.

Table 2.3 *The scope for confusion in usage of 'subjective/objective wellbeing'*

		THE FOCUS OF MEASUREMENT/ ESTIMATION (main criterion)	
		'Objective', as focused on externally approved non-feelings	*'Subjective', as focused on feelings*
METHOD OF MEASUREMENT/ ESTIMATION (subsidiary criterion)	*'Objective', as external measurement/estimation*	Case I: Focus on externally approved and estimated non-feelings; clearly 'OWB'	Case II
	'Subjective', as using subject's self-report	Case III	Case IV: clearly 'SWB'

The 'subjective' and 'objective' labels are often unsatisfactory. As Veenhoven, among others, stresses, the ambiguity in the meanings of OWB and SWB causes confusion and is pernicious yet soluble. Table 2.3 indicates that we need at least four categories not two. Feelings can be 'objectively' studied, by externals, as in case II in Table 2.3; and in case IV in the same table, self-reports on feelings are sometimes valid and reliable measures.[3]

The philosopher Derek Parfit's (1984) influential list went one step further than an SWB/OWB division and contained three types of notion of wellbeing:

1 Hedonism: wellbeing as pleasure;
2 Desire theories: wellbeing as the fulfilment of preferences/desires;
3 Objective list theories: wellbeing as the attainment of the elements in a list of what makes a life well-lived.

Hedonism represents a crude version of the SWB conceptualisation, crude because psychologists identify other aspects of feelings besides pleasure. Objective list theories correspond to OWB. Influenced by the practice of economics, Parfit adds preference fulfilment to the list. It is a distinct conception because preference fulfilment does not necessarily give pleasure and is not always in normatively approved forms. When we ask what the preferences are for or about, we get a hint that we may have to go further than a list of three. Are the preferences for commodities,

---

[3] From decades of research, Veenhoven (2006) advises that we should use a 3×3 rather than 2×2 matrix of categories, with nine possibilities rather than four, while recognising that we face a spectrum of possibilities along each axis rather than clearcut divides.

for characteristics, for satisfaction, for (in Sen's terms) other-oriented agency objectives, or for something else?

Seven concepts of wellbeing

If we take the categories added to micro- and welfare economics by Kelvin Lancaster, Sen and others, and connect them to traditional categories in economics and ethics, we obtain an extended narrative sequence of how control over resources connects through to human fulfilment, as outlined in Table 2.4 (to be read from bottom to top).

The role of the table is not to insist that this is exactly how wellbeing must be conceived. Many of the main determinants of wellbeing, such as family life and friendship, religion and other belief systems, culture and role designations, do not readily fit into this economics-derived perspective. However, the extended sequence indicates how several different conceptions of the content (rather than sources) of wellbeing can be seen as focusing on different levels in this sequence. It helps us to grasp the plurality of wellbeing conceptions.

Table 2.4's first column presents the following seven wellbeing concepts, some of which have variants.

1 To judge wellbeing in practice, economists have traditionally focused on level 1A: control over or power to acquire commodities, as indicated by income and wealth; and level 1B, the acquisition of commodities. In Sen's terms this focus on control over things is a focus on opulence.
2 Economists have also used the concept of revealed preference: the presumption that choices fully reflect preferences. There are two associated conceptions of wellbeing that focus neither on things nor on further outcomes. First, since the presumption that choices fully reflect preferences is empirically mistaken, the implied or sometimes explicit stance is that wellbeing lies in making choices, whether or not these prove to fulfil *ex ante* preferences or promote other valued results. Second is the stance that wellbeing consists in the fulfilment of (*ex ante*) preferences, regardless of the real outcomes they bring. Since preferences can be formulated and focused upon for outcomes at various levels/stages – commodities, characteristics, functionings and so on – the conception of WB as preference fulfilment in fact emerges at several levels. Two are indicated in Table 2.4: 6A – fulfilment of preferences for obtaining certain goods, and 6B – fulfilment of preferences for attaining certain functionings.
3 Somewhat outside economists' categories is a third broad conception of wellbeing – as activity *per se*. It perhaps spans aspects of choice, purchase and consumption, and also includes some functionings and

Table 2.4 *Relating concepts of wellbeing to the stages in Sen's enriched narrative of consumer choice, consumption and functioning*

CONCEPTS OF WELLBEING (based on Gasper 2005b)	ALTERNATIVE LEVELS OF FOCUS IN STUDIES OF WELLBEING: PUTATIVE NARRATIVE SEQUENCE (from bottom to top) (source: Gasper 2005c)	DOYAL and GOUGH'S LEVELS IN *A THEORY OF HUMAN NEED* (1991) (with some contents of the more limited variant on their p. 170, and broad equivalences to levels in the narrative sequence)
4D: Objective list IV	HUMAN FULFILMENT as value fulfilment	
7: Pleasure/satisfaction = SWB (if we presume a crude mental model)	'Utility' – as HAPPINESS &/OR SATISFACTION (this is, clearly, not a unitary category; different aspects can be distinguished)	
6B. Preference fulfilment II	'Utility' – as DESIRE-FULFILMENT	
4C. Objective list III (the central OWB focus)	FUNCTIONINGS (other than satisfaction)	'UNIVERSAL GOAL' = avoidance of serious harm to persons (incl. social exclusion),
5. Capability/positive freedom	CAPABILITY (the range of lives which a person could attain)	
4B. Objective list II	CAPABILITIES (people's skills, capacities); and other characteristics of people	'BASIC NEEDS' = an 'optimum' of physical health and autonomy of agency
4A. Objective list I	CHARACTERISTICS OF GOODS, which are acquired through consumption	'UNIVERSAL SATISFIER CHARACTERISTICS' = adequate nourishment, shelter, education, environment, security, personal relationships, etc.
3. Activity	CONSUMPTION proper – viz., actual *use* of purchases/acquisitions.	
1B. Opulence II	PURCHASES and other acquisitions	SPECIFIC SATISFIERS
6A. Preference fulfilment I 2. Choice	'Utility' as CHOICE, which is typically assumed to reflect preference, and (as default case) weighted according to purchasing power.	
1A. Opulence I	INCOME AND RESOURCES/POWER TO ACQUIRE GOODS/ COMMODITIES	SOCIETAL PRECONDITIONS (MATERIAL AND PROCEDURAL) FOR NEED SATISFACTION

the stages of activity that precede and lead up to income and resources. In face of the accumulated evidence of a 'hedonic treadmill' in materially affluent countries, where ever more activity leads to no or very few hedonic gains (and perhaps far smaller gains than if they were not pursued via the path of commodity-production, -acquisition, -bonding and -discarding), this activist conception of wellbeing represents an addicted resignation, Promethean defiance. Henry Bruton's *On the Search for Well-Being* (1997) gives one statement of such a stance, by a distinguished development economist of the 1960s through the 1990s.

4 Several stages in the narrative correspond to some 'objective-list' conception of wellbeing, or to some sort of component in an 'objective list': certain characteristics acquired through consumption (this is the level of 'universal satisfier characteristics' stressed by Doyal and Gough); certain capabilities, seen as skills and abilities; certain functionings, such as long and healthy life; and value fulfilment or eudaimonia. I have grouped them here as variant conceptions of OWB, but one could also treat some or all of them separately.

5 Treated separately in the classification is Sen's category of capability. It too could be treated as an objective-list conception, but it has achieved independent prominence. Arguably the degree of promi-nence is more than it deserves, for a plausible conception of wellbeing will span a number of aspects, as Sen periodically reminds us.

6 Preference fulfilment is purportedly central in economists' treatment of wellbeing. Economists, unlike psychologists, retreated from direct attention to utility (ophelimity) as felt wellbeing.[4] Utility thereby came to focus instead, in principle, on preference fulfilment. In practice, however, this was reduced to wellbeing as choice or as sheer activity (conceptions 2 and 3 above).

7 Lastly, our old friend, wellbeing as pleasure or satisfaction – SWB, or at least one version of it – has been rarely studied by economists, until very recently. It has been left to other disciplines, whose findings most of economics then ignored.

The final column of Table 2.4 presents key components of Doyal and Gough's theory of need, in the same levels/stages format that has been applied to the concepts of wellbeing. Doyal and Gough's book did not itself make this precise comparison or exact links to the capability

---

[4] Let alone attention to utility as the possession of useful characteristics or performance of useful functionings, as considered by many sociologists, psychologists, designers, engineers and planners.

approach or wellbeing discourse. In the more limited variant of their theory, the 'universal goal' is 'Avoidance of serious harm: minimally disabled social participation' (1991: 170). This corresponds in part to the level or narrative-stage of 'functionings' in Sen's sense, what people are and do. The implied basic needs of physical health and autonomy of agency correspond to a level of concrete capabilities, not to Sen's abstracted general notion of capability. Mental health needs enter as requirements of autonomy of agency.[5]

Interrelations between concepts of need and concepts of wellbeing

To probe further the relations between the conceptual fields of needs and wellbeing, Figure 2.1 reformats Table 2.1's modal analysis of types of need, as a Venn diagram. The intersections of the three need modes give five cases, five areas in the diagram.

- The uppermost rectangle represents needs which are wants and/or behavioural drives (in other words, needs in mode A). It consists of areas 1 + 2 + 3.
- The middle rectangle represents needs which are requirements for a given objective (in other words, in mode B). It consists of areas 2 + 3 + 4 + 5.
- The third rectangle is a subset of the middle one and represents needs as normative priority requirements (in other words, in mode C). It consists of areas 3 + 4. This normative concept of need links – somewhat ironically in terms of labelling, as we noted – to the concept of objective wellbeing.

Area/case 3 indicates behavioural drives or wants which fulfil normative priority requirements. In a humanist/welfarist conception the central priority may be human wellbeing, typically interpreted as OWB (the formulation of which may or may not subsume SWB). Behind much of the sloppy usage of the term 'need' lies a presumption that all drives are of the area 3 type. This rests on an exceptionally rosy theory of human nature: that evolution or Providence have selected for us only those drives which lead to the promotion of normative priorities; thus all drives are supposed to be found in area 3, and areas 1 and 2 are presumed empty. Also contributing to casual usage is a sister presumption,

---

[5] Doyal and Gough discussed 'capabilities/functionings' as a package notion (1991: 156) and thus did not make the precise links. They instead tried to link all their 'basic needs' to the level of functionings (1991: 156). Nor did they use the distinction between capability (Sen's category) and capabilities (Nussbaum's).

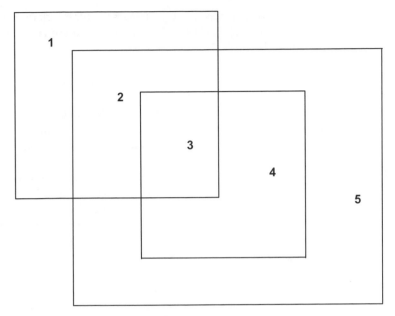

Figure 2.1 Venn diagram of the three modal usages of 'needs'

that we have no normative priorities which are not targeted by behavioural drives; in other words, that area 4 is empty.

In reality:

- Some drives fulfil no objective (see area 1 in Figure 2.1); they are non-functional, perhaps outmoded relics from prehistory.[6]
- Some drives fulfil an objective but not one that is a normative priority (case 2). This could be the case for some drives that promote SWB that is not considered OWB; possibly the drives of the addict. Some drives are even dysfunctional, leading to undesirable outcomes. They might be evolutionary experiments that failed but have not been eliminated, perhaps because too deeply wired-in, or, again, that may once have been functional but became outmoded.
- Many requisites for particular objectives are not drive-based (cases 4 and 5). Unfortunately, some of these concern normative priority objectives (case 4). Some case 4 instances may be examples that promote OWB but not SWB.

---

[6] In the case of wellbeing interpreted as activity, however, this category might be null, since all activity is deemed good.

- Case 5 concerns instances where a requisite serves some function but one that is not of normative priority and that, perhaps fortunately, has no behavioural drive behind it.

In sum, case 3 is the ideal or classical case, but is not the only one, contrary to those who treat the term 'need' in a way that does not distinguish modes. A more realistic assessment is that many drives do not promote normative priorities, some of these drives being dangerous and some indifferent; and that many functional requirements and normative priorities are not drive-based.

The danger case is case 2, where drives fulfil non-priority objectives, perhaps even anti-objectives. The other problem case is case 4, where normative priority objectives lack a behavioural motor behind them; a need's sheer lack does not itself 'serve to motivate or mobilise the subject' (Jackson *et al.* 2004: 11). Case 1 might be problematic too: drives that fulfil no objective instead divert us. Case 5 concerns undriven objectives of no significance and appears innocuous.

We have a number of interesting conclusions from this further step in modal analysis. Case 3 is not the only important case; and the value of needs discourse is not limited to or by the occurrence of case 3. Cases 1, 2 and 4, none of which matches the classical conception of needs, are all important cases for thinking about the promotion of wellbeing. Fulfilment of mode A needs is not the sole and guaranteed route to wellbeing.

2.5   Methodological and programmatic reflections

To draw conclusions on how wellbeing research can benefit from needs theory, let us review what needs theory is for, then ask in what ways it might serve wellbeing research, and wellbeing research in low-income countries in particular.

Needs theory for wellbeing research?

What is the goal of needs theory? First, it has an explanatory branch and purpose: to extend our explanatory repertoire beyond 'economic man' and other overly crude models. Second, it has a normative task: to structure, rationalise and humanise policy prioritisation, to extend our evaluative repertoire beyond the criterion of per capita income, and also beyond what is usually now embodied in Poverty Reduction Strategy Papers (PRSPs). Thirdly, in both cases it has a communicative function: to further the explanatory and normative tasks by frameworks that are simple enough, yet robust enough, to be both usable and not too misleading in routine professional and political discourse.

The post-fall revival in the 1990s of needs theory in both explanatory and normative branches, sometimes under new names and in more advanced versions, suggests that it can contribute helpfully in these roles. We see important explanatory work, such as that of Ryan and Deci, and normative and policy work on the HDI, Human Development Reports, Millennium Development Goals, humanitarian intervention and – insofar as human rights must often rest on claims about human needs (Doyal and Gough 1991; Galtung 1994; Gasper 2005b) – on rights-based approaches.

Specifically for wellbeing research, our Venn diagram analysis shows that needs discourse offers one valuable framework in the study of wellbeing, provided it is treated as a complex frame that gives space for our minds to work – as a tool in a research programme. It generates an agenda of three important types of situation for us to study (cases 1, 2 and 4), in addition to the optimistic case 3 that is widely presumed.

How far is Doyal and Gough's theory, a normative theory constructed for ethics and planning with primary reference to high-income countries, relevant for the study of wellbeing in low-income countries? Needs discourse has a role in critiquing income measures as extremely insufficient and quite often misleading. Most evidence suggests that income remains one significant contributor to subjective wellbeing for low-income countries but not beyond middle-income levels.[7] Doyal and Gough's approach, the spirit of which we presented in section 2.3, contributes an intellectual clarity and a refined framework for instrumental and normative analyses. It helps us think about modes, levels, indicators, the choices of normative priority criterion, and the use of available theory and evidence from many fields, together with practical reason, to specify the factors that influence key elements in real people's lives. At the same time, it is not itself a complex explanatory framework, and should be complemented by good explanatory analyses, including from within needs mode A. Arguably, the revival of needs approaches may only be sustained if backed and guided by such deeper explanatory research. Effective conceptualisations, albeit working simplifications, might be those that are informed by sustained investigation of the empirics. Let us look at two areas.

---

[7] Income remains a significant contributor until upper middle-income status (perhaps around $6,000 per capita p.a., in 1991 dollars, suggested by the World Values Survey (Dutt 2001)).

Research on the dynamics of need definition

Hamilton (2003) laments the divorce between, in our terms, mode-A analyses of needs and mode-C analysis of need, and the neglect, in his view, of the former. While showing limited insight into work in modes B and C, and exaggerating the difference between his conceptual framework and that of Doyal and Gough, his book on needs interestingly tackles interactions between the modes, notably the dynamics of transformation of mode A needs, and the processes of emergence of some felt needs as approved priorities. Hamilton notes that drives are not only instinctual in origin but are continually newly generated and also dissipated. He investigates the dynamics of transformation, including from pure wants to felt needs in the sense of drives, and how this mode-A need generation and transformation can affect what are instrumental requirements and agreed priorities. There can be moves from the status of pure want to the status of felt mode-C need, i.e. felt approved needs. Sometimes the reverse happens.

Figure 2.1 also arouses our curiosity concerning its area 4: normative needs which are not felt needs. In needs-mode A, needs which are not felt refers to unconscious drives; in mode B unfelt needs concern, for example, requirements for professional success which are not part of a person's desires-system and are sometimes even inconsistent with it; whereas in mode C they concern any requirements for *approved* goals (e.g. health) which are not part of the desire-system. To be part of a person's system of wants and desires is of course not sufficient for ensuring need fulfilment; in commodity-based societies, for example, law-abiding members who have no money are unable to fulfil many or most of their wants or needs. But for normative needs to be not part of the wants-system raises particular problems, which a wellbeing-oriented needs approach will investigate. Can space 4, the sphere of priority needs that are divorced from wants, be diminished – by developing wants corresponding to those needs, or finding functional substitutes for fulfilment of those needs?

*Research on substantive interconnections between
wellbeing and need fulfilment*

In mode A discourse, 'real needs' are drivers of behaviour; in mode C discourse, 'real needs' are those 'needs' whose fulfilment brings wellbeing. Not all (mode A) need fulfilment leads to wellbeing, whatever our interpretation of the latter – except perhaps in the bizarre yet influential interpretation of wellbeing as sheer activity. Using Manfred Max-Neef's language, we can speak of 'pseudo-needs': behavioural drives which fail to bring mature reflective satisfaction. Max-Neef's (1991) typology of needs and satisfiers is thought-provoking and should also be research-provoking. 'Pseudo satisfiers' give only fleeting fulfilment; 'violators' completely fail to satisfy, yet one may be habituated to them; 'inhibiting satisfiers' satisfy one need (often a short-term one) but at the cost of reducing satisfaction of other needs; and 'synergistic satisfiers' fulfil several needs at once, unlike 'singular satisfiers'. We do typically seek to fulfil several needs at once, as cultural theorists demonstrate – but how well our chosen satisfiers do this requires empirical evaluation and the answer is frequently critical. Modern market society can drive us onto commercialised hedonic treadmills which bring no enduring values but which destroy some values and destroy our habitat (Jackson et al. 2004).

The Venn diagram thus illustrates the sort of research agendas on wellbeing that arise in mode C needs discourse. These agendas are partly empirical, drawing from investigations in mode B: what leads to what, under which circumstances; and partly ethical, in arguments about the normative status of the outcomes and processes, for example in the discussion of different interpretations of 'wellbeing'. The empirical agenda has been insightfully pursued by, for example, Deci and Ryan, Diener, Illich, Robert Lane, Maslow, Theodore Roszak, Tibor Scitovsky and others. The ethical agenda has been pursued by philosophers. The deepest insights may come from authors who connect and cross-fertilise the two agendas, such as Fromm and Galtung, Giri, Nussbaum and Sen.

Politics of discourse

The research agendas of needs and wellbeing are of fundamental importance. How can these linked research programmes proceed effectively in political–intellectual–organisational space, aware not only of the precision, logic and empirical reference of discourse but also of its politics?

One lesson from the rise and fall of the basic needs approach in the 1960s to 1980s is the importance of clarification of concepts. We must in addition keep on monitoring them. Language in such territories is slippery and not stable, even if it appears stabilised in the short run. The word 'want', for example, evolved during the past two hundred years away from the meaning of lack or need, now to mean desire.

A second possible lesson is of the importance of labels. 'Basic needs' as a label was unappealing to many. 'Wellbeing' appears to work better. But how appealing, we should consider and check, really is 'wellbeing' as a label? When will it promote priority to the basic needs of the poorest and under what conditions?

A third lesson is that it is essential to invest not only in cross-disciplinary alliances but to build trans-disciplinary cooperation. The basic human needs work remained, despite the valiant efforts of thinkers such as Galtung, a weakly integrated product of a series of weakly cooperating intellectual communities, from economics, philosophy, psychology, health and nutrition. Many of the economists involved felt apparently that they could do nearly the whole job, or at least the job of synthesis; but they failed to build a structure with the depth and sophistication required to withstand the scepticism and even hostility of diverse stakeholders and other intellectual and political traditions. Presently too, the wellbeing and human development streams of work remain insufficiently connected. The UNDP-related Human Development work continues dominated by (broad-minded) economists, who are only recently and tentatively opening to the riches of research on wellbeing and needs. Fortunately, a strong feature of the WeD work is close long-term cooperation between researchers from psychology, health, economics, anthropology and social policy. Outreach to others, in philosophy, politics, sociology, planning, education and social work, and in the humanities, will be important too.

3 Basic psychological needs: a self-determination theory perspective on the promotion of wellness across development and cultures

Richard M. Ryan and Aislinn R. Sapp

3.1 Introduction

The concept of wellbeing concerns a person's capacity for optimal functioning, and encompasses not only the issue of physical health, but also a sense of interest in one's surroundings, a confidence in being able to formulate and act to fulfil important goals, and the motivation and energy to persist in the face of obstacles. A 'well' being is able to maintain its vitality and to thrive within its everyday ecological context. Accordingly, there is increasing recognition that the study of human wellbeing must consider more than merely the physical requirements of persons, but it must also address the nutriments and processes entailed in psychological and social fitness.

In this chapter, we discuss the concept of wellbeing and the psychological needs of individuals within social contexts that make this larger concept of thriving possible. Specifically we employ the framework of *Self-Determination Theory* (SDT, Deci and Ryan 2000; Ryan and Deci 2000b), an empirically based perspective on development and wellness. The theory specifies a small number of basic psychological needs whose fulfilment is necessary for psychological wellness, and whose importance is both cross-developmental (applies to all ages) and cross-cultural (applies to all humans). SDT also specifies criteria for wellness that go beyond hedonic definitions of happiness and include eudaimonic conceptions of wellness that concern the actualisation of intrinsic potentials (Ryan and Deci 2001). By specifying both basic needs and a broad conception of wellness that reflects a fully functioning person, SDT is in a prescriptive (and proscriptive) position to argue for specific supports in contexts where health and wellness are being promoted.

3.2   Needs as foundations of wellness

Among the properties that distinguish living things from inanimate entities is the dependence of the former on nourishment. Living things must draw from their surroundings certain essentials that allow them to maintain and enhance their existence. Put differently, living beings have *needs* that must be fulfilled if they are to thrive (Doyal and Gough 1991; Ehrlich 2000; Jacob 1973).

The concept of needs is relatively non-controversial in the field of biology, which focuses on the physical nature of organisms. There is agreement that there are specifiable requirements, the fulfilment of which is essential to the health of individual organisms. Some are even common across all organisms. For example, no organism could survive without water, and thus the idea that organisms need water is a testable hypothesis and ultimately a scientific question.

Employed in this way, the concept of needs is *objective* in the sense that if something is an essential need there should follow observable consequences stemming from its provision or deprivation. If one were to argue that water is not a need, this claim could be easily disproved simply by withholding water from an organism and observing the ensuing deterioration in functioning. Indeed, the concept of biological or physical needs rests fundamentally on the idea that deprivation of certain goods results in measurably degraded forms of growth and impaired integrity. Thus, for humans, it is observable and, in principle, testable that we have minimal daily requirements for nutrition which, if not met, lead to states of deterioration and ill health.

Also, when defined in this way, the identification of basic needs pertains prescriptively to life. If one wishes to care for an organism, one must know what the organism needs and supply the needed elements. If one cares about human beings, for example, one would want to ensure that they are afforded proper nutrition, clean water and adequate shelter from hostile elements. Failure to do so would be neglect.

A similar formulation can be applied with respect to the nutriments underlying psychological growth and integrity. By investigating how specific social conditions facilitate or undermine various forms of human motivation and wellbeing outcomes within and across domains and cultures, SDT, accordingly, identifies principles that directly inform effective social practice and organisation.

Basic needs as a psychological construct

As noted above, health or wellbeing is not simply a physical issue – a matter of bones, tissue and medicine. Rather, to be healthy entails not only physical capabilities but requires such psychological attributes as hope, vitality and confidence, attributes that allow one to engage in one's surroundings and to thrive within them.

SDT recognises both the psychological and the physical dimensions of health, and specifically focuses on the developmental and social conditions that foster optimal psychological growth, integrity and wellbeing versus those that lead to amotivation, fragmentation and unhappiness. SDT begins by explicitly positing that humans are inherently active, relational beings. Based on ethological, behavioural and developmental evidence, it is argued that from infancy on, people have inherent or natural developmental tendencies to take interest in and engage their inner and outer worlds, a fact manifest in the phenomenon of *intrinsic motivation* (Deci and Ryan 1985, 2000). These intrinsic inclinations, including the propensity to explore, manipulate, assimilate and understand, are essential to child development, education and, in later life, to personal vitality and self-restoration. In addition SDT argues that healthy development entails the psychological *internalisation and integration* of socio-cultural regulations and practices (Ryan and Connell 1989; Ryan 1995). These processes are important because integration represents an assimilative tendency that provides the basis by which individuals connect with, and find meaning and purpose within, a social organisation or community.

The postulate of such active, integrative tendencies in psychological development is not a new idea, nor is it one that even applies exclusively to humans. In fact, this SDT view of psychological development simply reflects a principle that in theoretical biology is called *organisation* – the tendency of living entities of all kinds to progress towards increased differentiation and integration (Jacob 1973; Kaufmann 2000; Mayr 1997). Simply stated, individuals are endowed with, and energised by, innate propensities to expand and elaborate themselves in the direction of organised complexity. This organismic tendency, which Maturana and Varela (1992) described as *autopoiesis*, is again what separates living entities from their inanimate counterparts. Living things, when their needs are met, actively maintain and extend their structure and functioning.

The applicability of this 'tendency toward organization' to psychological functioning has been recognised within a number of historically important psychological theories (Ryan 1995) that have embraced the idea that the human psyche, like living organisms in general, manifests a natural inclination towards growth and assimilation that allows for coherent functioning under changing conditions. This organisational assumption is reflected in cognitive-developmental (e.g. Piaget 1971;

Werner 1948), humanistic (e.g. Goldstein 1939; Rogers 1963), psychodynamic (e.g. Freud 1962; Loevinger 1976) and other (e.g. Ford 1992; Hermans 1989) approaches. Yet, unlike most of these previous approaches, SDT is explicit in its embrace of empirical methods to explore the necessary conditions for organismic growth. By accepting that it is possible to employ quantitative scientific methods to study growth and wellness, SDT raises hypotheses, unearths phenomena, and predicts dynamics that had remained only speculative in the hands of even some of our most astute predecessors.

An alternative definition of needs

While SDT's formulation of psychological needs closely parallels the way in which physical needs are framed from a biological perspective, it stands in stark contrast to the way some theorists have historically conceptualised psychological needs. In particular the work of Murray (1938) represents an altogether different approach to the concept of psychological needs. Murray defined a need as a construct that stands for a 'force which organizes perception, apperception, intellection, conation and action in such a way as to transform in a certain direction an existing, unsatisfying, situation' (1938: 124). In other words, the concept of needs denoted virtually any salient motivational force, organising behaviour and experience. Based on this broad definition Murray postulated over twenty-five needs, ranging from obvious and general needs such as that for affiliation to more specific desires, for example a need to dominate others, or its opposite, a need to defer and submit.

The problem with Murray's definition of *need* is that it concerns neither what is essential to growth and wellness, nor that which is universal or cross-cultural. His definition encompasses virtually *any* motivating force in the person insofar as people's desires, wants or strivings all represent 'forces which organize perception and action'. Murray's definition, therefore, fails to differentiate needs from other acquired desires and appetites. In fact, although all the motives Murray identified in his list of needs can energise behaviour, many may produce as much damage as good for the person's psychological health (e.g. his need for *abasement*), whereas others represent motivations that in no way apply universally to humans (e.g. his need for *exhibition*).

Needs as defined by SDT

An alternative and more restrictive definition of needs is used in self-determination theory. Specifically, within SDT a basic psychological need denotes only those *nutriments essential for psychological growth and integrity* (Ryan 1995). This definition of need, which is similar to the concept of biological needs with respect to physical growth and integrity, suggests that there are psychological supports that humans must experience to thrive, and that when deprived of these supports, empirically observable degradation results.

To say that psychological needs are essential does not mean that people will always be aware of their importance or even value them. This is another sense in which needs are objective rather than subjective (Braybrooke 1987; Doyal and Gough 1991; Plant, Lesser and Taylor-Gooby 1980; Samuels 1984). Note, for example, that without proper socialisation, children may not learn to value or prefer nutritious foods. But, regardless of preferences, lacking nutrition can cause serious harm, and this can be objectively ascertained. Similarly, people may block awareness of basic psychological needs, especially when they have been routinely unable to satisfy them. A person who denies a need for relatedness may be attempting to cope with a difficult history of harmful relationships, but his/her failure to obtain relatedness can nonetheless be related to psychological degradation.

Whether or not individuals are explicitly conscious of their basic needs as goal objects, the human psyche innately strives for these nutriments and gravitates to sources of their fulfilment, whether directly or indirectly through substitutes. Psychological needs therefore energise much of human behaviour. And, as much research demonstrates, many psychological desires are derived from the dynamics of basic needs.

A short list of needs: autonomy, competence and relatedness

Because of the restrictiveness of its definition, SDT's list of psychological needs is, unlike Murray's, very short, as there are few psychological nutriments or conditions that are universally required for humans to thrive. In other words, there are few desires or motives that, if cast off or unmet would, in and of themselves, lead to negative psychological effects for all individuals, unless of course the motives were dynamically intertwined with a basic need. Indeed, the list of basic psychological needs is so short that it boils down to three: those for *autonomy, competence and relatedness* (Deci and Ryan 1985, 2000; Ryan 1995). Deprivation of any of these three leads to decrements in growth, integrity and wellness irrespective of individual or cultural values for them.

Autonomy (de Charms 1968; Friedman 2003; Shapiro 1981) refers to the evolved propensity to self-regulate one's actions, a propensity that is experientially associated with feeling volitional and integrated. Autonomy does not herein mean independence or separateness, but rather refers to the self-endorsement of one's own behaviour – that is, feeling personal value and interest with respect to what one does (de Charms 1968; Ryan and Connell 1989). *Competence* (Heckhausen and Schultz 1995; Skinner 1995; White 1959) refers to the propensity towards effectance, or feeling able to attain outcomes and to operate effectively within the environment. The need for competence, that is, concerns experiencing opportunities to exercise, expand and express one's capacities. *Relatedness* (Baumeister and Leary 1995; Bowlby 1979; Harlow 1958) concerns feeling socially connected. Typically, one feels most related when one feels cared for and significant to others, but relatedness also pertains to a general sense of being integral to a social organisation that lies beyond the individual or what Angyal (1941) labelled homonomy.

3.3   Application of basic needs

Social contexts

Specifying fundamental human needs serves a variety of purposes. It gives content to human nature by describing natural tendencies and inclinations. It provides a basis for understanding the development of individual differences in integration versus fragmentation. And it represents a framework for making *a priori* predictions about which aspects of the social context will enhance versus undermine effective functioning, psychological wellbeing, and optimal development of the self. Simply stated, aspects of the social context that are likely to satisfy the fundamental needs for autonomy, competence and relatedness are predicted to promote effective functioning and integrated development, whereas aspects of the social context that are likely to thwart need satisfaction are predicted to diminish effective functioning and support non-optimal developmental trajectories.

We thus characterise social environments in terms of the extent to which they are: (1) autonomy supportive (versus controlling); (2) effectance supporting (versus over-challenging, inconsistent or otherwise discouraging); and (3) relationally supportive (versus impersonal or rejecting). We then make predictions about the effects of specific contextual factors (e.g. strong pressure to win a competition or positive feedback about one's work performance) based on a reasoned consideration of the relation of these factors to the basic psychological needs. Our predictions concern not only the experience of wellness, but also the quality of people's engagement, performance and attitudes in a given context.

Our conceptualisation of the effects of social contexts is pertinent both to motivation and behaviour in immediate situations and to development and wellbeing over time. In other words, supports for autonomy, competence and relatedness are theorised not only to facilitate self-determined functioning in the immediate situation, but they are also understood to promote the development of an integrated self and enduring psychological health over time. Indeed, the dynamics of psychological need satisfaction predict cultural, organisational, personal and within-person fluctuations in functioning and wellbeing.

The wellbeing that needs predict

Within SDT we have argued that psychological health can be more specifically characterised in terms of capacities for (a) growth rather than avoidance or stagnation; (b) integrity in one's functioning and identity, rather than fragmentation or lack of coherence; and (c) a subjective experience of wellness, rather than a sense of insecurity, distress or unhappiness (Deci and Ryan 2000; Ryan 1995). Put simply, psychological health or wellness entails growth, integrity and subjective wellbeing. These abstract elements of psychological health in turn are associated within the SDT framework with specific manifestations and tendencies in development, each of which can be related to basic psychological need supports.

Psychological growth is especially connected with the phenomeon of intrinsic motivation (Deci and Ryan 1985). Indeed, these three basic needs were initially identified on functional grounds, because they served well to integrate the results of experiments concerning the effects of social contexts on intrinsic motivation (Deci and Ryan 1980, 1985). Both experimental (e.g. Deci, Koestner and Ryan 1999) and field studies (e.g. Deci, Nezlek and Scheinman 1981; Ryan and Grolnick 1986) showed how lack of supports for autonomy, relatedness or competence derailed intrinsic motivational tendencies in children that are at the heart of active growth and assimilation, both in home and school contexts (Grolnick, Deci and Ryan 1997).

Beyond growth, SDT conceives of integrity in terms of the integration to the self of behavioural regulations, values and identity. The more integrated an individual, the more coherent and coordinated is the system of values and priorities that organise their actions and interests. As investigations of such integration based in SDT have amassed, they too confirmed that the three basic needs are essential to the process of

internalisation and integration of non-intrinsically motivated behaviours. Thus children were shown to be more likely to assimilate and
embrace societal values when they experienced those values being
transmitted in a context characterised by relatedness, support for
autonomy, and optimal challenges. That is, in interpersonally warm and
non-controlling contexts, children more readily take in the ambient
values of adults, and transform them into self-endorsed regulations
(Deci and Ryan 2000). Similarly, adult workers more readily accept the
values and goals of their organisations when they feel relatedness and
autonomy-support within them (e.g. Baard, Deci and Ryan 2004).

Finally, as we looked at how critical these three needs were for
intrinsic motivation and internalisation, we also repeatedly found evidence for the critical role these needs play in positive experience or
happiness (Ryan and Deci 2001). Unlike a variety of other human
desires that motivate behaviour, the basic needs are essential for effective functioning (Deci and Ryan 2000) and wellbeing (Ryan and Deci
2001). On the basis of both broad and deep forms of empirical evidence
we thus theorised that, when any of these three basic psychological
needs is frustrated or neglected in a given domain, or in general, the
individual will show lowered vitality, loss of volition, greater fragmentation and diminished wellbeing.

Accordingly, we define psychological health in terms of the robust-
ness of intrinsic motivation, integrated internalisation and positive
individual and relational experience, and see these outcomes as derived
from conditions that support the basic needs for autonomy, competence and relatedness. By focusing on these indicators of psychological
health, and using a restrictive and verifiable definition of needs, we
thus avoid what has been historically perhaps the most common criticism of need-related theories, namely that there is a potentially infinite list of needs that can be postulated. In fact, we have seen little
evidence for any psychological needs beyond the three we have isolated
(Ryan and Deci 2000a). We also avoid the trap of tautology, in that
need supports and satisfactions predict wellbeing outcomes, rather
than defining them.

3.4   Implications of STD's definition of needs

One important implication of our definition of psychological needs is
that they are innate and universal. Psychological needs are innate in the
sense that they are an invariant aspect of human nature. They are universal in that they apply to all humans in all cultures, whether collectivistic or individualistic, materially developed or underdeveloped.

The claim that needs are innate depends first and foremost on the generalisability of needs across individuals. Moreover, this claim depends upon establishing, from an evolutionary point of view, the basis by which psychological needs might have become so centrally anchored in our natures, not as specific adaptations, but as developmental thrusts that many specific adaptations evolved to support (Deci and Ryan 2000). However, as we already noted, it does not depend upon the claim that all individuals equally recognise or value their basic needs, nor that they are all equally equipped with respect to achieving their fulfilment.

The issue of generalisability is particularly relevant to cross-cultural applications. While the manifestation or expression of psychological needs, and the vehicles through which they are satisfied, may differ across societies, their necessity is unchanging. For example, although collectivistic and individualistic cultures vary in the relative primacy they give to either the group or the individual, the necessity of the three basic needs does not vary across the cultures.

Indeed, it will be a fundamental tenet of SDT that the reason people have a readiness to adopt and internalise ambient cultural values, no matter what their content, is that by doing so, they satisfy needs. It is by assimilating the values of one's group that one becomes more connected and related, and more competent and effective. Furthermore, the general tendency to make ambient values one's own, and to feel them as central to identity, is an expression of the need for and developmental tendency towards autonomy. Put differently, needs supply the underlying processes that explain how cultures become part of individual personality. These essentials are thus apparent across historical, cultural, political or economic contexts.

On the other hand, differing historical, economic and cultural contexts *can* be compared in terms of the degree to which they are (or have been) conducive to the fulfilment of basic needs. In this view, not all cultures, contexts or economic structures are equally 'good' for humans (Ryan, Sheldon, Kasser and Deci 1996). This point differentiates SDT from the absolute cultural relativism characterising much of modern psychology (e.g. Cross and Gore 2003; Schweder 1991) that views cultures as the absolute sculptor of human nature. If this were so, cultural transformation or instability could rarely be explained. A psychology of needs, on the other hand, suggests the limits of cultural impositions, and the bases by which people will seek change. A focus on needs can inform, that is, about where culture and 'human nature' collide.

Thus the concept of basic psychological needs brings to the foreground two important tenets of SDT. The first is that basic psychological needs are evolved and *universal*: people are inherently and fundamentally motivated to feel connected to others within a social milieu, to function effectively in that milieu, and to feel a sense of volition and integrity while doing so. Second, factors associated with variations in support for and experience of these needs being fulfilled thus should predict growth integrity and wellbeing across all domains, all epochs of human development and all cultural contexts. When basic needs are thwarted, development will be non-optimal and people will be less effective and healthy. Indeed, when needs are thwarted people often fall into passive, alienated or fragmented modes of functioning. In fact, many forms of psychopathology have their aetiology in deprivations of basic needs for autonomy, competence or relatedness (Ryan, Grolnick, La Guardia and Deci, forthcoming).

Another reaction to need thwarting is an attempt to adjust through substitute and compensatory activities. For example, on the basis of how contingent rewards often impact perceived autonomy, SDT has reliably predicted when rewards undermine rather than sustain subsequent motivation (Deci, Koestner and Ryan 1999). Similarly, SDT's analysis of materialism and status seeking shows these motives, when strong, often result from insecurities fostered by non-nurturing (specifically, rejecting or controlling) psychological conditions in earlier development (e.g. Kasser, Ryan, Zax and Sameroff 1995), as well as more proximal threats and frustrations (Kasser 2002). For example, materialists, who strongly desire possessions that convey to others their worth and importance, are frequently people whose developmental backgrounds are characterised by need deficits, and who are therefore insecure. Materialism, or Murray's 'need for acquisitiveness' (1938), is therefore a substitute for something more basic that has been missing. Still other analyses suggest that excessive motives for achievement and power are related to the conflict between needs for autonomy and relatedness resulting from contingent regard (Assor, Roth and Deci, 2004). Finally, SDT also details how people can come to live by inauthentic or introjected motives in order to gain or maintain approval and relatedness (Ryan and Deci 2004). These examples suggest how positing basic needs supplies a deep structure of the psyche, around which secondary motivations, desires and defences are built.

Multiple needs and the absence of a need hierarchy

Another implication of our needs framework is that people cannot psychologically thrive by one need alone, any more than people can live healthily with water but not food, or plants can thrive on soil without sunlight (Ryan, 2005). Social environments that afford, for example, opportunities to experience competence but fail to nurture relatedness are ones conducive to an impoverished human condition. For example, career development that requires so much time that one is unable to satisfy relational needs (a condition of epidemic proportions in modern market-based societies) will extract a cost on wellbeing regardless of how effective one is in that career. Worse yet are contexts that pit one need against another, thereby creating conflicts that inevitably produce ill-being and maladjustment.

This necessity of satisfying all three basic needs across the lifespan separates our theory from yet another type of need theory, namely, those that specify a *hierarchy* of needs in which one level of basic needs must be well satisfied before another level emerges as a salient motivator of behaviour (e.g. Maslow 1954). For Maslow, as for us, there are basic psychological needs whose fulfilment is considered essential to healthy development, but in his view they do not emerge until the physical needs are relatively well sated, and then they are addressed in a more or less serial fashion: first security, then love, then esteem, then self-actualisation. In our view, if the fulfilment of any of the three basic psychological needs is blocked within a given domain or in a given period of one's life, specifiable experiential and functional costs within that domain or in that life phase predictably follow. Even if the decision to forgo satisfaction of one need for another is rational or adaptive given the situation, there will be negative functional effects.

There is, of course, considerable variability in the beliefs, values and norms held within different cultures, which according to SDT means that the avenues through which basic need satisfaction is accomplished can differ greatly. For example, in a collectivist culture, people might resonate to and deeply endorse the collectivist values such that acting in accord with group norms within their culture could lead them to experience not only relatedness but also autonomy. In an individualistic culture, however, acting in accord with a group norm might have the functional significance of conformity or compliance and thus could represent a threat to autonomy rather than a reflection of it. As such, behaviours that are in accord with group norms could have different meanings in the two cultures and thus very different impacts on the individuals who enact them. The implication of this is that, when investigating issues related to basic needs in different cultures, it is necessary to take a dynamic perspective that goes deeply enough into psychological processes to find linkages that relate the basic psychological needs to the phenotypic behaviours that appear in different cultures.

3.5   Research on psychological needs and wellbeing

As outlined in the sections above, considerable research supports the contention that contextual supports for the three needs facilitate more healthy behavioural functioning and positive experience. This work demonstrates how supports for autonomy, relatedness and competence facilitate intrinsic motivation, integrated internalisation and wellbeing across a variety of contexts. From school (e.g. Ryan and Brown 2005) and work (e.g. Baard, Deci and Ryan 2004) to healthcare (e.g. Williams, Deci and Ryan 1998) and even to religious (e.g. Ryan, Rigby and King 1993) and political (e.g. Losier and Koestner 1999) activities, application of the basic principles of SDT show how basic science concerning human needs bears on practical endeavours in every domain of life. More central to this chapter, however, is the universality of needs and their saliency and applicability across cultures, and thus it is the burgeoning cross-cultural literature on SDT to which we now turn.

Research on the universality of needs for relatedness,
competence and autonomy

Although the concept of universal psychological needs appears in few empirically based theories, the notion that there exist basic needs for relatedness and competence is relatively non-controversial. For example, Bowlby (1979) proposed a need for relatedness or attachment that is basic to human beings, and that has been widely utilised by developmental and relationship researchers. Baumeister and Leary (1995) also proposed a fundamental need for belongingness and marshalled an impressive array of evidence in support of such a proposal. Thus, the concept of a need for relatedness has been proposed by theories other than SDT and has been well supported.

Similarly, White (1959) proposed a basic need for competence or effectance as a solution to the problems that had been encountered in the drive theories within both the empirical tradition and the psychoanalytic tradition. More recently, Elliot, McGregor and Thrash (2002) postulated a basic need for competence that underlies achievement goal pursuits. In addition, the concept of competence or efficacy is central to the theories of flow (Csikszentmihalyi 1990) and self-efficacy (Bandura 1989). Although not all of these theories explicitly endorse the concept of needs, the centrality of the need for competence has generated little debate.

The concept of a need for autonomy, however, represents a quite a different situation. Cross-cultural psychologists such as Miller (1997) have portrayed autonomy as a western concept not applicable to traditional societies. Oishi (2000) equated autonomy with individualism and argued that it is not an applicable concept for eastern culture. Iyengar and Lepper (1999) suggested that the value of autonomy is contradictory to the value of relatedness, which they argue is more central within eastern cultures. Markus, Kitayama and Heiman (1996) articulated a cultural relativist position suggesting that there are no universal needs for autonomy or relatedness, only culturally constructed values. To them, wellbeing is a matter of fulfilling cultural constructions, thus they see no functional importance for autonomy in collectivist cultures, which they describe as devaluing autonomy.

Chirkov, Ryan, Kim and Kaplan (2003) argued, however, that part of the reason why the cultural-relativist position appears to be so different from the SDT perspective is that relativists typically define autonomy very differently from the way it is defined in SDT. In spite of the fact that the SDT view of autonomy has consistently concerned volition or the self-endorsement of action (e.g. Deci and Ryan 1985), most of the opposing viewpoints have portrayed autonomy as if it meant independence, separateness or 'freedom from' any social-environmental influences. Although that is not an unreasonable view of individualism, it is a very different from SDT's definition of autonomy as volition and self-endorsement of one's actions.

When understood as the experience of self-endorsement of one's actions, SDT's view of autonomy is recognisable in the work of prominent eastern thinkers. For example, Lo (2003), reflecting on autonomy and authenticity in the writings of Confucius, stated that the Chinese word *ji* refers to one's core self or the authentic identity of one's self, and that the word *shen* refers to the outer embodiment of the *ji*, to the expression of one's authenticity, which can be harmonised. Chong similarly discusses autonomy as acting from one's authentic identity, and adds that in the view of Confucius, people as moral agents have 'a deep seated desire for directing [their] own lives' (2003: 277). Thus, when considering autonomy as volition rather than as independence, these Chinese thinkers express an SDT tenet that people have an abiding and deep need for autonomy or self-determination.

Ultimately, however, the claim that a need is universal is not simply a philosophical question, but an empirical one – a position completely fitting with our view of psychological needs as objective rather than subjective phenomena. Cross-cultural investigations focused on the needs for autonomy, competence and relatedness, which SDT claims to be fundamental and universal, are relatively new, but the initial results are very exciting. We focus especially on the issue of autonomy, the most controversial of the three.

Effects of autonomy in Japan and China

Initial support for the significance of the need for autonomy in an eastern context came from studies by Japanese scholars that conceptually replicated earlier SDT studies done in the USA. For example, Hayamizu (1997) assessed the degree of autonomy reported by Japanese students in grades seven and eight based on a model derived from Ryan and Connell (1989). Hayamizu reported that greater autonomy was related in Japanese students to more positive forms of motivation, deeper engagement with learning and higher wellbeing, findings comparable to numerous studies in US schools (e.g. Grolnick and Ryan 1989; Ryan and Connell 1989). Yamauchi and Tanaka (1998) similarly examined fifth- and sixth-grade Japanese students using a different Japanese version of the Ryan and Connell self-regulation model. They too found links between autonomy and more depth of processing, higher learning versus performance orientations and greater self-esteem among other outcomes. Tanaka and Yamauchi (2000) later extended these findings to college undergraduates in Japan.

Vansteenkiste, Zhou, Lens and Soenens[1] examined the role of autonomous self-regulation in young Chinese adults. Participants in the first of two studies were students in English-language classes in Shenyang. Results indicated that participants' relative autonomy for studying predicted positive attitudes about learning, self-reports of study behaviours and achievement level. A second study showed that among Chinese persons who had recently immigrated into Belgium, those who perceived their parents as autonomy-supportive rather than controlling evidenced both greater learning and wellbeing.

Comparative studies on the effects of autonomy

The studies just reviewed demonstrate the impact and importance of autonomy within eastern cultures. However, because they focused on within-culture differences in autonomy, they are not truly cross-cultural comparisons. We now turn to such comparative studies.

Chirkov and Ryan (2001) examined parents' and teachers' autonomy-support of high school students in Russia (a moderately collectivist culture) and the USA (a highly individualist culture). They predicted that autonomy-support from parents and teachers would predict both greater autonomous motivation and psychological health in both

---

[1] M. Vansteenkiste, W. Zhou, Lens and B. Soenens, 'Experiences of autonomy and control among Chinese learners: Vitalizing or immobilizing?' Unpublished manuscript, University of Leuven, Belgium, 2005.

countries. Results indicated that the constructs assessing autonomy-support and wellness were psychometrically comparable and understood in similar ways across these cultures (Little 1997). Further, although parent and teacher autonomy-support were, as predicted, lower in Russia than in the USA, autonomy-support related positively to more self-motivation in school and mental-health in both countries.

Applying an SDT perspective, Chirkov et al. (2003) proposed that values and practices reflecting collectivism and individualism can be internalised to differing degrees within cultures, which means they can be more or less autonomously embraced. It is, they argued, this degree of autonomy in the enactment of either collectivist or individualist values and behaviours, rather than the type of value embraced, that will determine individuals' psychological wellbeing.

To examine cultural practices, Chirkov et al. (2003) used Triandis and Gelfand's (1998) two-dimensional characterisation of cultural practices. The collectivism/individualism dimension concerns the relative priority given to the goals and norms of the relevant collective versus the desires and preferences of the individual within that collective. This is crossed with the dimension of horizontal/vertical, which refers to whether values and practices support equality and interchangeability of individuals within a society or emphasise the power differential implicit in superior–subordinate relationships. Four countries that varied greatly along these dimensions of individualism/collectivism and horizontal/vertical were then selected for this research, namely Russia, Turkey, South Korea and the USA. Participants in each country were first asked for their perceptions of the frequency and importance that other people in their culture place on a variety of cultural practices that reflect the four types of cultures specified by Triandis and Gelfand (1998). This provided information about the degree to which the participants saw the practices as prevalent within their own culture.

Next, participants were asked why they personally engage in each of these cultural practices. SDT posits that regulation for a given behaviour can vary with respect to how autonomous or self-determined it is. Cultural practices can thus be differentiated on the basis of how well they have been integrated and internalised into one's self by assessing the degree to which participants endorsed autonomous or self-determined (e.g. identified and intrinsic) versus heteronomous or controlled (e.g. extrinsic and introjected) reasons for engaging in each practice. For each practice, participants' ratings of extrinsic, introjected, identified and intrinsic reasons were combined to reflect an overall relative autonomy score (Ryan and Connell 1989). The primary hypothesis was that, within all four cultures and for all cultural practices, the degree to which a person is autonomous in enacting it will predict the person's wellbeing, as assessed by both hedonic and eudaimonic measures. Culture was not expected to moderate this relation.

Results provided strong support for these formulations. After establishing construct comparability across the four countries, the researchers calculated the relative autonomy for each cultural practice for each participant and then aggregated them within persons to form each participant's relative autonomy for the four types of cultural practices – namely, those consistent with horizontal collectivism, horizontal individualism, vertical collectivism and vertical individualism. Regression analyses showed that the degree of internalisation of each of the four types of cultural practices within each of the four cultures predicted varied wellbeing outcomes, a relation that was not moderated by culture. In short, autonomous behaviour was found to be positively associated with psychological health in all four cultures regardless of whether the practices being enacted were collectivist or individualist, horizontal or vertical.

Chirkov et al. (2003) also raised the question of whether all cultural values are equally assimilable. In other words, can people internalise and integrate all cultural values with equal ease? They speculated that some societal orientations would be more difficult to accept and endorse if they were less compatible with satisfaction of the psychological needs. Although these researchers suggested that there is likely to be no difference in the degree to which collectivist and individualist orientations would allow satisfaction of the basic needs, they postulated that vertical cultural values would be more difficult to integrate than horizontal, or more egalitarian, values. The fact of being subordinate to powerful others represents a high risk towards thwarting one's need for autonomy. Further, the fact that such powerful others can place limits on the people with whom one can experience intimacy and belongingness suggests that vertical policies, relative to horizontal ones, could be more thwarting of the need for relatedness. If those speculations were true, then vertical practices would have a lower relative autonomy index across cultural contexts than would horizontal practices. This is just what Chirkov et al. found. There was a highly significant difference between the internalisation scores for horizontal, relative to vertical, practices across all cultures. It does, therefore, seem that integrating vertical cultural forms is more difficult than assimilating horizontal forms, whose enactment may simply be more directly fulfilling basic needs for autonomy and relatedness.

In a subsequent related study by Chirkov, Ryan and Willnes (2005), Brazilian and Canadian students reported on the importance and frequency of cultural practices and values reflecting individualistic/collectivistic and horizontal/vertical orientations. They also rated their relative autonomy for these practices and the degree to which parents and teachers supported autonomy, competence and relatedness. It was predicted that in both samples, despite mean differences, greater relative autonomy and need support would be associated with greater wellbeing and perceived cultural fit. It was also expected that vertical cultural orientations would be less well internalised in both Brazilian and Canadian groups. Results supported these hypotheses, and were especially important in suggesting that the more individuals reported basic need satisfactions and autonomy supports, the more they felt that they 'fitted' with their culture and the less they reported either cultural estrangement or ill being.

Sheldon, Elliot, Ryan *et al.* (2004) examined the relations of autonomous motivation to wellness in three eastern cultures and the USA. Participants were asked to list the personal strivings (Emmons 1989) that were most important to them at that time. They were then asked to rate the degree to which they were pursuing each striving for external, introjected, identified and intrinsic reasons, and an overall relative autonomy score was calculated. Participants also completed measures of subjective wellbeing (Diener 1994). As anticipated, the level of autonomous motivation in the different cultures varied, with the USA and South Korea being relatively high and China and Taiwan being relatively low. Nonetheless, autonomous motivation was significantly related to subjective wellbeing in all four samples.

Another study of need satisfaction compared Bulgarian and US workers (Deci, Ryan, Gagné *et al.* 2001). Until 1989 Bulgaria had a totalitarian regime in the Stalinist tradition, and virtually all industries were owned by the State and operated by central-planning principles. Even five years after the country was freed from Soviet domination, none of the important state-owned companies had passed into private hands and the companies still operated primarily by central-planning principles. In this context Deci *et al.* (2001) collected data on psychological need satisfaction from employees of ten state-owned companies in Bulgaria and a US comparison company. Participants completed assessments of their work climate (assessing autonomy-support versus control), need satisfaction, motivation and psychological wellbeing. Analyses showed that autonomy-support from management was positively related to satisfaction of each of the basic needs for autonomy, competence and relatedness in the workplace. Extending this, a structural equation model supported the hypothesis that autonomy-support predicts need satisfaction, and that need satisfaction in turn predicts wellbeing and work motivation in both Bulgarian and US samples, in spite of the stark differences in work contexts and cultural backdrops.

Autonomy within relationships

SDT proposes that healthier functioning occurs within relationships characterised by need supports. A person is predicted to be best off with relational partners who support his/her autonomy, competence and relatedness, and to be less satisfied, vital and fully functioning in relationships with persons less responsive to needs.

Lynch, Ryan, La Guardia et al.[2] tested this idea by having US participants rate the degree of vitality and satisfaction experienced within different important relationships in their lives. It was expected that vitality and satisfaction would vary from partner to partner as a function of the amount of need satisfaction they experienced with that partner. They found that, to the extent that others were need supportive, individuals reported not only more vitality and satisfaction, but they also differed in the traits they displayed with that person. The more need supportive a particular relational partner was the more the participant reported being open, agreeable, conscientious and extraverted, and less neurotic, relative to their own baseline way of being. In short, people varied meaningfully on 'big five' personality traits from partner to partner, and need satisfaction within these relationships accounted for much of this variation.

Lynch et al.[3] then extended this by collecting similar data in samples from the USA, Russia and China. They focused primarily on the need for autonomy because that is the more controversial of the needs as they relate to collectivist cultures. Their expectation was that support for autonomy is important regardless of the culture in which one lives and that greater autonomy support within a relationship would lead to greater relationship satisfaction and to behaving more in accord with the positive end of each of the 'big five' traits. They found that, in all three samples, there was considerable variability in the way that people described themselves on traits when they were with different relational partners. Further, in all three countries the amount of autonomy support people experienced with a particular relational partner predicted the degree to which they felt vitality and satisfaction with that relationship. Moreover, autonomy support in any given relationship was

---

[2] M. L. Lynch, R. M. Ryan, J. G. La Guardia, L. Haiyan, R. Yan and T. N. Strabakhina, 'Variability of self-concept across personal relationships: The role of culture, autonomy-support and authenticity'. Unpublished manuscript, University of Rochester, 2004.
[3] *Ibid.*

associated with more extraversion, agreeableness, conscientiousness and openness to experience, and less neuroticism, a pattern that obtained with equal strength in all three samples. Even big five traits, it seems, are mutable as a function of need supports such that, regardless of one's culture, the more one experiences basic need satisfaction when with a relational partner, the more one will behave in ways that represent the healthy manifestations of the various traits.

Finally, Ryan, La Guardia, Solky *et al.* (2005) examined emotional reliance on family and friends in four countries – South Korea, Russia, Turkey and the USA. They reasoned that *emotional reliance* (feeling able to turn to others for emotional support when needed) would generally be beneficial for wellbeing, but that emotional reliance would occur more frequently in relationships where basic needs were supported, regardless of culture. Ryan *et al.* first showed in a US sample that people tend to turn for emotional support mainly to those whom they experience as supporting their autonomy. In a second study, they looked cross-nationally, finding that tendencies towards emotional reliance differed by country, as a function of cultural values and attitudes. Nonetheless, within each country, the degree to which people relied on others when having emotional experiences positively predicted wellbeing. In a subsequent study, Lynch and Ryan[4] replicated this latter result in Chinese, Russian and US samples, further showing that people are more apt to emotionally rely on partners who are autonomy-supportive, no matter what type of culture they find themselves in.

Goals and needs

Ryan, Chirkov, Little *et al.* (1999) examined the life goals of Russian and American college students. The study grew out of earlier work done in the USA by Kasser and Ryan (1996) which had shown that when people place strong importance on pursuit of extrinsic goals (accumulating wealth, becoming famous and presenting an attractive image) relative to intrinsic goals (personal growth, meaningful affiliation and contributing to one's community) the individuals also tended to be less psychologically healthy. In the Ryan *et al.* (1999) study the Russian and American students completed assessments of the importance or value they placed on each of the six categories of life goals. In addition, participants reported the extent to which they experienced attainment of

---

[4] M. L. Lynch and R. M. Ryan, 'Emotional Reliance and what it depends on: A cross-cultural test of self-determination theory'. Unpublished manuscript, University of South Florida, 2005.

those goals in their current lives. Finally, they completed measures of self-esteem, self-actualisation, life satisfaction and depressive symptoms.

The primary analyses indicated that those individuals in both Russia and America whose life goals were focused more on relationships, growth and community than on wealth, image, and fame evidenced greater self-esteem, self-actualisation and life satisfaction as well as less depression. Stated differently, the more people were oriented towards satisfaction of extrinsic life goals relative to intrinsic life goals, the poorer was their psychological wellbeing. Further, the data from Russia and the USA showed that whereas greater current attainment of intrinsic goals enhanced wellbeing, greater current attainment of extrinsic goals contributed very little. Thus, not only does strongly pursuing extrinsic goals bode poorly for one's mental health, but it also seems to be the case that attaining extrinsic goals is of little help for mental health.

Our interpretation of these results is that pursuit and attainment of the intrinsic aspirations for growth, relationships and community provides relatively direct satisfaction of psychological needs and thus contributes to wellbeing, whereas pursuit and attainment of extrinsic aspirations does not typically enhance basic need satisfaction, even if it does fulfil goals or motives. Indeed, an excessive focus on extrinsic goals not only does not satisfy basic needs, it also tends to focus people away from the activities that do provide need satisfaction. For example, a particularly strong pursuit of wealth and material possessions can interfere with building meaningful relationships (relatedness) or expressing one's abiding interests (autonomy). In this way, then, the extrinsic pursuits provide little satisfaction of basic psychological needs and can also distract from activities that do provide these satisfactions that are also critical to psychological health.

3.6   Some final comments

Families, organisations and cultures vary greatly in their approaches to socialisation, the salient values and goals embraced by their members, and in the opportunities and supports for functioning provided to individuals who reside within them. The focus of self-determination theory is on the relations of these practices, values and supports to the satisfaction of basic psychological needs. Insofar as different contexts afford greater or lesser satisfaction of basic psychological needs for competence, autonomy and relatedness, SDT proposes that they will also differ in the degree to which the people within them flourish in their vocational, social and cultural engagements. Indeed, considerable research has shown how variations in need supports predict vitality and persistence in a variety of domains from work, to school, to religion, and new cross-cultural work demonstrates the generalisability of such relations across even very distinct cultural backdrops.

Particularly important in the SDT perspective is support for autonomy. In our view supports for autonomy allow an individual to address all needs better, and in this sense we agree with Alkire (2005) concerning what she calls the *architectonic* role of autonomy with respect to the other dimensions of wellbeing and with Doyal and Gough's (1991) central emphasis on autonomy in their theory of needs. It is through autonomy that one most fully exercises capacities in the direction of growth and actualisation. The extent to which familial governmental, economic and cultural conditions either foster or inhibit autonomy thus becomes understood as especially critical. Indeed, we think our SDT view is consistent with the views of economist Sen (1999) in emphasising the critical role of freedom in supporting human thriving.

In saying this, however, one cannot diminish the importance of relatedness and competence needs. In fact, the very development of autonomy rests on a secure and responsive context of relatedness (e.g. Ryan 2005), and autonomy without competence still leads to frustration or helplessness. Thus all three are necessities, and are mutually interdependent.

SDT's proposal that some organisational and cultural contexts are far more antithetical to basic psychological needs than others also has important implications as work on needs extends into developing nations. Unlike the more radical cultural-relativist theories (e.g. Cross and Gore 2003; Schweder 1991) that assume that all of a culture's salient goals and values will yield positive outcomes if people succeed at them, SDT deals with the harder question of what goal contents are consistent with human nature and, in particular, with the universal human needs for autonomy, competence and relatedness. The enactment of need-incongruent goals, we maintain, will engender costs in terms of psychological growth, integrity and wellbeing even when culturally endorsed. This applies to goals from self-subjugation (Goodwin 1994) to materialism (Kasser 2002). Although such a position is controversial, it does suggest the possibility of a comparative cultural analysis of supports for human wellness and thriving, which relativist positions often eschew.

A final perspective derived from SDT concerns the relation of psychological needs to the ultimate stability of cultures and nations. Cultures transmit an array of values and practices more or less compatible with basic psychological needs. We suggest that the more a culture, through both its strategies of socialisation and regulation and through the content of its values and practices, engenders integrated internalisations and need fulfilment, the more satisfied and harmonious its members will be, and thus the more stable will be the culture itself (Chirkov, Ryan and Willnes 2005; Ingellheri 1999). Alternatively, when cultures use either controlling forms of socialisation or endorse values and cultural forms that are not compatible with basic needs, they will be characterised by greater alienation, unrest and conflict. Accordingly, it is not only by providing food, shelter and medicine that wellness or stability can be fostered in developing nations, but also by attention to opportunities to fulfil the basic psychological needs that are the foundation of healthy behavioural functioning and that characterise all members of our otherwise all too divided species.

4   Measuring freedoms alongside wellbeing

Sabina Alkire

4.1   Introduction

A new idea, it would seem, more easily moves into significance if it drives up with a novel methodological sidecar attached. So the *idea* of human capital arose together with the *methodology* that human capital variables should be on the right-hand side of growth equations. The *idea* of human development arose together with the *methodological* tool of the Human Development Index (HDI). And of course the *idea* of free trade drove up with *methodologies* of privatisation and liberalisation. While the relationship between the idea and the method is often publicly uneasy (usually because the methodology does not precisely match or compass the idea), the fact that such pairings are both common and fruitful can hardly pass notice. It follows that if potentially interesting ideas roar in without appropriate sidecars in tow, the research community sets about to craft them.

When such a community considers Sen's capability approach as a way of framing wellbeing and agency, they will immediately observe that the methodological sidecar seems unfinished. Even if one focuses purely on the issue of measuring the expansion or contraction of basic capabilities at the individual level, Sen's conceptual *approach* seems far richer and more compelling than the measurement companions thus crafted – and of course measurement is only one intermediary methodology that might be of use.[1] In particular, existing measures focus on *functionings* – beings and doings such as being nourished or education – but neglect *freedoms*. Yet it is the substantive role Sen gives to freedom which distinguishes the capability approach and informs *Development as Freedom* (1999). How might a methodological sidecar incorporate freedom? Promising measures have been developed in other disciplines but have not been integrated into or evaluated within the capability framework.

---

[1] Some of these are surveyed in Wiebke Kuklys and Ingrid Robeyns, 'Sen's capability approach to welfare economics', paper presented at the 2005 AEA meetings, Philadelphia.

The purpose of this chapter is to clarify the need for measures of freedom, and to map possible practical routes forward, which involve the communication of existing knowledge across disciplines as well as new empirical work.

4.2   Aspects of freedom in Sen's writings

Sen's work on the value and role of freedom in development is one of the literatures often cited among economists interested in development and wellbeing as giving credence and philosophical grounding for including freedom in poverty reduction initiatives in developing countries (poverty being understood here as a deficit of wellbeing). Even the 2000/2001 *World Development Report* of the World Bank, entitled 'Attacking Poverty', argued that poverty reduction entailed 'empowerment' of the poor. The first footnote in that report cites Sen's *Development as Freedom* and its description of deprivation includes 'voicelessness' and 'powerlessness' (as well as low levels of education and health) (World Bank 2001: 15, citing Sen 1999: 87). Sen's capability approach is clearly but one of many approaches – academic, practical, even spiritual – that try to articulate the value and appeal of considering freedom alongside wellbeing. Related and sometimes overlapping terms such as 'self-reliance', 'autonomy', 'democratic practice' and 'participation' likewise relate to the ability of groups to make informed decisions and advance valued goals on their own behalf.[2] However, this chapter will confine itself to Sen's conceptual terms.

The considered presentation of Sen's concept of freedom appears in the Arrow lectures.[3] 'Freedom', Sen there argues, 'is an irreducibly plural concept' (2002: 585). Some aspects of freedom relate to opportunities that people face (often called capabilities), others, to processes that they command (which may be called agency) and experience. The elements of valued opportunities and processes are themselves plural and diverse.

First, more freedom gives us more *opportunity* to achieve those things that we value and have reason to value. This aspect of freedom is concerned primarily with our *ability to achieve*, rather than with the process through which that achievement comes about. Second, the *process* through which things happen may also be of fundamental importance in assessing freedom. For example, it may be thought, reasonably enough, that the procedure of free decision by the person herself (no matter how

---

[2] I have tried to study participation in development, and its connections to the capability approach, in Alkire (2002a: chs 3 and 4), and in Alkire (2006).
[3] Published in Sen (2002).

successful the person is in getting what she would like to achieve) is an important requirement of freedom (Sen 2002: 585).

The process and opportunity aspects of freedom overlap, but are distinct – neither subsumes the other. In terms of opportunity, Sen argues that besides considering people's actual choices, achievements and their space for personal liberty, separate regard should be given to the opportunities that are available to people which they value and have reason to value – their freedom to achieve valued outcomes. Characteristically, Sen clarifies the distinction between different types of information related to the 'freedom to achieve', insists on their difference, and gives certain examples of why a sole focus on actual choices or achievements or a sphere of personal liberty would be insufficient. But he does not argue that it would always be either adequate or necessary to take note only of opportunities. Also characteristically, Sen builds into the description of opportunities the condition that they are valuable: the opportunities that matter for an assessment of freedom are those that people value and have reason to value. Opportunities that people might consider horrid are not to be expanded; nor should an assessment of freedom be formulated by considering all opportunities without taking note of whether or not these opportunities are strongly valued, mildly valued or objectionable. Furthermore, what people value may change over time, and an adequate assessment of freedom must allow for this evolution – for the ongoing development of preferences and of meta-rankings of preferences – and not freeze people's values at one point in time and extrapolate them inflexibly into the future. There are a number of familiar ambiguities and potential conflicts in this formulation that we will consider presently, because people may or may not *actually* value all that they have reason to value. Alternatively, things they value may be actively detrimental to others.

In regards to the process aspect of freedom, Sen argues that 'We are, of course, interested in outcomes such as being affluent, or creative, or fulfilled, or happy, but we can also value being able to choose freely, or not having interference by others in the way we live' (2002: 623). The process aspect of freedom concerns things such as autonomy and immunity – 'whether the person was free to choose herself, whether others intruded or obstructed, and so on' (Sen 2002: 10). Sen identifies two ways in which people's preferences regularly encompass processes:

1 Personal process concern: individuals may have preferences over the processes that occur in their own lives;
2 Systemic process concern: they may also have preferences over the processes that operate as general rules in the working of the society (Sen 2002: 624).

He argues that, in addition to considering opportunities, an adequate consideration of freedom should include processes, and that these should include systemic processes or social concerns such as rights and justice. This is important even though the systemic process concerns that people value may conflict with one another.

Sen asks, 'Why is it that both in formal welfare economics and in a good deal of modern moral philosophy, processes have tended to be ignored at the *fundamental valuational level*?' (Sen 2002: 627). Sen observes that utilitarianism has taken extensive note of the consequences of action but not attended to processes. Libertarianism, on the other hand, gave priority to processes but treated them as 'admission rules' that should in all cases be given priority. In contrast, Sen argues that the appropriate approach would be to take an 'integrated view' in which both processes and culmination outcomes are considered, and compete with one another for attention, with none dominating *a priori* but the merits – and conflicts – and trade-offs – all being scrutinised explicitly.

An 'informational analysis' of Sen's own work would lead one to conclude that information on freedom was indeed required in order for an adequate assessment of social arrangements.[4] Thus we need to craft a methodological sidecar containing one or a handful of indicators – qualitative and/or quantitative, subjective, objective and/or participatory – that are imperfect and crude, yet represent empirically the value of freedoms better than current approaches. But how do we obtain this information – how can we measure change in individual freedoms in a sufficiently sensitive and policy-relevant way?

4.3   Freedom and measurement: focusing the question

Before beginning to survey measurement approaches, as the remainder of the chapter will do, it is important to focus in such a way that an imperfect measurement approach or set of measures might emerge that would add value to present methodologies. This is inherently a less than satisfactory task. For practical methodologies – as the introduction suggested – almost always fail to compass the depth of the idea they accompany. Their one advantage is that they may, in comparison to current methodologies, add value.

---

[4] The first of Sen's Dewey Lectures, on the moral role of information, makes this point (1985b), as does Sen (1979a).

We might break the measurement question into two (or three) components of individual freedoms:

- *Opportunity freedoms* – which are the freedoms to achieve valued functionings. This entails the identification and measurement of valued functionings:
   Functionings – which are 'valuable beings and doings' (or needs) such as being nourished, being safe, being educated, being healthy, and so on.
- *Process freedoms* – which relate to a person's ability to take action in certain spheres of life – to empowerment, to self-determination, to participation, and to practical reason.

At present, a clear emphasis of wellbeing research is to expand the indicators of functionings that, taken together, comprise wellbeing. For example, Geof Wood's chapter in this volume explores how functionings related to security could be expanded. More crudely, in 1990 the HDI explored how life expectancy and education could supplement income as a measure of wellbeing. Others explore how subjective measures of wellbeing can enrich our understanding of the functionings people enjoy.

Research on measures of *opportunity and process freedoms*, however, is less prominent. This of course is partly because a precise *measure* of opportunity freedoms is difficult and has been argued to be impossible. It would need to include not only the opportunities that people had actually chosen, or into which they had been coerced (both would be captured by functionings measures) but also the counterfactual opportunities that had been open to them that they had not chosen. In other words, a full measure of opportunity freedoms, like a complete budget set, would list all of the possible options open to the agent, all of the 'roads not taken'. And as many have noted, such a set could be theoretically constructed, but would be challenging to measure empirically (Carter 1999; Foster and Sen 1997; Sugden 2003). However, as we shall see shortly, the empowerment framework proposed by Alsop and Heinsohn (2005) does attempt to identify opportunities that are present structurally but not chosen. If the empirical work achieves this aim, it could shift the discussion on opportunity freedom measurement significantly.

Even if it is not possible to measure unchosen opportunities, I have argued that it would be interesting to explore a different approach to capabilities that are in some sense basic, that might pertain to poverty or, as Sen's 2004, 'Elements of a theory of human rights' article argues, that, by virtue of their *special importance* and *social influenceability*, might be claimed by people as a human right.[5]

Consider a person who is undernourished, or who lacks any of the capabilities that are especially important and socially influenceable. If these capabilities are accurately identified (and the participatory processes by which they may be identified is an important question that lies beyond the scope of this chapter) then one might expect that were this 'opportunity freedom' present, the vast majority of people would choose it. However, we do not know why a particular person is undernourished, and, in particular, we do not know whether or not he or she would eat or would choose to fast for some period of time instead. We can only measure nutritional levels. Now, there are at least four possible ways in which observable functionings measures could intersect with capability or opportunity freedoms and with coercion – which might be considered to be a subset of process freedoms violations.

- Person A could be Undernourished because she could have eaten but chose not to.
- Person B could be Undernourished because she lacked the capability to eat.
- Person C could be Nourished because she had the capability to eat and enjoyed it.
- Person D could be Nourished because she was coerced into eating against her will.

Thus we previously established that opportunity freedoms – being counterfactuals – could not be empirically estimated. And we have now pointed out that it is not possible to evaluate capabilities only from the observed functionings of 'nourished' or 'undernourished'; more information is required. What empirical paths might be explored?

One way ahead would be to focus not on the opportunity freedom at all, but rather on the coercion or process freedom with respect to the functioning of interest. If we could establish, for example, that a person was or was not coerced (or if we could establish that a person had autonomously taken action – these are not necessarily polar opposites), then we would be able to distinguish between person C and person D. We could still not distinguish person A from person B, of course. Yet if the reason that the measurement exercise was important was that there were efforts under way to expand the chosen functioning, and if the

[5] For a fuller exposition of this see Sabina Alkire, 'Measuring the freedom aspects of capabilities', paper presented at the 2005 AEA meetings, Philadelphia. Available at http://www.aeaweb.org/annual_mtg_papers/2005/0107_1430_0104.pdf

functionings were specially important, then these measures might suffice for the purposes of the exercise.

An alternative approach would be to focus on the side effects an action had on other basic functionings. It might be argued that any adequate measure of freedom must consider not only the functioning and autonomy directly related to it, but also whether the process undermined other basic capabilities and human rights (for example, if the process of obtaining food was degrading or dangerous or dis-empowering). Indeed in some cases this might be a central criterion, for example in situations involving young children's nutrition, immunisation and primary school attendance. In the case of a headstrong yet brilliant young child, a period of parental cajoling, reasoning, convincing and requiring the child to attend school (or eat her dinner) may make the child's educational (nutritional) achievements a shade less than autonomous, and this may be constructive rather than otherwise (Nussbaum 2000). Yet it *would* be relevant to know whether the process involved in securing the headstrong young child's primary education significantly undermined her other basic capabilities in the same or subsequent time periods. To return to the case of the fasting person, if they were forced to eat, then such an approach (were it feasible – and we'll return to this issue!) might detect a detrimental impact on their spiritual state, or on their ability to advance the social cause which occasioned the fast in the first place. Thus were we able to measure side effects, this might also provide, in a different way, sufficient information to distinguish person C from person D.

4.4   Measurement approaches

The nature of the measures of individual freedom either in use or under construction is a significant topic in itself which this chapter can only summarise. This chapter will focus on two measurement approaches:

1 Empowerment measures and opportunity freedoms;[6]
2 Agency measures.[7]

---

[6] Surveys are found in Alsop and Heinsohn (2005), Malhotra, Schuler and Boender (2002), Narayan (2005) and Roy and Niranjan (2004).
[7] Biswas-Diener and Diener 2001; Christopher 1999; Diener and Biswas-Diener 2002; Alkire 2005; Diener and Diener 1995; Diener, Oishi and Lucas 2003; Diener and Suh 1997; Diener, Suh, Lucas and Smith 1999; Frey and Stutzer 1999, 2002; Gregg and Salisbury 2001; Gullone and Cummins 1999; Hampton and Marshall 2000; Hayo and Seifert 2003; Helliwell 2003; Helm 2000; Ng 2003; Ravallion and Lokshin 2001, 2002; Ryan and Deci 2001; Suh 2002; Wissing and van Eeden 2002.

To draw upon existing literature well is more difficult than might be anticipated, because it is evolving at a rapid pace and in an increasingly decentralised manner. Furthermore current measures are dispersed across disciplines (psychology, sociology, economics, politics) and occur in literatures related to distinct issues (quality-of-life and living-standard work, opportunity sets, multidimensional measures), distinct measurement schools (participatory, qualitative, quantitative-objective and quantitative-subjective), and use distinct quantitative techniques of aggregation and internal cross-checking. These measures also relate to differently 'named' concepts (efficacy, esteem, empowerment, agency, freedom, creativity, self-reliance, autonomy, etc.). To further complicate the problem, the same terminology is used with different definitions. Aware of limitations and involuntary omissions, some of the papers that shed light directly upon this topic are presented below.

4.5   Empowerment measures

Many approaches to measuring empowerment have traditionally used proxies – functioning measures that are easy to use and that, it has been assumed, are strongly correlated with the unobservable variable of empowerment. For example, studies of women's empowerment often used women's education, mothers' education, women's labour force participation, mothers' labour force participation, and so on. Another set of variables involve decision-making power of women, for example over cooking decisions or child-spacing, or, specifically in the case of women, such things as gender preferences for children.[8]

This section will focus instead on a framework for measuring degrees of empowerment proposed by Alsop and Heinsohn (2005). They argue that degrees of empowerment can be understood as comprising two factors: agency and opportunity structure. 'Agency is defined as an actor's ability to make meaningful choices; that is, the actor is able to envisage options and make a choice. Opportunity structure is defined as the formal and informal contexts within which actors operate' (Alsop and Heinsohn 2005: 6). They measure 'degrees of empowerment' by assessing:

1 'Whether a person has the opportunity to make a choice';
2 'Whether a person actually uses the opportunity to choose';

---

[8] P. Princy Yesudian, 'Impact of women's empowerment, autonomy and attitude on maternal health care utilization in India', Global Forum for Health Research, Forum 8, Mexico City, 2004. A range of studies that employ various proxies are surveyed in Malhotra *et al.* (2002) and in Annex one of Alsop and Heinsohn (2005).

3 'Once the choice is made, whether it brings the desired outcome' (Alsop and Heinsohn 2005: 7).

For example, 'if the woman in Benin wants to send her daughter to school, is there a school for the daughter to go to? If yes, does the woman actually make the decision to send her daughter to school? If yes, does the daughter actually attend school?' (Alsop and Heinsohn 2005: 7).

In order to complete the framework, Alsop and Heinsohn suggest that empowerment should be assessed relative to three different domains of people's lives:

- the state – in which a person acts as a citizen (*justice, politics, service delivery*);
- the market – in which a person is an economic actor (*credit, labour, goods* – for production and consumption);
- society – in which a person is a social actor (*family, community, etc.*).

To complete their framework, they observe that each domain can be analysed at three levels: macro-, intermediary and local. How these levels are specified will vary in different contexts. Often the macro-level will coincide with the nation; the intermediary will be the state or province, and the local, the village or neighbourhood.

Thus this approach situates individual empowerment firmly within a social, political and economic context, and explores how informal and formal institutions at many levels impinge on individual empowerment.

This framework guides a five-country study of empowerment, being undertaken by various teams within the World Bank. In addition to draft participatory exercises and an individual survey questionnaire, Alsop and Heinsohn present the indicators used in Ethiopia, Nepal, Honduras and Mexico to illustrate the kinds of indicators that are used to fill in this framework. The indicators from Ethiopia are:

- Extent to which women are equally represented in district councils (compared with men). *State: intermediary*;
- Extent to which women are equally represented in village councils (compared with men). *State: local*;
- Extent to which women choose their type of employment. *Market: local and intermediary*;
- Extent to which women negotiate working conditions with their employers. *Market: local and intermediary*;

- Extent to which women have access to credit. *Market: local and intermediary*;
- Distance to nearest bank or credit institution (measured in hours/minutes). *Market: local and intermediary*;
- Number of times women have asked for (1) loans from bank, (2) loans from moneylenders, (3) loans from family and friends, (4) store credits, (5) forward sales in the last year. *Market: local and intermediary*;
- Number of times women received (1) to (5) over the last year *Market: local and intermediary*;
- Percentage of women who take action against harmful traditional practices (female genital mutilation, milk tooth extraction, etc.). *Society: local and intermediary*;
- Percentage of women who take action against domestic violence. *Society: local and intermediary*;
- Extent to which women can make independent decisions over investments in (1) house durables, (2) kitchen utensils, (3) farm tools, (4) yard animals, (5) farm inputs and (6) business inputs. *Society: local*;
- Percentage of women having an equal say over (1) the spacing of children, (2) using contraceptives, (3) having sex. *Society: local*;
- Ratio of women vs. men who attend (1) political, (2) social, (3) religious community meetings. *Society: local*;
- Extent to which women vs. men (1) speak up at these meetings, (2) have their views taken into consideration, (3) affect decisions. *Society: local*.

Alsop and Heinsohn also identify questions from other survey instruments, including the World Bank's Living Standard Measurement Survey modules (LSMS) and its Integrated Questionnaire for the Measurement of Social Capital (IQMSC), as well as other data sources such as that of Freedom House, which can be drawn upon for assessing certain aspects of empowerment. This planned approach uses objective quantitative indicators, combined with participatory and qualitative techniques.

What can we learn regarding the measurement of capabilities from Alsop and Heinsohn's framework? The first observation is that, like this approach, the analysis of degrees of empowerment distinguishes between opportunity structures (which correspond to opportunity freedom in Sen's work – and can be provided by social, economic or political institutions) and agency.

Here the terms differ somewhat. It is not necessary to expend too much effort on conceptual matters given that the present task is to generate a narrow but sufficient methodology. Yet it might prevent confusion to observe that agency, as defined by Alsop and Heinsohn, includes only a subset of Sen's concept of process freedom. That is, Alsop and Heinsohn focus on instances in which people exercise agency on behalf of themselves or their family or community to choose functionings from within a feasible capability set. It will be interesting to learn more precisely what aspects of agency the quantitative measures of choice represent, and qualitative, subjective, participatory and ethnographic studies should clarify this. Given the discussion of 'individualism' that will be presented in the next section, it will also be interesting to observe the extent to which choice-related empowerment measures (such as many of those used in Ethiopia) are correlated with cultural individualism vs. collectivism. Some questions are left unaddressed, such as how information on agency and opportunity structures will be combined during the analysis to establish 'degrees of empowerment'.

However, the main contribution of this approach becomes evident when we return to the four-fold division between persons, which is crude, but does highlight a slightly different set of issues:

• Person A could be Undernourished because she could have eaten but chose not to.
• Person B could be Undernourished because she lacked the capability to eat.
• Person C could be Nourished because she had the capability to eat and enjoyed it.
• Person D could be Nourished because she was coerced into eating against her will.

Theoretically, Alsop and Heinsohn's framework could distinguish person A from person B, because they could identify persons who enjoyed an opportunity structure of nourishment but chose not to use it. That is, theoretically, they could actually identify a counterfactual opportunity freedom, a 'road not chosen'. If the empirical work bears this out, it will be of tremendous importance to those working on capability measurement. We will be able to distinguish persons who are 'starving' from those who are 'fasting'. What is not yet clear is how persons C and D will be distinguished from one another, or in the case of children, for example, how destructive forms of coercion will be identified. Alsop and Heinsohn have provided a masterful and promising map of the range of variables that potentially impact on the measurement of both opportunity and process freedoms.

4.6   Domain-specific agency measures

Another fertile and significant literature is that of *subjective measures of autonomy at the individual level*. For there are a number of large-scale cross-cultural psychological studies of creativity, of autonomy, of self-esteem, of personal freedom, of self-determination – some or all of which may pertain to freedoms.[9]

Rather than approaching agency only as a 'dimension of wellbeing', however, I have argued that it is also appropriate to consider agency with respect to each domain of wellbeing. The reason for this is drawn from Sen's analysis, which rejects the view (held by some basic needs theorists) that agency (or, for that matter, opportunity freedom) can adequately be represented *only* as a dimension of wellbeing (Alkire 2002a: ch. 5). Sen acknowledges that agency can have intrinsic value, and insofar as it does, I have argued that it can take its place as one domain or dimension of wellbeing alongside other dimensions that have intrinsic value, such as friendship, meaningful work, knowledge, relationships, inner peace, or being healthy (Alkire 2002a; Finnis 1980; Grisez, Boyle and Finnis 1987). However, Sen's capability approach argues that freedoms must be evaluated with respect to *each* valuable functioning – freedom also plays an architectonic role with respect to the other dimensions of wellbeing (Nussbaum 2000). It would seem consonant with this approach to suggest that, similarly, agency might be more accurately evaluated with respect to different functionings rather than globally.

This can be stated quite simply. A person who is 'empowered' as a citizen because she can vote and speak in local meetings may nonetheless be excluded from the labour market because of her gender and low levels of education, or be abused by her husband. A domain-specific measure of agency can distinguish between the freedom that she experiences in different domains of her life, whereas a 'global' measure of agency would conflate these diverse measures into an aggregate that would be of less practical value.

One significant empirical approach to domain-specific measures of human agency is the self-efficacy scales, initiated by Albert Bandura.[10] The social-cognitive theory he uses distinguishes between *personal, proxy and collective* forms of agency. For example, in one recent application of Bandura's approach, individuals rank three kinds of 'efficacy' on scales from 1 to 5. These are: perceived personal efficacy (handling activities in family, in partnership, at work, managing personal finances and health); individual social efficacy (perceived capabilities to contribute individually

---

[9] A recent survey of these may be found in Alkire (2005).
[10] Bandura's and related work has been collected in Bandura (1997).

to improvements in social problems); and collective social efficacy (capabilities of society as a whole to effect desired improvements in unemployment, corruption, criminal and drug activities, economic crises, and terrorism) (Fernandez-Ballesteros, Diez-Nicolas and Bandura 2002). While Bandura's own interest focuses on the way that individuals' beliefs about personal efficacy can be cultivated in order to increase efficacy itself, the measures may also be of interest to those whose primary variables are external to the person or community.

Another very fruitful potential subjective approach to measuring agency and autonomy empirically and across cultures is the Self-Determination Theory (SDT) of Ryan and Deci (2000b), and this approach will be explored in greater depth. This approach resonates very strongly at a conceptual level with Sen's own work because it focuses on capabilities that the person *values* (in contrast to self-efficacy, which identifies capabilities a person understands herself to *have* – whether or not she values them).

According to the SDT formulation, a person is autonomous when his or her behaviour is experienced as willingly enacted and when he or she fully endorses the actions in which he or she is engaged and/or the values expressed by them. People are therefore most autonomous when they act in accord with their authentic interests or integrated values and desires (Chirkov, Ryan, Kim and Kaplan 2003; Deci and Ryan 1985, 2000; Ryan, Deci and Grolnick 1995).

SDT contrasts autonomy with its [presumed] opposite, *heteronomy*, 'in which one's actions are experienced as controlled by forces that are phenomenally alien to the self, or that compel one to behave in specific ways regardless of one's values or interests' (Chirkov *et al.* 2003: 98).

To determine autonomy, a study first asks respondents whether they engaged in certain practices (these could relate to health, to education, to employment, or to any other domain of poverty or wellbeing). Respondents are then asked to rate, from 1 to 5, four possible reasons why they felt or believed or engaged in the practice (1 = *not at all because of this reason*; 5 = *completely because of this reason*). The possible reasons range from less autonomous (1) to more autonomous (4) and were as follows:

1 *External regulation*: because of external pressures (to get rewards or avoid punishments). I would engage in this behaviour because someone insists on my doing this, or I expect to get some kind of reward, or avoid some punishment for behaving this way.

2 *Introjected regulation*: to get approval or avoid guilt. I would engage in this behaviour because people around me would approve of me for

doing so, or because I think I should do it. If I did not do this I might feel guilty, ashamed or anxious.

3 *Identified regulation*: because it is important. I would engage in this behaviour because I personally believe that it is important and worthwhile to behave this way.

4 *Integrated regulation*: because I have thoughtfully considered and fully chosen this. I have thought about this behaviour and fully considered alternatives. It makes good sense to me to act this way. I feel free in choosing and doing it (Chirkov *et al.* 2003: 102).[11]

The attention within SDT to autonomy, which Deci and Ryan describe as 'the experience of integration and freedom, and ... an essential aspect of healthy human functioning' (Deci and Ryan 2000: 231), generated a vigorous empirical debate within the field. Some argued and attempted to demonstrate empirically that autonomy is not universally valued, but is rather valued by, and useful in, more individualist cultures and societies alone. In a powerful rebuttal to this attack, Chirkov *et al.* distinguished autonomy – conceptually as well as empirically – from several related concepts: dependence / independence, and individualism/ collectivism and vertical/horizontal.[12]

It is worthwhile to note their distinction between dependence and independence. Of particular interest, given the other measures surveyed, is the possibility that a person could be *autonomously dependent*. The basic terms are defined as follows:

SDT defines *dependence* as reliance on others for guidance, support or needed supplies (Ryan and Lynch 1989). Within SDT, the opposite of dependence is not autonomy but rather *independence*, the circumstance of not relying on others for support, help or supplies.

Thus SDT argues that a person can be autonomously *dependent* or autonomously *independent* – that these categories are orthogonal to one another. An autonomous person might, for example, welcome others' influence and be responsive to good advice – or she might be inclined to resist any external influences. Similarly, they argue that an autonomous person may be more *individualist* (ascribing 'relative priority ... to the individual's goals and preferences' (Chirkov *et al.* 2003: 98–99)), or more *collectivist* ('priority placed on the needs, norms, and goals of one's group or collective' (Chirkov *et al.* 2003: 99)). Finally, they argue that individualism and collectivism can be fruitfully distinguished from *horizontal* and *vertical* aspects of culture, where these refer to 'practices and

[11] These four are explained at greater length in Deci and Ryan (2000).
[12] Following Triandis (1995). See also Oyserman, Coon and Kemmelmeier (2002), who do not mention SDT, however.

norms supporting equality or interchangeability among people versus hierarchical or subordinate social relations' (Chirkov et al. 2003: 99).

Testing autonomy thus defined across four countries (Turkey, Russia, USA and South Korea) produced a series of findings that broadly supported the SDT claims, and established that autonomy can be distinguished from individualism,[13] as well as from horizontal vs. vertical outlooks, and that autonomy is correlated with wellbeing for persons in individualist as well as collectivist cultures (Chirkov et al. 2003).

What is particularly useful in this conceptual approach is the clarification of how autonomy is distinct from both dependence/independence and individualism/collectivism. Thus a person could be acting within rules set by a parent or by social norms or by law, but doing so autonomously because one internally endorsed those rules. Alternatively, one could be acting in the same way but feeling utterly coerced and oppressed by the parent, the norms or the law. In the first instance, autonomy – and indeed agency – is not threatened; in the second it is. This distinction Sen, too, has cultivated – in his example that freedom is expanded by the government spraying malaria ponds even if it did not consult every person, because they would probably have endorsed this if asked (Sen 1982, 1988, 1992).

The SDT approach to measuring autonomy is of considerable interest for several reasons. First, previous empirical studies have apparently been able to use variants of this instrument to discern changes in autonomy, so the instrument has the potential of being sensitive to policy-changes. Second, the concept of autonomy is carefully distinguished and empirically distinguishable from individualism and independence, and thus potentially relevant across cultures and societies in much the same way that Sen understands agency to be relevant across cultures. Third, the self-regulation scales can be adapted to measure autonomy with respect to different practices or to different dimensions of wellbeing. Indeed, the proponents of SDT have developed separate questionnaires for autonomy related to education (from elementary age on up, including persons with learning disorders), health-related behaviours, religion, pro-social behaviours, friendship and exercise. Agency can be differently exhibited in different spheres – within the household, in gender relations, in health practices, in political domains. The SDT autonomy tool could, conceivably, be used to map agency in different domains. Fourth, the tool is relatively brief, which improves feasibility and reduces costs.

---

[13] Seen Oyserman et al. (2002), whose in-depth review of empirical psychological studies of individualism and collectivism between European Americans and non-Americans or African/Latino/Asian Americans, found that 'these differences were neither as large nor as systematic as often perceived' (2002: 40).

But how could this tool contribute to a measure of capability freedom? What is terribly evident is that this measure is incomplete. It must be complemented by a functioning measure. That is, for each domain of wellbeing under consideration, one could anticipate two empirical representations: one for the functioning(s) (related, for example, to health, employment, nutritional status, education, safety, self-respect, and so on), and the other for the 'autonomy' associated with each functioning. So a wellbeing questionnaire would include functioning measure(s) and one agency measure per domain of wellbeing. How the (functioning, autonomy) set of wellbeing measures would be compared across persons or across time – whether by dominance rankings or by aggregation – is a separate topic for study.[14]

If the autonomy measures are accurate, then what is clear is that if a person was highly autonomous but undernourished, this might suggest that they pertained to the category A; if they were nourished and had a high autonomy ranking, they would almost certainly pertain to category C. If the person had a low autonomy ranking and was nourished, it could not be definitely concluded that she was being forced to eat (category D), but it would definitely suggest that empowerment was required. If this information were further supplemented by data on the opportunity structure that Alsop and Heinsohn propose, then it would be possible to map individual freedoms more fully.

4.7   Conclusion

In 1985, Sen made a plea that wellbeing not be considered in isolation from human agency (Sen 1985b). At present, the explosion of research on empowerment in development similarly draws attention to the need for increases in wellbeing to be in part generated by and sustained by the communities in question. Measures of empowerment and opportunity structure, such as Alsop and Heinsohn propose, would contribute clarity regarding the exterior environment. Measures of individual autonomy, such as Ryan and Deci have developed, could potentially provide accurate domain-specific measures of autonomy. The methods by which these data would be combined for comparative purposes, and the accuracy of the proposed indicators, are still appropriately the subjects of ongoing empirical research. However, these streams could be the building blocks for a methodological sidecar that would expand the functioning measures with key aspects of individual freedom.

---

[14] For a fuller exposition of this see Alkire, 'Measuring the Freedom aspects of capabilities'.

5   Using security to indicate wellbeing

Geof Wood

5.1   Introduction

This chapter argues for socio-economic security to be included as a key component of wellbeing. It moves from theory to a discussion of principles and indicators, which could constitute part of an agenda for ongoing empirical research into wellbeing.

The chapter does not claim to present a comprehensive account of wellbeing or of socio-economic security (see ILO 2004, for example, for a labour-related agenda). Instead it addresses, axiomatically, a sub-set of ideas within a broader set of conceptions about wellbeing and security. It sees the problem of human security as a major element in the understanding of wellbeing. The approach adopted here reflects debates about vulnerability and livelihoods[1] (Wood 2005), and operates with a strong sense of time, opportunity, choice and risk. Although the idea of security is inextricably associated with law and order and rights, here the focus is more upon the informal and social conditions for predictability of wellbeing rather than the statutory context for it. It tries to identify those ingredients of behaviour which are, or could be, in the control of ordinary people in poor situations, given modest policy support. The issue of predictability is central to the approach in this chapter, and, given prevailing hostile conditions in the political economy, there is an emphasis upon ordinary people's agency as the route to this predictability. The overall context for this discussion is conditions of rapid change in which expectations alter and uncertainty prevails especially for the poorer, politically weaker actors in society (Webster and Engberg-Pedersen 2002). In contrast to the Doyal and Gough human needs architecture of 'needs satisfiers', this chapter offers the corollary idea of 'risk averters' as a further set of institutions and practices essential for the reduction of uncertainty.

---

[1] G. Nooteboom, 'A matter of style: Social security and livelihood in upland East Java' Ph.D thesis, University of Nijmegen, The Netherlands 2003.

The next section traces the evolving discourse from human development to human security, before contrasting autonomous and dependent security. It then offers comparative observer (etic) and actor (emic) accounts of this contrast, concluding that for poor people, dependent forms of security become the main realistic option. That perspective is then explored, before deriving a set of seven 'principles of improvement' in security, supported by illustrative indicators. Throughout the following discussion, the concept of individual security evolves through elaboration of the imperative for individuals, households and groups to reduce uncertainty as part of risk mitigation.

5.2   Individual and societal security

The discourse about security has evolved from military defence themes and the practices of social protection in welfare state regimes, although both continue in changing forms. Human Security (HS) is becoming the umbrella term moving us beyond the more familiar human development discourse. 'Human security' emphasises the relationship between individual and societal security via the processes of claiming and the presence of rights rather than more top-down policy intervention to deliver needs. Some propositions about individual security, as in the *Human Security Now* papers (Ogata-Sen Commission 2003), clearly have their origins in the 'agency' nexus of capabilities and functionings, but also in a rights perspective about freedoms. However there is a crucial difference between 'freedom to' and 'freedom from'.[2] Thus the capability and functioning perspective, as embodied in Human Development (HD), is about the freedom to act successfully in the pursuit of livelihoods and wellbeing. Thus within HD there are intrinsic assumptions about the duties of top-down providers, especially in support of human capital development via health and education, primarily directed at the 'freedom to' objective. Clearly the performance of such duties contributes to security, because they are intended directly to improve the conditions and chances for successful agency, which in turn would bring about personal security.

The human security discourse, while not discarding the 'HD – freedom to' agenda, additionally embraces the 'freedom from' agenda. In a banal or tautological sense, this is 'freedom from insecurity' thus elevating security, its opposite, to an irreducible element of wellbeing Dissecting this further, this is a freedom from all things that are

---

[2] The UNDP Human Development Reports of 1993 and especially 1994 elaborate the notion of human security and set up this distinction.

perceived as potentially threatening to wellbeing, as well as those things that actually threaten wellbeing[3]; thus freedom from future as well as present danger. This also means that there is objective insecurity as well as subjective, the latter especially represented by the concept of fear about harm and consequent ill-being.

The HS perspective certainly 'ups the ante' from the HD one. It extends the framework of correlative duties in order to match and support 'freedom from' needs in addition to 'freedom to' needs. It thus makes a stronger connection between the individual and institutional arenas of responsibility (Von Benda-Beckmann and Von Benda-Beckmann 1994). It extends the notion of rights from top-down intervention for human investment (i.e. via support for education and health) to universalist social protection. This represents a shift from a liberal perspective about enabling opportunities and choice towards the more pervasive rationale for the state as the guarantor of order and basic needs. It thus takes us from limited permissive rights to fuller protective rights. This is exceedingly ambitious in terms of social or political economy expectations about governance, about justice, about redress, about comprehensiveness.

At the same time, there is another kind of developmental danger about pushing the security agenda to these limits of comprehensiveness, even if that were achievable. The downside of a risk-free, fearless society is the potential loss of the adventure of agency, and the alienation arising from the absence of a need to choose. Some balance has to be struck between the limited liberal and the comprehensive 'nanny' state, a balance which offers incentives within a reasonable but not exhaustive framework of protection. The problem is that this balance does not work in the same way for everyone given inequalities of power and resources. And the paradox is that those with the greatest need to claim risk averters (the corollary of Doyal and Gough's 'needs satisfiers') are in the weakest position to do so given the social origins of the state. Those with extensive personal resources are more equipped to manage their own 'freedom from' agenda independently of the state and its repertoire of statutory rights and entitlements. In this sense, the individual security for the select few may come at the expense of security for the many.[4] Contrast gated communities with the slums in highly unequal parts of the world.

[3] Thus Alkire, a member of the Commission for Human Security, states 'the objective of human security is to safeguard the vital core of all human lives from pervasive threats, without impeding long term fulfilment' (2003: 24).

[4] Bob Deacon makes this point indirectly when he argues that richer people have wider options to pursue personal welfare in global markets, not only deserting but undermining more localised provision (Deacon, Hulse and Stubbs 1997).

The reference to 'alienation' in the previous paragraph has wider ramifications for the relation between security and wellbeing. Since alienation is about the lack of control, it therefore has to be about agency within a local–universal context, the individual's room for manoeuvre. This is a central preoccupation for the WeD Research Group, because it is including the dimension of subjective awareness. But part of the problem of understanding wellbeing through subjective awareness concerns the extent to which power structures,[5] through processes of conformity and alienation, deny the self-actualisation of culture as expressed through the words and deeds of the subjective good life. In other debates, this has been represented as the problem of false consciousness.

This alienation problem was the intellectual basis of more recent 'development' themes about participation and governance (Cooke and Kothari 2001) as practical additions to the more fundamental lexicon about senses of belonging, membership, choice and influence over personal destiny. In other words, how to metamorphise local social rights (associated with identity and membership of locally functioning institutions) into political and universal ones. Even counter, alternative and post-development ideas (Pieterse 2001) can be understood as a continuation of the self-actualisation theme, celebrating cultural relativism over modern universalism. Indeed there is some paradox that the universalist proposition about autonomy (Doyal and Gough 1991) is actually more consistent with a relativist agenda of self-actualisation than with globalised, or universalist, modernist welfare principles.

However, within this there is a further paradox to resolve: alienation arises from both the presence and absence of protection via enabling structures/institutions. Comprehensive protection entails such an extensive performance of correlative duties by others than oneself that one's rights are entirely dependent upon the actions of others: i.e. alienation. But the absence of protection, certainly in the sense of formal rights and claims, obliges forms of informal dependency behaviour which are themselves demeaning and alienating. To put it another way: one can have too much security and have no agency, no personal responsibility, no dignity; or too little of it and only have options for degraded agency and also no dignity. A further version of the proposition is that excessive loyalty is the undignified route to security. So while, universally, security is understood as a precondition for dignity

---

[5] (Especially Lukes's second and third dimensions, 1974).

(Goldewijk and Fortman 1999) and thus wellbeing, an excessive reliance upon either formal or informal types of security can only be achieved at the price of dignity and self-respect.

Again, not all are equal with respect to this dilemma. It is helpful, therefore, to distinguish between autonomous security and dependent security.[6] Autonomous security refers to confident social actors with capabilities and functionings in a Rawlsian (Rawls 1970) as well as Sen sense (Sen 1999),[7] whose agency enables them to operate in a successful mix of public and private domains: both enjoying rights as competent citizens (Rawls), but also enabled to provide personally for their welfare through property, labour and financial markets (Sen). Dependent security refers to those who are either excessively reliant upon the state, or upon philanthropy or clientelism. Clearly there are people in rich societies experiencing dependent security due to idiosyncratic disadvantage (e.g. the disabled, elderly and infirm, and chronically ill) and systemic poverty. In poorer societies, the incidence of dependent security arising from systemic poverty is much higher, entailing a reliance upon clientelism more than either the state or philanthropy. While dependent security may be the enforced choice/option for many under conditions of a problematic institutional responsibility matrix (i.e. dysfunctional state and imperfect/segmented markets, see Gough and Wood 2004), autonomous security is the avowed goal of HS modernisers since it is, *inter alia*, compatible with dignity and thus broader conceptions of wellbeing. The prevalence of dependent security across the poor regions of the world has profound, systemic, negative reproductive consequences for the goal of autonomous security: a Faustian bargain is at work (Wood 2003) whereby informal, clientelised rights are deepened, thus foreclosing the prospects for an enabling political economy to emerge which responds to individual capabilities and functionings. In other words, the weakness of the 'freedom from' conditions undermines the 'freedom to' possibilities.

Connecting this reasoning to the Gough and Wood (2004) 'welfare regimes continuum', we can end up with a clear linkage between regime type and forms of insecurity/security in Table 5.1.[8]

---

[6] This distinction became clearer to me in debates with Guy Standing, Director of the ILO In-Focus Programme on Socio-Economic Security, during the production of Economic Security for a Better World (ILO 2004).

[7] The contrast between Rawls and Sen is essentially a contrast between political competence within legal frameworks of justice, and a capacity to activate economic and social entitlements through the trading of assets and skills, especially when relative values suddenly change or are continuously uncertain.

[8] I am grateful to Ian Gough for suggesting this table.

Table 5.1 *Linkage between regime type and forms of security/insecurity*

Insecurity	Dependent security	Autonomous security	Excessively imposed security
Insecurity regime (Bevan 2004b)	Informal security regime (Wood 2004)	Many welfare state regimes (Esping-Andersen 1990)	Communist 'dictatorship over needs' or German Fascist 'Versorgungstaat' ('warden state')

5.3   Security and wellbeing

Embedded within this dilemma between autonomous and dependent security and its implications for wellbeing is the relation for social actors between time, perception and opportunity. Thus present decisions about risk and agency are partially determined by perceptions of what the future will provide.

Thus all these themes come into the story about predictability and security as a function of wellbeing. It is a primordial instinct to seek safety for oneself and valued others. So there is an additional aspect to be opened up in our discourse: the avoidance of fear about safety. The subjective and fearful feelings of anxiety and panic about safety are common to all humans as a sense of ill-being, but these are exaggerated for some categories of the population due to non-idiosyncratic, systemic vulnerability, characterised by a chronically weak control over personal destiny.[9] But essentially, for poor people in poor societies, fear and security are inversely related.[10] If fear is a key element of ill-being, so security is a key part of its resolution and thus a feature of wellbeing. Fear is strongly associated with the unknown, with uncertainty and unpredictability. It is associated with not knowing if one has the resources (mental, material and social) to cope with unassessable challenges. It is not knowing if one can discharge emotional and cultural responsibilities for kin and friends. It is not knowing whether one can protect oneself or offer protection to valued others in the present and future. Those who can, invest considerable resources in mitigating fear by reducing risk of

[9] Clearly there are a multitude of propositions about political economy, inequality and powerlessness which lie behind that weak control.
[10] This is not a general statement about the relation between fear and security. The studies of risk and fear in rich countries indicate that people who are objectively very secure, nevertheless feel very insecure. This is well observed, for example, in relation to crime trends (actual crime down, fear of crime up). This would suggest that the fear/security comparison between poor and rich people can be expressed as a 'U' curve, with subjective fear as the vertical axis and objective security as the horizontal one.

failure and decline in all forms of wellbeing (emotional, material, objective and subjective). Those who cannot, remain in fear, which thus becomes a prevalent condition in countries with a high incidence of poverty. And an inability to invest derives not only internally from constrained resources (of all kinds) but also externally from uncertainty.

These arguments touch on the Doyal and Gough (1991) proposition that autonomy and health are the key two universals for all, to be pursued through varying sets of needs satisfiers. Health, of course, is a form of security or safety. But the relation between autonomy and security is more problematical. As indicated in the previous section, autonomy is not always a precondition for security, even if, as Doyal and Gough argue, security is a universal satisfier for autonomy. In other words, the notion of security has to be unpacked into its autonomous and dependent dimensions. The realities of power and inequality mean that autonomy and security need to be disentangled conceptually, even though we may all agree that sustained or 'quality' security can only be an outcome of autonomy.[11] However, the reality of wellbeing for many poor people globally is that their security is achieved through asymmetrical loyalty to, or dependence on, other powerholders, whether formal or informal: i.e. under constrained conditions of choice and agency. Indeed, depending on the timeline chosen for the analysis, is there a trade-off between autonomy and security for poor people with weak control over personal destiny as manifested through weak capability, access and their related inferior profile of resources? The timeline issue distinguishes between, on the one hand, value-driven and, on the other, analytic judgements about the quality of security. Short-term security achieved at the expense of dependency may be valued less by the universalist observer than the impossible dream of higher-value security which embodies the principle of autonomy, even if our poor actors have to settle for the reverse. In other words, the etic normative objective stance is subordinated to the emic pragmatic, subjective stance.

To summarise this part of the discussion, this etic–emic distinction can be represented in Table 5.2.

The next section elaborates this emic account via a series of propositions, which link the problem of security and the search for wellbeing to the condition of poverty as a determinant of agency. In the penultimate section a series of seven principles for improving the security dimension of wellbeing are derived. Each of these principles is illustrated through boxed summaries of behavioural change and structural conditions which would indicate that wellbeing via security is being realised.

---

[11] As clearly argued at different times by Doyal and Gough (1991) and Standing (ILO 2004).

Table 5.2 *Autonomy and security trade-off*

Etic account	Emic account
Normative	Pragmatic
Emphasis on quality of security	Willingness to settle for less
Autonomy	Dependency
Needs satisfiers	Risk averters
Longer-term, sustained timeline, reflecting greater predictability of conditions	Shorter-term perspectives, reflecting higher discounting under conditions of change and uncertainty

5.4   The problem of security for poor people

When considering the conditions of poverty for poor people in developing countries (and to a lesser extent elsewhere too, especially in more unprotected rich countries such as the USA), a major feature of those conditions is uncertainty. Apart from the general conditions of uncertainty that afflict the total population and threaten a general sense of personal wellbeing, the poor experience an exaggerated sense of uncertainty. This derives from: the paucity of effective resources under their command; their consequent inferior position in relation to other, superior, power-holders in the society; and their resulting vulnerability to hazards and shocks. Such uncertainty comprises therefore a series of risks, which have to be managed effectively.

However, these risks are likely to be co-variant, occurring in small pools, which increases their probability as well as intensity and significance of impact.[12] The co-variance arises from the narrow spread of activity through which livelihoods are pursued. This is an absence of diversity in a portfolio of options, a lack of choice. In agriculture, a climate disaster not only damages the crop of the small farmer, but at the same time reduces the prospects of off-farm employment on the cropland of neighbouring farmers similarly affected. It also has knock-on effects in reducing post-harvest employment opportunities, including for women, which historically deliver not just incomes but crop shares (as a hedge against price inflation). Consequent scarcity of food products in local markets increases local prices and reduces family entitlements in the Sen sense of tradable exchange (Sen 1981b). If assets have to be sold to meet extra prices (including, typically, livestock), an

---

[12] I am grateful to Steen Jorgensen, Head of the Social Development Division at the World Bank, for helpful insight on this point.

over-supply of assets also reduces their market value. But at the same time, the excess supply of labour has also reduced the labour price. All these co-variant problems occur within a small pool of relationships and options, characterised by inequalities and interlocked transactions. They are only relieved by 'migration' of some family members into wider risk or option pools.[13] Although the conditions for the urban poor vary from the rural conditions, many rural conditions are reproduced in the cities of peasants (Loughhead, Mittal and Wood 2001; Roberts 1978; Wood and Salway 2000), with segmented and imperfect labour markets dominated by brokers and intermediaries who also control residential areas and access to public goods and entitlements (in a non-Sen sense). Their risks are thus interlocked with few exit options, since other parts of the city and the other labour markets within the city are also managed in similar ways and thus difficult to enter.

Risks have many dimensions, but can also be classified into shocks and hazards.[14] Of course everyone is vulnerable to *shocks*, although perhaps not equally. Thus the impact of an earthquake shock will vary according to the quality of house construction, and the insurance provision upon it. Likewise with flooding as we know from Bangladesh. Disease epidemics, even class-neutral ones with respect to incidence like HIV/AIDS, can have a differential impact upon families of different classes. However, the poor are more vulnerable to *hazards* than others because they have less resistance to them and less room for manoeuvre to prepare for them in terms of resource mobilisation. Hazards are what we can expect to happen at different stages in a family life-cycle, as well as the predictable threats more widespread in the society. Thus we can expect illness to occur for key adult income earners. Richer families can prepare for such eventualities through savings, insurance and other risk spreading, such as job diversity among family members. Not only can they cover the costs of treatment, but they can also ride out the loss of income. Weddings, dowry expenses and funerals are all predictably heavy demands (often derived from social and cultural expectations and thus important for the maintenance of social and cultural resources) which constitute hazards to ongoing livelihoods. Some dimensions of wellbeing have to be served through meeting these obligations.[15] But the poor are compelled to make key sacrifices in order to do this, such as

---

[13] Which is why migration is becoming such a dominant analytical theme across the four WeD countries: Peru, Ethiopia, Bangladesh and Thailand.

[14] I am grateful to Sarah White at the University of Bath for insight into this distinction.

[15] Funerals arising from HIV/AIDS infections have become a major issue in many parts of Africa as cultural expectations and social obligations are honoured by the bereaved families and immediate kin and associates.

deepening their dependence on others for liquidity and in-kind resources, and thereby further removing their freedom of action subsequently. The alternative is exclusion and a deepening of risk and vulnerability as a result.[16]

Poor people, operating under conditions of severe inequality and hostile political economies, have less control over the institutions through which they must seek their livelihoods and wellbeing, in all four of the wellbeing dimensions (emotional, material, subjective and objective). They have weak statutory rights and entitlements to welfare (in both a Sen and a non-Sen sense). This draws our attention to the multiple dimensions of inequality and asymmetries of power across many arenas. Poor people face daily and repeated humiliation and reminders of their inferiority, lack of worth and respect. They are continuously forced to act in ways that undermine a personal sense of dignity. Those family members who experience this externally in wider interaction outside the family bring back those frustrations and senses of inadequacy internally. Shame can easily translate into other emotional states and problematic behaviour: depression and domestic violence. These are fears which gnaw away at the psyche.

This is how we return to the autonomy/security issue. Clearly there is dignity in autonomy, a sense of personal worth and direction. Thus it is valid, as argued above, for wellbeing analysis to distinguish between two forms of security: autonomous and dependent. And this is not just a distinction between means, between needs satisfiers and risk averters, as it were. The means certainly entail the ends – i.e. the quality of that security. This is akin to the proposition that rights gained are far more meaningful than rights awarded (Wood 2004: 72–79). Thus autonomous security can be seen as fundamentally enabling, both reflecting adequate control over personal destiny as well as providing the basis for further options and choices, and thus risk spreading. By contrast, with dependent security, the means subvert the quality of the end achieved. It is ultimately a disabling process, which repeatedly forecloses future options for autonomous security. Thus the sustainability of one's personal security and safety depends upon the arbitrary, non-statutory, non-rights based behaviour and favours of others. Some might argue (Standing at ILO for example) that this is not security at all, just insecure clientelism. But this is the etic–emic dilemma for analysis: what is a second best, debased option for the comfortable observer is the only game in town for others. Clientelism at least entails predictable flows of

---

[16] Much of the livelihoods literature refers only to the notion of shocks in the analysis of vulnerability (see Wood 2005 for a review of the livelihoods discourse).

goods, services and even constrained opportunities in return for loyalty[17] and loss of independence.

In this context, what induces poor people to accept dependent security rather than take on the added risk of asserting broader rights to choice? There is an irony here with risk aversion being both a feature of wellbeing and contradictory to it. Risk aversion has long been associated with peasantries around the world ever since Chayanov saw it as the rational response to uncertainty. The proposition here is that the poor are distinguished from other classes by their induced discount rate.[18] Looking at the composition of household budgets for the poor, in which for example much higher proportions are spent on food, as compared to other classes, a much higher proportion of their budgets are allocated to short-term needs rather than medium to longer-term ones over their own or children's life-cycle. In addition to non-stored food (which for very poor families can account for 70% of expenditure), shelter and clothing are the other priorities. Everything else, including health spending (except at moments of crisis), is much less significant. For non-poor families, these proportions, including significantly spending on education, are allocated very differently and over a longer timeline. For poor families, this reveals a high discounting of the future over the present. Of course, this discount rate is induced. So poor people's time preference for the immediate present over even the near future is not a wilful choice associated with cultures of poverty and such like. But to secure the present is not just a matter of time-constrained household budget allocation. It also involves entering relationships and agreements which will deliver these immediate needs, agreements which are immediately attractive even if they foreclose choices and investment for the future, in other words, risk averting behaviour – taking what is on offer as a response to uncertainty rather than looking for more tenuous options even if of longer-term value. The classic example is the imme-diately available high interest loan, which has trapped the poor the world over.[19] But interlocked transactions abound: credit linked to labour obligations; job access in return for commission; shelter and services in return for loyalty and labour obligations; sexual favours; the bonding of one's children; mortgaging of land to other's use; vacating prime real estate sites; trading at below market prices and perhaps on non-repayable credit; protection charges; early committal of children to work; and so on.

---

[17] As in Hirschman's 'exit, voice and loyalty' schema (1970).

[18] In Wood (2004) I refer to the 'peasant analogue' in order to extend this analytical point to non-peasants in changing and urbanising societies.

[19] This, of course, is the main rationale for microfinance programmes.

These are all better described as 'risk averters' in the real world rather than 'needs satisfiers' in an imagined world.

In other writing (Gough and Wood 2004; Wood 2000), the idea of an institutional responsibility matrix has been advanced as a framework within which to analyse the variation of welfare regimes within which people pursue livelihoods and wellbeing. This matrix has domestic and global dimensions, but at these two levels it essentially represents the four arenas of state, market, community and household. For different classes in different countries, these arenas are more or less problematical, more or less dysfunctional. Although wellbeing is a function of agency in all of these arenas simultaneously, the problems associated with particular arenas require more reliance upon others in the framework which might be working better for the social actor. Thus in countries with problematic states and highly imperfect markets, poor people at least have to rely more upon community and household arenas, even though these arenas, too, may have their own problems (i.e. communities may comprise arbitrary hierarchies and untamed power; households may be over-patriarchal for the wellbeing of women). Poor people in overall conditions of insecurity are less able to manipulate these problematical institutional arenas to their advantage. And indeed their relative weakness in one arena (e.g. in their encounters with the state – Schaffer and Huang 1975) forces their increased reliance and dependence upon another arena (e.g. the community) where their revealed powerlessness exposes them to more intensive exploitation, since they do not have a demonstrable exit option. This entails a further erosion of self-respect via the negative trade-off between security and autonomy.

These outcomes of insecurity can be further understood by distinguishing between social capital and social resources. In effect, the above describes the conditions of weak social capital not just for the society as a whole but especially for sub-sections of the population. That is to say: the overall capability environment is sufficiently problematical to prevent the realisation of entitlements (in both the Sen and non-Sen senses) through formal institutional behaviour. The sense of a formal capital stock of transparent, rights-based institutions characterised by the principles of equity is missing. The capital that may exist instead is 'dark' (Putzel 1997): functional to those classes and groups who can play in the darkness, but exclusionary to those who need to rely upon 'light'. Under those conditions, poor people's wellbeing can only be pursued through the deployment of personal social resources (in contrast to public social capital) in imperfect market arrangements (especially labour markets, but also the trading of goods and services in the informal sector) and in the community and household arenas. It is this reasoning that places the 'resources profile' approach so centrally in the arguments about wellbeing. It is also important to recognise that such resources (social and cultural ones especially) are not just means towards wellbeing; their possession is also part of the meaning of wellbeing itself. In other words, they have affective value, not just instrumental value as in the contrast made by Weber. They are in part a measure of the quality of life. And their possession also brings the principles of security and autonomy closer together towards an objective of enabling autonomous security, reducing risk and thereby fear. It would also either enable the possessors to play better in the darkness, or, with others, create the light.[20]

However, such possession of functional resources is an idealistic jump in the argument. The road is strewn with boulders. Keeping in mind the broader version of capability (i.e. beyond the simpler notion of human capital or human resources), we should distinguish between those who have a capacity or potential capacity for meaningful agency in respect of their security and those who do not. Many labels have been invented for the latter (Wood 1985[21]), but clearly a feature of their condition is complete dependency on whatever is the quality of institutions and relationships within which they are situated. They are completely reliant upon the protection of others (formal and statutory, or informal but predictable) for any version of wellbeing. So they possess few, if any, meaningful resources and have few, if any, choices for action. But even for those with a capacity for meaningful agency,[22] they require forms of social protection from somewhere in the institutional responsibility framework to alter their time preference behaviour away from the induced immediacy of the present, with all its dark relational and institutional connotations, towards investment in the future. In other words, a support mechanism which assists a more optimistic perception of risk over time leading to a reduced discount rate, and thus enables them even at the margin within poor households to reallocate their household budgets away from the present towards the future. In this way, they would be realising the condition of security and in the process displaying the presence of it too.

At this point, the distinction between autonomous and dependent security comes back into play. While a policy objective may be to reach

---

[20] Hence the title 'Prisoners and escapees' in Wood (2000).

[21] This work on authoritative labelling for the purposes of managing scarcity is now being re-visited in a collection of essays, edited by R. Eyben and J. Moncrieffe, provisionally entitled *The Power of Categorisation* (forthcoming from Earthscan).

[22] In a policy context, one might refer to this as a capacity for counterpart social action.

the state of autonomous security, the reality within the political economies of developing countries, as discussed above, is that this is a difficult state to reach. Under present conditions in many of these societies, poor people with agency are trying to find that social protection informally, through relationships and institutions which work more predictably for them than the state. Thus their current strategies for reaching security beyond the immediate point in time still rely upon socially guaranteed or informal rights rather than statutory ones.

The problem is that these 'rights'[23] are subject either to adverse incorporation or to low value reciprocity. The dependency entailed in such security arrangements either has the function of foreclosing more ambitious and stable options in the longer term because they require commitments and obligations to present power-holders (adverse incorporation); or the mutual interdependence between poor people themselves cannot deliver anything on sufficient scale to alter the discount rate (low value reciprocity).

5.5   Improving the security dimension of wellbeing

This section outlines seven principles of improvement which derive from the preceding discussion. It is proposed that if each of these were achieved, then the wellbeing of poor people in developing countries would be enhanced. More importantly for elaborating the agenda of 'researching wellbeing', each of these principles can be illustrated by discrete sets of indicators which then comprise the elements of what we understand by the security dimension of wellbeing.

Of course, these indicators are not exhaustive. Some can be demonstrated from existing data sets, whereas others would require new, primary data. Some are unambiguously concrete and measurable, though thresholds of significance are always a problem. Others are, at this stage, less easily convertible into observable measures. Some may be more obvious illustrations of the principle than others. The criteria for selecting some and not others here may be simply due to the lack of social science imagination. Thus the following discussion is necessarily explorative. The main objective is to derive potential indicators from the theoretical propositions about human security behaviour outlined above, rather than to be constrained by the presence or absence of these data at this stage. Certainly the next stage of the 'project' is to assess the fit between what is proposed here and the existence and comparative comprehensiveness of presently available data sets. It is certainly expected

---

[23] Which some political philosophers deny are rights at all.

that the four country data arising from the WeD Research Group will plug some of the gaps identified, and thus give rise to the beginnings of a more global, and theoretically informed, comparative analysis. Furthermore, while these theoretically grounded indicators do lead to measurement or at least narrative trend analysis, they also reveal policy objectives and thus offer a link between aspects of WeD research and development policy.

The first principle is the alteration of time preference behaviour. The more that people are able to commit resources to the avoidance of risk and the management of uncertainty in the future, the more secure and happy they will feel in the present. In other words, the prospect of wellbeing is a vital, even necessary, condition of ongoing wellbeing. If people feel confident in the future in terms of stable prices, law and order, well-functioning relationships, then they are more prepared to forgo aspects of present, even desirable, consumption and risk some investment in that future. This helps to achieve security (means) but is also evidence of a stronger sense of it in the present. In other words, they are more willing to trade-off aspects of present happiness for the promise of happiness in the future. This is not only a trade-off between time periods, but can also be between different kinds of resources within an individual or household profile of resources. Perhaps most obviously the time trade is likely to be between present material resources and future human ones, as in educational investment. But less obviously, and maybe less attractively to a modernist, an expensive dowry commitment for a daughter will involve immediate material cost to maintain cultural resources and indeed invest in future social resources.[24]

Proposed indicators:
- Clear perceptions and action for desired family size, enabling more targeted child investment;
- Redistributing family budgets away from immediate basic needs;
- Redistribution of intergenerational transfers either to elderly welfare, and/or children's education;
- Larger-scale, longer-term borrowing (as argued in Sharif and Wood 2001);

[24] This was a very conscious strategy for aspirant, but vulnerable, families in the villages of North Bihar, India where dowry costs were rising above the rate of local inflation in the 1990s during my last fieldwork there. The aim was to access the superior social networks of slightly richer families within the same caste by offering daughters to those families.

- Longer-term and reduced access deposits (in contrast to open access, higher savings rate argument, Wright 1997);
- Wider access to social insurance products;
- Use of debt for human capital investment (e.g. children's education and skills training).

The second principle, closely related to the first, is an enhanced capacity to prepare for hazards. We might think of this essentially as insurance, saving and planning. The point made above about hazards, in contrast to shocks, is that they are predictable as events, with high probability attached to them. There may be uncertainty about actual impact, depending on other conditions prevailing at the same time as the predictable event. Vulnerability and insecurity occurs when it has been impossible to prepare for these eventualities, either because the resources are simply not available for this objective, or because other factors and perceptions have induced a higher discount rate than is rationally necessary. Such perceptions may be a function of past family history, with structurally induced sub-cultures of despair and fatalism. But the absence of preparation is a loss of autonomy, as it compels the poor to rely upon others who can exploit the emergency and significance of the event to be countered. Peasant families who live on the margin of subsistence in South Asia (Chakraverti 2001) have long experienced an erosion of key productive resources (e.g. land and livestock) when being unprepared for disaster has driven them into the clutches of landlords and moneylenders.[25]

Proposed indicators:
- Higher availability and use of insurance products to meet predictable costs, such as: health, shelter, dowry/brideprice, membership/entry costs to forms of collective action (including collective insurance itself);
- Provision of public goods: vaccination (including for HIV/AIDS[26]); for storage and market intervention for price stabilisation, to offset entitlement loss and famine; common emergency facilities (e.g. cyclone shelters in South Bangladesh); fire proofing measures in urban slums; seed storage for replanting (after co-variant crop damage).

---

[25] A further extreme example of this process has been struggling families in Badakhshan, Northern Afghanistan, where the combined siege and drought for three years preceding spring 2002 induced them to give up significant land, and therefore future security, in return for immediate food support from the few richer, often 'commander' families in their locality.
[26] There is an international public goods dimension to this example, currently being pursued under the auspices of the World Bank, through the Global Fund.

The third principle of formalising rights is more utopian, and perhaps guilty of ethnocentric, western modernism. It certainly connects closely to the universal–local theme of the WeD research objectives. In a sense, we are dealing here with a hierarchy of preferences. Some security is better than none. Forms of security which reflect local relations of dependency and adverse incorporation are preferable to an absence of security, so that informal security regimes are preferable to insecurity regimes (Gough and Wood 2004). However, security obtained through the predictability of informal rights still retains elements of arbitrariness and preferentialism and thus constitutes a threat to sustained security. It remains trapped within local social relations and cultures which contain inequities and uncertainties, as well as foreclosures. So universal, formal rights would be preferable to local, informal ones, if only the state was characterised by good governance, accountability and bureaucratic principles (in a positive, Weberian sense) of equity.[27] Thus predictability would be enshrined in legal process. Protection would be guaranteed. And the prospect of security would positively contribute to present wellbeing. People would feel safe, and these dimensions of fear, at least, would be removed.[28]

Proposed indicators:

- Written bylaws or voluntary codification of practices for local charitable institutions;
- Introduction of formal criteria for entitlements at community philanthropy level (Wood with Shakil 2006, for illustration re Northern Pakistan);
- Agreed queuing and access arrangements (a key effective rights issue, see Schaffer and Huang 1975);
- Voluntary registration and external audits, especially among service NGOs;
- Improved access to formal justice (increases voice and reduces dependent security).

The fourth principle is almost another version of the third one: de-clientelisation. This term is deliberately etymologically constructed as a conceptual alternative to de-commodification. It refers, then, to the process

---

[27] Within AKRSP in Northern Pakistan, we have been exploring prospects for enhancing the predictability of local philanthropy via the mosques (Sunni), imambarga (Shia), and jamaatkhana (Ismaili), by encouraging a move towards more transparent 'needs' criteria in the local allocation of zakat and other similar funds.

[28] Idiosyncratic fears are something else.

of de-linking client dependants from their personalised, arbitrary and discretionary entrapment to persons around them with intimate power over them. Institutionalised micro-credit has been a classic widespread attempt at de-linking poor people from rapacious and usurious moneylenders. Mutual assurance societies, cooperatives, trade unions and other civil society forms of mobilisation are all contributors to the principle of de-clientelisation.

The proposition behind this principle may be contentious since it refers to the pervasiveness of clientelism as both the source of immediate security for most poor people across the world and the constraint to autonomous security. While this may appear as a sweeping generalisation, and over-emphasised as a defining element of political economy in this chapter, I challenge those with any empathy for the condition of the poor world-wide to refute the proposition. Some critics of this proposition argue that it comes from a particularly South Asian perspective. But some of those critics, for example with African experience, are often obliged to counter that the poor in Africa do not even have the luxury of clientelism, and are more clearly excluded than adversely included. So other remedying principles may apply to them rather than de-clientelisation. But do we have examples at the other end of the continuum, where the poor in developing countries are not dependent upon informal patronage of some kind? It seems that one would have to argue for the non-existence of hierarchy, inequality and class stratification and a well-functioning state offering widespread social protection in order to sustain such a position. While it is true that some societies in South America have been able to offer limited social insurance via employee rights, those rights have never extended to all (Barrientos 2004), and under conditions of increasing flexibilisation and casualisation of labour the provision of social insurance attached to employment is also eroding (Standing 1999, 2002). And such discussions about social insurance have rarely investigated the circumstances of the labour market in terms of recruitment and segmentation, in which access to such limited rights has itself been achieved via patronage, at a price.

Thus the principle of de-clientelisation is defended. As a principle it is akin to Esping-Andersen's notion of de-familialisation (Esping-Andersen 1999) – namely here is an institution which is close to and dominant over the determination of poor people's livelihoods both socially and culturally, yet it comprises a set of informal rights which systemically discriminate against particular sub-sets of the population. The family, with its pervasive patriarchalism, discriminates against women and sometimes children and the elderly, hence de-familialisation as a condition of universalist social policy in social democratic or liberal countries where the state is assumed as a well-functioning and superior substitute. While the family may remain a problem for similar reasons in other countries, neither the state nor the community (the two arenas within which clientelism thrives) can yet be favoured as a substitute for the family.[29] So in such countries, de-clientelisation is the first pervasive, dysfunctional condition to resolve as a precondition for poor people's wellbeing. No one is suggesting a magic wand will remove this fundamental feature of the structure–agency relationship in those societies where it is prevalent, and neither would that be desirable in the absence of improvement in formal rights and good governance. However, there are indicators to track moves in that direction, moves which are often the agenda of rights-based NGOs and civil society.

Proposed indicators:

- Seasonal wages compatible with overall patterns of market demand (a key contraindicator of interlocked labour and credit/patronage markets);
- De-linking of employment and credit markets (e.g. alternative to employer borrowing options for clients);
- Wider spread of employment and income sources;
- Increased migratory behaviour (though can indicate new patronage, as in Khan[30]), or deepen patronage for other family members (personal research in N.Bihar);
- Non-directed voting behaviour;
- Higher levels (value and frequency) of reciprocal exchange (e.g. through ROSCAs and ASCAs), as alternative to hierarchical dependency;
- Claiming and seizure of untitled assets (see Kramsjo and Wood 1992 for Bangladesh, but a general indicator of willingness to take political risk);
- Participation in local and informal judicial processes.

---

[29] Although the theme of de-clientelisation as the equivalent of de-commodification for non-transformed societies in the Polanyian sense is explained in Gough and Wood (2004), there may even be an associated logical argument for de-communitisation as well. However, with the state not superior to community in welfare terms, the prevailing development paradigm is to reform community and remain optimistic about collective action.

[30] I. A. Khan, 'Struggle for survival: Networks and relationships in a Bangladesh slum' Ph.D thesis, University of Bath, UK, 2000.

The fifth principle is enlarging choice and the risk pool. As noted above, a key problem for the poor is the narrowness of their risk pool, exacerbated by co-variance.[31] Too many of their eggs are in one basket.[32] It is interesting to observe that pre-Green Revolution farming peasants practised far greater crop and management diversification as a conscious risk-spreading strategy, though this was undermined by the mono-cropping tendencies of the Green Revolution technologies. Of course the limited skill base of poor rural people outside agriculture and agricultural services limits their employment either to that agriculture, or to unskilled labour in rural works, construction or trading where competition is fierce. Families would minimise their exposure to income risk if they were able to extend their skill base and/or diversify their access to employment in a wider range of sectors, and across wider economic space. The same argument applies with personal relationships and thus the social aspects of their resource base. Reducing their sole dependence upon one patron, a limited form of de-clientelisation, would also reduce the negative consequences of that one relationship going sour. It might also offer some opportunities for a stronger bargaining stance over local rights and obligations. Diversifying the skill base as well as the functional spread of one's resources across different access points is, of course, also a function of investment and altered time preferences. This can be done via different family members. There are salutary lessons from Bangladesh or Bihar in India, where key families spread their risk across different political parties, business sectors and indeed countries. This gives them a resilience to changes in regime and the disruption to patronage and favouritism that accompanies such changes. So, to summarise: the poor need to extend the options and arenas through which to deploy their profile of resources as a way of coping with shocks, hazards and the continuous constraints of the clientelist political economy. In this way, their grip on security is strengthened, the prospects for it are enhanced, and thus present wellbeing too.

Proposed indicators:

- Non-local circulation of savings (as argued for in Sharif and Wood 2001) which spreads risk away from local, often low productivity, markets;
- Diversification of employment opportunities;

---

[31] I am grateful for a discussion with Steen Jorgensen, Director of the Social Development Division at the World Bank on this point.

[32] Perhaps one should say 'apples' to capture the co-variance point, since rotten eggs do not tend to infect others, unlike apples.

- De-segmentation of labour markets;
- Proliferation of easily accessed service providers (including financial products);
- Within-family risk spreads through migration and remittances;
- Wider associational membership (e.g. professional, artisan or sector) with mutual insurance services (i.e. evidence of people going beyond their immediate social resources and networks to participate in wider institutions, not vulnerable to the principle of subtraction[33]).

The sixth principle refers to the improvement of the quality and predictability of institutional performance, which of course must, at least partially, be achieved via poor people's agency through their empowerment and voice. This is a familiar governance and accountability point when considered in terms of the problematic state within the institutional responsibility matrix. It refers to a process whereby poor people's long-term and sustainable wellbeing can only be achieved by transferring their rights-based claims from the informal, personalised domain to the formal, bureaucratic domain, in other words, the counterpart principle to de-clientelisation. It also emphasises that security is not only achieved through immediate, personal activity but requires successful and institutionalised processes of claiming opportunities, services and benefits from other agencies with guarantees. However, outside the state (including the internationalised state), the market also needs to operate in non-arbitrary, non-exclusionary ways without monopolies and associated rent-seeking. Well-regulated markets maintain contractual rights, reduce uncertainty of employment and offer dimensions of social insurance. It has been interesting that the focus of much attention and advocacy has been upon governance and accountability in relation to the state, but not upon the improvement of regulated markets.

Proposed indicators:
- Media 'pro-poor' critiques of annual government budgets (evidence that poor have recruited opinion formers from the middle classes to their security and wellbeing project);

---

[33] The distinction between social resources and social capital is that the former is sensitive to the problem of subtraction, namely that if actors are removed through death or migration from the social network (resources) then the quality of the network changes for the remaining members. This does not apply to the more universalist, abstract conception of social capital, characterised by a level of institutionalisation which insulates systemic behaviour from idiosyncratic, personalised behaviour. (See also McGregor 2004 on the need to distinguish 'capital' and 'resources'.)

- Shifts in budget priorities towards human resource investment (standard UNDP measures for this);
- Pro-poor commitments in political party manifestos;
- Electoral outcomes correlated to indices of constituency mobilisation by civil society organisations;
- Court cases against politicians and bureaucrats as a result of popular criticism;
- Access to justice (speed of time queue, acceptance of documentation, speed of outcome, implementation of court decisions).

The seventh and final principle is the strengthening for poor people of well-functioning collective institutions, which, especially at the local level, reduce adverse incorporation by offering an institutional alternative which is both instrumental and affective. In contrast to the sixth principle, the seventh emphasises the community aspects of the institutional responsibility matrix, and thus reflects some pessimism about improvements in the institutional quality of the state and market, at least in the short and medium term. In other words, people cannot rely exclusively upon the successful reform of national or global level institutions, but also have to rely upon forms of collective action which are sufficiently stable and rule-bound as to offer services and benefits in a reasonably guaranteed and predictable manner: i.e. successful common property management of key basic needs and opportunities, mutual social protection and so on. This would represent a process of improving the value and quality of low-level reciprocity, and is thus a parallel objective to de-clientelisation. Given footnote 29 above, the argument would be that an element of de-communitisation (i.e. the moderation or even removal of iniquitous community-level practices) is a necessary condition for the sustainability of well-functioning forms of collective action which contribute towards security. In many ways, this has been the objective of mobilising, development, NGOs which have not naively over-celebrated extant community practices, but have sought to modify and improve them. In India, the community development and panchayati raj movements were directed towards the same objectives, as indeed is the case for present decentralisation attempts, and the Rural Support Programme movement in Pakistan. It is interesting that local activists have also understood the case for more formal organisational practices at the community level to manage productive infrastructure (Lawson-McDowall[34]) and philanthropy (Wood with Shakil 2006).

[34]   B. Lawson-MacDowall 'Handshakes and smiles: The role of social and symbolic resources in the management of a new common property' July, Ph.D, University of Bath, 2000.

Proposed indicators:

- Clear rules for determining eligibility for membership;
- Clear rules for indicating rights of members and behavioural expectations;
- Rules for conduct of business, basis of decisions and sanctions for non-compliance and free-riding;
- Breadth of services and degree of inclusivity (a 'security' reassurance to all who might fall on hard times at the community level, even if the 'price' of inclusivity is charity to destitute members);
- Extent of internal cross-subsidies between families in a group;
- Length of cycles for membership and entitlements (as an indicator of stability, and thus security).

5.6   Conclusion

This chapter represents a conceptual stage in a longer research agenda, with definite implications for operational research. It has focused upon aspects of personal human security within an epistemological framework, which relies strongly upon the 'peasant analogue' (Wood 2004)[35] in which 'freedom from' takes precedence over 'freedom to' in poor people's agency. It promotes the argument that such security is an inextricable dimension of wellbeing as both presently enjoyed, hedonic happiness and the eudaimonic prospect of it (Ryan and Deci 2001). It has tried to bring together into the same conceptual schema the objective analysis of poor people's vulnerability and insecurity with insight, gained from many years of fieldwork in South Asia, into poor people's subjective perceptions of the institutional and relational landscape which frames their agency. In this respect, it has made use of the etic–emic contrast. It recognises that poor people are especially differentiated from richer people with respect to a sense of security because they face greater uncertainty and discount the future to a greater extent. A feature of their ill-being is the fear which arises from not being able to control or significantly influence their immediate or longer-term operational environment for survival. This fear induces both a heightened sense of risk and an acceptance of dependent over autonomous security. Thus while the etic discourse of human development emphasises the principle of 'needs satisfiers', the emic account relies more on 'risk averters', which marry dependency and short-termism closely

---

[35] See also Bailey (1966) and Redfield (1969) for discussions of peasant views of the bad life and good life, respectively.

together. The chapter has then identified a series of 'security-improving' principles, which reflect these issues of discounting, risk reduction, dependency, and the institutional and relational landscape. To each of these principles is attached an illustrative series of quantitative and qualitative (trend narrative) indicators which would confirm or refute improvements in the security and wellbeing of poor people. These indicators are offered as a refinement, arising from conceptual thinking about wellbeing and security, to human development (UNDP-HDI) and democracy (World Bank Social Development Division) indicators. This refinement seeks to inject the agency and perceptual perspectives of the poor, while remaining sensitive to the structural realities of political economy and institutional landscapes which frame the boundaries and limit their room for manoeuvre. The conceptual improvement and empirical presentation and analysis of these indicators defines the ongoing research agenda. The quantitative and qualitative data arising from the four WeD countries has been explicitly designed around the local–universal, the emic–etic dialogue. Such data are therefore well placed to support the analysis of human security.

6 Towards a measure of non-economic wellbeing achievement

Mark McGillivray

6.1 Introduction

It has become commonplace to treat wellbeing as a multidimensional concept, enveloping diverse, separable or behaviourally distinct components, domains or dimensions.[1] Accordingly, a wide and growing range of national wellbeing achievement indicators now exists, with each intended to capture one or more of these dimensions.[2] Indicators of health and education status are widely used and available for large samples of countries. Multidimensional indicators are also popular. The best known and most widely used multidimensional indicator is the Human Development Index (HDI), which is published annually and now available for more than 170 countries (UNDP 2004). These indicators, along with most of their counterparts, are often seen as

Earlier versions of this chapter were presented at a WIDER research seminar in Helsinki in April 2003, at the WIDER Conference on Inequality, Poverty and Human Wellbeing in Helsinki in May 2003, at the Development Studies Association Annual Conference in Glasgow in September 2003, at a research seminar at the Institute of Social Studies in The Hague in February 2004 and at the WeD-WIDER International Workshop on 'Researching Wellbeing in Developing Countries' at the Hanse Institute for Advanced Study in Delmenhorst, Germany in July 2004. The author is grateful to participants of these events, in particular James Copestake, David Fielding, Charles Gore, Ian Gough, Nanak Kakwani, Stephan Klasen, Massoud Karshenas, Mozaffar Qizilbash, Oliver Morrissey, Mansoob Murshed, Farhad Noorbakhsh, Matthew Odedokun, Mariano Rojas, Richard Ryan, Tony Shorrocks, Frances Stewart, Subbu Subramanian, Erik Thorbecke, Rob Vos, Guanghua Wan and Adrian Wood for useful comments. The author is particularly grateful to Allister McGregor, who can claim partial responsibility for the selection of ôçi as the label for the non-economic wellbeing indicator proposed in this chapter, and to Sarah White, for many stimulating conversations on wellbeing and its measurement that influenced parts of this chapter. The usual disclaimer applies.

[1] See, for example, Cummins (1996), Doyal and Gough (1991, 1993), Finnis (1980), Galtung (1994), Narayan (2000), Nussbaum (1988), Qizilbash (1996), Sen (1990, 1993), Stewart (1996) and UNDP (1990). Alkire (2002b) provides an excellent survey of the literature.

[2] For the purposes of this chapter, notions such as human wellbeing, quality of human life, human development, and basic human needs fulfilment are treated as synonymous.

alternatives to income per capita and are hoped to shed light on wellbeing achievement that economic indicators cannot. This is obviously consistent with a multidimensional conceptualisation of wellbeing: income per capita might be a valid indicator of achievement in a material or economic dimension of wellbeing, but not of achievement in others.

Yet as valid as the preceding case might sound, the commonly used or standard indicators of non-economic wellbeing achievement are often highly correlated, both ordinally and cardinally, among countries with income per capita.[3] Inter-country variation in non-economic wellbeing achievement, measured using these standard measures, is, therefore, well predicted by variation in economic wellbeing. An implication of this relationship is that these measures might not capture the richness or vitality of the wellbeing concept, giving an incomplete picture of it or at least the part of it that they are intended to capture. The contribution of the standard non-economic measures has been questioned on these grounds, with some commentators going so far as to claim they are empirically redundant *vis-à-vis* income per capita.[4]

Yet a simple and instructive point has been given insufficient attention in the literature. While there is a high correlation between income per capita and the standard non-economic indicators in large and diverse samples of countries, some countries perform better in the latter than predicted by the former and some countries perform worse. What would seem, therefore, to be more interesting and informative, than correlations between indicators, is that variation in measures of standard

---

[3] See Cahill (2005), Hicks and Streeten (1979), Larson and Wilford (1979), McGillivray (1991), McGillivray and White (1993), Noorbakhsh (1998) and Srinivasan (1994). These correlations hold for large samples of countries, both developed and developing. One can speculate why this might be so, but it is entirely reasonable to posit that higher per capita incomes facilitate private and public expenditure on goods relevant to higher non-economic wellbeing achievement. Smaller country samples yield much lower correlation coefficients, although in most cases these coefficients are statistically significant. Larger correlations do not necessarily hold for samples of individuals or households at the sub-national level, however (see, for example, Klasen 2000). As such it must be emphasised that the context referred to in this chapter is for countries, not individuals or households.

[4] See Cahill (2005), Larson and Wilford (1979), McGillivray (1991) and McGillivray and White (1993). The redundancy label has been assigned on the basis of correlation coefficients between the non-economic indicators and per capita income typically ranging from the low 0.70s upwards. Larson and Wilford (1979), for example, considered the PQLI to be empirically redundant based on the correlation between it and GNP per capita of 0.776. McGillivray (1991) draws this conclusion for the HDI based on a correlation coefficient between it and GNP per capita of 0.889. More generally, it is not uncommon for correlations between non-economic indicators to range from 0.70 to 0.90 or higher. It should of course be emphasised that the HDI includes an economic component indicator. For convenience we simply refer to it as a non-economic indicator. As is outlined below, a non-economic indicator is, for the purposes of this chapter, treated simply as one not entirely based on some measure of income per capita.

non-economic wellbeing achievement not accounted for by income per capita. Amartya Sen, in various publications, and the UNDP, in its *Human Development Reports*, address this variation, but stop short of providing a formal analysis of it.[5] A formal measure of this wellbeing achievement, on which international comparisons might be based, would thus appear to be warranted. While one should always view empirical measures with some degree of caution, among the insights provided by such a measure is the systematic identification of those countries that have better non-economic wellbeing achievement than their economic achievement predicts. This information is important if we accept that there is more to wellbeing achievement than what has been achieved in its economic sphere. It also allows us to begin to ask why some countries do better in this regard than others.

This chapter commences by extracting, using principal components analysis, the maximum possible information from various standard national non-economic wellbeing achievement measures. It then empirically identifies the variation in this extraction not accounted for by variation in income per capita, in the form of a variable called μ_i. This variable is the residual yielded by a cross-country regression of the extraction on the logarithm of Purchasing Power Parity (PPP) GDP per capita. μ_i is interpreted *inter alia* as a measure of non-economic human wellbeing achievement *per se*, in the sense that it captures wellbeing achieved independently of income. Given that μ_i is purely a statistical construct, obtained econometrically, the chapter then looks at correlations between this measure and variants of it and other wellbeing or wellbeing-related indicators in an attempt to find the variable or group of variables that best captures non-economic wellbeing achievement. It should be emphasised that this is a pure measurement exercise, in that inferences regarding causality are not drawn explicitly. It is of potential practical benefit, however, as it provides a case for allocating more resources to the collection and reporting of the variables, especially if the variable or variables are available or reported for relatively small samples of countries. Alternatively, it provides a case for more use of the variables in wellbeing assessments if they are available for reasonably large samples of countries. Among the measures not as widely reported or available across countries or not as widely used as those mentioned above, two variables perform best in this regard. One is a measure of gender empowerment and the other is a measure of educational attainment. It is

---

[5] See, for example, Drèze and Sen (1991). The UNDP examines this variation by reporting the difference between each country's GDP per capita and HDI rankings (see, for example, UNDP 2004: 139–142).

found though that none of these measures perform consistently better than a very widely used one, that measure being adult literacy.

6.2   Non-economic wellbeing achievement

We commence by identifying a class of non-economic variables, each of which is rather highly correlated with income per capita, which is available for large samples of countries and is widely used. For convenience, and following on from the discussion of the preceding section, we shall label them as 'standard indicators'. The chosen standard indicators are years of life expectancy $(x_{1,i}^t)$, the adult literacy rate $(x_{2,i}^t)$ and the gross school enrolments ratio $(x_{3,i}^t)$. Thus there are three variables $(x_{k,i}^t$ where $k = 1,$ $\ldots, m)$ for a sample of i countries (where $i = 1, \ldots, n$). The superscript t indicates that these variables are transformed in a way for subsequent statistical application. Data on these variables are taken from the UNDP's *Human Development Report* 2002 (UNDP 2002). These variables are three of the four components of the HDI. As Tables 6.1 and 6.2 show, they are indeed quite highly correlated among each other, with PPP GDP per capita and the HDI as a whole. The Pearson (zero-order) coefficients between these variables and the logarithm of PPP GDP per capita in Table 6.1 range from 0.701 to 0.794 and the corresponding Spearman (rank-order) coefficients in Table 6.2 range from 0.695 to 0.840.

Our next step is to combine the three variables above into a single index, denoted W_i. We extract the maximum amount of information from these variables, subject to a normalisation condition, using principal components analysis.[6] This extraction, the first principal component, is treated as a 'standard' index of non-economic wellbeing. W_i shares some similarities with the HDI, given that they share a number of variables, but at the same time is seen as a wellbeing indicator in its own right.[7] The first principal component is a linear combination of the variables under consideration $(x_{k,i}^t)$ that exhibits the maximum variation permitted by the

---

[6] Ram (1982), Ogwang (1994) and Lai (2000) also use the principal components technique to derive wellbeing measures.

[7] The HDI is a weighted average of life expectancy, adult literacy, gross school enrolment and the logarithm of PPP GDP per capita, each scaled within theoretical ranges of zero and one hundred. The first and fourth of these variables are assigned weights of one third, while the second and third variables are assigned weights of two ninths and one ninth, respectively. It follows that W_i differs from the HDI in that it assigns different weights to each variable (income per capita receives a weight of zero through its exclusion) and that the variables are transformed using a different procedure, outlined below. Ranis, Stewart and Ramirez (2000) use a similar index, which is identical to the HDI in all respects other than assigning a zero weighting to income per capita. W_i is preferred here mainly because it captures more variation in the component variables but also because its weights are less arbitrary (although of ambiguous theoretical interpretation).

Table 6.1 *Zero-order (Pearson) correlation coefficients between commonly used wellbeing indicators (n = 173)*

	Life expectancy $(x_{1,i})$	Adult literacy $(x_{2,i})$	Gross enrolment $(x_{3,i})$	HDI	PPP GDP per capita (log) $(\ln y_i)$
Life expectancy $(x_{1,i})$	1.000				
Adult literacy $(x_{2,i})$	0.726	1.000			
Gross enrolment $(x_{3,i})$	0.736	0.803	1.000		
HDI	0.925	0.870	0.881	1.000	
PPP GDP per capita (log) $(\ln y_i)$	0.794	0.701	0.792	0.923	1.000

Table 6.2 *Rank-order (Spearman) correlation coefficients between commonly used wellbeing indicators (n = 173)*

	Life expectancy $(x_{1,i})$	Adult literacy $(x_{2,i})$	Gross enrolment $(x_{3,i})$	HDI	PPP GDP per capita $(\ln y_i)$
Life expectancy $(x_{1,i})$	1.000				
Adult literacy $(x_{2,i})$	0.724	1.000			
Gross enrolment $(x_{3,i})$	0.715	0.773	1.000		
HDI	0.938	0.841	0.833	1.000	
PPP GDP per capita (log) $(\ln y_i)$	0.840	0.695	0.780	0.938	1.000

chosen normalisation condition. This combination is the weighted sum of the three variables. The weights are denoted as ϕ_k. Further details are provided in Appendix A, which provides a technical outline of the analysis conducted in this section.

Correlation coefficients between W_i, and its component variables, shown in Table 6.3, are all very high, ranging from 0.895 to 0.927 and 0.894 to 0.908 for the zero- and rank-order coefficients, respectively. Each of the preceding results is consistent with the rather high correlations between the three component variables reported above. W_i is also very highly correlated with the HDI and with PPP GDP per capita measured in logarithmic terms. The zero-order and rank-order coefficients between W_i and the HDI are 0.976 and 0.956, respectively. The corresponding coefficients between W_i and the logarithm of PPP GDP per capita $(\ln y_i)$ are 0.833 and 0.838, respectively.

Table 6.3 *Correlation coefficients between wellbeing indicators*

		Wellbeing index ($W_i = PC_{1,i}$)	
		Zero-order	Rank-order
Life expectancy	($x_{1,i}$)	0.895	0.894
Adult literacy	($x_{2,i}$)	0.923	0.908
Gross enrolment	($x_{3,i}$)	0.927	0.905
HDI		0.976	0.956
PPP GDP per capita (log)	($\ln y_i$)	0.833	0.838

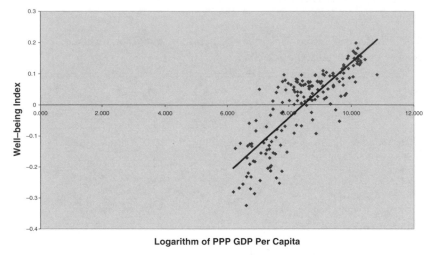

Logarithm of PPP GDP Per Capita

Figure 6.1 Scatter plot of wellbeing index and income per capita

A scatter plot of W_i on the logarithm of PPP GDP per capita is shown below in Figure 6.1. There is a close empirical association between the two variables, consistent with the correlation coefficients shown in the last row of Table 6.3. The line of best fit in Figure 6.1 emphasises this point. This line has been obtained using the regression analysis outlined in Appendix 6A. Not all points lie on the line, given that the income variable does not perfectly explain or account for the inter-country variation in W_i, as one would of course expect. Money cannot buy everything. The vertical distance between each point and the line is that variation or component of W_i that is not explained by income per capita or economic wellbeing. A measure of this distance is provided by the

Table 6.4 *Correlations between μ_i and wellbeing indicators*

Variables	Zero-order[a]	Rank-order[a]	n
HDI	0.373[a]	0.242[a]	173
Life expectancy $(x^t_{1,i})$	0.421[a]	0.262[a]	173
Adult literacy $(x^t_{2,i})$	0.612[a]	0.513[a]	173
Gross enrolment $(x^t_{3,i})$	0.482[a]	0.398[a]	173
Wellbeing index (w_i)	0.554[a]	0.438[a]	173

Note: [a] Significantly different from zero at the 90 per cent confidence level

residual or error term, μ_i, in the regression equation outlined in Appendix 6A. μ_i is central to our analysis. It is, by definition, orthogonal with respect to $\ln y_i$, and, as such, is not subject to the criticism that it reveals disappointingly little additional information in inter-country wellbeing compared to income per capita. More pointedly, it is interpreted as a measure of non-economic or income-independent human wellbeing achievement. It is also interpreted, possibly contentiously, as a measure both of the success in converting economic wellbeing into non-economic wellbeing and of the non-economic wellbeing component, dimension or domain within the space of W_i.

Estimates of μ_i values of W_i and all other variables mentioned for the full 173 country sample are reported in McGillivray (2005). Correlation coefficients between μ_i and the standard indicators are shown in Table 6.4. Of the latter variables, that variable most highly correlated with μ_i is adult literacy. Those countries with the fifteen highest and fifteen lowest residual values are shown in Table 6.5. High residual values indicate that countries do better in terms of non-economic or non-income predicted wellbeing achievement. The group of countries that does best in terms of this wellbeing is dominated by those which either still have or in their recent pasts have had non-market, centrally planned economies. Eleven of the top fifteen and each of the top ten countries in terms of this wellbeing fall into this category. More generally, most of these fifteen countries have moderately low incomes per capita and, albeit to a lesser extent, HDI values. These are characteristics of all but three of the thirty countries listed in Table 6.5. These three countries are each in the bottom fifteen group. They are Luxembourg, Oman and Equatorial Guinea, which are ranked among the top 25 per cent of the 173 country sample in terms of income per capita. Luxembourg has by far the highest PPP GDP per capita of this sample, but its ranking in terms of μ_i is 163, the eleventh lowest in the sample. The bottom fifteen countries also include Botswana, a middle-ranked country in terms of income per capita.

Table 6.5 *Wellbeing data: selected countries*

Country	PPP GDP per capita			HDI		Wellbeing Index		Residual	
	Value (y_i)	Value $(\ln y_i)$	Rank	Value	Rank	Value (W_i)	Rank	Value (μ_i)	Rank
Tajikistan	1152	7.049	151	0.667	112	0.050	81	0.177	1
Armenia	2559	7.847	117	0.754	77	0.096	33	0.152	2
Uzbekistan	2441	7.800	119	0.727	95	0.075	50	0.135	3
Georgia	2664	7.888	115	0.748	81	0.079	46	0.131	4
Moldova, Rep. of	2109	7.654	126	0.701	105	0.056	78	0.130	5
Viet Nam	1996	7.599	128	0.688	109	0.040	89	0.118	6
Azerbaijan	2936	7.985	112	0.741	89	0.069	61	0.113	7
Suriname	3799	8.242	103	0.756	74	0.083	44	0.103	8
Cuba	4519	8.416	90	0.795	55	0.095	35	0.101	9
Mongolia	1783	7.486	134	0.655	113	0.012	106	0.100	10
Ecuador	3203	8.072	110	0.732	93	0.064	64	0.100	11
Kyrgyzstan	2711	7.905	114	0.712	102	0.048	84	0.099	12
Congo	825	6.715	163	0.512	136	−0.059	123	0.098	13
Philippines	3971	8.287	97	0.754	76	0.081	45	0.097	14
Ukraine	3816	8.247	102	0.748	80	0.074	52	0.095	15
Mauritania	1677	7.425	136	0.438	152	−0.196	157	−0.102	159
Cote d'Ivoire	1630	7.396	139	0.428	156	−0.200	158	−0.104	160
Vanuatu	2802	7.938	113	0.542	131	−0.152	147	−0.104	161
Oman	13356	9.500	40	0.751	78	−0.016	114	−0.108	162
Luxembourg	50061	10.821	1	0.925	16	0.097	32	−0.112	163
Mozambique	854	6.750	160	0.322	170	−0.270	170	−0.117	164
Gambia	1649	7.408	137	0.405	160	−0.213	160	−0.118	165
Central African Rep.	1172	7.066	150	0.375	165	−0.244	166	−0.118	166
Botswana	7184	8.880	64	0.572	126	−0.093	132	−0.129	167
Burkina Faso	976	6.883	155	0.325	169	−0.286	172	−0.144	168
Djibouti	2377	7.774	121	0.445	149	−0.214	161	−0.151	169
Equatorial Guinea	15073	9.621	38	0.679	111	−0.053	122	−0.155	170
Guinea	1982	7.592	129	0.414	159	−0.235	165	−0.157	171
Niger	746	6.615	168	0.277	172	−0.324	173	−0.158	172
Angola	2187	7.690	125	0.403	161	−0.253	167	−0.183	173

6.3   Correlates with μ_i: data and results

μ_i is a purely statistical construct. Policy makers might be reluctant to, for example, monitor a residual obtained from a linear regression of a principal component on the logarithm of income per capita. A key question, therefore, concerns that variable which best individually accounts for the variation in μ_i across countries. Of particular interest is whether less widely available, reported or used wellbeing or wellbeing-related indicators perform better than the standard indicators, the $x^t_{k,i}$ and the HDI.[8] If so, then this would appear to be an *a priori* case for the relevant bodies to further develop and report these indicators, including expanding their country coverage. It could also provide a case for greater use of the available data on them in reporting and analysing wellbeing achievement. The following simple hypotheses were therefore evaluated:

$$H_0 : |\rho_{ns,j}| \leq |\rho_s^{max}|$$
$$H_1 : |\rho_{ns,j}| > |\rho_s^{max}|$$

where $\rho_{ns,j}$ is the correlation coefficient between μ_i and the jth less widely available, reported or used indicator and ρ_s^{max} is the highest correlation coefficient between μ_i and the non-economic standard indicators, respectively, for the sample of countries under consideration. We shall, for convenience, label the former as non-standard indicators.[9] The null hypothesis is that the non-standard indicator under consideration accounts for no more of the variation in μ_i than the standard one that does best in this regard. The alternative hypothesis is that the former does better than the latter in empirically capturing this variation. Both zero-order (Pearson) and rank-order (Spearman) coefficients are reported. All coefficients are also subjected to the standard hypothesis test; that being whether they are significantly different from zero.[10] Two issues relevant to and which seriously complicate the hypothesis testing are discussed in Appendix 6A. They relate to the erroneous rejection of the null hypothesis due to measurement error and the manner in which μ_i is constructed.

The non-standard variables were taken from or constructed using data from the *Human Development Report* 2002 (UNDP 2002) and the *World Happiness Database* (Veenhoven 2002a, 2002b). The variables are categorised as follows: Human Poverty, Health Services Provision,

---

[8] Note that it makes no difference whether one uses $x^t_{k,i}$ or $x_{k,i}$ (the non-transformed variables) given the nature of the transformation.

[9] It is acknowledged that this term is used quite loosely, as the distinction between non-standard and standard indicators is not always clear. In particular, a number of the non-standard indicators have been used for some time and are available for large samples of countries. In this case, an indicator is in effect deemed 'standard' if it has been used to form the HDI. Similarly, the term non-economic indicator, used throughout this chapter, is used simply to describe an indicator that is not based solely on some measure of income per capita.

[10] μ_i and its variants were re-estimated for each of the samples for which data the non-standard indicators were available. This is necessary to ensure that they are orthogonal with respect to $\ln y_i$.

Health Status, Survival, Education Status, Gender Bias, Gender Empowerment, Income Inequality, Governance and Happiness. There is, of course, overlap between these categories. The governance indicators are subjective and relate to wellbeing derived from civil liberties, political rights, non-violence and the like. The happiness variables are intended to measure subjective, self-assessed wellbeing. A full list of variables and their definitions is provided in McGillivray (2005).

Results are reported in Table 6.6.[11] Fifty-six zero- and rank-order coefficients between the non-standard indicators and μ_i are reported (see the second and seventh columns of Table 6.6, headed $\rho_{ns,j}$). Thirty-five of the former and thirty of the latter are significantly different from zero. Those with the highest correlations with μ_i are the contraceptive prevalence, youth literacy and women professionals and technicians variables. The zero-order coefficients between these variables and μ_i are 0.535, 0.581 and 0.569, respectively. The corresponding rank-order coefficients are 0.538, 0.559 and 0.374. Only two of the variables in the income inequality, governance and happiness groups, life enjoyment and happy life years, are significantly correlated with μ_i.[12]

Evaluation of the hypotheses relating to whether the non-standard indicators perform better than their standard counterparts in accounting for the variation in estimates of μ_i and its non-biased alternatives, $v'_{q,k,i}$, produced interesting results.[13] The above-outlined null hypothesis, that $|\rho_{ns,j}| \leq |\rho_s^{max}|$, cannot be rejected in favour of the alternative in almost all cases if former coefficients are obtained using estimates of μ_i. As is shown in Table 6.6, the estimates of ρ_s^{max} obtained using μ_i are larger in absolute value than the corresponding $\rho_{ns,j}$ in all samples. These estimates are shown in the third and eighth columns of Table 6.6, headed μ_i. Moreover, in almost all cases the standard variable that was most correlated with μ_i was adult literacy ($x_{2,i}^t$) (see the fourth and ninth columns of Table 6.6).[14]

---

[11] Estimates of the residuals were obtained using different, non-logarithmic transformations of y_i consistent with various alternative values of ε in equation (6A.4). Broadly similar results were obtained. These details are also available, on request, from the author.

[12] It has been suggested that the correlations between these variables and μ_i will be a decreasing function of their correlations with lny_i, with, in particular, the indicator most highly correlated with μ_i being that which is most lowly correlated with lny_i. In McGillivray (2005) it is shown that while variables highly correlated with lny_i tend to be lowly correlated with μ_i the relationship is not a systematic one in the sense suggested.

[13] Note that the term 'bias' here is used loosely, simply to refer to estimates of μ_i that do not cause the erroneous rejection of the null hypothesis due to the problems discussed in Appendix 6B.

[14] The result is also broadly consistent with a position taken in Doyal and Gough (1991: 181–184), which was to measure the basic need for autonomy using adult literacy.

Table 6.6 *Correlation coefficients between estimates of μ_i and wellbeing indicators*

Variables	Zero-order						Rank-order				n
			ρ_s^{max}						ρ_s^{max}		
	$\rho_{ns,i}$	μ_i	Variable	$v_{q,k,i}^{/}$	Variable	$\rho_{ns,i}$	μ_i	Variable	$v_{q,k,i}^{/}$	Variable	
Human poverty											
Human poverty index	−0.483[a]	0.629[a]	$x_{2,i}^t$	0.374[a]	$x_{3,i}^t$	−0.470[a]	0.627[a]	$x_{3,i}^t$	0.381[a]	$x_{3,i}^t$	87
Survival to 40	−0.428[a]	0.615[a]	$x_{2,i}^t$	0.390[a]	$x_{2,i}^t$	−0.342[a]	0.595[a]	$x_{2,i}^t$	0.410[a]	$x_{2,i}^t$	116
Water usage	−0.182	0.636[a]	$x_{2,i}^t$	0.393[a]	$x_{2,i}^t$	−0.221[a]	0.623[a]	$x_{2,i}^t$	0.411[a]	$x_{2,i}^t$	108
Poverty headcount ($1)	−0.278[a]	0.586[a]	$x_{2,i}^t$	0.275[a]	$x_{2,i}^t$	−0.215	0.546[a]	$x_{2,i}^t$	0.336[a]	$x_{2,i}^t$	60
Poverty headcount ($2)	−0.200	0.588[a]	$x_{2,i}^t$	0.276[a]	$x_{2,i}^t$	−0.196	0.546[a]	$x_{2,i}^t$	0.336[a]	$x_{2,i}^t$	60
Health services											
Sanitation facilities	0.199[a]	0.615[a]	$x_{2,i}^t$	0.357[a]	$x_{2,i}^t$	0.139	0.512[a]	$x_{2,i}^t$	0.328[a]	$x_{2,i}^t$	123
Drug access	−0.042	0.610[a]	$x_{2,i}^t$	0.433[a]	$x_{2,i}^t$	−0.094	0.510[a]	$x_{2,i}^t$	0.380[a]	$x_{2,i}^t$	170
Water services	0.185[a]	0.572[a]	$x_{2,i}^t$	0.352[a]	$x_{2,i}^t$	0.076	0.497[a]	$x_{2,i}^t$	0.320[a]	$x_{2,i}^t$	165
Measles immunisation	0.456[a]	0.609[a]	$x_{2,i}^t$	0.459[a]	$x_{2,i}^t$	0.416[a]	0.593[a]	$x_{2,i}^t$	0.439[a]	$x_{2,i}^t$	165
Tuberculosis immunisation	0.394[a]	0.636[a]	$x_{2,i}^t$	0.431[a]	$x_{2,i}^t$	0.398[a]	0.514[a]	$x_{2,i}^t$	0.385[a]	$x_{2,i}^t$	140
Oral rehydration	−0.205	0.769[a]	$x_{2,i}^t$	0.615[a]	$x_{2,i}^t$	−0.015	0.784[a]	$x_{2,i}^t$	0.666[a]	$x_{2,i}^t$	56
Contraceptive prevalence	0.535[a]	0.682[a]	$x_{2,i}^t$	0.483[a]	$x_{2,i}^t$	0.538[a]	0.629[a]	$x_{2,i}^t$	0.442[a]	$x_{2,i}^t$	91
Birth attendance	0.371[a]	0.651[a]	$x_{2,i}^t$	0.460[a]	$x_{2,i}^t$	0.327[a]	0.610[a]	$x_{2,i}^t$	0.452[a]	$x_{2,i}^t$	122
Physicians	0.389[a]	0.632[a]	$x_{2,i}^t$	0.445[a]	$x_{2,i}^t$	0.413[a]	0.516[a]	$x_{2,i}^t$	0.394[a]	$x_{2,i}^t$	165
Health status											
Undernourishment	−0.132	0.671[a]	$x_{2,i}^t$	0.486[a]	$x_{2,i}^t$	−0.120	0.678[a]	$x_{2,i}^t$	0.517[a]	$x_{2,i}^t$	101
Underweight children	−0.257[a]	0.662[a]	$x_{2,i}^t$	0.456[a]	$x_{2,i}^t$	−0.286[a]	0.634[a]	$x_{2,i}^t$	0.452[a]	$x_{2,i}^t$	124
Underheight children	−0.186[a]	0.667[a]	$x_{2,i}^t$	0.454[a]	$x_{2,i}^t$	−0.186[a]	0.639[a]	$x_{2,i}^t$	0.443[a]	$x_{2,i}^t$	118

Table 6.6 (cont.)

Variables	Zero-order					Rank-order					n
	$\rho_{ns,j}$	μ_i	Variable	ρ_s^{max} $v'_{q,k,i}$	Variable	$\rho_{ns,j}$	μ_i	Variable	ρ_s^{max} $v'_{q,k,i}$	Variable	
Underweight infants	−0.281[a]	0.619[a]	$x_{2,i}^t$	0.448[a]	$x_{2,i}^t$	−0.286[a]	0.474[a]	$x_{2,i}^t$	0.381[a]	$x_{2,i}^t$	150
Adults with HIV/AIDS	−0.290[a]	0.587[a]	$x_{2,i}^t$	0.408[a]	$x_{2,i}^t$	−0.325[a]	0.485[a]	$x_{2,i}^t$	0.392[a]	$x_{2,i}^t$	144
Women with HIV/AIDS	−0.213[a]	0.717[a]	$x_{2,i}^t$	0.505[a]	$x_{2,i}^t$	−0.197[a]	0.461[a]	$x_{2,i}^t$	0.348[a]	$x_{2,i}^t$	73
Malaria cases	−0.346[a]	0.697[a]	$x_{2,i}^t$	0.514[a]	$x_{2,i}^t$	−0.342[a]	0.723[a]	$x_{2,i}^t$	0.494[a]	$x_{2,i}^t$	84
Tuberculosis cases	−0.205[a]	0.617[a]	$x_{2,i}^t$	0.437[a]	$x_{2,i}^t$	−0.038	0.516[a]	$x_{2,i}^t$	0.384[a]	$x_{2,i}^t$	170
Cigarette consumption	0.132	0.569[a]	$x_{2,i}^t$	0.359[a]	$x_{2,i}^t$	0.143	0.358[a]	$x_{2,i}^t$	0.216[a]	$x_{2,i}^t$	110
Survival											
Infant mortality rate	−0.393[a]	0.612[a]	$x_{2,i}^t$	0.429[a]	$x_{2,i}^t$	−0.203[a]	0.509[a]	$x_{2,i}^t$	0.376[a]	$x_{2,i}^t$	172
Child mortality rate	−0.419[a]	0.513[a]	$x_{2,i}^t$	0.429[a]	$x_{2,i}^t$	−0.204[a]	0.509[a]	$x_{2,i}^t$	0.376[a]	$x_{2,i}^t$	172
Survival to 65 (females)	0.425[a]	0.613[a]	$x_{2,i}^t$	0.434[a]	$x_{2,i}^t$	0.273[a]	0.517[a]	$x_{2,i}^t$	0.391[a]	$x_{2,i}^t$	166
Survival to 65 (males)	0.347[a]	0.613[a]	$x_{2,i}^t$	0.434[a]	$x_{2,i}^t$	0.233[a]	0.517[a]	$x_{2,i}^t$	0.391[a]	$x_{2,i}^t$	166
Maternal mortality rate	−0.416[a]	0.640[a]	$x_{2,i}^t$	0.446[a]	$x_{2,i}^t$	−0.174[a]	0.571[a]	$x_{2,i}^t$	0.343[a]	$x_{2,i}^t$	144
Education status											
Youth literacy rate	0.581[a]	0.630[a]	$x_{2,i}^t$	0.426[a]	$x_{2,i}^t$	0.559[ab]	0.611[a]	$x_{2,i}^t$	0.428[a]	$x_{2,i}^t$	128
Primary school enrolment	0.445[a]	0.548[a]	$x_{2,i}^t$	0.368[a]	$x_{2,i}^t$	0.349[a]	0.451[a]	$x_{2,i}^t$	0.345[a]	$x_{2,i}^t$	122
Secondary school enrolment	0.317[a]	0.550[a]	$x_{2,i}^t$	0.394[a]	$x_{2,i}^t$	0.186	0.369[a]	$x_{2,i}^t$	0.279[a]	$x_{2,i}^t$	95
Children grade 5	0.062	0.507[a]	$x_{2,i}^t$	0.397[a]	$x_{2,i}^t$	0.092	0.482[a]	$x_{2,i}^t$	0.289[a]	$x_{2,i}^t$	48
Gender bias											
Gender-related development index	0.357[a]	0.587[a]	$x_{2,i}^t$	0.389[a]	$x_{2,i}^t$	0.243[a]	0.495[a]	$x_{2,i}^t$	0.355[a]	$x_{2,i}^t$	146
Human development disparity	−0.390[a]	0.587[a]	$x_{2,i}^t$	0.389[a]	$x_{2,i}^t$	−0.436[a]	0.495[a]	$x_{2,i}^t$	0.355[a]	$x_{2,i}^t$	146
Life expectancy ratio	0.340[a]	0.613[a]	$x_{2,i}^t$	0.434[a]	$x_{2,i}^t$	0.380[a]	0.517[a]	$x_{2,i}^t$	0.390[a]	$x_{2,i}^t$	166
Adult literacy ratio	0.456[a]	0.583[a]	$x_{2,i}^t$	0.387[a]	$x_{2,i}^t$	0.358[a]	0.490[a]	$x_{2,i}^t$	0.351[a]	$x_{2,i}^t$	149

											N
School enrolment ratio	0.460^a	0.609^a	$x^t_{2,i}$	0.435^a	$x^t_{2,i}$	0.372^a	0.509^a	$x^t_{2,i}$	0.382^a	$x^t_{2,i}$	162
Earned income ratio	0.130	0.659^a	$x^t_{2,i}$	0.418^a	$x^t_{2,i}$	0.115	0.662^a	$x^t_{2,i}$	0.450^a	$x^t_{2,i}$	90
Gender empowerment											
Gender empowerment measure	0.265^a	0.629^a	$x^t_{3,i}$	0.306^a	$x^t_{2,i}$	0.127	0.478^a	$x^t_{2,i}$	0.141	$x^t_{2,i}$	66
Women in parliament	0.113	0.594^a	$x^t_{2,i}$	0.411^a	$x^t_{2,i}$	0.127	0.458^a	$x^t_{2,i}$	0.338^a	$x^t_{2,i}$	170
Women in senior positions	0.457^a	0.680^a	$x^t_{3,i}$	0.409^a	$x^t_{2,i}$	0.364^a	0.483^a	$x^t_{2,i}$	0.225^a	$x^t_{2,i}$	77
Women professionals & technicians	$0.569^{a,b}$	0.680^a	$x^t_{3,i}$	0.409^a	$x^t_{2,i}$	0.374^a	0.480^a	$x^t_{2,i}$	0.218^a	$x^t_{2,i}$	78
Income inequality											
Gini coefficient	-0.117	0.609^a	$x^t_{2,i}$	0.420^a	$x^t_{2,i}$	-0.048	0.404^a	$x^t_{2,i}$	0.301^a	$x^t_{2,i}$	116
Income share ratio (20%)	-0.154	0.609^a	$x^t_{2,i}$	0.420^a	$x^t_{2,i}$	-0.040	0.404^a	$x^t_{2,i}$	0.301^a	$x^t_{2,i}$	116
Income share ratio (10%)	-0.128	0.609^a	$x^t_{2,i}$	0.420^a	$x^t_{2,i}$	-0.049	0.404^a	$x^t_{2,i}$	0.301^a	$x^t_{2,i}$	116
Governance											
Polity score	0.144	0.614^a	$x^t_{2,i}$	0.439^a	$x^t_{2,i}$	0.111	0.625	$x^t_{2,i}$	0.395^a	$x^t_{2,i}$	147
Civil liberties	-0.100	0.612^a	$x^t_{2,i}$	0.429^a	$x^t_{2,i}$	-0.107	0.513	$x^t_{2,i}$	0.381^a	$x^t_{2,i}$	173
Political rights	-0.113	0.612^a	$x^t_{2,i}$	0.429^a	$x^t_{2,i}$	-0.103	0.513	$x^t_{2,i}$	0.381^a	$x^t_{2,i}$	173
Press freedom	-0.067	0.613^a	$x^t_{2,i}$	0.429^a	$x^t_{2,i}$	-0.078	0.509	$x^t_{2,i}$	0.376^a	$x^t_{2,i}$	173
Voice and accountability	0.058	0.621^a	$x^t_{2,i}$	0.453^a	$x^t_{2,i}$	0.064	0.497	$x^t_{2,i}$	0.367^a	$x^t_{2,i}$	156
Political stability and non-violence	-0.046	0.628^a	$x^t_{2,i}$	0.455^a	$x^t_{2,i}$	-0.074	0.509	$x^t_{2,i}$	0.373^a	$x^t_{2,i}$	151
Law and order	-0.087	0.611^a	$x^t_{2,i}$	0.432^a	$x^t_{2,i}$	-0.117	0.510	$x^t_{2,i}$	0.380^a	$x^t_{2,i}$	159
Rule of law	-0.046	0.628^a	$x^t_{2,i}$	0.455^a	$x^t_{2,i}$	-0.074	0.509	$x^t_{2,i}$	0.373^a	$x^t_{2,i}$	151
Happiness											
Life enjoyment	-0.410^a	0.653^a	$x^t_{2,i}$	0.453^*	$x^t_{2,i}$	-0.361^a	0.317	$x^t_{2,i}$	0.203	$x^t_{2,i}$	66
Happy life years	-0.209^a	0.653^a	$x^t_{2,i}$	0.433^*	$x^t_{2,i}$	-0.228^a	0.317	$x^t_{2,i}$	0.203	$x^t_{2,i}$	66
Life enjoyment inequality	-0.036	0.691^a	$x^t_{2,i}$	0.507^*	$x^t_{2,i}$	-0.030	0.319	$x^t_{2,i}$	0.273^a	$x^t_{2,i}$	55

Notes:

[a] – significantly different from zero at the 90 per cent confidence level or greater.

[b] – significantly greater than adjusted ρ_s^{max} at the 90 per cent confidence level or greater.

$x^t_{2,i}$ – is transformed adult literacy.

$x^t_{3,i}$ – is transformed gross school enrolment.

That the null hypothesis cannot be rejected is not surprising given the measurement error and construction issues and resultant inflation of $\rho_s^{\max}$, as discussed above. Much lower values of these coefficients were obtained from regressing $v'_{q,k,i}$ on the standard indicators. These coefficients are shown in the fifth and tenth columns of Table 6.6, headed $v'_{q,k,i}$.[15] The null hypothesis still cannot be rejected in almost all cases. The only sample for which adult literacy was not the most highly correlated variable with these adjusted residuals was that determined by the availability of the Human Poverty Index (HPI). For that sample, school enrolment $(x^t_{3,i})$ was the standard indicator most highly correlated cardinally and ordinally with the chosen $v'_{q,k,i}$. It should be noted, however, that these coefficients were not significantly higher those that between adult literacy and this residual for the same sample.

The null hypothesis, that $|\rho_{ns,j}| \leq |\rho_s^{\max}|$ was ultimately rejected for two variables only: youth literacy and women professionals and technicians. That is, both variables are significantly more highly correlated with this chapter's measure of non-economic wellbeing than any of the three standard variables. This was the case for both the zero- and rank-order correlation coefficients for the former, but for only the zero-order correlation for the latter indicator. There would appear, therefore, to be case for further development and use of these indicators in the ways mentioned above.

6.4   Conclusion

A range of indicators has been used over recent decades in an attempt to capture non-economic dimensions of human wellbeing empirically. Most of the commonly used indicators, available for large country samples, are very highly correlated with various measures of income per capita. Given this, they have been criticised for not being able to tell us much more than income per capita alone and, as a consequence, for not sufficiently capturing non-economic dimensions of cross-country wellbeing achievement. This chapter has responded to this criticism. It identified the variation in a composite of the most widely used non-economic wellbeing indicators not accounted for by income per capita. It did this by regressing this composite on the logarithm of PPP GDP per capita, observing the values of the residual term of the regression. This residual was interpreted as an income-independent, or non-economic, measure of

---

[15] Columns 5 and 10 of Table 6.6 report the largest correlation coefficients obtained regressing each $v'_{q,k,i}$ on each $x^t_{k,i}$.

national wellbeing achievement. Estimates of this residual were provided for 173 countries. An interesting result is that the top-ranked countries, in terms of non-economic wellbeing achieved measured according to this residual, were dominated by those which either still have or in their recent pasts have had non-market, centrally planned economies. The bottom-ranked countries were far more diverse, seemingly without a unifying, common characteristic.

The chapter then looked at correlations between its measure and other less widely used wellbeing indicators in an attempt to find the indicator which best captures non-economic wellbeing achievement. The rationale for this is that the above-mentioned residual is a purely statistical construct, derived from a series of econometric procedures. It is not what might be described as a direct measure of wellbeing, therefore. As it turned out, only two of the less widely used indicators perform better in this regard than a standard indicator. Those variables were youth literacy and a gender empowerment variable, the female share of professional and technical employment. In all other cases a standard, widely used measure performed best in this regard. That variable was the adult literacy rate. This was a particularly robust result, which was obtained consistently across different samples of countries and under different assumed error measurement scenarios.

What are the implications of these results? Most obviously, it suggests that if we wish to use a measure of wellbeing, in the sense defined above, that best captures this chapter's notion of non-economic wellbeing achievement, across different samples of countries, we should be using the adult literacy rate. This is an interesting finding, to the extent that the adult literacy rate is subject to the above-mentioned criticism regarding correlations with income. It is also disappointing, on the one hand, that there have been many attempts to shift the focus away from the standard measures, including adult literacy, towards newer, hopefully more enlightening indicators. On the other hand, it is not disappointing, given that such a widely used measure performs so consistently well in capturing non-economic wellbeing achievement. With regard to the female share of technical and professional employment and youth literacy variables, there would appear to be a case for expanding the coverage, reporting and usage of these indicators if one is to measure non-economic wellbeing achievement comprehensively with a variable other than one obtained by construction, using econometric techniques. Greater coverage of the former variable would appear to be especially warranted, given that it is available for a relatively small sample of countries. A message for policy from this result is that if we want to promote non-economic wellbeing, as defined in this chapter, we should continue to strive for improvements in adult literacy. This message is made stronger given the result for youth literacy.

Finally, let us consider some possible directions for future research. First, while this chapter has made some attempt to account for measurement error in the standard indicators, further work on this is clearly required both at a conceptual level, involving further consideration of the source of measurement error and at the purely empirical level. The nature of the errors might be different or more complicated than envisaged in this chapter. As such, it is not beyond the bounds of imagination to speculate that the correlation between the variants of μ_i and adult literacy is due to errors in measurement not captured in this chapter. Further tests for the sensitivity of this result to possible measurement error would appear to be warranted, therefore. Second, there is far from universal acceptance that a logarithmic transformation of income per capita, used in this chapter, is appropriate. Alternative transformations could be investigated. Third, non-economic achievement could be measured using period-averages of the relevant data instead of data for a single year. This might better capture long-run relationships between income and the non-economic indicators. Fourth, one could account for possible endogeneity between income and the non-economic indicators in estimating the residual between them. Fifth, rather than seeking to correlate this chapter's measure of non-economic wellbeing achievement on a single variable, one could look at correlating it against a composite of a number of indicators, thereby providing a multidimensional non-economic wellbeing achievement indicator. Finally, rather than seeking a variable or variables which are merely associated with the chapter's constructed measure of wellbeing achievement, one could undertake a far more sophisticated analysis that looks for causal relationships.

Appendix 6A: estimation of a non-economic wellbeing measure

We commence with the following composite, 'standard' index of non-economic wellbeing for country i:

$$W_i = \sum_{k=l}^{m} \phi_k \, x_{k,i}^t \qquad i = l, \ldots, n. \tag{6A.1}$$

where $x_{k,i}^t$ are appropriately transformed values of the wellbeing indicators $x_{k,i}$ and the ϕ_k are weights. The $x_{k,i}$ are 'standard' non-economic

Table 6A.1 *Principal components analysis results*

		Principal components		
		First $(PC_{1,i}=W_i)$	Second $(PC_{2,i})$	Third $(PC_{3,i})$
Eigenvalue		2.510	0.293	0.197
Cumulative per centage of eigenvalues		83.654	93.424	100.000
Component weights (ϕ_k):	Life Expectancy $(x_{1,i})$	0.565	−0.824	−0.051
	Adult literacy $(x_{2,i})$	0.582	0.441	−0.683
	Gross enrolment $(x_{3,i})$	0.585	0.356	0.729

wellbeing indicators, defined above. W_i captures the maximum obtainable information from the $x_{k,i}$ subject to an appropriate condition. This is achieved by choosing the ϕ_k that maximises the variance of W_i subject to a normalisation condition. ϕ_ks are therefore obtained by principal components analysis, with W_i being the first principal component extracted from the $x_{k,i}^t$ and ϕ_k being an (m×1) eigenvector. The corresponding eigenvalue is λ_k and the normalisation condition is that ϕ_k^2 equals λ_k.

The principal components analysis was conducted using the computer program SHAZAM, which allows the analysis to be done on a number of alternative matrices. The correlation matrix was chosen, which is appropriate when the original variables are measured in different units, as is the case with the $x_{k,i}$. This dictated that the $x_{k,i}^t$, in equation (6A.1) above, from which W_i were extracted, were obtained through the following transformation of the $x_{k,i}$:

$$x_{k,i}^t = \frac{x_{k,i} - \overline{x}_{k,i}}{\left[\sum_{i=1}^{n}\left(x_{k,i} - \overline{x}_{k,i}\right)^2\right]^{\frac{1}{2}}} \tag{6A.2}$$

where the bar denotes a mean value. This is a linear transformation. For further details see Whistler, White, Wong and Bates (2001).

Results of the principal components analysis, which is based on the transformed components, $x_{1,i}^t$, are shown in Table 6A.1. W_i, the first principal component performs very well in extracting information from the three component variables, capturing 84 per cent of the eigenvalues. The component variable weights ϕ_k are very similar, varying from 0.565 to 0.585.

Values of μ_i were obtained by estimating the following regression equation:

$$W_i = \alpha + \ln y_i + \mu_i \qquad (6A.3)$$

where $\ln y_i$ is the logarithm of PPP GDP per capita. The logarithm is used to reflect diminishing returns to the conversion of income into economic wellbeing. The use of logarithmic values is consistent with the well-known Atkinson formula for the utility or wellbeing derived from income. This formula is written as follows:

$$W(y_i) = \frac{1}{1 - \varepsilon} \, y_i^{1-\varepsilon} \qquad (6A.4)$$

where $W(y_i)$ is the utility or wellbeing derived from income and ε measures the extent of diminishing returns. As ε approaches 1 $W(y_i)$ becomes the logarithm of y_i. Selecting values for ε can be contentious, and for this reason alternative transformations of y_i, obtained from Equation 6A.3 but with different values of , are also used later in this chapter. Anand and Sen (2000) provide a detailed discussion of this issue in the context of the HDI. Note also that while income is seen as a wellbeing indicator in its own right, it is also seen as a means for converting economic wellbeing into non-economic wellbeing. Allowing for diminishing returns is justified in this context given the boundedness of many non-economic indicators and the increasing costs associated with greater achievement in others (such as life expectancy).

Regressing W_i, on $\ln \gamma_i$ yielded the following equation:

$$\hat{W}_i = -0.755 + 0.089 \ln y_i.$$
$$(-19.50) \ (19.67) \qquad (6A.5)$$

The numbers in parentheses are t ratios. The R^2 and $\bar{R}^2$ are 0.694 and 0.692, respectively.

Appendix 6B: hypothesis testing issues

First consider measurement error. While few if any wellbeing indicators considered thus far are free of measurement error, arguably those subject to greatest error are the standard non-economic indicators, as defined. This is of relevance to the above hypothesis tests given its implications for W_i, as can now be demonstrated. Let the true, unobservable and measurement error-free variable be $W_i^\star$. Its relationship with W_i is:

$$W_i = W_i^* + \mu_i^* \tag{6B.1}$$

where μ_i^* is the error in measuring $W_i^\star$. It follows from (76B.1) that μ_i is a composite variable, defined as:

$$\mu_i = v_i + \mu_i^* \tag{6B.2}$$

where v_i is the true measure of non-economic wellbeing achievement, as defined above.

Given (6A.1), μ_i^* is defined as:

$$\mu_i^* = \sum_{k=1}^{m} \phi_k \; \mu_{k,i}^{t,*} \tag{6B.3}$$

where $\mu_{k,i}^{t,*}$ are the errors in measuring $x_{k,i}^{t,*}$. μ_i^* is thus a composite error term, with the same general structure as the wellbeing indicator W_i. It follows from (6A.1), (6B.1) and (6B.2) that regressing μ_i on $x_{1,i}^t$, $x_{2,i}^t$ or $x_{3,i}^t$, $x_{1,i}^t$, $x_{2,i}^t$ or $x_{3,i}^t$ is the equivalent of regressing $(v_i + \mu_i^*)$ on $(x_{1,i}^{t,*} + \phi_1 \mu_{1,i}^{t,*})$, $(x_{2,i}^{t,*} + \phi_2 \mu_{2,i}^{t,*})$ or $(x_{3,i}^{t,*} + \phi_3 \mu_{3,i}^{t,*})$, respectively. A regression of μ_i on the HDI also involves regressing of μ_i^* on itself given that the HDI shares variables with W_i. The resulting correlation coefficients will therefore be distorted upwards, in absolute terms, in the sense that each regression involves regressing μ_i^* on itself or on one of its components. This in turn means that $\rho_s^{\max}$ will be distorted upwards, therefore, possibly leading to the erroneous rejection of the null hypothesis outlined above. The nature of this measurement error problem is different to that usually discussed in econometrics textbooks, as it involves coefficients which are pushed away from zero rather than being biased towards them.

Addressing this issue is less than straightforward as we are required to speculate as to likely values of μ_i^* to obtain v_i. v_i can then be regressed on $x_{1,i}^t$, $x_{2,i}^t$, $x_{3,i}^t$ and the HDI to obtain a less distorted $\rho_s^{\max}$. The issue was finally addressed as follows. Given (6B.1) and (6B.2), we can, after some algebraic manipulation, write the following equation:

$$W_i = \alpha + \ln y_i + \gamma_q \pi_{q,i} + v_{q,i} \tag{6B.4}$$

where $\gamma_q \pi_{q,i}$ are alternative estimates of μ_i^*. $\pi_{q,i}$ is one of q variables and γ_q are the corresponding parameters. A number of different formulations of $\pi_{q,i}$ and values of γ_q were considered. Three formulations and values were, in the final analysis, adopted. These formulations are, of course, necessarily no more than informed guesses as to the likely values of μ_i^*. No attempt was made to guestimate the $\mu_{k,i}^{t,*}$, and, as such, each of the $x_{k,i}^t$ are assumed to be approximately equally erroneously measured.

It is reasonable to assume that error in measuring W_i will be subject to a random process but also be a decreasing function of the resources a country allocates to the collection and reporting of aggregate wellbeing data and the effectiveness with which these resources have been allocated. Moreover, it is also reasonable to posit that both of the second of these factors will be an increasing function of the income per capita. The formulations of $\pi_{q,i}$ are based on these assumptions. The first, $\pi_{q,i}$, was defined as a standard random variable with a mean of zero and variance of one, expressed as a ratio of the reciprocal of $\ln y_i$. For a given random value, therefore, $\pi_{1,i}$ will be smaller the larger a country's income per capita is and vice versa. In estimating (6B.4) with $\pi_{1,i}$, the value of γ_1 was unrestricted, being determined purely by the data. This is appropriate, as the resulting estimate of μ_i^* will be scaled in proportion to W_i. $\pi_{2,i}$ was defined as a random normal variable but with a mean, standard deviation and variance differing according to country group. For low- and middle-income countries the standard deviation was four and two times that of the high-income countries, respectively. γ_2 was determined by the data to ensure that the corresponding estimate of μ_i^* is in proportion to W_i. Finally, $\pi_{3,i}$ was defined as a uniform random number, but with its range being set according to some fraction of W_i. This fraction was set at 0.025, 0.05 and 0.20 for high-, middle- and low-income countries, respectively. γ_3 was restricted to one in estimating (6B.4) with $\pi_{3,i}$.

The second issue also relates to ρ_s^{max} and the possible erroneous rejection of the null hypothesis outlined above. It is obvious from (6A.1) and (6A.2) that:

$$\mu_i = \sum_{k=1}^m \phi_k \, x_{k,i}^t - (\alpha + \ln y_i) \tag{6B.5}$$

It follows from (6B.5) that regressing μ_i on $x_{1,i}^t$, $x_{2,i}^t$, or $x_{3,i}^t$ to obtain ρ_s^{max} is the equivalent of regressing μ_i partly on itself. This also applies to regressing μ_i on the HDI. As is the case with measurement error, this in turn means that ρ_s^{max} will be pushed upwards, purely by construction. It might hardly be surprising, therefore, if the null is rarely rejected. This issue was addressed by first subtracting each $\phi_k x_{k,i}^t$ from W_i prior to regressing the latter on $\ln y_i$ and $\gamma_q \pi_{q,i}$ to obtain adjusted estimates of

$v_{q,i}$, denoted as $v'_{q,k,i}$. That is, $W_i - \phi_1 x^t_{1,i}$ was regressed on $\ln y_i$ and $\gamma_1 \pi_{1,i}$ to obtain $v'_{1,1,i}$. This was repeated, subtracting $\phi_2 x^t_{2,i}$ and then $\phi_3 x^t_{3,i}$ from W_i to eventually obtain $v'_{1,2,i}$ through to $v'_{3,3,i}$. Given that $k = 1, 2, 3$ and $q = 1,2,3$, this resulted in nine residuals and in turn nine zero-order correlation coefficients and nine rank-order coefficients, for each sample, from which the ρ^{max}_s were obtained. The residuals obtained from these processes were then regressed separately on $x^t_{k,i}$ to obtain adjusted correlation coefficients, from which ρ^{max}_s is ultimately selected.

No attempt was made to obtain adjusted correlation coefficients between μ_i and the HDI. This was of no practical consequence, given that the unadjusted coefficients between these variables did not qualify as ρ^{max}_s. Note also that another method of addressing this issue is to re-estimate (6A.1), successfully dropping each of the component variables, one at a time. This method was also used, but produced very similar results to that described above.

Part II

Resources, agency and meaning

7 Wellbeing, livelihoods and resources in social practice

Sarah White and Mark Ellison

7.1 Introduction

When in 1334 the Duchess of Tyrol, Margareta Maultasch, encircled the castle of Hochosterwitz in the province of Carinthia, she knew only too well that the fortress, situated on an incredibly steep rock rising high above the valley floor, was impregnable to direct attack and would yield only to a long siege. In due course, the situation of the defenders became critical: they were down to their last ox and had only two bags of barley corn left. Margareta's situation was becoming equally pressing, albeit for different reasons: her troops were beginning to be unruly, there seemed to be no end to the siege in sight, and she had similarly urgent military business elsewhere. At this point the commandant of the castle decided on a desperate course of action which to his men must have seemed sheer folly: he had the last ox slaughtered, had its abdominal cavity filled with the remaining barley, and ordered the carcass thrown down the steep cliff onto a meadow in front of the enemy camp. Upon receiving this scornful message from above, the discouraged duchess abandoned the siege and moved on. (Watzlawick, Weakland and Fisch 1974: xi)

This story gives an example of comic reversal in the definition and deployment of resources. Faced with a desperate situation of chronic food shortage and imminent military and political defeat, the commandant resorts to a reckless, apparently irrational act. Rather than have the remaining food consumed in a final attempt to rally his people's flagging strength, he has the ox and barley hurled over the barricades in a last-ditch, winner-takes-all, symbolic act of resistance. The gamble pays off. The duchess, already wearied by her recalcitrant troops and the lure of other battles to fight, has had enough. The commandant's transformatory interpretation of the resources at his disposal has a transformatory outcome. The use of ox and barley as symbol of scorn and defiance has a material impact far beyond their 'innate' capacity.

We would like to thank Douglas Saltmarshe, Allister McGregor and Ian Gough for helpful comments on an earlier draft of this chapter.

157

From simply enabling an insupportable situation to be continued a little longer, they become the means for liberation.

The story offers a number of challenges to conventional ways of thinking about resources. It suggests, first, that the character of resources is not simply given, but varies according to the context in which they are perceived – and the potentially radical ways in which they may be re-conceived and creatively deployed. Second, and linked to this, it shows the importance of agency, that it is human subjects and their reading of their needs and what they wish to achieve in the situation they face, that defines how resources are understood. Third, it points to the significance of social identities and power relations for both the capacity to use resources and the outcomes of that use – if one of the ordinary soldiers had suggested throwing away their remaining food, he might well have found himself hurled over the barricades instead. Finally, it points to the indeterminacy of social practice. However great the creative inspiration of the commandant, the success of his action depended on the response of his opponent. Had she reacted otherwise, the fate of the besieged community and our history of that part of the world would have been very different.

This chapter considers the significance of these points for the use of 'resources' as a conceptual category in researching wellbeing. Rather than seeing resources as stable, fixed categories of assets, we argue that what constitutes a resource in any given context depends primarily on the *purposes* of the people involved. Resources offer means to an end. Both the ends people identify and the perceptions of resources available are constituted in and through culture and social relations. We begin with a brief introduction to the concept of wellbeing and the livelihood frameworks which inform approaches to wellbeing in development studies. This leads into more general discussion of the points made above: the importance of agency; the difficulty of fixing categories of resources; and the place of subjectivity, social identities and contingency in the definition and use of resources. We then explore these issues in closer focus, through examination of a specific piece of social interaction described by Paule Marshall in her novel, *The Chosen Place, The Timeless People*. In conclusion, we consider the significance of the arguments made here, and their implications for researching wellbeing.

7.2   Wellbeing and livelihood frameworks

Building on established critiques of narrowly economic approaches to poverty or development and restrictively medical understandings of health, wellbeing offers a rounded, positive focus which includes not only material resources and social relationships, but also the psychological states and subjective perceptions of people themselves. The stakes are high: at the core of 'wellbeing' lies the question of what are the essential conditions for human flourishing. On the one hand it invokes the universal: the notion that there are core dimensions of human wellbeing which are common across time and space (e.g. Alkire 2002b; Doyal and Gough 1991; Nussbaum 2000; Ryan and Deci 2001; Sen 1999). As post-colonial scholarship attests, however, frameworks that aspire to be 'universal' nevertheless remain caught within a particular set of cultural co-ordinates (e.g. Mehta 1997; Parekh 1995). On the other hand, therefore, the notion of 'wellbeing' appeals to the local, and the particularities of culture and personal experience. In the policy context its key promise is to provide a more holistic, accurate profile of what is really important to people, challenging the default biases of the professionals and enabling them to shape their programmes in more effective ways.

Within Development Studies, it is livelihood frameworks which aim to offer such a rounded, bottom-up perspective, reflecting a reaction against a narrow emphasis on one-off, income measures of economic status, and seek to give a more holistic, people-centred approach. They recognise that household livelihoods are often diverse, combining various activities of various members, with multiple priorities, strategies, influences and therefore outcomes. They seek to overcome the compartmentalisation of people's lives according to the arbitrary 'sectoral' divisions of government departments and development agencies: urban/rural, formal/informal, education/health/industry/agriculture. They also aim to move beyond single 'snap-shot' views of poverty, recognising seasonality changes with the turning year, as well as longer-term cycles and shifts. Through the concepts of 'vulnerability' (Chambers 1989), 'sensitivity' and 'resilience' (Bayliss-Smith 1991) they also seek to capture the hazards that households face and the shocks that these engender, and the capacities of households to respond to them. Echoing the move towards 'wellbeing' as focus, the overall inspiration of livelihoods approaches is to move away from negative, outsider categories which dissect people's lives according to areas of professional specialisation. Instead, they aim to offer a positive, actor-oriented focus which emphasises 'strengths' rather than 'needs', and draws on people's own perspectives through participatory methods of research. In aspiration at least, such approaches seek, rather than abstracting particulars from their context, to show how the system works in context: how the whole gives character to the parts through the interrelation of the social and economic, the human and environmental, people's action and the policy and political context.

The notions of 'resources', 'assets' or 'capitals', and the categories into which these are seen to fall, play a key role in the ways that livelihoods approaches conceptualise different facets of people's lives. The Sustainable Livelihoods Framework advanced by the UK Department for International Development (DfID) and researchers at the Institute of Development Studies in Sussex, for example, categorises the types of resource at people's disposal into natural, social, physical, financial, and human 'capital'. Diagrammatically, this allows household livelihoods to be represented as a pentagon whose points rest on each of these different forms of capital. The larger the area that the pentagon occupies, the stronger and more resilient the livelihood it represents (Carney 1998). An alternative approach is offered by Caroline Moser's Asset Vulnerability Framework, derived from urban research (Moser 1998). This identifies five categories of assets: labour; human capital; productive assets (especially housing); household relations (the composition and structure of households and cohesion of relations within them); and social capital (co-operation and cohesion within the community).[1] This has the great advantage of including explicit reference to asset-holding at various levels within its core terms: figuring in differentiation within households on the one hand and within communities on the other. Other frameworks, by contrast, tend to focus primarily on 'the household' and so are vulnerable to producing an over-homogenous view of this. The Resource Profiles Framework (RPF), developed at the University of Bath, is distinctive in including culture as a separate resource category. This points to the significance of status and symbolic value in the social interactions which constitute livelihoods. To be seen as 'poor but pious', for example, may enable people to advance claims beyond those justified by their material position or social relationships alone.[2]

7.3   The importance of agency

With the view having been broken that 'resources' or 'capital' comprise only income and productive assets, the question arises as to how much more such frameworks can do. Does dividing up household characteristics and assets according to various categories tell us anything new, or simply re-describe tangible and observable features in rather

---

[1] Although it does not include this within the five asset categories, the framework also recognises the importance of social and economic infrastructure, and the mix of public and private provision of this, to people's welfare positions.

[2] J. A. McGregor, 'A poverty of agency: Resource management amongst the poor in Bangladesh', paper presented at the Fifth Workshop of the European Network of Bangladesh Studies, 18–20 April 1998.

abstract and alienated ways? Do the frameworks genuinely incorporate the importance of social and cultural dynamics, or simply re-cast these in economic terms? What do such approaches add to our understanding of the practical problems poor people face and the processes by which poverty and inequality are produced, reproduced and potentially transformed?

The Sustainable Livelihoods Framework seeks to answer such questions by setting the 'asset pentagon' within a broader diagram showing the additional factors of 'vulnerability context' and 'structures and processes' that impact on livelihoods and the flows of influence between them.[3] This has the advantage of relieving the 'asset pentagon' of much work. Variability apparently derives from these other factors, which will affect the specific content of a particular asset bundle, but leave the basic model untouched. The disadvantage, of course, is that this introduces a whole further set of variables which again need more investigation, both in terms of their definition and in their relationship to one another and to the whole. Rather than simply building more *around* the notion of types of capital, it is important to investigate further the notion of capital or resources itself, and in particular to explore the social and cultural processes through which they are constituted and deployed (see e.g. Molyneux 2002).

The first step towards investigating the notions of 'capital', 'assets' or 'resources' is to question the reification which can arise from their uncritical transplantation from one context into another. The 'home' context of 'capital', for instance, lies in the discourses of economics and political economy, where it indicates the presence of tangible assets with particular functions in systems of production and exchange. Within these discursive conventions, it then becomes possible to extend the term metaphorically, and to talk of 'human capital' and 'social capital'. As these have come into common usage, however, they are increasingly used in apparently literal ways, as representing 'real things' 'out there', rather than categories of economic thought. The difficulties this brings can be seen at quite an immediate, practical level. In applying livelihoods approaches, decisions have to be made about how to allocate goods, services or characteristics between the various resource categories. As with any framework, in practice it can be difficult to know what goes where. Take education. In all of the livelihoods frameworks this appears as a type of human resource, as providing skills or aptitudes

---

[3] The 'vulnerability context' comprises: 'trends' – in natural resource stocks, population, technology, politics and economics; 'shocks' – climate or conflict; and 'culture'. The 'structures' comprise levels of government and private sector, and 'processes', laws, policies, incentives and institutions (Carney 1998).

that add value, basically, to the household stocks of labour. In Bourdieu's (1984) work on the makings of elites and social distinctions, however, education appears primarily as a cultural resource. It is at once a highly transactable sign of status (symbolic capital, in Bourdieu's terms), and the means through which values are inculcated and tastes are refined, which in turn drives the reproduction of social and cultural difference. Should education be classified as a human resource, or a cultural resource? The obvious answer is that it may function in both ways.

Recognising this dual potential of education challenges us to move beyond simply generating inventories of the goods and relationships people have at their disposal, to ask how different categories of resource are related to each other. This may be done in different ways. For mathematically minded economists, the question becomes how to quantify the social and cultural, and how to model the terms of exchange whereby more of these may compensate for fewer material goods. For those more interested in the social processes through which people generate their livelihoods, it is here that the importance of distinguishing between the languages of 'capital', 'assets' and 'resources' becomes clear. Far from being simply semantic, the choice of terms points to more profound distinctions which bear importantly on the key issues for this chapter. As Wood (2005: 5) points out, the term 'capital': 'implies fixed rather than variable value, somehow existing with relative autonomy from the actor(s)'.

The choice of the RPF to talk of 'resources' thus points to an active relationship between householders, the material and other assets to which they have access, and the strategies which they use to deploy them. It aims to prioritise the social and see this as the context for the economic, rather than the other way around. Thus McGregor (1994) argues that if you wish to understand the livelihood dynamics of poor people in Bangladesh, you need to focus on credit *relationships*, rather than the exchange of credit as an inert asset in itself. To grasp the utility of different kinds of intervention, you need similarly to explore the social relations which mediate their entry into villages, since these can result in formal government programmes reinforcing the very relations of patronage they are designed to overcome (*ibid*). Wood (2005) makes an allied argument in the form of a metaphor, likening the agency of the household members to the shine given by a bowler to the cricket ball of the household assets, the critical element that determines its swing, and thus the outcome it secures. As in our initial story of the siege of Hochosterwitz, these more social approaches suggest that the character of resources is given by their *use*. Resources are not things that can be abstracted simplistically from their context and categorised without reference to the people to whom they belong. They are already infused with meanings and intentions which reside in the relationship between the 'thing' itself and the person who values it and deploys it as a resource within a social and cultural context.[4]

7.4   Reviewing resource categories

Recognising the importance of agency to the character of resources opens up a very different way of approaching the classification of resources and the relations between them, involving two major departures from the literalist account of 'capitals' or asset types. In this section we discuss the first of these, the de-stabilising of the conventional, reified categories. In the following section we move on from this, to see how different categories of resource are not mutually exclusive, but rather help to constitute each other.

The common usage of the terms 'capital' or 'resource' conjures specific, if sometimes intangible, identifiable goods whose character is given and stable. The siege of Hochosterwitz, however, indicates that the features that 'goods' can assume differ markedly by context and use. It is vital, therefore, to open the space to differentiate between (tangible and intangible) goods, services, activities and relationships (Doyal and Gough 1991) that can be observed objectively to exist, and the transformation of these into *resources* when they are perceived by people as offering the means to meet a particular end. Let us return to the example of education. In both the wellbeing and development literature, this is typically seen as a fundamental prerequisite for a good life. In fact, however, historically many communities have existed quite successfully without anyone knowing how to read or write. Literacy is certainly an objectively identifiable good (though the means for assessing it obviously vary) but it becomes a *resource* only when people have the need to read. This is not simply a semantic point, it has practical consequences. As numerous adult education programmes have found to their cost, enthusiasm falls and skills quickly fade where there is no immediate need to put classroom learning into practice. To categorise literacy as a resource is thus ultimately a cultural act. Goods, services, relationships, etc. objectively exist, but they become *resources* only when they are perceived by a subject as offering the means to achieve a desired end.

---

[4] Cf. J. A. McGregor and B. Kebede 'Resource profiles and the social and cultural construction of wellbeing', paper presented at the inaugural workshop of the ESRC Research Group on Wellbeing in Developing Countries, University of Bath, 13–17 January 2003.

This claim may seem too bold. We do, after all, generally regard resources as having an objective existence, that is, of existing, *qua* resources, independently of the subject. There are, we believe, four important reasons for this. Two of these are general, and two relate specifically to the formation of livelihood frameworks and the development discourse which they reflect. The first reason that resources appear to have a 'real' existence, independent of any actor, is that agency and subjecthood are not properties of individuals alone, but also carry a collective aspect. We recognise that oil is a resource, for example, even if we personally do not run a car, or operate oil-powered heating systems. The structure of our social and economic systems and the technologies on which these depend construct oil as a critical resource. If we as individuals were to die tomorrow, this would not change. Through history and anthropology we can, however, look to other social and economic systems in which oil has not been a resource because people have not identified a need for the functions that it can offer. We can even, although with perhaps more difficulty, imagine a future where oil might again become redundant, and so slip once more out of the category of resources. 'New' resources also emerge as circumstances change. The global market in human organs, where poorer people come to see parts of their bodies as saleable assets, and richer people parts of other people's bodies as items for purchase or theft, perhaps offers one of the most striking, and shocking, instances of the emergence of a new category of 'livelihood resource' (see e.g. Scheper-Hughes 2000).

Second, there is also a psychological dimension to the reification of resources. As Bourdieu (1977: 79) notes, over time 'history [is] turned into nature'. What we need to learn at one point in our life is with habitual use taken for granted, since it becomes second nature to us. The move from learning a conscious set of actions which enable us to drive a car to 'just knowing' how to drive is an example of this. Our everyday knowledge has of course been learned through identifiable steps that can be consciously reconstructed when called for. This is what happens, for example, when one teaches someone else to drive. For everyday purposes, however, our association of certain goods with certain purposes is so habitual that we forget that what these things *mean* to us is not given to us by the things themselves. Our use of pieces of paper as money is a prime example of this. For the most part, to use Bourdieu's (1977: 19) term, we operate out of 'a *learned ignorance*'. When circumstances shift, however, and our default responses are no longer adequate, a creativity is called for to reinterpret the potential of resources in new ways. This, of course, was the crowning achievement of the commandant in the story of the siege. But this creativity is not the sole preserve of desperate commandants; it may be the very stuff of any effective agency and is clearly evident in the livelihood activities of many very poor people.

The third part of the explanation of why resources appear to have an existence independent of the subjects who employ them is more specific to the formation of livelihoods frameworks and the assumptions and values they express. Although it has become commonplace in development studies, the value of broadening definitions of 'capital', 'assets' or 'resources' from the material or financial to include the social or cultural is not self-evident. It becomes meaningful in the context of a policy discourse which privileges economic understandings of what is important. When the framing shifts so the meaning changes. A woman feeding her children probably does not consider what she is doing as the reproduction of human capital. For an economic analysis to express it in this way is to capture something critical about what is going on, which challenges more conventional views of 'productive' (read valued) activity. This is undoubtedly useful, reflecting as it does feminist arguments regarding the essential interrelationship of 'productive' and 'reproductive' labour, and hence the importance of women's work, much of which might otherwise be discounted. However, to analyse what is happening *simply* in these terms is to commit what Spivak (1988: 271) has called in another context 'epistemic violence'. It distorts what is taking place, posing it in quasi-market, calculative terms, and suppresses what it means for the woman and children themselves. Most importantly, perhaps, it obscures the primacy of identity and relationship (motherhood, love, family, belonging) which is the 'home' context that makes the action meaningful to those involved. It over-writes the subjectivity and concerns of the actors with the perspectives and interests of external observers.

This dominance of economic terminology and perspectives on livelihoods and resources reflects more widely the structural formation of development discourse and practice. As critics from Karl Marx to Karl Polanyi to Pierre Bourdieu have pointed out, the economic thinking that dominates current intellectual approaches is one that obscures its own particularity, and effectively silences other voices. What is critical for the argument here is that the economics of capitalism mystifies the primacy of social relations between people and re-presents them as relations between people and things, or even as between objects themselves. This is a major argument that cannot be taken further here, but we believe it is an important issue for future discussions.

The final part of the explanation for the apparently universal characterisation of resources brings us back to agency. We believe that there are, in fact, subjects of the livelihoods analyses, subjects whose interests and purposes define which goods are featured as resources and how these are classified. Despite the claims to the contrary, these subjects are not the local people whose lives the frameworks claim to describe. In fact, they may not be real people at all. Rather, the subjects are constituted through the discursive practices of development bureaucracies and the geopolitical relations which underlie them. It is these institutions, their values, techniques and procedures that define the purposes of 'alleviating poverty' or 'sustainable development' that govern particular readings of 'resources'. In addition, as Mudimbe (1988) argues with respect to colonialism, they construct the identities and subject positions not only of those who are to be developed, but also of planners and policy makers. While the subjecthood of 'local people' receives celebration in contemporary development discourse, however, that of planners and policymakers is implicit. Part of the 'necessary self-deception of planning' (Chatterjee 1993: 207), the 'unmarked', supposedly neutral presence of planners and policymakers facilitates an elision between their interests and those of development subjects. Whereas in fact, as Bernard Schaffer (1985: title) pointed out two decades ago, 'policy makers have their needs too'. The construction of the development industry tends to mask this, making it easy for development bureaucrats to mistake their own tools and assumptions for the perspectives of the people themselves.

7.5   From types of resource to dimensions of resources

The importance of agency, and a more flexible and interactive approach to resources, is very clear when we come to the category of 'culture'. In the Sustainable Livelihoods Framework, 'culture' appears along with 'shocks' and 'trends' as part of the 'vulnerability context'. Diana Carney (1998: 11) sets out the 'key issue' that this raises as follows: 'What effect, if any, does culture have on the way people manage their assets and the livelihood choices they make?'

This question is deeply problematic. It casts culture as residual, exterior, implying a profoundly materialist understanding of the ways that people conduct their lives. This reflects a broader poverty in the understanding of culture within development circles – it often appears, as indeed in that book, almost exclusively in relation to gender issues, with 'religion' now perhaps more frequently added in. This renders 'culture' as not only externally located, outside of the nitty gritty of everyday (economic) life, but also localised, significant only in parti-cular, marked, areas of society. As noted above, the RPF gives more space to culture than the other livelihoods frameworks, by identifying a specific category of cultural resources. This offers both an opportunity and a danger. The opportunity is that the framework directs users to look for cultural resources, and to recognise the significance these have. The danger is that treated crudely this can rigidify rather than overcome the localisation of culture, implying that other 'material' or 'human' or 'natural' assets are somehow a-cultural. Culture may then again become a residual category, containing only those 'pure' markers of status – such as honorific titles – that cannot be fitted anywhere else. As is clear in the papers which apply the RPF, however, this is very far from the intention (see e.g. McGregor 1994, 1998; Saltmarshe 2001, 2002; Wood 2003, 2005). In fact, of course, all of social life is constituted through culture. To be human is to speak a particular language, wear a particular kind of clothes, eat a certain kind of food, use a particular set of tools, marry according to certain rules, value some kinds of goods over others. This is not to deny the existence of some biological universals – the needs that human organisms have to survive – but to recognise that nowhere do we have access to these outside of the mediation of culture. Recent reflection on the RPF under the WeD programme thus recognises that there is a duality to culture: it forms at once a specific form of resource and the context through which all resources are constituted.[5]

Once this point is accepted for culture, we can go on to see that it holds for other resource categories also. Whether material, social or symbolic, *they all represent at once specific forms of resource and the means through which resources are constituted*. Land, for example, is classified in all the livelihoods frameworks as a material, physical, or 'natural' endowment. However, land only becomes *a livelihood resource* when transformed through the *human* activity of labour, the *social* contracts of ownership or use-rights, and the *cultural* meanings of value and status. Its value is not simply given, but varies markedly depending on the state of the market, the social and political context, and the personal circumstances and relationship of the would-be buyer and seller. In transactions between kin, transfers between strangers in times of plenty, or distress sales in times of famine, violent conflict or forced migration, the cash value and livelihood significance of the apparently fixed material resource of land may differ almost beyond recognition. Similarly *cultural* values – such as beauty, or piety – are not free-floating in the ether, but always embedded – or embodied – materially and socially.

The importance of recognising that the conventional categories of resource do not represent mutually exclusive types, but rather co-constituting dimensions, is especially evident when we come to consider social

[5] *Ibid.*

resources. Certain links, such as close kinship ties, have a strong institutional element that exists relatively independently of any affective
element or active celebration – the 'I may not like him but he is still my
brother' syndrome. Such relationships and other forms of institutionalised networks may, as Wood (2005: 6) suggests, have such a robust
existence, functioning 'independently of the idiosyncrasies of any party
to them' that they may be categorised as social capital. The 'social
capital' of a household is then the sum of all such structural relationships
in which the household is engaged. As quantitatively inclined economists have found, this leads into considerable technical difficulties of
how to assign values to relationships of differential intensity or utility.
But proceeding in this way may not only be technically difficult but also
philosophically mistaken. It is helpful that economics and the dominant
development actors now recognise that relatedness and social connections are critical to people's psychological welfare, social status and
economic potential. The challenge is to go beyond seeing this as
representing one area of life, set apart from others. At base, the term
'social capital' is a metaphor, which draws our attention to the importance of social relationships, not a 'real thing' which exists somehow 'out
there'. And relationships are not inert, fixed assets, but rather exist as
they are *lived*. Any negotiation, any aspect of the pursuit of livelihoods or
wellbeing will necessarily have a social side. Issues such as the politics of
who is entitled to what, the negotiation of values, the terms of access to
key goods, and the significance of social identities, interpersonal and
social group dynamics in structuring these, are constantly present.

Rather than seeing specific goods, services, relationships and activities as
constituting always a particular type of resource, therefore, we may also say
these all have the potential for use as material, social or relational and
symbolic resources. As in the opening story, this brings to the definition of
resources a certain indeterminacy: the 'obvious' way of looking at resources
(the ox and grain as food) is not the only way, nor necessarily the most
useful in a given context. As noted above in the case of education, whether
a particular item constitutes a resource in the first place, and then whether
it is performing a primarily symbolic, or social, or material function will
differ according to the setting, and these functions may in practice be
intertwined. As Bourdieu (1998/2001: 53) rather chillingly notes: 'the most
brutal relations of force are always simultaneously symbolic relations'.

7.6   Subjectivity and contingency

Having set out a general framework above, in this section we go micro,
re-locating to the dingy kitchen of a couple of Caribbean share-croppers,

courtesy of Paule Marshall's novel, *The Chosen Place, The Timeless People*. The headline issue is one beloved of development studies: food security. Although the passage is a little long, we relate it here as a powerful cameo of the use of resources in social practice.[6] To draw on such a text in a chapter like this might itself be seen as a somewhat creative interpretation of resources, since novels are not typically seen as material for use in social science analysis. However, the acute observation of personal interaction contained within it offers the opportunity to explore a further important aspect of resources which is often overlooked. Where livelihood frameworks have been criticised for failing to offer an adequate account of power and social identities, this episode clearly demonstrates the interplay of different perspectives and priorities amongst differently placed actors. It also offers an opportunity to reflect further on our earlier claims regarding the importance of subjectivity in determining the character of resources, and to consider how issues of social structure and human agency articulate with this.

We enter as Harriet, the elite, White Anglo-Saxon Protestant wife of a North American Jewish anthropologist, visits a neighbouring house and finds the children alone and hungry.

Harriet had gone that late afternoon to the hopelessly overcrowded house where Stinger and Gwen lived with their innumerable children ... She arrived to find that Gwen had not yet returned from the fields although it was past five, and the children, left alone in the house all day, had had nothing to eat since the mid-morning meal at eleven. She could barely make out their individual faces in the interior dimness of the two tiny cluttered rooms ... But she could sense their hunger, almost see it ...

The oldest child, a girl, had been left in charge, and Harriet called her over ...

'Isn't there anything at all to eat, Brenda?' she said. She could not bring herself to look at her.

The child also kept her gaze averted. 'No, please,' she said.

'Are you sure? Isn't there perhaps something left over from this morning?'

'No, please. We've eaten the last.'

But there was nothing in Harriet that could comprehend such a fact, and on sudden impulse she turned from Brenda and made her way out to the kitchen, ... remaining the longest time gazing with a kind of numb fixity at the soot-covered pot in which the day's rice had been cooked. It had been scraped clean. Even the burnt part at the bottom had been eaten ...

And then she saw them: a half-dozen brown-speckled eggs in a cracked bowl inside the otherwise empty larder. Never thinking to ask herself why they had been left there unused, she strode over to the larder ... and took out the bowl ...

---

[6] We have abridged the original text for the sake of brevity.

'Brenda.' . . .

'Yes, Miss Harriet?'

'Is there a frying pan?'

She didn't turn to look at Brenda as she spoke, or at the other children who, curious and intrigued, had slipped silently up behind their sister, filling the doorway.

'Yes, please.' Brenda said.

'Would you bring it for me, please.'

The child held back a moment, her troubled eyes on the eggs, wanting to say something but not bold enough; and then brought her the heavy iron skillet . . . .

Her most severe test came during the actual cooking, when she had to struggle with nausea at the sight of the littered, food-stained hearth, the grease-encrusted pan, and the suspiciously rancid smell of the butter as she heated it . . . But finally, there lay the finished omelette . . . [Harriet was] inordinately proud of it. There was something of a miracle about it almost; the fishes and loaves. Above all, she felt an immense relief. She had done her part, she told herself, gazing down at it steaming gently on the plate, to quiet that ravenous presence charging up and down the two rooms . . . .

[Harriet leaves Brenda with instructions to share out the omelette between them, and makes her way home. When her husband comes in, however, he is furious at what she has done.]

'Could you please tell me just what the hell you thought you were doing over at Stinger's today?'

For a moment she couldn't imagine he was speaking to her . . .

'What did I think I was doing?' Her voice, her frown, expressed her bewilderment . . .

In face of her distress he turned aside, ashamed of his anger. 'Oh, Christ, Hatt, I know you meant well,' he said . . . 'But if only you had thought to ask somebody first . . . ' . . . On his way home . . . he had stopped off at Stinger's, . . . only to find Gwen quarrelling and the child Brenda in tears. Gwen, it seemed, had a long-standing agreement with the postmaster to sell him all of her eggs. This money was then used toward purchasing the family's weekly supply of staples. It was a very carefully worked out arrangement of which Gwen was proud.

'Gwen's not mad at you for having cooked the eggs,' he said. 'She understands why you did it, but she blames poor Brenda for not speaking up and telling you who they were for. I'm afraid she gave her quite a thrashing.'

'Oh, no!' she cried, and her mind wheeling back she saw Brenda standing bowed and silent amid her sisters and brothers in the doorway . . .

'Well, it'll all blow over, I guess.' he said. . . . 'If only you would stop and ask, Harriet, before taking things into your own hands! I am sure it never even occurred to you to find out if the eggs hadn't been left there for a reason. I don't know,' he said, slowly shaking his head, 'there's this thing in you which makes you want to take over and manage everything and everybody on your own terms. . . . And it's not to say you don't mean well most of the time, but it still makes for complications.'

'But they were hungry!' Her voice was sharp and emphatic; she had not permitted herself to hear what he had just said. 'Besides, it doesn't make any sense to sell perfectly good, nourishing eggs to buy that awful rice they all eat.'

'It might not make sense to you,' he said .... 'but it obviously does to Gwen. She's probably discovered she can feed more mouths doing it her way. I don't know. What I do know is that you can't go around ordering other people's lives and trying to make them change long-standing habits overnight ... Everybody doesn't live by your standards. Your values aren't necessarily the world's. Why, the kids didn't even eat the goddamn omelette.'

'They didn't eat it?' And she was perhaps more stunned by this than anything else he had said. ... 'Perfectly good, nourishing eggs ... I don't understand ... '
(Marshall 1969/84: 175–181, abridged)

As noted above, resources are what people can use to meet their needs and purposes. Logically, therefore, a need must precede the identification of a resource to meet it. But the story above gives a further twist to this. Simply having a need is not enough. The children's hunger is not in doubt. But for them, the eggs were not a resource they could use to meet that need. Why not, when they were, as Harriet appreciates, perfectly good, nourishing food? Because, in that household's livelihood strategy, the eggs were for sale, not for consumption. This is worth underlining. For those children, the eggs were not food – and even when Harriet had cooked the omelette, they did not become so. Probably the children did not even think of eating the eggs – maybe they were not part of their diet, or maybe they had simply internalised their mother's absolute rights over their disposal. What was critical was not which of the conventional asset categories they fitted into – no one doubts that they were material – but rather the *purpose* to which they had been assigned, and the power relations which circumscribed their use.

Admitting that the identification of a resource is ultimately subjective is not, however, to suggest that it is somehow random or indiscriminate. Harriet making the omelette was a (rather catastrophic) assertion of agency, to be sure, but it was an agency both enabled and constrained by structure. At base, this structure is configured by international relations, the imperialism of US interests over the Caribbean. At its simplest, this gives the context for Harriet's presence on the island. At a deeper level, it also shapes her entire understanding of the place and her relationships within it as well as the island people's responses to her. Just as Said (1985) argues with respect to nineteenth-century European writers on the Orient, the patterns of international dominance are so strong that *no* interaction across these lines can be innocent of it. The beauty of this passage, however, is that it illustrates graphically how such structures operate not only at the 'public' or macro-level, but also within the most intimate, inter- and intra-personal relations. The macro-political structures intertwine with the 'everyday' dominance of adult over child. The eggs did not belong to Harriet, were not in any sense hers to dispose of, and yet because of who she was she assumed the rights to use them. The children were silenced by fear, the power of Harriet's person even greater than their fear of their mother's reaction. Gwen's anger is vented not against Harriet, the high-status perpetrator, but against Brenda, the child who had been pressed into service as unwilling accomplice. Power is not something inert, 'out there', but expressed graphically through speech and silence, action and passivity, the meeting and avoidance of eyes.

These links between macro-patterns and micro-interaction and the ways that structure and agency together inform subjectivity are powerfully conceptualised by Bourdieu in his notion of 'habitus'. This is particularly apposite for a focus on wellbeing because it offers an unusually holistic view of human experience, connecting the bodily to the social, and the social to the psychological. Bourdieu describes 'habitus' variously as a 'system of dispositions', propensities, or ways of being in the world; the 'feel for the game' which is so deeply embedded within one that it seems like second nature (Bourdieu 1977, 1990). Its role is to generate regular practices, perceptions and attitudes that are not governed by rule or conscious calculation. The habitus is developed through childhood and experience and is shaped by the social structures in which these take place. Far from a set template which always marks out a predetermined pattern, the habitus is a principle for the 'improvisations' that for Bourdieu are the stuff of social life. Critically, however, inscribed within it is awareness of one's own social location and hence the different locations of others and how these are placed in relation to one's own. In linking structure and agency, it also offers a critical orientation towards *social practice*. Social (and economic) life is seen as something done, achieved through time in risky interaction with others, never settled or utterly predictable, but requiring new and creative responses as established attitudes and propensities confront the demands of a new context or 'field'.

Finally, however, Harriet's intervention offers a paradox to this picture of power and the agency related to it. As bell hooks (1984) argues, there is a power that belongs to the margins and limitations for those who live at the centre and assume that the centre is the whole world. For the children, hunger could be borne for the present. It was probably not unusual for them and they understood the domestic economy was one in which they had to endure. For Harriet, on the other hand, the children's hunger was literally unbearable: she could not look at them. Her agency was both an expression of power and of weakness: it was predicated on her ignorance of the ways Gwen made ends meet and her refusal or inability to quieten the clamour within herself and see the world through the children's eyes. It gives an example, once more, of the indeterminacy of social practice. In this case Harriet 'got it wrong': she misread the 'field' of action. Though she could push through with her own intention to make the omelette, the children refused to eat it as she intended, and Gwen was furious rather than grateful when she found out what had happened. These responses transformed the character of Harriet's behaviour. From a salvific act of altruism, it became an insulting and wasteful imposition. Her action came out of her own desperate need to act, to resolve things, to find herself valid through their reception of her gifts. The needs that Harriet was responding to were not so much the children's, but her own. The outcome was that Harriet made things worse: materially, of course, in wasting the assets Gwen had carefully set aside for sale. But beyond this, the incident is shot through with symbolism. Harriet's actions at once betrayed her lack of faith in Gwen's capacity to care for her family, and undermined the strategies Gwen had set in place. Gwen's fury at Brenda was not only an expression of her grief at the material loss she had suffered. It was also borne of humiliation, that her struggles to feed her family should be so shamelessly exposed, and anger, that the settlement that she had made in a difficult situation should be so thoughtlessly overturned.

At one level, of course, Harriet stands as a metaphor for ill-informed and ill-advised development intervention by outsiders. Many of us who have been involved in development practice may recognise aspects of Harriet in our projects, our colleagues, and even ourselves, just as we wish to distance ourselves from other elements. Indeed the novel as a whole may be read as a study in the resistance of the islanders to the development they are offered, and its framing of the issues in political rather than technical terms offers a powerful caution to the blithe assumptions of much development planning. This is worthy of further study in its own right. However, the main point here is rather different. Pursuing our concerns with social process and the social and cultural construction of resources is to see, through a practical encounter, how resources are critically associated with social identities and power relations, both within and beyond the household. At one level the passage takes us right down to the level of individuals, and intensely personal interaction. But it is not *simply* personal or free-standing. As noted above, structural inequalities by race, class, age and gender are implicated in Harriet's need to feed the children and their unwilling accession to her demands. In order fully to grasp this piece of micro interaction, we need to look outward and upward at the international political economy and policy regimes which structure the poverty and dependence of the share-croppers' livelihoods on the one hand, and Harriet's assumption of the right and necessity to intervene on the other. This takes us on a further step in our understanding of resources. The character of what these *are*, is not only intrinsically related to agency, purposes, and what is *done*, but these are in turn fundamentally related to subjectivity and *who* does what, and the structural forms of power which these identities embody.

7.7   Conclusion

How, then, does this discussion of resources contribute to research into wellbeing? First, there are a number of ways in which the arguments we have made in relation to resources can be applied directly to the study of wellbeing. The most important aspect of this is the need to retain openness to a people- and context-centred view. The tendency in our intellectual culture towards reification, and emphasising relations between things rather than between people, can affect understandings of wellbeing, just as it does resources. There may indeed be universal determinants of wellbeing, and conventional indicators of human development such as maternal or infant mortality may offer shorthand indices to these. However, such 'hard' statistics need to be held lightly, as probable indicators of factors which promote or inhibit wellbeing, rather than 'the thing itself'. For ultimately the meanings of wellbeing will differ, like resources, according to the cultural context, purposes, agency, and social identities of the people concerned.

Second, there is an implicit plea here for greater rigour on the part of sociologists and anthropologists involved in development studies. If the promise of 'wellbeing' to offer a genuinely new, more holistic and more people-centred approach is to be fulfilled, there is a vital need for much more critical, sociologically and politically engaged thinking. This must go beyond the rhetoric of 'it all depends on the context' so beloved of social development specialists, which elides their own proto-disciplinary perspectives with those of 'the people', and leaves all powerful explanatory models in the hands of economists. The point is not to deny the importance of the economic, but to broaden our understanding of what that may comprise, and to situate it securely within the social, cultural and political. Instead of being shy of theory, it is vitally important that social analysts of development draw on the wealth of critical thinking that exists in the disciplines they represent. The test of such an approach will be that it adds explanatory value to simple observation, and genuinely explicates the particular, rather than simply re-describing it in alienated terms. This chapter, we hope, offers some suggestions as to how to move this forward.

For effective policy making, what is required is not a template through which diverse realities can be 'read' in standardised terms. Rather, the need is for a model which is sufficiently open and dynamic that it can be used in a variety of contexts in order to expose the specificity of each. In place of an abstract, universalised notion derived externally, research needs to build up a dynamic picture of what wellbeing means in practice for particular people faced with particular challenges, and the politics involved in their struggles to achieve it.

Critically, of course, attending to the relations between people rather than the 'resources' which are exchanged also suggests the importance of the terms on which exchanges take place. This is to approach livelihoods and the attempts to secure wellbeing as a form of social practice: recognising that interactions are fundamentally constructed through social and cultural structures and power relations; recognising that our own positions as planners or analysts are not 'unmarked' or innocent, but utterly implicated in these patterns of power; letting go of the conceit of agency which is predicated on structures of global injustice; admitting the primacy of people's own priorities and purposes; and seeking ways of listening better to these, rather than assuming we already know what they are or should be; and, finally, recognising the creativity and indeterminacy of social practice, and expecting to be surprised.

8   Livelihoods and resource accessing in the Andes: *desencuentros* in theory and practice

Anthony Bebbington, Leonith Hinojosa-Valencia,
Diego Muñoz and Rafael Enrique Rojas Lizarazú

8.1   Introduction

As much as development is about encounters (Escobar 1995; Long 1989; Peters 2000), it is also about *desencuentros* – discontinuities, misunderstandings, conflicting interpretations, impositions and resistances. The discussions of livelihoods (or often sustainable livelihoods) that came increasingly into vogue during the 1990s reflect such a sense of *desencuentro*. Scholars, practitioners and activists have invoked the notion of livelihood in order to argue that the ways in which poor people[1] get by are far more complex than most interventions allow for. The idea has also been used by those working within the 'they know how' (Chambers 1983; Meehan 1978) tradition of populist, *basista*[2] approaches to development, in order to argue that the only livelihoods that stand any hope of being sustainable will be those that build on the ways in which poor people currently live, that reflect people's own knowledge and that are grown from the grassroots (Chambers 1987; Chambers and Conway 1992).

We are grateful to the Dutch Ministry of Foreign Affairs/Stuurgroep for financing the fieldwork reported here. The support of the Economic and Social Research Council (UK) is also gratefully acknowledged. The analytical work underlying the preparation of this chapter was part of the programme of the ESRC Global Poverty Research Group. Continuing thanks are given to the co-financing agencies and the NGOs involved, and for the comments of Nico van Niekerk, Allister MacGregor, Cris Kay and participants at a seminar at the Institute of Social Studies in the Hague at which the paper on which this chapter is based was also presented.

[1] There is far less work on the livelihoods of wealthier people and professionals but it is quite possible that the ways in which they get by and get on are equally complex, convoluted and inadequately captured simply by talking of their principal occupation. Certainly it feels that way.

[2] The term *basista* was coined by David Lehmann (1990) to refer to a brand of grassroots development and social justice work that characterised those Latin American NGOs, social movements and their northern supporters who traced their roots to anti-authoritarian and left-inspired movements for social and political change.

This chapter explores such encounters and *desencuentros* between livelihoods and development interventions – in this case, the interventions of aid chains involving Dutch and Andean NGOs.[3] Specifically, the chapter focuses on the asset (resource) management dimensions of rural livelihoods to explore the points at which household strategies of resource accessing converge with and diverge from the strategies through which actors within the nongovernmental aid chain[4] aim to enhance household asset bases. As will be clear, the degree of convergence/divergence varies according to type of household and – to some extent – type of NGO. This appears to reflect dissonances between what it is that intervention strategies imply rural people want for their and their children's future, and what it is that rural people appear to be seeking for this future. Such dissonances sometimes reflect differences in views on what is feasible (rural people may well identify with the goals espoused by NGOs but find them impracticable given the current context in which they live), and at other times differences in view over what is desirable (such as differences in viewpoint over identities and cultural mores to be privileged in livelihood strategies, or over the roles of particular institutions in regulating social life). Put in other words, these are sometimes differences of perspective on human needs, and sometimes on needs satisfiers (cf. Gough 2004; Gough and McGregor 2004). Furthermore, these *desencuentros* can reflect real differences in the underlying concerns and politics of rural people and external agencies. Often, though, they are an effect of the different bodies of information available to these different actors. External actors do not have to be operating at a global scale to lack the information that would allow them to adapt their understandings of 'community,' 'wellbeing' or 'rural economy' to the underlying relationships and dynamics of particular localities (Gough 2004; McGregor 2004) – they need only be thirty miles away in the capital city.[5]

---

[3] Other parts of this research are reported elsewhere, and references to the wider study will be kept to a minimum here. See Bebbington (2004b, 2005) and Bebbington, Hinojosa and Rojas (2002). The research – which was not part of the WeD initiative – was funded by the Dutch Ministry of Foreign Affairs via the Steering Committee for the Evaluation of the Dutch Co-financing Programme.

[4] The notion of aid chain was taken to refer to the networks linking both individuals and organisations and making possible the wider social relationships and flows of ideas, knowledge and finance on which much local development intervention is based.

[5] These observations are made with some humility, for of course the same applies to us as researchers. Our own distance – physical, cultural, existential – can equally lead to information gaps, mis-specified concepts, and inappropriate abstractions. It is thus far too easy to be judgemental, and that is not the spirit of this chapter. The issues raised are ones of structure more than of culpability.

Second, the chapter explores the ways in which political economic forces and relationships influence rural people's aspirations for the future, and the quality of the life and livelihoods that they build. That discussion suggests that (practical or academic) interventions in people's livelihood practices ought to pay as much attention to the structures and relationships that govern access to resources and the productivity and quality of those resources, as to actual asset bases and resource accessing strategies of rural households.

The chapter proceeds as follows. Section 8.2 discusses livelihood approaches to rural poverty and development. In particular, it explores the potentials and drawbacks of approaches that focus on household asset bases, and discusses ways in which questions of political economy have been brought into such approaches. Section 8.3 presents recent evidence on household resource accessing strategies in municipalities in which the authors have conducted research and explore how far external interventions have responded to the dynamics underlying these strategies. The section first discusses methodological issues. It then outlines general patterns in the resource accessing and broader livelihood strategies used by families and the extent to which external interventions have helped improve the outcomes of these strategies. Section 8.4 discusses socio-political and political economic factors that have influenced livelihood possibilities and resource accessing preferences. Section 8.5 concludes with a discussion of the *encuentros* (encounters) and *desencuentros* between livelihoods and nongovernmental interventions in these communities.

8.2   Livelihoods agency, resources, structures

Notwithstanding the recent enthusiasm for 'the livelihoods approach', a concern for livelihoods is nothing new. In the 1970–80s, research informed by dependency and world systems theory often drew links between processes of underdevelopment in Latin America and the dependent nature of poor people's livelihoods. This work emphasised the extent to which the broader development model constrained and undermined people's livelihoods. The concept of functional dualism (de Janvry 1981), for instance, embodied the notion of structural relations among modernising and popular sectors of the economy in which the modern economy *needed* the popular economy as a source of cheap labour, foodstuffs, goods and services. This work suggested that given this structural need for cheap labour and products, poor people would hardly ever escape from their poverty. They would always be sources of something cheap, and this structural relationship would define their livelihood possibilities and strategies. Similar ideas characterised work on urban survival strategies, and took on particular force in critiques of self-help housing and of de Soto's interpretation of the informal economy (Bromley 1994; Bromley and Gerry 1979; de Soto 1989).

Other approaches – while not eschewing the ways in which broad processes of capitalist development exclude people and limit their livelihood options – have taken a somewhat different approach. They have argued that a careful analysis of how people compose livelihood strategies can suggest ways in which openings, however small, in the overall development model might be reworked and exploited by poor people and organisations that work alongside them.[6] These approaches combine a concern for poor people's agency, an interest in the asset bases of their livelihoods, and an acknowledgement of the ways in which institutions and structures affect livelihood options. Some such approaches focus particularly on the ways in which people – through both struggle and creativity – gain access to and control over resources. In this concern for both assets and agency, there is considerable overlap between concepts of livelihoods and of environmental entitlements (Leach, Mearns and Scoones 1999). Where the balance lies between focusing on changes in stocks of resources, and on strategies and practices of resource access and control, is perhaps what determines whether livelihoods approaches tend towards utopianism, populism and mild reformism (Altamirano, Copestake, Figueroa and Wright 2003: 21) or not.

The notion that people draw on a diversity of assets, combining them in different ways in order to pursue their aspirations, has been emphasised in recent efforts to conceptualise livelihoods.[7] While these conceptualisations have much in common, they differ in emphasis. One such difference – which has both methodological and interpretative implications – is the extent to which approaches emphasise what people *think and do*, or what they *have and control*. While all livelihood approaches are actor-oriented in the sense that they focus on individuals' and households' concerns, those with intellectual roots in actor-oriented sociology and cultural ecology place great emphasis on actors' intentions and perceptions, and on the ethnographic details of their practices and strategies (Zimmerer 1996; Zoomers 1998, 1999). Other approaches, tracing their roots to farming systems research, participatory and rapid rural appraisal and to discussions of the multidimensionality of poverty, focus more on the ways in which people aim to access, control and combine different asset types (Carney 1998). While these approaches also lay importance on peoples' intentions

---

[6] This paragraph draws on Bebbington (2004a).
[7] See for instance: Bebbington (1997, 1999); Carney (1998); Moser (1998); Scoones (1998); Zoomers (1999).

and concerns, they tend to focus more on changes in asset bases and the effects of institutions and social structures on these changes. They tend towards less ethnographic, often shorter-term, studies of the (above all) rural economy.[8]

The research reported here fell somewhere between these two emphases. We shared the cultural and political ecological concerns to understand agency, intention and perception, and the political economic structures (see below) in which agency is embedded – but it was not ethnographic. Furthermore, our concern to say something comparative (across families and locations) about the effects of interventions on rural poverty and livelihood led us to focus on changes in asset bases over time and space. In that sense, we adopted an assets-based approach to livelihoods. Such frameworks focus on 'what the poor have, rather than what they do not have' (Moser 1998: 1) and understand livelihood strategies as the ways in which people gain access to these assets, combine them and transform them into livelihood outcomes (see Figure 8.1). In particular the following types of asset tend to be emphasised (Bebbington 1999):

- Human capital – the assets that one has as a consequence of one's body: knowledge, health, skills, etc.;
- Social capital – the assets that one has as a consequence of one's relationships with others and one's membership in organisations, and which also facilitate access to other resources;
- Produced capital – both physical assets (infrastructure, technology, livestock, seeds, etc.) and financial assets (money, working capital and assets easily converted into money);
- Natural capital – the quality and quantity of the natural resources to which one has access;
- Cultural capital – the resources and symbols that one has as a result of the social structures within which one is embedded.

In addition to having a broad view of the assets upon which people draw, the framework also has a wide view of what people pursue in their

---

[8] This bias towards rural applications of asset-based approaches to livelihoods is perhaps not surprising. Not only does it reflect the intellectual roots of such approaches (in farming systems research etc.), but it may also reflect the work that such approaches are made to do – in particular, they have been used to draw attention to the increasing importance of non-farm dimensions of rural life and economy, and to the (relatively) diminishing significance of natural resources in rural livelihoods (Escobál 2001; Reardon, Berdegué and Escobar 2001; Zoomers 1999). Indirectly, they have also been caught up in those discussions of agricultural extension and technology transfer that have implied – or directly argued – that for poorer rural households, public resources would be better spent on education (directly or via vouchers) than on agricultural extension (López 1995).

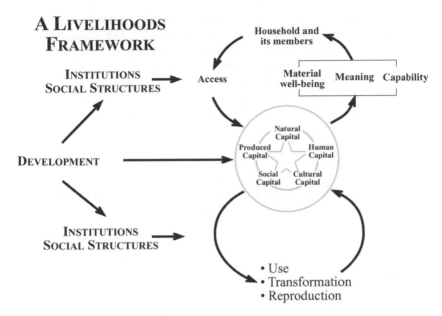

Figure 8.1 A livelihoods framework. From Bebbington 2004a. Reproduced by permission of Edward Arnold.

livelihoods – or, in another language, what they produce when they transform these assets. These frameworks thus work with a multi-dimensional view of poverty (Moser 1998) and aspiration (Appadurai 2004). The framework portrayed in Figure 8.1 conveys the notion that through their practices and strategies of asset management, people seek not only to generate material income (or income in kind), but also meaning and socio-political capabilities. There is thus an inherent relationship between livelihood and culture, and between livelihood and political capacity: livelihoods are in and of themselves meaningful, and a change or loss of livelihood possibilities necessarily implies cultural change. Likewise, a reworking of assets necessarily means a change in a person's ability to participate politically and in the concerns they will pursue in that political participation. Furthermore, just as livelihood trajectories and decisions have cultural and political consequences, they are also driven by cultural and political concerns.

As they combine their assets in pursuit of their objectives, it is supposed that people tend to pursue those livelihood strategies that: are the most consistent with the portfolio of assets that they control at that point in time; reflect both long-term aspirations and immediate needs; and seem the most viable given the opportunities and constraints of the circumstances within which they live. In such conceptions of livelihoods, it is important to introduce a time dimension[9] in the sense that people's livelihood practices at the present may differ from their strategies for the future, i.e. where people invest the majority of their time and effort now may not reflect their aspirations for the future. Indeed, livelihood strategies may work at two levels simultaneously, with people accessing and using the resources they need to meet immediate family needs, while also trying to build up those assets which, when accumulated over time, will allow them or their children to pursue a different sort of livelihood. An example is where rural families not only pursue agriculture to meet immediate needs, but are also investing in those assets that allow their children to gain education so that they can shift out of agriculture (and even out of the countryside). This 'capital switching' (Batterbury 2001) is a dynamic process that likely reflects what is happening (or is desired) in much of the countryside, but which agrarian (and at times essentialised) conceptions of the peasant/*campesino*[10] may not catch.

In emphasising the importance of *access* to resources, such frameworks also emphasise the ways in which broader social structures, and market, state and civil society institutions affect this access and people's abilities to transform, reproduce and accumulate their resources (see Figure 8.1). The influence of the state on livelihoods can be profound, and is exercised in many ways through: laws that influence who has access to resources; public policies and programmes that provide resources and influence market conditions; state-sanctioned violence that renders assets insecure and depresses local economies; levels of repression or democratisation that influence the relative inclination of more powerful social groups to steal the assets of the poor; and so on. The influences of racisms (Figueroa 2000), patriarchy (Moser 1998), and dominant notions of authority are equally significant. The politics of economic policy making – that privileges particular macro-economic strategies, sectors of the economy and regions over others – also has a critical influence on what people can do with their assets and on their long term livelihood aspirations. While a policy framework that does little to offset the stagnation of *campesino* agriculture might elicit forms of collective rural radicalism as a response, at an individual level, it is at least as likely to translate into family strategies that aim to lay the bases

---

[9] A point also made in the WeD Research Group: see for instance Bevan (2004b).

[10] *Campesino* can be taken to mean 'peasant', a family-based subsistence production unit. However, here we give it a broader meaning to refer to rural residents whose livelihoods are partly based on agriculture and whose identities are partly based on this link to rural areas. It is also taken to imply residents who tend to be income poor.

for children to leave – to leave agriculture, to leave the countryside and to leave economically depressed regions.

Of course, it is easier to state such joint concerns for agency and structure, assets and political economy, static and dynamic analysis, than it is to operationalise them. In this sense, livelihoods approaches suffer similar problems to structuration approaches to agency and structure (Giddens 1979, 1984) – that is at any one time they either bracket agency or bracket structure, but rarely explore how agency and structure co-produce each other. Furthermore, in contrast to those bodies of earlier work that emphasised the dependent nature of livelihoods, the more recent approaches noted above have tended to focus more on people's agency and less on questions of power, politics and violence. While for some authors this emphasis constituted a desire to seek more 'room for manoeuvre' than earlier approaches, it might be argued that too little attention has been paid to the more entrenched social and political relationships that structure what room is and is not available.

8.3   Livelihoods and asset management strategies in the Andes

The research reported here (see Bebbington 2004b, 2005; Bebbington, Hinojosa and Rojas 2002) traced the evolution over time of rural development strategies within aid chains linking Dutch nongovernmental aid and Andean NGOs, and their effects on livelihood possibilities of people living in the rural communities in which the NGOs worked.[11] Methods included focus groups, structured household interviews and semi-structured key informant interviews. To assess changes in assets, descriptive indicators were developed and grouped loosely into the five asset types noted above (Bebbington 1999, see Figure 8.1).[12] Families were asked to describe the changes in these assets over time, to discuss, in their own terms, the economic and socio-political consequences of these changes and to explain these changes. People's explanations were compared with those coming from key informants and other sources. This was very much an interpretive process – with no attempts at formalist explanations.

---

[11] The Dutch NGOs were Cordaid, Novib and Icco – referred to here as co-financing agencies (CFAs); the Peruvian NGOs studied in depth were CCAIJO, Asociación Arariwa and IAA-Canas; in Bolivia, research focused on the NGOs CIPCA, Qhana, IPTK and ACLO.

[12] This operationalisation of this framework (Bebbington 1999) bears interesting similarities to WeD's Resources And Needs Questionnaire (RANQ) which operates with five categories of resources: material, human, environmental, social and cultural.

Figure 8.2 Map of Peru and Bolivia

Work was conducted in twenty-five separate communities across seven municipalities in La Paz, Cusco, Potosí and Chuquisaca (see map in Figure 8.2). In all sites (except one, where resources were more constrained) we worked in two or three communities in which the NGO worked and a broadly comparable community in which the NGO did not operate. In the former type of community, interviews were conducted with families with different intensities of contact with the NGO (from intensive to no direct contact). These are all high-altitude areas with economies based historically on rain-fed agriculture and livestock. Levels of commercialisation vary among regions and households, with wealthier households and areas closer to roads having the more commercialised production systems.

Livelihood strategies

While it is risky to generalise about livelihood trends across the seven micro-regions studied, certain patterns were apparent in livelihood dynamics and the effects of the aid chain on them. The first is that most people (above all most women) are still primarily or significantly engaged in farming. This is so in different ways and for different reasons. Some families – those on the pathway of the capitalised family farm – are primarily farmers because this is part of their accumulation strategy. Others are because their survival strategy revolves around ensuring food security. Even those who are diversifying income sources still spend considerable time farming to secure the food needs of the family members living both in the countryside and in the city.

This continuing agricultural orientation is evident both in how people talk about themselves and in time allocation data showing that, especially in higher-altitude communities further from roads, men and women dedicate most of their time to crops and livestock. However, in communities closer to roads, men dedicate considerable time working outside the community as agricultural labourers and in non-agricultural activities. Time dedicated to non-agricultural activities has increased over the decade, and in lower-slope communities women are also beginning to dedicate time to non-agricultural work outside the community.

A second striking similarity across the cases is the extent to and complex ways in which families organise their resources, activities and time in order to enhance children's educational opportunities. Many families aimed to reduce the distance between themselves and quality schooling, in particular post-elementary schooling. Those with most resources do this by purchasing a small lot on which they build small shacks and then homes in primary urban centres offering greater educational opportunities. Those with somewhat fewer assets (though still far from the poorest) acquire land and lodging in lower-order urban centres with secondary schools. In other cases, people with fewer assets still aim to invest in particular social relationships so that their children can stay overnight with other people whose homes are closer to schools.

A complementary set of strategies has been to shift gender and generational roles within the family so as to facilitate school attendance. Adults do more and more of the pasturing of animals, freeing up time so that children – most strikingly, young girls – can attend school. As a result, some families appear to have smaller herds than previously, reflecting labour constraints on herd management deriving from the decision to keep children of both sexes in school.

While families give many reasons for this emphasis on human capital formation, parents' main concern is to ensure that their children have more opportunities than they themselves enjoyed. Many parents neither wanted nor expected their children to be *campesinos*.[13] Some also argued that investing in education constitutes a way of reducing pressure on natural capital. Parents were quite explicit that increasing their children's educational and thus employment options would mean that the farm could be passed on to just one or two children, reducing the rate and degree of subdivision of the property.

This reasoning relates to another pattern across the cases – the increasing pressure on natural resources. This pressure is both demographic – most communities registered stable or slightly increasing population levels, notwithstanding out-migration – and environmental – many families perceive that climate changes have increased erosion hazard. Responses to this pressure on natural capital vary depending on the resources at a family's disposal, its alternative options and the overall availability of land (cf. Turner and Brush 1987). Farmers' main responses have been to: expand the agricultural/pasture frontier and reduce fallow; intensify in those few cases where families have access to the means to do so; and to seek off-farm income sources (see also VMPPFM and Banco Mundial 1998). One community was explicitly discussing the possibility of an organised group migration to the humid lowlands of Quispicanchi. NGO responses to this pressure have revolved around agro-pastoral intensification, generally through promoting small-scale irrigation and stall-feeding of cattle. This option has been absorbed by families benefiting from direct NGO assistance, but, given the costs involved, has spread mostly among wealthier *campesinos*.

In this instance, it is not that there is a *desencuentro* between NGO models of intensification and what farmers would like to do about pressure on natural resources, but rather that the NGO response is affordable for only a minority, unless they receive the direct subsidy from the NGO (which the NGO can give to only a very few families). Other NGO responses (or non-responses) do reflect *desencuentros*. Most have promoted conservation measures – run-off ditches, slow-forming terraces and tree planting (each of the NGOs have done some of this). These have had far less success: tree failure has been high, maintenance of conservation measures poor and installation of terraces limited. On the other hand, only one of the NGOs has directly addressed family planning, in which (at least in Cusco, the only site where this question was pursued) there did appear to be interest among women. There are understandable reasons for this (it is a sensitive topic; it has been associated with heavy-handed government

---

[13] For a similar conclusion in Cusco see María Elena Garca, '"To be Quechua is to belong": Citizenship, Identity, and Intercultural Bilingual Education in Cuzco, Peru'. Ph.D dissertation, Brown University, Rhode Island, USA., 2000.

sterilisation programmes; and it is almost impossible for a Catholic Church-linked NGO to address): yet, the implication is that NGOs have not responded to felt needs of those women expressing a preference for smaller families and greater ability to control fertility, and to assure they can finish school before becoming a parent.

Combining the concern for education and this pressure on natural capital, while one might say that many livelihoods still depend on the *use* of natural capital, the asset in which families seem much more concerned to *invest* is human capital. Put another way, this implies that while current livelihood practices are still primarily agricultural, the medium- and long-term strategy of many households is to allocate resources in such a way as to help members escape from farming. One might also say that families are drawing down their natural capital assets out of necessity (cf. Bernstein 1979) and as part of a strategy of building up human capital across generations. This human capital is perceived to offer an 'escape' clause for children. It also increases the productivity of other assets, both in the present and in the future. In some communities, tangible capital assets appeared to have more impact on income among families who had greater stocks of human capital; these families then invested this income from tangible capital in their children's education. In this respect, synergies among particular sets of assets at a point in time can allow a family to accumulate specific types of asset over time and thus slowly shift the balance of their asset portfolio – in this case from natural to human capital.[14] Thus, while people *are* still mainly farmers, their goal is not always that they or their children continue being so. This objective (rather than current practice) goes a long way in determining people's relative propensity to invest in particular assets.

Finally, livelihood possibilities are differentiated among social and economic strata and so it is not only that overall access to and control over assets is socially differentiated – so also is the possibility of exploiting synergies among assets. Two points merit emphasis. First, a significant part of the rural population has no option but to continue farming because of their asset bases, age and gender (though they may hope that their children do not farm); another segment (those on the path towards capitalised family farming)[15] has the option and wants to farm; another segment (younger, married adults) may want to remain in the community, but not

---

[14] It is in recognition of these types of (context-specific) interactions among different resources that the WeD programme talks of resource profiles, in order to capture not just information on stocks that families control, but the particular interactions among those assets within given structural and location-specific conditions.

[15] The path to capitalised family farming in the Andes has been discussed by Lehmann (1986) and Llambi (1989), among others.

as farmers; and yet another segment (the young and single) is more inclined to leave the community altogether. NGO proposals have mainly addressed the conditions and aspirations of the second of these segments – leaving the first caught in agricultural marginalisation with little chance of prospering, and the latter two to develop their own options.

The second point is that – consistent with the findings of Reardon, Berdegué and Escobar (2001) – for the wealthy, livelihood diversification is a strategy of accumulation, while for the poor, it is one of survival. Furthermore, these two types of diversification are structurally related. In communities in the *altiplano* of La Paz, Bolivia, wealthier families who had built up large dairy farms deliberately created opportunities for their children to work in more profitable activities as tailors, builders or drivers in the city. This increased the need for non-family agricultural labour and so less wealthy *campesinos* from the community were employed.[16] Thus, in diversifying their own family strategies, they created employment opportunities allowing poor families to diversify *their* income sources. These two types of diversification are thus different parts of a larger process of increasing differentiation in the types of opportunities open to families. Thus, just as it is important to understand the synergies among assets, so it is important to understand the synergies among different families' livelihoods, both at a given point in time and across time.

Livelihood outcomes

Livelihood frameworks and the aid chains discussed in this study are alike in making the reasonable assumption that improvements in rural people's asset bases will translate into improvements in their wellbeing, and more specifically into their economic opportunities and human and socio-political capacities (empowerment for short). However, shifts in certain assets and asset-mixes are more likely than others to translate into such improvements. Political economic conditions, for instance, determine the relative productivity and security of different assets, and thus help determine which assets are more, and less, likely to contribute to overall improvement in livelihoods and wellbeing. Furthermore, how effective and sustainable such asset changes are in leading to enhanced wellbeing depends on the institutional and political economic contexts of rural livelihoods. This section comments on the extent to which

---

[16] It merits comment that such processes were among the core concerns of earlier literature on the peasantry and rural development (see Harriss 1982 and the *Journal of Peasant Studies*). Thus, even if *campesinista* views of the rural economy might have led to *desencuentros*, many of the concerns of this traditional peasant economy literature remain relevant for the analysis of contemporary rural dynamics.

certain changes in asset bases were perceived by *comuneros* (community leaders) as having translated into such improvements.

From assets to empowerment This research began with the informal hypothesis that the greatest impact of the aid chains studied would be on rural people's empowerment, manifested above all in the form of stronger, more visible and more influential social organisations. This was based on the view that the aid chains studied had long emphasised the political dimensions of development and the promotion of popular participation in political and economic processes. Yet, while we encountered spaces of some rural empowerment, these were rarely associated with NGO's politically oriented interventions.

The NGOs studied had certainly aimed to enhance social capital (though not using this language), primarily through supporting rural people's organisations, strengthening municipal governments and reducing the distance between them and rural citizens. Yet many respondents barely mentioned the role of supra-communal forms of organisation in their livelihoods. In one site in the Bolivian *altiplano*, people failed even to mention (let alone judge the relative significance of) the supra-communal organisation that one NGO had been supporting for many years, and at another site in the *altiplano*, where a different NGO worked, people appeared blissfully unaware that the NGO's main goal, and identity, was to foster empowerment: respondents saw it as a source of technology. In other cases, while respondents recognised NGO's attempts to strengthen supra-communal organisations, they were ambivalent about the effectiveness or relevance of this for their livelihoods. In one site (and reflecting a more generally held view in the region) respondents viewed the NGO's social capital building work as too influenced by party politics, and while some *campesino* leaders trained by the NGO had gained positions of authority in municipal government, this was rarely seen as generating benefits for communities. In another site, people questioned the representativeness and relevance of the departmental *campesino* federation that one of the NGOs had long supported and certainly doubted its effectiveness in opening up local development options.[17] In contrast to these supra-communal forms of social capital, community-level organisations consistently emerged as important in people's livelihoods, ensuring a degree of local political participation and representation.

---

[17] The federation remains one of the few significant departmental *campesino* federations in Peru. This might be deemed important in and of itself, even if the communities in which research was conducted were less convinced.

While organisations have been only modest sources of rural empowerment, changes in human capital were perceived as having contributed to people's sense of self and of power. Among the most valued changes identified by rural people in all communities were those related to improvements in human capital and human capabilities (cf. Sen 1997). Compared with a decade ago, people are healthier, have a broader view of the world, enjoy more (if still limited) options, and have greater self-confidence.[18] There is also an important gendered component here. In several of the communities, the suggestion was that over the last decade women had become more self-confident and assertive and gender relations had shifted somewhat. Even if women's participation in formal social organisations was still lower than that of men, it had increased. More telling is the extent to which girls' access to school (and adult women's concerns to acquire basic literacy skills) had increased.

The link between human capital and empowerment raises the issue of social capital again, for a number of families had tried to build social networks as a means of facilitating their children's access to (above all secondary) education. Building social capital thus had an important role to play in families' own search for empowerment – the form of social capital prioritised was, however, that of personalised networks and relations of reciprocity, rather than formal social organisations. A more general point, perhaps, is that what matters more than stocks of particular forms of capital are the types of synergies among them – synergies whose possibility depends on structural and contingent conditions. Assets and capitals must then be understood in context rather than discussed as having any meaningful existence or value out of context (cf. Bebbington 2002).

Assets and economic opportunities The extent to which asset accumulation has translated into enhanced economic opportunities for community members varies greatly. The translation is far more apparent in some regions (above all those with more buoyant agricultural economies) than others. It is also clearer for some families than others. Indeed, the most striking relationship across the sites is that those families best able to enhance their incomes have been those who have had most intense contact with NGOs – families who may well have been the most dynamic in the first place, a dynamism that drew the NGO to them, and them to the NGO. The net effect of this has been greater (real and perceived) socio-economic differentiation within all communities studied.

---

[18] At the centre of this improvement is the extension of basic social services – education, health, electricity, roads, etc. While some of the NGOs have played a role in this extension, it is primarily an effect of increased state provision of services.

The most significant, but also most socially concentrated increases in income have been among those families who have been the direct clients of NGO programmes supporting production. The financial and physical assets for dairy production systems transferred by NGOs in La Paz, for instance, have opened up new income opportunities for farmers. They allowed them to produce more milk for sale to the La Paz dairying plant and the income generated was then invested in further physical assets, as well as in children's education and start-up economic activities. The income deriving from increased potato production among farmers working with IPTK in Ravelo was translated into assets such as trucks and urban properties (themselves a bridgehead to help children gain access to secondary schools).

While NGO intervention helps explain this increase in assets, the translation of assets into income depends on the opportunities opened up (or closed) by other factors, above all the structure of the market. When prices have been higher and levels of demand stable, accumulation has occurred. Conversely, when markets have become depressed and unstable, the income effects of changes in asset bases have been greatly reduced. Where markets have been generally stagnant, the income effects of increased asset bases have been far more modest.

This asset accumulation among direct beneficiaries means that across a number of the cases intra-community socio-economic differentiation has increased, as is clear from a comparison of families' asset bases (Bebbington et al. 2002). This is most acutely the case where NGOs have provided significant subsidies to a necessarily small (because of the cost of the subsidies) number of families. Examples of such individually targeted subsidies include livestock, feedstalls, greenhouses, credit, sprinkler irrigation systems, potato seed, etc. It would be easy to explain such targeting of significant subsidies to a small number of families as simple clientelism or 'another failure of NGOs to understand the Andean community', but it also reflects pressures within international aid. Indeed, the tendency to provide subsidies to targeted and already better-endowed households has increased in recent years as NGOs feel the need to show visible impacts. While many NGOs have also provided group- and community-wide assets at the same time, the per capita significance of these is far smaller and does not offset the differentiating effect of significant household-level subsidies.

That socio-economic differentiation has increased in most cases is one point. How to interpret the phenomenon in terms of wellbeing is more complex. There is a tendency to automatically dismiss differentiation as undesirable, yet there may be good reason for NGOs to focus on more viable producers as these are the most able to respond to new productive options and the most able to take risks. Indeed, Peru and Bolivia desperately need rural economic growth, and focusing on a group within the peasantry that can become capitalised family farms can foster important and slightly more inclusive rural economic growth than that fostered by public policy. The effects of this on the wellbeing of others – and on collective senses of wellbeing – may, however, be negative. It is not only that others gain less, but also that they are aware of gaining less. This can further weaken community-wide solidarities and collective action. Meanwhile there was only limited evidence that asset accumulation among more 'viable' peasants had trickle-down benefits for poorer families. Such interventions reflected *encuentros* with one form of livelihood in these communities, but significant *desencuentros* with many other forms of livelihood.

8.4   Structural constraints on access

Livelihood frameworks emphasise the importance of access to and control of resources in determining livelihood possibilities. They also emphasise the importance of broader socio-economic structures (policies, institutions and relations of power) in determining the extent to which people are able to turn these resources into satisfying, stable and progressively 'better' lives, and to rework policies and institutions in order to improve the quantity and productivity of the resources to which they have access.

The interventions of the case study NGOs can be viewed as efforts to address problems of access directly. For those families able to participate directly in their programmes, they reduce barriers to access to irrigation, credit, knowledge, technology, etc. In some cases, their interventions also remove access constraints for people who do not benefit directly – for instance when these people learn from innovations of direct beneficiaries and incorporate this learning in their livelihoods.

However, most of the NGOs studied worked on enhancing access to resources directly. They have done less to tackle the structures and institutions that have a more general effect on families' access to resources and on the extent to which those resources translate into improved livelihood outcomes. Yet macro-level and structural barriers to rural people's access to resources are profound. These macro-barriers might be thought of as: infrastructural, institutional and political economic.

Broader *political economic and trade policy* barriers constituted the most serious political economic barrier to improved livelihoods – reducing rural peoples' access to markets and sometimes the overall value and productivity of their assets. In Ravelo, for instance, the cumulative effects of interventions improving potato production were greatly diminished after the mid 1990s when cheap potatoes from Argentina (and oversupply in Chuquisaca itself) brought prices down in the Sucre market. In the *altiplano* of La Paz, when multinational owners of the recently privatised dairy processing plant decided to close it during a rationalisation of its regional operations, market opportunities for farmers who for a decade had worked with NGOs on increasing milk production were dramatically reduced. In other words, global structures impinge on everyday livelihoods in all these sites, in ways that can be both enabling and highly constraining.

More generally, the stagnation of Andean regional economies constrained resource accessing possibilities, and weakly developed markets limited people's capacity to convert assets into livelihood outcomes. In Sopachuy, the unit value of many family assets appears to have decreased over the last decade, meaning that the accumulation of physical assets does not necessarily translate into realisable monetary accumulation – this all depends on the structural context in which that asset accumulation occurs.[19] In Cusco, the generally depressed regional and rural economy limits market possibilities. In each of these cases, any effects of interventions that increase local access to resources are overshadowed by these obstacles to market access or to the ability to convert tangible assets into income.

In a similar sense, the overall absence or weakness of *institutions* reduced access to resources in a way that small-scale interventions could do little to address. There were many examples of this phenomenon. Particularly acute was the weakness of state institutions to deliver education and health services. While the presence of state institutions had increased significantly during the last decade, the *quality* of education and health care was still very poor. This limits the quantity and quality of education and health care that families can access, requiring them to develop other strategies to access these services, often outside the community. This clearly weakens the long-term (sustainable) impact of these NGO asset-building programmes.

Among the most critical *infrastructural* barriers to access were those related to roads, electricity and water supply. Indeed, roads emerged as perhaps the most important determinant of local development possibilities. Where roads had been built, their construction was viewed by communities as one of the most critical moments in recent community history. Their building allowed trucks and ambulances to enter communities, facilitated access to markets, allowed people to bring in

---

[19] Cf. McGregor and Kebede, 'Resource profiles', 2003.

building materials to improve their houses, eased access to schools (especially secondary schools), etc. In cases where NGOs had helped build the road, this had largely been in order to facilitate other elements of their programme, yet communities seemed to view the roads as more important than these other activities.

In those cases where electricity had been installed, it was also viewed as one of the most important changes in the community in the decade. Lack of electricity is also a serious barrier to taking full advantage of educational and organisational resources: light enables evening study and evening meetings, and electricity can facilitate the emergence of small family enterprises. The relative value of electricity was reflected in one community where *comuneros* working on an NGO's natural resource conservation activities used the payment they received to cover the cost of their contributions for an electricity connection. Meanwhile the maintenance of the conservation measures has been poor.

While a number of the NGOs have worked on installing micro-irrigation systems, these have had the effect of better using existing water resources (at least for a small group of families in the communities), but do not resolve problems of overall water availability, which is the more significant constraint on access. None of the case study NGOs had addressed the macro-barrier to water access. Resolving infrastructural barriers to access such as these is a less glamorous aspect of enhancing people's wellbeing and is actively resisted as a hallmark of modernisation projects. Still, in the communities studied during this research, these were deemed important problems that, if resolved, would enhance the impact of other interventions and bring other multiplier effects.

Given the significant effect of such structural limits on access to and the productivity of resources, it is not surprising that the greatest impacts of smaller-scale NGO interventions occurred where such macro-constraints to access have not been as severe. The clearest case of this was that of dairying in the Bolivian *altiplano* (up until the privatisation of the processing plants). In this case, there was a stable market created by public policy (and then transferred to the private sector); there was good road infrastructure built by the state and bilaterally funded dairy development programmes; and there had been targeted interventions increasing the ability of specific families to negotiate their market relations and increase the productivity of their other land and human assets. Under circumstances such as these, one can speak of synergies between more favourable policy and economic contexts, favourable conditions of basic service and infrastructure provision, and specific NGO interventions. In other cases, such synergies are rarer.

These observations clearly have implications for the roles that NGOs might play in addressing macro-barriers to access. Some of the NGOs had engaged in advocacy and lobbying for policy change. However, their lobbying has tended to be on themes such as bilingual education, educational reform, land and territory, etc. While obviously important topics, the implication is that there is also a quite different terrain in which lobbying is needed: on infrastructural investment policy; on the future of the dairy sector in Bolivia; on the future of the alpaca sector in Peru; on sector-specific trade policies, and so on. Yet these NGOs have done very little in this regard. This is a serious gap. On the one hand it is a reflection that – notwithstanding their intentions – these NGOs have not scaled up their experiments with production systems into proposals for policy change. More fundamentally, it means that the NGOs have at best removed micro-barriers to access while macro-barriers limiting access to and transformation of assets have remained in place and often become more severe.

A surprisingly consistent theme in each of the case studies is the perception of environmental and climatic change. In almost every community, people perceived a change in climate, with more extreme storms and winds, and an overall decline in rainfall and more general water availability. The perception is that these changes have led to increased soil degradation and increased drought hazard (see also VMPPFM Banco Mundial 1998). There is a need for caution before accepting perception as truth – research in Tarija has suggested that perceptions far exceed geomorphological estimations of either soil erosion or overgrazing (Beck and Preston 2001; Preston 1998; Preston, Macklin and Warburton 1997). Still, if it is the case that climate is changing, and if the effect of this is to increase drought, climatic hazard and erosion proneness, then this intensifies some of the most critical constraints on livelihoods in the region. To the extent that much *campesino* agriculture is constrained by ecological disadvantage,[20] then such climatic stress only aggravates the problem of fostering agriculturally based livelihoods. It also makes interventions aimed at increasing water availability and managing run-off from high magnitude storms that much more relevant.

---

[20] 'When all is said and done, one can't change environmental limitations', commented one project official quoted by van Niekerk, in 'La cooperación internacional y las polticas públicas: el caso de las zonas andinas de altura de Bolivia', paper presented at the Seminario Internacional sobre Estrategias Campesinas, Sucre, Bolivia, 3–4 April 1997.

8.5   Livelihoods and NGO interventions: encuentros and desencuentros

Several recent studies of livelihoods in the Andes have talked of a '*desencuentro*' between rural livelihood strategies and project interventions (le Grand 1998a, 1998b; Zoomers 1998; see also van Niekerk[21]). At their core, such studies suggest two main problems. One is that the selection of project sites, contents and ways of working are not necessarily based on a prior analysis of priorities and current conditions in the rural economy; instead they are driven by institutional concerns, pre-existing networks of contacts, existing human resource capabilities of the institutions, pre-existing theoretical commitments, etc.

A second and related claim of these studies is that interventions have often been based on misconceptions of contemporary rural livelihoods. In the words of another study of interventions in highland Peru and Bolivia, 'NGOs' development proposals are insufficiently based in a thorough understanding of *campesinos*' strategies for using time and managing natural resources – this reduces the effectiveness of their programmes' (de Zeeuw, Baumeister, Kolmans and Rens 1994: 132). A frequent misconception is to view rural livelihoods as essentially agricultural and therefore geographically static, when they are often geographically mobile and based on multiple income sources and activities, pursued in a range of locations (Zoomers 1998, 1999). This 'agro-centric' view of livelihoods leads to *desencuentros* between the geographical structure of project interventions that tend to be based on one delimited site (community, municipality, watershed, etc.), and the geographical structure of livelihoods that are often discontiguous and combine activities within the community and watershed with others in distant rural and urban locations. Our study suggests a similar phenomenon. All the aid chains reviewed included activities related to agriculture, livestock or natural resource management. They all worked in geographically bounded areas, and in all these areas, the livelihoods of many families included important economic and social activities in other locations.

As a consequence, projects and families appear to differ in the assets that they prioritise. Projects have spent considerable resources investing in tangible assets, while families also invest much of their effort in building up human and social capital (in the form of social networks). In Laja, for instance, families estimated that they spent from 25 per cent to 30 per cent of their income on their children's education in order to

[21] *Ibid.*

prepare them for a non-agricultural future. Many parents have also invested in their own human capital – particularly by participating in literacy programmes. Literacy – and education more generally – are viewed as crucial for empowerment and advancement, and to reduce mistreatment when working and living as migrants in other areas.

Another *desencuentro* between interventions and communities – particularly in the first half of the decade – was derived from NGOs' conceptions of community economic organisation and culture. Reflecting the tradition of community studies and community development in the Andes (Degregori 2000), all the NGOs studied had at some point promoted collective production. These initiatives almost all failed, reflecting a misperception of the organisation of production in many communities. The community has rarely governed production, and while it has governed resource management (land, water, pasture), in all the case studies, this role is also under pressure as *comuneros* want ever more private tenure in natural resources. The community continues to play an important role in providing collective assets and NGOs *have* been able to build on this by mobilising communal labour for building infrastructure. However, because, in many cases, this infrastructure has been a group asset open to some rather than a collective asset open to all, this has sometimes generated dissatisfaction and tensions among those *comuneros* who do not benefit. These problems reflect a related 'misconception' – the continuing tendency of these NGOs to understate or skate over the implications of social differentiation within the community (de Zeeuw *et al.*, 1994). This has meant that the productive options promoted within aid chains have tended to be relevant for the more 'viable' – i.e. wealthier – families, but not for the livelihoods of poorer people. As a result, interventions seem to have fostered yet further differentiation. *Desencuentros* in intervention can thus have significant effects in the dynamics of agrarian structure.

Such reflections lead to a larger, more strategic question – how far ought actors within the aid chain to pursue strategies that prioritise direct support to families' asset building strategies, and how far ought they to direct their attention to the structures and institutions that govern overall patterns of access to resources in Peru and Bolivia?[22] A related question is whether livelihoods frameworks – at least those that focus attention on asset management strategies – have the effect of encouraging intervention strategies to focus on direct asset building rather than

---

[22] A question that has taken on new meaning for the Dutch co-financing agencies as they endeavour to rethink their own roles within the aid chain.

on the social and political economic arrangements that do so much to structure overall patterns of wellbeing. This chapter began by arguing that livelihoods approaches do not need to divert attention from these structural questions, and the research reported here suggests that such approaches can be used to demonstrate that grassroots asset-building strategies are only a small part of poverty alleviation and the enhancement of wellbeing. It has also argued that a livelihoods lens *can* help illuminate the logics inhering in popular strategies, as well as the ways they are embedded in broader sets of social and economic relationships (and thus they can help work across scales of analysis: cf. Gough and McGregor 2004). However, at the very least, the research makes palpably clear the dangers inherent in focusing too much on assets and too little on political economy, too much on popular agency and too little on social structure.

9 Poverty and exclusion, resources and relationships: theorising the links between economic and social development

James Copestake

9.1 Introduction

Debates about development hinge in no small measure on the importance people attach to material resources versus social relationships, both as ends and as means. These are particularly evident when one person or group seeks to help another. A food transfer, for example, can be condemned as patronage or applauded as social protection, depending upon the social and symbolic compromises bundled up with it. Development is never as simple as it seems, and the full significance of any one action can only be assessed as part of a wider analysis of how poverty and other welfare outcomes are produced in a particular time and place. While ultimately interested in the general question of how best to identify opportunities (public and private) for action to reduce poverty, the chapter is more modest in scope. Its method is to summarise one particular approach to structural analysis of poverty (social exclusion theory as elaborated by the Peruvian economist Adolfo Figueroa) and to subject it to constructive criticism. In so doing, it seeks to contribute towards general understanding of how inventories of resource endowments are only as useful as the accompanying analysis of exclusionary/inclusionary processes arising from their use.

There is a strong Latin American tradition – embracing dependency theory, structuralism, liberation theology, Freirian pedagogy and post-developmentalism – of emphasising the importance of relational dimensions of development alongside the material. In a study sponsored by the International Labour Organization, Figueroa, Altamirano and Sulmont (2001) add to this tradition by applying the concept of social exclusion to the Peruvian context. They start by classifying people according to their holdings of human, material, political and cultural resources. They then

This chapter has benefited from numerous criticisms of earlier drafts, particularly those of Allister McGregor, although I cannot claim to have done justice to them all.

199

explore how social exclusion processes affect the way resources are used to produce welfare outcomes in three domains: cultural, political and economic. Cultural exclusion – on racial and ethno-linguistic lines – is particularly important in Peru, they argue, providing the basis for a horizontal/hierarchical stratification of social networks. These networks in turn underpin political exclusion of non-native Spanish speakers from adequate social protection and formal education, and this in turn reinforces economic exclusion, particularly in the labour market.

Figueroa (2001a, 2001b, 2003) extends this approach into a more formal and general theory of economic development. Section 9.2 presents a non-technical summary of how one part of this theory (the *sigma* society model) explains persistent inequality and relative poverty as a low-level equilibrium trap. The *sigma* model's theoretical originality rests in demonstrating that economic dualism can be endogenous to a general equilibrium model that assumes all actors are rational and self-interested in pursuit of their material interests. As an exercise in positivist analysis, its main empirical claim is to be able to explain the persistence of high levels of inequality not only in Peru but in several Latin American countries and perhaps beyond. As such, the model provides a counter to the optimistic assumption of most (particularly western) development economists that the onslaught of capitalism inevitably erodes economic dualism and other forms of market segmentation, and that economic development can usefully be analysed independently of social development. This may seem a rather pessimistic finding, but it can also be viewed more constructively as a way of highlighting the extent to which economic growth and inequality reduction are dependent upon cultural and political mobilisation, not least through advocacy of human rights. This is in stark opposition to the more common assumption of economists that improved human rights are more likely to *follow* economic development than to be a *precondition* for it.

Section 9.3 looks more critically at Figueroa's *sigma* model. Part of the problem with it is that, in rising to economists' norms of rigour, it introduces simplifying assumptions that put off other social scientists. The deterministic exposition (linked to the ambition to turn the argument into a mathematically precise and rigorous model) also appears to rule out potentially important possibilities for change. I argue that there is scope for recasting the model within a broader and more open *inclusion/exclusion framework*. This partially represents a reversion to the original exposition of Figueroa *et al.* (2001). However, some of the criticisms made of the *sigma* model apply to this chapter too.

Section 9.4 considers briefly the potential relevance of an inclusion/exclusion approach to development policy and practice. I argue that its more negative and realistic flavour is helpful in identifying potential 'pressure points' and 'drivers of change' that take into account system interests of others and the development agencies' own limitations. A simple diagrammatic model is presented to emphasise these points. More specifically, I argue that the *sigma* model, for all its limitations, indicates how the intellectual basis for a human-rights based approach to development can be grounded not only in moral philosophy but also in a hard-headed analysis of how to confront key structural constraints to economic progress.

9.2   Figueroa's 'sigma economy' model of social exclusion

In addition to explaining the persistence of high rates of inequality within some countries, Figueroa (2001a, 2001b, 2003) is also concerned to explain the slow pace of convergence of per capita income between countries. To this end, he develops three distinct models of capitalism at the country level. The *epsilon* economy has homogeneous skilled labour, though unemployment persists as a device for disciplining workers (Shapiro and Stiglitz 1984). The *omega* economy is characterised by excess labour supply, divided between direct employment by capitalists, unemployed and self-employment in an informal sector with limited access to financial services. The *sigma* economy has two types of labour: y-workers are skilled, and divided among the same three activities as workers in the *omega* economy. Z-workers, in contrast, lack the skills to secure high-productivity employment and can secure income only through self-employment, and in generally lower productivity activities than y-workers due to their lack of skills (see Figure 9.1). Those y-workers unable to find employment in the high-productivity sector choose either to remain unemployed or opt for self-employment. Subsistence employment of z-workers is completely separate.

The main emphasis in this chapter is on the *sigma* model because it is the most elaborate of the three, and the one that Figueroa argues is consistent with the persistence of inequality in Peru and countries with a similar colonial past. Two questions immediately arise. First, what prevents z-workers from acquiring skills and thus becoming y-workers? In other words, what stops the *sigma* economy from transforming into an *omega* economy? Second, what prevents capital accumulation proceeding to the point at which all y-workers are either unemployed or employed in high-productivity activities? In other words, what prevents the *omega* economy from transforming into an *epsilon* economy?

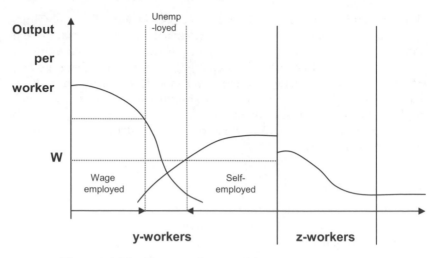

Figure 9.1 The Figueroa *sigma* model

To answer these questions it is first necessary to provide a fuller description of the *sigma* economy model. This is first an exercise in static equilibrium: establishing the distribution of employment and income for a given distribution of assets, and set of goals. Dynamics of economic development are then explored by considering how this equilibrium changes in line with capital accumulation, as well as various exogenous shocks, such as a rise in the money supply and trade liberalisation. The economy comprises four 'stakeholder' groups: capitalists, politicians, y-workers (skilled labour) and z-workers (unskilled labour). Capitalists seek profits. To do so they are willing to take risks, so long as these do not expose them to such large losses that they could cease to belong to the capitalist class. Politicians seek to maximise political power, and the utility of workers is positively related to income and negatively to the drudgery of labour. Capitalists, self-employed y-workers and self-employed z-workers all produce a standard good, B. In other words, the *sigma* model ignores specialisation in production.

There are three types of economic asset: physical capital, skilled human capital and unskilled human capital. There are also two kinds of social asset: political capital and cultural capital. The former consists of influence over government powers to tax, to spend and to regulate. The latter consists mainly of hierarchically ordered social networks through which political capital is mobilised, protected and used. Cultural capital is strongly linked to race, ethnicity and language – personal attributes that change over time, but cannot easily be traded or transferred to others.

The initial endowment of social and political assets is taken to be the outcome of a historical or foundational shock, typically colonial incorporation (on racial lines) into global capitalism. Capitalists own most physical capital and derive most of their income from profits. They are also rich in political and cultural capital. Y-workers own little physical capital, but are skilled. Their endowment of political and cultural capital is less than that of capitalists, but greater than that of z-workers, who have the least human, physical, political and cultural capital.

Static equilibrium positions of each group of stakeholders are explored in two stages. First, Figueroa reviews what he calls *basic* markets for labour, capital and insurance. Second, he considers the quasi-market for power, with politicians acting as power brokers between other stakeholders. In the labour market, the private marginal cost of training z-workers exceeds the private marginal benefits to capitalists. As a result they are excluded from wage employment, and restricted only to self-employment at relatively low levels of productivity. Y-workers face three possibilities, as already briefly discussed and as illustrated by the diagram. Their first preference is to work for capitalists at an efficiency wage, W, that is set at a premium over and above that which would clear the market for y-workers. Second, they can be self-employed and earn income equal to their marginal product, subject to their limited access to capital and to diminishing returns. Third, they can be unemployed but available to work for capitalists. Equilibrium in the market for y-workers is set by the condition that W multiplied by the probability of getting a job must be equal to the marginal product of y-labour in self-employment.

Z-workers are self-employed and produce B, but less efficiently and also subject to diminishing marginal returns. They are prevented from transforming into y-workers principally by lack of education (see below), but also by exclusion from opportunities for learning-by-doing through employment within the capitalist sector and the small businesses of y-workers. Migration, as formalised in the Harris–Todaro model is concerned with rural–urban and inter-sector movement. But the dualism in the *sigma* model is primarily social not geographical. Z-workers can move to the cities and from agriculture to services in large numbers, but they still face huge barriers to acquiring skilled employment – entry barriers that may be shored up by y-workers as fast as z-workers pull them down.[1]

---

[1] Even if z-workers succeed in educating themselves and improving their skills, y-workers raise the barriers by educating themselves even more. Thus the model is more potent in explaining the reproduction of relative poverty than absolute poverty.

Table 9.1 *Stakeholder analysis of options for reducing economic exclusion*

	Provide free education	Provide subsidised financial services	Provide social protection
Z-workers		Z-workers would be the main beneficiary in each case. But Figueroa emphasises their inability to turn strength of numbers into political capital for at least two reasons. First, poverty limits their incentive to do anything other than meet immediate material needs (Maslow 1970). Second, they face the standard collective action problem: rather than initiate struggle for access to resources, it is rational to free-ride on the efforts of others to do so (Lichbach 1998; Olson 1965).	
Y-workers	Opposition due to fiscal cost, plus fear of seeing their own employment opportunities weakened (a labour aristocracy argument)	Support, to the extent that this could strengthen their prospects for self-employment and low-level capital accumulation, but opposition from those for whom benefits are likely to be more than offset by the fiscal cost	
Capitalists	Support to the extent that there are skill shortages, and W can be lowered by increasing the supply of skilled labour	Opposition to the extent that increased self-employment raises the opportunity cost of labour, hence W, and reduces profits; for some it may also undermine their powers of patronage	

Turning to the capital market, y- and z-workers with small businesses have vastly inferior access to credit because their capacity to service debts relative to the fixed costs of providing them is small, and this greatly reduces risk-adjusted net returns to private sector suppliers. They also have less means and opportunity to save. Segmentation of the formal insurance market is also critically important. Capitalists have sufficient wealth and income to be able to at least partially insure against the failure of risky investments. As a result they not only invest more, but can also commit to high-risk, high-return investments. Self-employed workers, in contrast, are limited in their ability to make risky investments by fear of losing the little physical capital they have. Their lack of access to financial services helps to explain why output from self-employment is less productive than in capitalist wage employment. Lower productivity of z-workers can also be explained partially by lack of physical capital as well as by inferior skills.

Given this exclusion from capitalist-controlled credit and insurance markets, both y- and z-workers seek their own personalised, informal and inter-linked forms of credit and security. These institutions are an effective form of collective social protection, given lack of access to other institutions, but rules of 'reciprocity and redistribution' limit the scope for individual accumulation (Figueroa 2001b). The nature of this financial dualism is complex, but is reinforced by the distribution of cultural assets. These embed z-workers more firmly in a micro-economy dominated by non-market exchange rules, supported by some patronage from y-workers.[2] The cultural capital of y-workers enables them to access a mixture of mutual forms of social protection and patronage from capitalists and government.

Why does the government fail to raise taxes from the rich in order to address the market failures identified above? A simple (substantivist) explanation is that they may be inhibited by ethnic prejudice towards the subaltern group (Lewis 1985). However, Figueroa is interested in explaining such a decision also in terms of rational material self-interest. There are three policy propositions to consider. First, government could provide free education so as to turn unskilled workers into skilled workers. Second, they could subsidise financial services. Third, they could provide a social protection system. Table 19.1 takes a first look at each of these policy propositions from the perspective of each stakeholder.

Z-workers should benefit from political intervention in each market. However, Figueroa suggests that their ability to bring mass support to

---

[2] The latter corresponds to what Wood (2003) refers to as the Faustian bargain of the poor: security at the expense of autonomy.

bear on politicians is weakened by preoccupation with material needs combined with a lack of incentives on the part of any individual to lead such a movement. In the case of education, they also face opposition led by those y-workers most likely to face competition from an erosion of education as a barrier to entry into skilled jobs. In the case of financial services and social protection, opposition is led by capitalists fearful of a resulting rise in the opportunity cost of skilled labour and hence W. Both groups are better endowed than z-workers with the political and cultural resources to ensure politicians respond to their wishes. International capitalists can also threaten politicians with disinvestment if political intervention demands too much on behalf of workers. These arguments suggest formidable political obstacles to any government programme to address social and economic exclusion.

Moving from comparative statics to dynamics, Figueroa assumes that the profits of capitalists are all reinvested in the following period, and that they are more than sufficient to offset capital depreciation. The increase in the capital stock invested in high-productivity activities is likely to be further augmented by technological progress. The resulting economic growth has no effect on z-workers, but y-workers benefit from increased wage employment. Their wages also rise as excess skilled labour supply is absorbed, and technical progress may also raise the efficiency wage premium. On the other hand, this effect may be delayed by displacement of self-employed y-workers (a Ricardian machinery effect). The overall effect on income inequality is indeterminate, depending on whether the 'enrichment and enlargement effects' on the income share of y-workers outweighs the falling income share of z-workers (cf. Fields 1980: 30).

Political reactions to these changes in income distribution cannot be predicted without more detailed specification and analysis of particular contexts. But what even this simple analysis illustrates is how relative income changes of any kind are a threat to the social order. This argument establishes a potentially powerful negative feedback loop: capitalist growth disturbs income distribution; this upsets the political order and undermines the confidence of capitalist investors; hence capital accumulation dries up. A key question is then whether govern-ments can sustain economic growth by mitigating the destabilising effects of induced changes in income distribution. An even more searching question is why political elites in some countries have been more successful in developing political institutions for reducing inequality, while others have more often resorted to frequently violent forms of repression (Bardhan 2001; Gough and Wood 2004; North 1990; Powelson 1997).

This line of argument runs counter to the more common assumption that capitalist growth is stabilising precisely because it creates new jobs. A possible explanation for this is that many workers perceive themselves to be excluded from securing those new jobs. Hirschman's (1973) 'tunnel effect' argument (that people will tolerate temporary inequality so long as they believe that their turn is about to follow) cuts no ice. On the other hand, government may have some discretion to alter fiscal and spending policies in response. Capitalists should accept higher taxes to pay for actions to reduce cultural, political and hence economic exclusion of z-workers if this reduces political instability, as well as reducing skilled labour shortages. However, y-workers' support for continued capital accumulation and job creation will eventually disappear if the price of this is a policy regime that undermines their cultural, political and labour market privileges.

This is a delicate balance, and Figueroa adds a final twist by advancing a new political economy explanation for doubting the ability of politicians to manage it. The reaction to social and economic exclusion in richer societies, he notes (following Okun 1975) is a political process of establishment of universal rights. But this is not necessarily an effective way for politicians in a *sigma* economy to maximise power. First, no credit is given to those who deliver them, since a right is, by definition, an entitlement, not a gift. Second, universal provision limits powers of patronage. Third, rights are not easily reversed. Other strategies include restricting access to information about the process of government (hiding costs) and repression.[3]

In sum, the model presents a profoundly pessimistic analysis of an inegalitarian development path that is consistent with the self-interested actions of the main domestic actors. Both z-workers and capitalists would benefit from labour market integration. But in isolation from each other – and perhaps even if they could form an improbable alliance – they lack the political resources to force the pace of integration in the face of resistance from y-workers and government. Figueroa asks whether development agencies might help to overcome these collective action problems. If the main issue was one of income or asset redistribution then this might, he suggests, be the case. But reflecting on the historical failure of land reform to transform *sigma* economies in Latin America, he observes that the key battles have to be fought in sensitive cultural and political domains where external support can be counterproductive. There is also, of course, the

---

[3] The argument presented here ignores the importance (positive and negative) of external forces in moulding political culture. But the key point being made is that local economic incentives cannot be relied upon on their own to bring about a fall in inequality.

issue of how to model the incentives of the intervening development agencies themselves.

9.3   An assessment of the theory

For economists, the *sigma* model's theoretical originality rests in demonstrating that dualism can be endogenous to a general equilibrium model based on the assumption that all actors are rational and self-interested in pursuit of their material interests. As an exercise in positivism, its main empirical claim is to be consistent with the persistence of high levels of inequality in several Latin American countries. As such, the model provides a counter to the tendency of most (particularly western) development economists to assume that the onslaught of capitalism will inevitably erode segmentation of the labour market, and that the resulting process of economic development can usefully be analysed in isolation from cultural and political relationships and changes.

If labour market dualism is primarily geographical and sectoral (as most theories of economic development since Fei and Ranis assume) then it can be eroded by migration and by investment in improved transport and communication. Early attempts to construct a more detailed explanation of 'an immutable economic dualism' (Boeke 1942) were undermined by the criticism that they ultimately rested on questionable empirical evidence of the resilience of non-capitalist values in the traditional sector (Higgins 1956). In contrast, Figueroa's model of persistent dualism rests on a universal application of orthodox economic assumptions of methodological individualism (i.e. rational pursuit of individual utility). The historical creation of a highly unequal capitalist society is a necessary condition for the model. But the *persistence* of dualism becomes endogenous or a *consequence* of exclusion rather than its prime determinant.[4] Hence Figueroa helps to fill a gap noted by Kanbur and McIntosh (1989: 119), who observed that 'there are non-dual economy models of growth but there are no models which treat factor immobility and asymmetry as endogenous, and, hence, there are no models which analyse the path of dualism itself. This is clearly a major area for further research'.

---

[4] This does not contradict the view that race is a core problem of development in Latin America and elsewhere. The point is that racial and ethnic differences (and indeed gender differences too) are perpetuated not only by cultural inertia but by a combination of resource distribution and the constrained material self-interest of each group. A major strength of this theory is that it explains persistent inequality even when lines of ethnic division are themselves fluid.

A second important feature of Figueroa's model is that segmentation (of the financial market as well as the labour market) is linked back to endogenous inequalities of political power between different social groups. Members of these groups actively invest in status differences and cultural barriers to defend these unequal power relations. Thus social development, such as promoting good governance or building social movements in support of an extension of social and economic rights, becomes a precondition for economic development, rather than part of some parallel and distinct development policy agenda. In contrast, economists have tended to argue the other way around: that economic development (particularly job creation) is a precondition for social development. Having suggested a low-level equilibrium trap for the economy that can only be broken by political struggle, Figueroa then uses 'rational choice' political economy arguments to explain why he thinks this is unlikely.

While Figueroa's precise but narrow *sigma* model specification of social exclusion theory renders it more accessible and challenging to economic theorists, it risks at the same time alienating other social scientists and development practitioners. For example, by emphasising the way variation in incentives to collective action for different groups perpetuates cultural, political and economic dualism, the model can be criticised for neglecting opportunities for individual upward social mobility through learning-by-doing and parallel development of informal networks.[5] This serves as a reminder that the *sigma* model is partially prevented from evolving into the *omega* and ultimately the *epsilon* model by the persistence of population growth as a mechanism for replenishing the number of z-workers and by the limited labour absorption that results from highly capital-intensive growth in the capitalist sector. But social (especially gender) relationships, which are exogenous to his theory, are again possibly more important factors behind fertility than economic factors (such as education, job prospects and potential returns to children) which are endogenous to the theory.

One way to re-emphasise the potential wider relevance of the social exclusion thinking behind Figueroa's theories, without at the same time downplaying the importance of relationships relative to material resources, would be to regard it as just one relatively narrow theoretical

---

[5] There is a strong analogy here with the 'Ricardian ladder' theory of dynamic comparative advantage. To be sure, some social groups (countries) succeed in graduating to higher productivity activities. But their very success can result in these forms of employment (sectors) becoming more competitive and therefore less remunerative. Meanwhile higher-status groups (richer countries) have graduated into new fields that offer still higher returns. Thus absolute growth is possible, but inequality is maintained.

development of a wider but still distinct exclusion/inclusion approach to thinking about development. The remainder of this section advances six arguments for adopting such a position. These constructive criticisms of Figueroa's general theories in part hark back to the original paper he jointly wrote on social exclusion (Figueroa *et al.* 2001). However, this paper also can be criticised for being too narrow in its discussion of the way unequal access to multiple resources is reproduced.

The first argument for a broader inclusion/exclusion framework is partially but not entirely semantic. Exclusion of some people, by definition, entails privileged inclusion of others: elite business associations, and rent-extracting coalitions of politicians and labour aristocracies on the one side; local and low-cost forms of natural resource management and reciprocal forms of social protection on the other. While most people are forced to commit to one 'club' or another, the ability of others to establish intermediate status, to sustain multiple cultural performances, and to broker between groups is also importantly moulded by their inherited resource endowments.

Second, and more fundamentally, the term social exclusion suggests that inclusion is always a good thing, whereas it can of course also be ugly and exploitative. One way of addressing this criticism is to emphasise how coercive *inclusion* in the economic sphere arises precisely because it is embedded in forms of *exclusion* in the political and cultural spheres. Thus a wider inclusion/exclusion framework has no difficulty in dealing with the concept 'adverse incorporation' and other criticisms of social exclusion theory that have emanated particularly from South Asia (Gough and Wood 2004), but also echo much earlier discussion of internal colonialism and inclusive dependency in Latin America. Likewise, political inclusion in the form of patron–client relations can be harmful to the extent that it is embedded in status inequality (cultural exclusion) and/or economic inequality (economic exclusion).

Third, an expanded inclusion/exclusion framework could also easily accommodate more complex and fluid analysis of social identity and networking than that built into the *sigma* model. Language is only one indicator of racial and class divisions defending different and overlapping degrees of market access, political influence and social protection (Altamirano, Copestake, Figueroa and Wright 2004). For example, it is obvious that not all Andean regions are equally impoverished (Bebbington 1997), nor all peasant farmers within them. A broader framework could also accommodate the existence of skill acquisition through learning-by-doing and hence some upward mobility in the labour market. A key question is then whether the effect of such mobility on relative wages and hence inequality is sufficient to offset population growth, and the continuous erection and fortification of market barriers.

Fourth, while Figueroa's assumption of the limited scope for collective and especially political action of subordinate groups (and of the responsiveness to them of politicians) serves as warning against populist wishful thinking, it is obviously also very restrictive and can usefully be challenged. One reason for this is to accommodate the growing strength of indigenous movements in Latin America, fuelled in part by external alliances and an appropriation of the language of rights – sufficient even to attract the attention of *The Economist* (2004). More generally, an overly narrow rational choice approach to analysing politics and the state risks understating the influence of leadership, culture, popular resistance and the unexpected on political processes and outcomes, as readily acknowledged by institutional economists such as North (1990) and Powelson (1997).[6]

A fifth argument concerns the nature of wellbeing. Like Marx and most economists, Figueroa's model emphasised the primacy of material wealth.[7] The *sigma* model highlights cultural and political relationships as the means to improving material relations and hence material outcomes. However, it is not hard to broaden the framework to allow for the intrinsic as well as instrumental worth of material, cultural and political relations, as discussed at length elsewhere in this book. Support in doing so comes from the various attempts to construct a universal theory of wellbeing. Thus for Doyal and Gough (1991) primary universal needs are both material (capability) and relational (autonomy). Likewise, self-determination theory emphasises not only competence, but also *two* relationship variables – relatedness and autonomy (see Ryan, this volume).[8]

A sixth argument for a wider framework is that actions cannot be classified unambiguously as belonging to distinct cultural, political and economic spheres. Rather, most activities simultaneously have

---

[6] Barrantes and Iguiniz (2004: 145) also make this point:
'Figueroa is very pessimistic about the political possibilities for reducing social exclusion. Despite this it remains necessary to study the characteristics of excluded groups and the means by which they remedy their position.'

[7] Wealth in turn generates not only income, but also freedom (from enforced wage labour, for example).

[8] The universality of autonomy, particularly its significance in more collectivist cultures, remains a matter of debate, even if it is defined narrowly as freedom from coercion. Part of the controversy can perhaps be attributed to the western tradition that *belonging* (or relatedness) is symbolically affirmed through social recognition of individual action, which requires individual autonomy. This issue is not central to the argument of this note, since it seeks only to emphasise the independent importance of relationships (whether autonomous or based on belonging) and resources.

consequences in all three (see White and Ellison, this volume) Indeed, classifying activities into spheres is potentially dangerous in the way it appears to sanction blinkered discipline-specific analysis over integrated analysis. To gain access to credit by joining a village bank entails entering into a complex set of social relationships. To intervene in the material domain by providing food aid, for example, without appraising the political and cultural aspects of the act is likely to have unanticipated and potentially counterproductive effects. These may indeed be so harmful as to render such narrowly conceived intervention deeply irresponsible. Hence a safer framework for analysis is to emphasise that any action can have consequences in all three spheres.

At this point it is appropriate to ask what remains of the idea of social exclusion that is not also captured by other conceptual frameworks that incorporate the relational dimension of development through terms such as 'social capital' and 'cultural and political' resources (e.g. Bebbington 1999; McGregor 2004; Rakodi 1999). The difference is perhaps mostly semantic, but the word 'capital' and even 'resource' suggest stocks of things that can be accumulated and traded, while the words 'inclusion' and 'exclusion' emphasise the primacy of social relationships as interactive processes. Resources cannot be used in isolation: they have inevitable consequences for others. The *sigma* model, for all its limiting assumptions, serves as a powerful reminder that an inventory of individual asset endowments is only the starting point for any analysis of poverty, which ends only when opportunities and obstacles to change arising from interaction with other parties have been fully explored. More fundamental still, it is open to debate whether social assets are 'traded' in a sufficiently routine and predictable way to make their valuation possible or useful at all.

9.4   Relevance for development policy and practice

Development organisations face a tension between acting consistently and in a 'joined-up' way (in line with some universal understanding of what they are doing), and flexibly (in response to local understandings).[9] They are generally more able to operate effectively, consistently and on a larger scale if they have clear, universal and measurable indicators of what they are trying to achieve. At the same time, the very specification of measurable goals can severely constrain their scope of activity, including

[9] See McGregor (2004) for a discussion of the idea of local and universal understandings, centred particularly on the concept of poverty, and Copestake (2005) for a fuller discussion of the tension between consistency and flexibility in development practice.

learning-by-doing and responsiveness to local priorities and needs. The history of the development industry can to some degree be viewed as the rise to and fall from favour of different frameworks for defining goals and means. For example, the Millennium Development Goals embody a multi-dimensional understanding of wellbeing and basic needs (informed by capability theory) which has to some extent superseded an exclusive focus on GDP growth and income (informed by modernisation theory). Meanwhile, the Comprehensive Development Framework of the World Bank signifies a shift towards a more pluralist view of the respective roles of public, private and civil society organisations in promoting development in different contexts. Looking to the future, current academic debates point towards a new conceptual framework that attaches more importance to subjective dimensions of development (including the quality of relationships), both as means and ends, than has been the case in the past. The growing influence of rights-based approaches can be viewed as part of this (DfID 2005), as can the increased attention paid by development agencies to participation, process and reflexivity (e.g. Chambers 1997). The WeD research is one of many efforts to develop new ways of thinking and operating that can contribute towards such a potential paradigm shift.

In one sense, the idea of social exclusion is not a very promising source for inspiration in this project. This is because its contribution is primarily analytical, rather than prescriptive in intent. If its central purpose is to explain the persistence of inequality and relative poverty, then it is no accident that it is pessimistic in its analysis of the scope for effective development intervention. The *sigma* model further reinforces this pessimism by formally modelling the reproduction of inequality as a low-level equilibrium trap. Nevertheless, the theory is in part valuable precisely because it counters the institutionalised optimism of frameworks elaborated by and for development agencies to emphasise opportunities over obstacles. A seemingly more negative approach can also be constructive if it provides a more realistic analytical foundation for identifying more precisely where scope for positive intervention might be, and how it fits into a larger political picture. By presenting comprehensive theory of why inequality persists, the model invites practitioners to identify the restrictive assumptions that can be challenged. This echoes the current fashion for being more strategic and selective in identifying 'drivers of change' in development or 'neuralgic pressure points' (DfID 2005).

A modest step towards incorporating inclusion/exclusion thinking into development practice is for development agencies to include themselves as well as other actors in their framework of analysis. This is

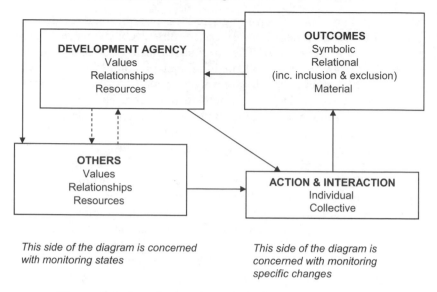

Figure 9.2 A reflexive framework for appraisal of development interventions

illustrated at a general level by Figure 9.2.[10] It goes beyond the discussion in this chapter so far by explicitly acknowledging the importance to development of symbolic as well as material and social dimensions of all actions. Agencies (including intervening development agencies) are defined by their values, relationships and resources. Values include formal goals but also the importance attached implicitly to different states and roles. Relationships may be both positive (e.g. membership of strategic networks and coalitions) and antagonistic. Resources include claims over material, natural and human assets as well as personal capabilities. Together they influence how different agencies act and interact with each other over time, with outcomes (symbolic, relational and material) which in turn alter their states.[11] If development agencies do nothing, then cycles of action, outcomes and altered states of 'others' continue without them. But the downward dotted line is a reminder that the mere existence of a development agency can affect the way others perceive themselves and behave. The upward dotted line, on the other

---

[10] This diagram is distinct from but fully compatible with the WeD conceptual framework (to be found in McGregor 2004: 7), which is more concerned with ordering ideas than informing action.

[11] See Bevan (2004b) for a thorough discussion of the time dimension.

hand, serves as a reminder that the values, relationships and resources of development agencies are also determined by how they perceive others.

The inclusion exclusion theory explored in this chapter provides some initial pointers for this kind of analysis. The mere presence of a development agency strengthens some values and latent relationships while weakening others. These symbolic and relational effects are reinforced in the way they act, e.g. through choice of language, staff recruitment, forms of consultation and collaboration. Thus development agencies unavoidably reinforce or weaken overall social stratification and the relative political influence of different groups. These symbolic and relational effects can be more important (in both their direct and indirect effect on wellbeing) than intended material effects, yet they are often ignored or downplayed. Much scope still remains for strengthening our analysis of the negative as well as positive consequences when one group of people use their resources and relationships as a means to the end of adding to the resources and relationships of others.

Part III

Quality of life and subjective wellbeing

10 Cross-cultural quality of life assessment approaches and experiences from the health care field

Silke Schmidt and Monika Bullinger

10.1 Introduction

As a result of increased international attention to the topic of Quality of Life (QoL), there has been an increase in demand for cross-culturally applicable measures of it. However, there are conceptual, methodological and practical problems in assessing quality of life across cultures. For example, the quality of life construct or modes of assessment may not be transferable from one cultural context to another, and there may be practical difficulties with the application of quality of life measures in developing countries.

Quality of Life is a concept with a complex and multiple history that incorporates perspectives from psychology, politics, economics, and philosophy. QoL was established as an area of study in sociology and social policy from the second half of the last century by researchers like Andrews and Withey, Campbell, and Flanagan who formed part of the Social Indicators movement (now represented by the international network ISQOLS). A couple of decades later QoL was adopted by health scientists and psychologists and defined in terms of people's perception of their health status, effectively becoming Health-Related

---

The reason for the slightly decreased fit in these centres seems to be associated with the different samples in these centres; they have comparably low scores across all groups. This is particularly a result of the clinical samples with a worse health status involved in these groups: strongest differences were identified for the relation between a quality-of-life higher-order factor and the Sensory Abilities scale (e.g. $r_{all} = 0.47$ vs. $r_{turkey} = 0.18$) and for quality-of-life and Intimacy (e.g. $r_{all} = 0.55$ vs. $r_{turkey} = 0.78$). Although this suggests different internal structures of QoL in older adults in Izmir, at this stage of the analysis one cannot make a final statement, taking both alternatives into account, if there are measurement biases (translation problems, cultural shift) or true score differences causing these observations. Such findings should be used to discuss the different conceptualisation of quality of life in specific samples, and not as a general critique towards a specific QoL instrument.

QoL (now represented by the separate international network ISOQOL). Although there has been little communication between these research traditions and their membership organisations, this may be starting to change with the advent of multi-disciplinary projects such as the Well-being in Developing Countries ESRC Research Group (WeD).

A potential area for collaborative development is the extension of individual QoL measurement to developing countries. This is not surprising as even within social development, understanding how people in developing countries view themselves, their lives, their immediate surroundings, as well as their larger social situation, is a relatively recent undertaking. The project also raises questions about how one can explore, measure and understand people's quality of life, and what this knowledge would be used for. To facilitate this discussion we need to achieve consensus on a definition of Quality of Life and methods for its assessment, drawn from a review of the current state of knowledge in this area.

This chapter addresses these issues by critically reviewing the 'state of the art' in the cross-cultural development of quality of life measures, using examples from the medical field where cross-cultural assessment of individual QoL is well established. It explores both conceptual issues, relating to the universality of definitions of QoL, and methodological concerns such as the development and validation of measures. It aims to develop a framework for the study of Quality of Life in developing countries and to identify ways in which this data can be used to inform policy and practice.

10.2   Cross-cultural issues in quality of life research

While social policy and sociology have experience of applying quality of life indicators across cultures and nations, this research mainly concerns so-called objective indicators of quality of life. Subjective indicators of quality of life have been included in population surveys, initially in the United States (Campbell *et al.* 1976) and Europe (e.g. Germany, Glatzer and Zapf 1984), but more recently in Latin America, Asia, and Africa (see Chapter 11 by Møller, also the Afro, Japan-ASEAN, and Latino Barometer population surveys). These surveys focus on quality of life in terms of satisfaction with different areas of life (or domains), for example, material, financial, social, and political.

Within the past twenty-five years, the field of 'health-related quality of life' has received increasing attention from researchers and practitioners. This partly reflects an increasing demand for cross-national quality of life research from the organisers of international clinical trials and bodies like the World Health Organization which are engaged in healthcare planning and intervention. This has required conceptual clarification, development of methodological approaches, and increased experience of practical applications in the international context (Berzon *et al.* 1993, Schmidt and Bullinger, 2003).

Such cross-cultural research into health-related QoL (HRQoL) raises big conceptual, epistemological as well as methodological questions, which cannot be tackled comprehensively here. Basically, there are two major poles of interpretation: on the one hand, anthropology and the different cultural meanings of disease, and on the other, more universalist western medical approaches to disease which assume fixed and culturally invariant aetiologies. The latter have developed international classification systems of diseases and disorders, such as the International Classification of Diseases (ICD), and the Diagnostic and Statistical Manual of disorders (DSM) in its various editions. However, these clinical taxonomies have been criticised for not appropriately reflecting the specific understanding of health, functioning and quality of life by individuals in specific cultures. International research in psychiatric epidemiology has shown that specific concepts – such as those concerned with negative emotions – cannot be assessed in the same way across specific cultures, as shown for India and China (Kleinman 1986; Mesquita and Frijda 1992; Sartorius *et al.* 1978). It is interesting to note that in the recent versions of the ICF, the International Classification of Functioning, research activities have been redirected to cross-cultural issues of daily activities and functioning.

At the other extreme, anthropology is one of the research traditions that have most extensively focused on the cultural specificity of health and quality of life. The observation that illness comprises the meaning a person attributes to their disease (largely determined by cultural schemata) and the way this shapes their response to it is particularly salient when working across cultures. According to Hutchinson (1996) these personal and cultural meanings are most visible in 'folk-illnesses' or 'culture bound syndromes' (see also Helman 2001). These include conditions like *susto* in Latin Americans (depressive anxiety), *koro* in China and South-East Asia (the fear of penis withdrawal into the body), *anorexia nervosa* in Europe and North America, and *heart distress* in Arabia (a condition occurring under specific distressing life conditions). Conversely, well-established medical conditions may not be perceived as such due to their high prevalence (for example, malaria among the Mano in Liberia, or measles, mumps and whooping cough in rural Greece).

If disease, as anthropological research suggests, is culture bound, how could quality of life be culture free? This concern, particularly on the part of anthropologists, is expressed in the following quote:

Although some researchers may desire a scale or similar measures for global assessments of cultures, permitting comparison of the "nature" of one culture with that of another, no such scale exists. In fact, given the multiplicity of variables or domains comprising a culture, that goal is unrealistic, both theoretically and methodologically. (Johnson 1996: 511)

This concern has deterred anthropologists from contributing to the development of cross-cultural measures. Possibly as a result of this the call for measures that are sensitive to language and dialect, customs, beliefs and traditions, as well as the education and socio-economic status of respondents has remained largely unheard (Guarnaccia *et al.* 1996; Hunt and Mc Kenna 1999). The anthropological perspective has therefore rarely been integrated in quality of life measures that may be cross-culturally applicable because its culturally specific approach to QoL has the potential to destabilise the whole quality of life project.

Cross-cultural quality of life research has tried to bridge the gap between the universalist view and the culture-specific view. Despite the scepticism of anthropologists, international research groups have been formed with the aim of empirically addressing cultural conceptions of (health-related) quality of life. These groups also addressed the question of whether it is possible to preserve the different cultural meanings of health and quality of life in an assessment approach.

A particular challenge is posed by language, which reflects the society, culture, and identity of its users. For the following discussion it might be helpful to distinguish between the terms 'international' and 'cross-cultural' in cross-cultural quality of life research. Usually the term 'international' is used to refer to phenomena concerning more than one nation or national cultural group, with a possible extension to non-dominant cultural groups within one nation. In the context of quality of life research, however, the term 'international' refers to activities by individual countries in the quality of life field (i.e. studies from different countries concerning specific research questions). By contrast, 'cross-cultural' quality of life research involves activities that are also collaborative and comparative (i.e. using the same instrument to assess quality of life in different countries to enable cross-national comparison). International and cross-cultural work therefore pose slightly different challenges, although both usually involve the use of quality of life measures in a different culture from the one in which they were developed.

In the quality of life literature, another controversial issue concerns (a) the type of components that are involved in the definition and measurement of quality of life, and (b) the operational level at which components are assessed. The most prominent measure of health-related quality of life, the SF-36, has used both the mental and physical health components and has assessed various operational levels ranging from subjective evaluations to functional assessment (Ware 2003). In contrast, the WHOQOL approach represents a greater number of components (physical, psychological, social, environmental, economic, and spiritual) and relies less on 'self-report objective' questions, for example, 'Does your health now limit you in climbing several flights of stairs?' The multi-dimensional definition of the WHOQOL Group (1995) defines

Quality of life (as) an individual's perceptions of their position in life in the context of the culture and value systems in which they live, and in relation to their goals, expectations, standards and concerns. It is a broad ranging concept affected in a complex way by the person's physical health, psychological state, level of independence, social relationships and their relationship to salient features of their environment. (WHOQOL 1995: 495)

In this chapter, we give a state-of-the-art overview of the development of cross-cultural instruments by some of these groups. The number of conceptual and methodological issues raised suggests that it may be time for researchers to pause and ask themselves the following questions:

1. Is the concept of quality of life comprehensible and relevant in a given location?
2. Do nations and cultural groups share an identical set of concepts about quality of life?
3. Can quality of life concepts be assessed with quality of life measures?
4. Is quality of life measurable across nations and cultural groups with the same instrument?
5. Can quality of life data be compared across nations and cultural groups?
6. Do the results of cross-cultural studies of quality of life provide a sound basis for decision making in the health care field?

10.3   Approaches to developing cross-cultural measures

There are three approaches to developing cross-cultural measures (see Schmidt and Bullinger 2003). The first and most ambitious is to develop a universal measure that is applicable across all cultures. The second involves the development of a universally applicable core measure with additional national modules. The third is to develop a series of national measures. So far, the majority of researchers have taken the first approach and focused their activity around a specific measure. For example, the following popular generic measures have been translated into European, African, and Asian languages:

- The General Health Questionnaire (GHQ; Goldberg and Williams 1988): available in French, Italian, Spanish, Norwegian, Dutch, Japanese, Chinese and Yoruba
- The Psychological General Wellbeing Index (Dupuy 1984): available in Swedish, Norwegian, German and English; used in a clinical trial for hypertension in Austria, Denmark, Finland, France, Holland and Italy
- The Nottingham Health Profile (NHP, Hunt et al. 1981): translated and validated in several languages by the European Group for Quality of Life and Health Measurement (EGQLHM Group 1992)
- The Sickness Impact Profile (SIP, Bergner et al. 1981): translated and validated in several languages (Anderson et al. 1993)
- The International Quality of Life Assessment Project Group (IQOLA) was founded in 1991 to work with the *SF-36* Health Survey (Aaronson et al. 1992; Ware and Sherbourne 1992)
- as was the European Quality of Life Project Group which developed the EUROQOL/EQ-5D Questionnaire (Kind 1996)
- The World Health Organization Quality of Life (WHOQOL) Group was established at the same time but took a simultaneous or 'spoke wheel' approach to developing a cross-cultural quality of life measure (WHOQOL 1994).

There has also been extensive development and translation of disease-specific measures, for example the European Organization for Research and Treatment of Cancer (EORTC) which began development of the EORTC Quality of Life Questionnaire in 1986 (Aaronson et al. 1996). International research groups have subsequently developed the Functional Assessment of Cancer Treatment Questionnaire (FACT Group, Cella and Bonomi 1996) and the Functional Living Index-Cancer (FLIC Group, Schipper et al. 1996).

The Cantril Self-Anchoring Striving Scale (Cantril 1965) has also been used in general population studies in over forty western and non-western countries with a sample of over 20,000 people. However, strictly speaking the scale is not a quality of life measure because it is not multi-dimensional and bears a closer resemblance to a single or 'global' question of QoL, happiness, or life satisfaction. Its link to QoL is its use of person-defined endpoints, which can also be seen in individualised QoL measures like the *Schedule for the Evaluation of Individual Quality of Life* (SEIQOL, O'Boyle *et al.* 1996) which were developed in the mid 1990s.

The above overview of generic and disease-specific quality of life measures demonstrates that most popular measures have undergone translation. Testing has been completed for some measures, but population data still has to be collected ('norming'). The languages in which measures are available are mostly European, with the exception of Eastern Europe. Indigenous South American, Asian, Arabic or African languages are underrepresented. Although international adaptation work is performed outside the working groups listed above, this research is not always published, which makes it difficult to assess the quality of the respective measures. International review committees and clearing houses have been founded to maintain standards in international quality of life assessment. For example, the Medical Outcomes Trust in Boston only approves measures for international use after they have been translated, tested, and normed, following the procedures described below.

This plenitude of measures in cross-cultural research suggests that not only the initial conceptualisation of HRQoL, but also the process of instrument development differs. In particular, three approaches can be distinguished in developing a cross-cultural measure (Bullinger *et al.* 1996). The first is the *sequential approach*, which involves transferring an existing questionnaire from one language to another. This approach was used with the SF-36 Health Survey (Ware *et al.* 1996), the Functional Assessment of Cancer Treatment questionnaire (Cella and Bonomi 1996), and the Nottingham Health Profile (Hunt *et al.* 1981). The second is the *parallel approach*, which involves assembling a measure from existing scales developed in different countries, for example the EORTC Quality of Life Questionnaire (Aaronson *et al.* 1996). The third is the *simultaneous approach*, which involves the cooperative cross-cultural development of a questionnaire, an approach that has so far only been used by the WHOQOL group (1994).

All of these approaches involve the following four steps: (1) Identification of relevant items; (2) Translation of the questionnaire; (3) Psychometric testing; (4) Collection of data to provide population norms. The following section will address these steps one by one and make comparisons between measures on the basis of issues in translation, psychometric testing, and norming (Chwalow 1995).

Identifying items

When exploring quality of life under certain conditions, such as among populations with specific health conditions or living situations, it is important to sample the items that are relevant to the topic. A common way of doing this is to conduct *focus groups* or *interviews* where people affected by the conditions under study are asked to describe and discuss the issues surrounding the condition. In both cases – interviews or focus groups – it is important to use open-ended questions that enable the respondents to reflect on their experiences. Interview schedules that are semi-standardised (with a predefined topic) are preferable to highly structured ones. Similarly, it is useful for focus groups to have a manual or study protocol describing the sequence of the procedure. Careful recording of the discussions is important in order to be able to derive adequate items from statements, which need to be recorded, selected, sorted, screened, and modified. For example, women might talk about the effect of breast cancer on their body image, and on their partnership, and on their feelings. These statements should be transcribed and then sorted to different domains, and similar statements can be compared in terms of different meanings. These discussions should be carried out in a multinational group. After agreeing on statements and their major content, an item writing process is started. It is aimed at keeping the items as close to the original wording that came from patients. This procedure could, for instance, produce an item asking 'has your experience of cancer reduced your self-esteem?' or 'has your experience of cancer affected your family life?'

Item development is a complicated issue because sentences or statements have to be recorded adequately, selected appropriately, and adapted or modified in order to avoid redundancy. Nevertheless, it is important to capture the meaning of each statement as closely as possible, taking into account language considerations. Cross-cultural research in item development requires that several persons from different cultures are involved in reviewing the statements and that original wordings of statements are preserved while at the same time having the English translation. Once item identification is completed the measure can be piloted with potential respondents. This usually involves 'cognitive debriefing' where items are presented to potential respondents in order to find out whether they are understandable and capture their experiences of the phenomena under investigation. This can be done when the items are presented by conducting an interview, or providing space for written comments on the questionnaire so that respondents can rate the performance of the items and suggest alternative formulations.

After generating the items, cognitive debriefing, and piloting of the response scales, a preliminary questionnaire can be compiled for the next step, which is pilot testing and subsequently psychometric testing. The answer categories need to be appropriate for both single country use and translation into different languages so that their meaning is comparable between countries. To ensure comparability, several international working groups have already compiled lists of scale descriptors (e.g. 'satisfied', 'fairly satisfied') that constitute an interval scale by virtue of the empirically established distance between descriptors. The equidistance of scale descriptors was then tested after their translation, so that appropriate answer cases were available for questions about the intensity, frequency, or satisfaction with the domain in question. The choice of an adequate answer scale is important because it affects the degree to which the measure can be reliably scaled and scored. For instance, different translations of answer scale descriptors (e.g. for the word 'sometimes' in a frequency scale) might evoke a different nuance across cultures.

Translating existing QoL measures

Brislin (Brislin *et al.* 1973) was one of the first researchers to distinguish different types of equivalence when translating measures from one culture to another: for example *semantic equivalence* (i.e. comparable meaning), *content equivalence* (the relevance of questions across cultures), *technical equivalence* (the types of question used), and *criterion equivalence* (the functioning of the questionnaire in the respective culture). He concluded that translation should be supported by a set of basic criteria to judge the equivalence of different versions of the same measure across cultures (see Herdman *et al.* 1998 or Hui and Triandis 1985). Later versions of the criteria were extended to include the following types of equivalence: *functional* (adequacy of translation), *scalar* (comparability of response scales), *operational* (standardisation of psychometric testing procedures), and *metric* (the order of scale values across a continuum).

Translation is the most thoroughly studied aspect of cross-cultural measure adaptation and development (Guillemin *et al.* 1993, Sartorius and Kuyken 1994). Theoretical foundations and methodological approaches to translating measures from one culture to another have been suggested from cross-cultural and comparative sociological research, as well as from cross-cultural psychiatry and educational psychology. Although each QoL working group has developed its own procedures for translation, these are essentially based upon 'forward translation'. Areas for debate include the number of translators required, and the use of 'back translations' (translations back into the original language by a native speaker of the original language who hasn't seen the original measure) to check the quality of the translation and the degree of linguistic equivalence. For example, the Nottingham Health Profile Group emphasised the importance of discussing forward translations in a focus group of health care professionals and people living with the condition, while the use of back translators was emphasised in the translation of the *SF-36 Health Survey*. The FACT Group highlighted the issue of translation by the use of several translators from each country, a group of experts in the field who reviewed the translations, and a linguist who revised them. In the WHOQOL Group, translations were complicated by the fact that they had to be made from a wide variety of original languages into English. This process also involved assessing the quality of translations, as was the case in the IQOLA Group (SF-36). The translation issue was pragmatically resolved in the EORTC Group by obtaining different translations, which were then reviewed by the national coordinators in each country. The FACT Group relies on both forward and back translations (a 'double translation' methodology), the use of an expert advisory committee, pilot testing, and thorough revision of the translations by linguists.

In reviewing different approaches to translation, Acquadro *et al.* (1996) stress the need to include at least two forward translations (with a comparative discussion) and are sceptical about the use of back translations, which are often of inferior quality, unduly affecting the evaluation of the forward translations. Most important is the international harmonisation of translations from different countries, which is done by assembling a group of bilingual people from different countries who are able to interact and critically review each other's translations.

While most guidelines for translation focus on the adequacy of the translation from the original into the 'target' language, Guyatt (1993) questions the attempt to transpose the measure from one language to another as closely as possible. He argues that during translation inconsistencies, illogical formulations, and culturally untranslatable expressions can appear, which should be the basis for reformulation of the original question, rather than adaptation in the target language. In spite of the differences between the translation approaches, most authors agree that the use of two forward translators is mandatory, the use of a back translator is potentially useful, and the use of focus groups to evaluate the applicability of the translated questionnaire in a specific country is recommended.

Testing the metric quality of QoL measures

Cross-cultural pilot studies need to be carried out in order to determine how different operationalisations of quality of life perform in different cultures. Culture-specific items may be preserved in this process. Data from these tests need to be saved in an international database. Psychometric testing is then carried out in order to determine whether different concepts have been reliably tested across nations and whether the conceptualisation has a high validity concerning other indicators. Psychometric testing relies on methods and procedures from psychometric theory and is valuable for establishing the validity and reliability of measures. For example, do the items in the measures correlate without duplication? Testing includes the generation of item descriptive statistics and measures of reliability, validity, and sensitivity.

The international working groups, however, differ in the procedures employed for psychometric testing. For example, the IQOLA Group (SF-36) emphasises the items' discriminant validity and uses item response theory to distinguish patterns of responses to items across cultures. They also observe the performance of the questionnaire in terms of known group differences, for example whether the SF-36 is able to differentiate between people differing in the degree of disease severity. In contrast, the FACT Group uses item analysis based on the Rasch model, structural equation models, and multivariate statistics to replicate the factor structure of the measure across countries. The WHOQOL group and IQOLA also employ structural equation models to test the measurement model of the questionnaire across countries. The WHOQOL group uses a model that is first fitted for the global data set and then replicated in each country (Power *et al.* 1999). Item descriptive statistics and scale correlations are then used to test whether items are applicable across cultures. The EORTC Group similarly uses item and scale statistics to decide whether specific items follow the measurement model of one country rather than another.

Collecting data to provide population norms

'Norming' is necessary in order to compare scores that have been assessed in specific populations (in terms of age, health and socio economic status) with the general population reference values that are based on representative samples having tested a QoL field instrument. Of all the international working groups on quality of life assessment, only the IQOLA Group had the opportunity to rely on population-based data to assess the quality of life of the general population. So far, data from seven countries are available; these include the US, Great Britain, Germany, the Netherlands, Sweden, Denmark and Italy. More IQOLA member countries are in the process of collecting national norms (for instance in Denmark, or France). A comparison of the measurement model of the SF-36 dimensional structure across countries showed that western countries are highly similar in these models. To date, the database to test the universality of the model in developing countries is still too small. In addition, comparisons of scale values of SF-36 subscores across countries show a similarity in rating with only slight differences in country profiles. This, however, only applies to industrialised western countries. The similarity of the SF-36 structure as well as convergent scale values across cultures suggests that identical weighting systems can be used. The normative data of the SF-36 can be employed in each country to obtain age- and gender-specific reference groups for clinical quality of life data, which can be expressed as deviation from the respective age- and gender-specific norm.

Other working groups such as the NHP Group were able to collect a convenience sample of the general population, which could be traced back using available census data. Thus, for example, the NHP in Germany was used within a sample of over 500 inhabitants of a north German city, which can now be used as reference data for clinical groups (Kohlmann *et al.* 1997). Similar data sets on a norm study basis recently emerged also for the WHOQOL (e.g. Germany), however, the number of countries is still small.

State of the art in international instrument testing

An overview of information regarding the state of international work with generic and specific quality of life instruments shows that most widely known instruments have undergone translation. Testing has been completed in some instruments but norming still has to be carried out. In general the languages in which instruments are available so far include mainly European languages (north, south, west, and more recently eastern European languages). South American (with exception of Spanish), Asian, Arabic or African languages are definitely under-represented. However, the approach that has been taken towards cross-cultural instrument development strongly diverges between the measures. Most adaptations have been performed sequentially so that it is difficult to discern the cross-cultural validity of the measures (e.g. Perkins *et al.* 2004). As described below, only a few working groups have used a simultaneous cross-cultural approach.

Furthermore, international adaptation is also ongoing outside the respective working groups, in particular those activities that have been performed in specific cultures. Reviewing the available literature on non-generic (targeted) measures, there is only a little literature on country-specific efforts in instrument development involving not only items with wording, but as figures and symbols. This may be a result of the fact that some culturally specific working groups do not necessarily publish their research. A disadvantage of these measures is that they do not allow concluding references outside a particular culture. To achieve high-quality QoL instruments, international review committees and clearing houses for international quality of life assessment have been founded (e.g. the Medical Outcomes Trust in Boston, which after strict review approves instruments for international use after sufficient translation, testing and – if possible – norming).

Sequential translations into developing countries Quality of life instrument development has so far mainly evolved from developed countries and has only subsequently been applied to developing countries. As a consequence QoL instruments have been developed to reflect the values and concerns of clinicians, patients and the general public of the country of origin. Bowden and Fox-Rushby (2003) have conducted a systematic and critical review of the process of translation and adaptation of generic health-related quality of life measures in Africa, Asia, Eastern Europe, the Middle East, and South America. Specifically, the review evaluated how the nine most prominent generic HRQoL instruments (15D, Dartmouth COOP/WONCA Charts, EuroQol, HUI, NHP, SIP, SF-36, QWB, WHOQOL) were translated and adapted for use in Africa, Asia, Eastern Europe, the Middle East, and South America. The review adopted a universal model of equivalence (Herdman *et al.* 1998) and evaluated conceptual, item, semantic, operational, measurement and functional equivalence of the approaches.

Fifty-eight papers were reviewed that came from twenty-three countries. A majority of studies came from the East Asia and Pacific region, and the SF-36 dominated the research. Bowden and Fox-Rushby (2003) showed that currently most adaptations focused on measurement and scale equivalence rather than on conceptual equivalence with the exception of the WHOQOL approach. In the WHOQOL approach conceptual equivalence was prioritised which was presumably a result of the simultaneous, rather than sequential approach to instrument development. For instance, it has been shown that items related to emotions can have very ambiguous meanings in Asian languages. Table 10.1 shows the extent to which the nine generic measures have been tested in terms of different

Table 10.1 *Types of equivalence tested in publication reviewed and adapted from Bowden and Fox-Rushby (2003) across nine measures of QoL (in %)*

Category		15D	COOP	EQ5D	HUI	NHP	SF-36	SIP	WHOQOL
Conceptual equivalence	None	100	77.0	80.0	100	50.0	69.6	100	27.3
	Partial	0.0	25.0	20.0	0	50.0	30.4	0.0	45.5
	Extensive	0.0	0.0	0.0	0	0.0	0.0	0.0	27.3
Item equivalence	None	50.0	62.5	100	50.0	75.0	91.3	66.7	20.0
	Partial	50.0	37.5	0	50.0	25.0	30.4	33.3	60.0
	Extensive	0	0	0	0	0	8.7	0	20.0
Semantic equivalence	None	100	62.5	60.0	50.0	50.0	60.9	100	81.8
	Partial	0	37.5	20.0	50.0	50.0	26.1	0	18.2
	Extensive	0	0	20.0	0	0	13.0	0	0
Measurement equivalence	None	0	37.5	40.0	50.0	25.0	21.7	66.7	54.5
	Partial	100	37.5	40.0	0	50.0	30.4	33.3	33.0
	Extensive	0	25.0	20.0	50.0	25.0	47.8	0	27.3
Assessment of local conceptions of health and QOL		0	37.5	0	0	50.0	8.7	66.7	54.5

Notes: Numbers represent the extent to which the particular type of equivalence has been assessed in various field studies of these measures.

types of equivalence and suggests that most measures focus on measurement equivalence.

Concerning the World Bank regions, conceptual equivalence has been more frequently tested in Southern American than in Asian and Pacific, African and Middle East regions. The conclusion of this review is that research practice and translation guidelines still need to change to facilitate more effective and inclusive assessments of equivalence of HRQoL measures across countries.

Simultaneous cross-cultural instrument development   There have been approaches towards preserving culture-specificity in the development of subjective wellbeing measures. To ensure cross-cultural validity in developing countries during instrument construction and validation, multinational collaboration is required at three levels. The conceptual model must reflect different cultural nuances (Sartorius and Kuyken 1994; Skevington *et al.* 2004); the manifest model – an instrument's descriptive system – must measure, in a representative sense, the universe of interest as defined cross-culturally in order to take account of emic (those effects that are specific to a culture) and etic effects (those effects that are invariant across cultures); and the observed model of

QoL elicited by the instrument must demonstrate validity in different cultural settings (Orley and Kuyken 1993).

A key reason why validation at these three levels is rarely performed is the well-known challenge associated with conducting multinational and multi-centre research. For instance, problems arising with international adherence to protocols have been reported. There is little published information in relation to the processes involved with this collaboration and the problems of embarking on large scale, multi-centre, cross-cultural research. One group with wide international representation that is tackling this difficult area is the World Health Organization's QoL group (WHOQOL Group 1995, 1999).

The experience of simultaneous cross-cultural instrument development
To date, only a few research groups have addressed instrument development as a simultaneous approach. The WHOQOL Group has used a common international protocol to develop two generic QoL profile measures, the WHOQOL-100 and the WHOQOL-BREF, and one age-specific module, the WHOQOL-Old for older adults. The group made use of a method of the simultaneous approach to instrument development described by Bullinger *et al.* (1996). All WHOQOL centres contributed to the definition of the domains and facets that were agreed to characterise Quality of Life, and, subsequently, all centres contributed items to the pilot version of the WHOQOL measure. Questions were drafted by focus groups, which generated ideas within each centre as to how and in which form to ask questions relating to quality of life. A second step of retaining cross-cultural equivalence was to rank order the importance of questions in each centre. This research showed that despite a high equivalence of the importance of domains and items across countries, a few culture-specific national items (these were culture-specific items from focus groups entered into the global item pool as national items) showed high importance in some countries, such as items on energy and food in Asian countries, and items on security in Israel (WHOQOL Group 1999). As a consequence, these items were retained as national items in the specific language version of the WHOQOL. Similar care was taken to generate cross-culturally comparable response scales by using three types of Likert scales which were worded in each culture according to the spacing of words falling at the 25 per cent, 50 per cent and 75 per cent distances between the two anchors (low and high) of each scale.

To date, research with the different WHOQOL versions has shown that although country populations show different levels of QoL across domains, the overall structure has a high cross-cultural validity (see Skevington 2004) suggesting a high degree of universality in this simultaneously developed measure. To date, the WHOQOL-BREF has been tested for its cross-cultural applicability in more than fifty countries. The work of the WHOQOL group is thus a good example for an approach that aimed at developing a universal model but nevertheless preserving the possibility of retaining culture-specific items and modules.

Nevertheless, a range of criticisms have been raised concerning the conceptualisation and the metric quality of some subdimensions of the WHOQOL measures (Skevington 2004). One considers that the social domain has not been adequately operationalised in the initial WHOQOL assessment instruments. It should be noted that in other quality of life instruments, such as the SF-36, there has been no conceptualisation of a higher-order social domain. Recent studies (Schmidt *et al.* 2006a, 2006b) suggest that it is particularly the social domain that – on the one hand – shows differential item functioning across cultures but on the other hand is most suitable in assessing cross-cultural differences in quality of life assessment. In recent approaches towards cross-cultural quality of life assessment, such as in the WHOQOL-Old study, or the European DIS-ABKIDS conditions (Bullinger *et al.* 2002; Schmidt *et al.* 2006a) and the KIDSCREEN study (Ravens-Sieberer *et al.* 2001), the conceptualisation of a higher-order social domain and its subfacets have been addressed. In the WHOQOL group it has been proposed to reanalyse the conceptual structure on the basis of different international field studies and data sets.

In our own recent research on *simultaneously developed measures*, many indices for a better cross-cultural performance of simultaneously developed measures were found because they have conceptualised higher-order domains on the basis of cross-cultural definitions. Simultaneous approaches were applied to a range of specific patient populations in international studies: examples are the cross-culturally developed DIS-ABKIDS measure for children with chronic conditions (Bullinger *et al.* 2002; Schmidt *et al.* 2006a), as well as in the EUROHIS measure (Schmidt *et al.* 2006b), the WHOQOL-Old measure (Power *et al.* 2005) and KIDSCREEN (healthy children).

We will briefly report some of the outcomes of simultaneously developed measures, i.e. those measures that have been based on a cross-cultural definition of QoL, that have involved different nations in each step of instrument development and that have also conducted international field tests. For instance, the EUROHIS study, an instrument development enterprise on health determinants and health outcomes in national health surveys in Europe, showed that quality of life scores from countries of the former Soviet block showed significantly lower scores across all items of the EUROHIS WHOQOL short index than in other European countries. However, item and structural equivalence were the same with some initial exceptions (see Figure 1; see Schmidt *et al.* 2006a).

The EUROHIS-QOL eight-item index showed good reliabilities in terms of internal consistency across all countries, good and equal discriminant validity in terms of distinctions between conditions as well as associations with health status in all countries. The measure also showed a good internal structure, for example from the loading of all items on the overall quality of life factor in each country, with the initial exception of the Romanian sample. The model fit in Romania was low, both as compared to other country samples and in terms of cut-off criteria for the fit of structural equation models (Hu and Bentler 1999). What reasons can be assumed for the decreased fit in this country? In the Romanian data, two items showed an extremely high impact on the overall QoL factor that led to an improvement of the structure when covariance terms were included. This finding could result from different mechanisms: it could be assumed that the lower fit results from the fact that there is no direct translation of the term 'quality of life' in Romanian, which has been evident in focus groups. So therefore connotations to the QoL in terms of money and or living conditions may have a strong and pervasive impact on overall quality of life so that they reflect more closely the QoL concept in Romania than the other items of the EUROHIS-QOL index. Conceptually, this finding may also illustrate a link between objective and subjective measures of quality of life for countries where living conditions are a current concern for the respondent, or may reflect effects on respondents that result from political and economic transitions in countries.

As the DISABKIDS and KIDSCREEN groups are examples for European cooperation in the area of child health, the WHOQOL-Old measure (Power *et al.* 2005) is a cross-cultural quality of life measure that has been designed for older adults.

The overall fit of the model (Figure 2) was high and similar across all centres and countries. Better fit statistics were obtained for the Porto Alegre, Budapest, Vilnius and Leipzig centre (>0.93), while a lower fit (<0.86) was observed in the Paris and Izmir centres.*

In our recent work we have focused on the conceptual interrelationship between health determinants and quality of life from a cross-cultural scale (Schmidt and Power, 2006). To date the lack of conceptual studies on health determinants and quality of life make it difficult to draw conclusions about the relation between determinants and outcomes. We have published work that has shown major differences between the interrelationship between health indicators and quality of life between different cultures (Schmidt *et al.* 2004; Schmidt and Power 2006). However, future studies will require larger and representative samples to test models on latent factors of mental health, physical health and quality of life, and on the basis of these findings to identify overall structural models across countries.

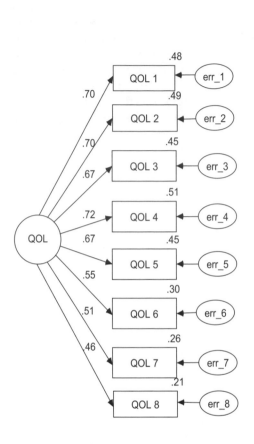

Country	CFI
France	>.90
Germany	>.90
United Kingdom	>.90
Lithuania	>.90
Latvia	>.90
Croatia	>.90
Romania	.78
Slovakia	>.90
Czech Republic	>.90
Israel	.89
Total	**.91**

Figure 10.1 Results of measuring the same structure for eight items of the EUROHIS-QoL eight-item index with one latent variable QoL, overall and for each country in the EUROHIS study ($n = 4,849$)

Note: QoL1-QoL8 reflect the different items of the WHOQOL EUROHIS quality of life instrument; the term err (= error) reflects measurement errors. CFI = Comparative fit index. CFIs greater than 0.90 are generally considered to have an acceptable fit.

In this particular sample a decreased fit was observed in the Romanian sample particularly as a result of a different conceptualisation of QoL (with strong loading of financial needs on a QoL concept).

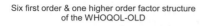

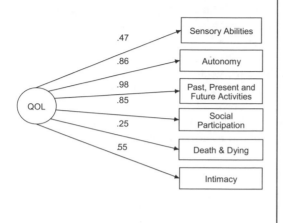

Centre	N	CFI
Edinburgh	116	>.90
Bath	145	>.90
Leipzig	354	>.90
Barcelona	271	>.90
Copenhagen	384	>.90
Paris	164	<.90
Prague	325	>.90
Budapest	333	>.90
Oslo	324	>.90
Victoria	202	>.90
Melbourne	376	>.90
Seattle	295	>.90
Beer-Sheva	250	<.90
Tokyo	188	<.90
Umea	455	>.90
Porto Alegre	328	>.90
Montevideo	248	>.90
Izmir	327	>.90
Geneva	139	>.90
Vilnius	342	>.90
Overall	*5.566*	>.90

Figure 10.2 Structural model of WHOQoL-old (The WHOQoL adaptation for older adults) and universal fit statistics
CFI = Comparative fit index. CFIs greater 0.90 are generally considered to have an acceptable fit. N = sample size.

10.4 Six problems in cross-cultural quality of life assessment

We return to the six key questions for QoL researchers listed earlier in this chapter and draw some conclusions.

Is the concept of quality of life comprehensible and relevant in a given location?

To date, the conceptualisation of quality of life has rarely been approached from a cross-cultural point of view. The viability of the quality of life concept across nations or cultural groups has been explicitly addressed by only a few research groups, such as the WHOQOL Group in a general measure, the DISABKIDS and KIDSCREEN group in paediatric QoL measures, and the WHOQOL-Old group in an older adults adaptation of the WHOQOL measure. These groups created space for nationally or culturally specific items to evolve by developing a common definition of quality of life, common domain structure, and protocols for formulating quality of life questions (using an international expert group), and subsequently developing the items in each country. The process resulted in the development of different national forms of these different measures, which increased the likelihood of producing a culturally relevant questionnaire. To summarise, the initial definition of a QoL concept in a cross-cultural group has rarely taken place. Cross-cultural QoL research should be initiated from the beginning with an internationally valid definition.

Do nations and cultural groups share an identical set of concepts about quality of life?

The above-mentioned quality of life groups are also the only ones to have addressed the putative existence of an identical set of concepts shared by nations and cultural groups. Although each country was given the opportunity to produce national items when the common data pool was analysed, there was a noticeable overlap of nationally produced items. This overlap was so strong that national items did not significantly increase the amount of variance the questionnaire explained. Thus it seems possible that different nations and cultural groups share a similar set of concepts about quality of life.

Can quality of life concepts be assessed with quality of life measures?

None of the international working groups have addressed the different forms in which assessment of quality of life is performed, largely because all have worked with quality of life measures in the form of questionnaires or interviews. It is not clear whether other forms of communication might be better able to represent the cultural nuances of experiences of quality of life (e.g. pictures, colours, etc.).

Is quality of life measurable across nations and cultural groups with the same instrument?

The measurability of quality of life across nations and cultural groups using the same measure has been addressed by almost all of the international working groups mentioned in the previous/section. There is empirical evidence in the form of psychometric data that quality of life can be measured across nations and cultures using the same measure; however, it may be that the culturally specific connotations of quality of life have not been grasped. Item analysis as well as the structural equation models employed by almost all the international working groups show that there is a high similarity between concepts of quality of life found in western industrialised countries. For example, the IQOLA Project found that the psychometric properties of the SF-36 were acceptable in the cultures studied, that there is considerable overlap in the dimensional structure, and that the scale scores of the SF-36 questionnaire differ only slightly in population studies. Similarly, the WHOQOL Project showed that items constructed by different cultures were similar, national items did not contribute significantly to the instrument's explanatory power, and structural equation modelling did not show substantial differences in the relationship of dimensions across cultures. This lends support to the notion that the concept of quality of life is a cross-cultural universal.

However, recent analyses of differential item function across cultures (see Schmidt *et al.* 2006a, 2006b) highlight that in particular the social domain shows cross-cultural differences in item functioning and the overall validity of the scale structure. At the same time, this is one of the most useful research domains for analysing cross-cultural differences in health status. Further research is needed in order to find answers to these cross-cultural nuances in the conceptualisation of quality of life and its impact on psychometric testing across cultures.

Can quality of life data be compared across nations and cultural groups?

The question of the comparability of quality of life data across cultures has already been addressed, however, comparisons can be hampered by the question of whether the response scales are cross-culturally comparable. This has explicitly been addressed in several international working groups; for example, the IQOLA group used a Thurstone scaling exercise to identify the relative distance of descriptors in the SF-36 answer scale across countries. It found that in western countries such differences were minimal (Ware *et al.* 1996). The WHOQOL Group also employed a procedure to assess the relative distance between answer response scales across countries and chose descriptors that best reflected the distance in each country. We can therefore conclude that as long as we have tested the comparability of answer scores, as well as their cross-cultural applicability, quality of life data can be compared across nations and cultural groups.

Do the results of cross-cultural studies of quality of life provide a sound basis for decision making in the health care field?

The final concern is whether cross-cultural quality of life results can be used as a basis of decision making. This question has not been addressed sufficiently in international quality of life research. There has been reluctance among international research groups, especially the WHOQOL, to conduct an epidemiological analysis across countries using quality of life data. This perspective is very different from that of members of the social indicators movement who routinely compare 'objective' indicators of quality of life across countries. This seems like a missed opportunity as the data collected so far by the international working groups suggests that there are differences in quality of life that do not arise from age, gender, educational status, or employment; these findings could have great political relevance.

Conclusions

An underlying issue in the general discussion about the use of quality of life instruments in the health care field of developing countries is to what extent those instruments produce information that is valuable for decision making in the health care field – either on a health political level or in the individual physician–patient interaction. The decision about the principal usefulness of quality of life assessment certainly should not be limited to being made from the so-called developed world, but should necessarily take into account the perspectives and needs of the general public as well as the health care professionals in the respective countries. To implement these measures, not only their methodological quality or their clinical interpretability is of importance, but also the willingness to accept such assessment tools and outcome indicators in research and practice. The general ethical demand of development policies also holds true for quality of life assessment in the health care field: provide possibilities, but leave individual decisions to the people concerned.

In general, the following three concerns have to be kept in mind. The first relates to the possible ethnocentrism of the measures and approaches used. All of the measures developed so far are based on the idea that people can articulate their inner feelings and experiences, which is an outlook that may be more common among white, middle class, Anglo-Saxon researchers than the people they are working with. A second problem is the possible normativity of the quality of life concept. For example, the selected domains of quality of life may not be value-neutral but act as standards which the individual is expected to live up to. Biases may also occur from the choice of convenience samples for quality of life assessment and the mode of questioning employed. Finally, the potential ethical consequences of cross-cultural quality of life research must be considered, for example protecting respondents' personal information and ensuring that quality of life data collected for one purpose in a specific setting are not then included in clinical trials (Bernhard et al. 1996; Cella et al. 1993; Mathias et al. 1994).

To sum up, there are international projects assessing quality of life across cultures. The measures they are using have been translated and are currently in a testing phase where they will be reviewed for their cross-cultural performance. Initial results with measures that have been tested suggest that these measures are cross-culturally applicable; however, this premise has not been tested in developing countries. For cross-cultural quality of life research in particular, the underlying quality of life concept needs to be transparent and the researchers should be circumspect in using specific measurement approaches. Measure administration and data analysis should be done rigorously and researchers should take responsibility for the results after their publication.

Quality of life research has a descriptive as well as a prescriptive aspect, which suggests that people think and care about their wellbeing independent of race, gender, age, social status, occupation, and mental or physical health status. Every society should engage in trying to study and improve the quality of life of its members. Quality of life data, by providing information about the respective status of different social groups, may suggest specific interventions to improve their quality of life, or show the effects of such interventions, which could contribute to minimising the gap between the 'developed' and the 'developing' world.

11 Researching quality of life in a developing country: lessons from the South African case

Valerie Møller

11.1 Introduction

Situated on the tip of the world's poorest continent, South Africa serves as a social laboratory for studying quality of life in developing countries. Classified as a middle-income country, it straddles the Developed and Developing World divide. It is a nation characterised by vast income inequalities, many levels of development and cultural diversity in terms of language, religion, ethnicity and settlement patterns. It is this rich mix of material and cultural differences that lends itself to experimenting with concepts and measurement instruments that capture the essence of quality of life.

This chapter reports the South African Quality of Life Trends Project, which commenced in the late 1970s and spans twenty-five years. Currently managed by Rhodes University's Institute of Social and Economic Research in Grahamstown,[1] the project has tracked the satisfaction and happiness of South Africans against the backdrop of changes occurring in society before and after the coming of democracy (Møller 1988b, 1989, 1992a, 1994b, 1995a, 1998, 1999a; Møller and Dickow 2002; Møller and Schlemmer 1983, 1989). The South African initiative was a child of its time and, to a certain degree, reflects the developments and the sophistications that have occurred in quality of life studies and the social indicators movement during its forty-year history. There may be lessons to be learnt from its successes and shortcomings which have become evident with the wisdom of hindsight.

---

[1] The project was initiated by researchers at the University of KwaZuluNatal, Durban, in collaboration with colleagues at the Human Sciences Research Council in Pretoria. Depending on the focus of each round of research or case study, the members of the original team have worked with partners representing a broad spectrum of social science disciplines including sociology, political studies, psychology, anthropology, social work, social gerontology, development studies, economics and statistics.

242

The story of the project is divided into three parts: the experimental, consolidation and innovation phases of the project.

11.2 The experimental phase: definition of concepts and the development of models and instruments

Because there is no generally accepted scientific theory of a good society, whoever sets out to describe and evaluate all the important features of a society must consult widely with the people living in that society. Clearly, this task increases in difficulty as the size and diversity of the society to be evaluated increases. (Michalos 2003: 7)

Initially, we were preoccupied with identifying and defining key concepts, developing a theoretical model to guide the research and fine tuning the research instrument. According to Alex Michalos (2003), quality of life has both descriptive and evaluative connotations; we need to know the nature of the good society as well as the value of the essential qualities of life. Our first task then was to define the essence of the good life in South Africa and to develop the method that would tell us to what extent real life matched the good life.

The classical works on quality of life by Andrews and Withey (1976) and Campbell, Converse and Rodgers (1976) that had just become available to South African researchers in the late 1970s served as our research guides. Following the lead of our US mentors, we sifted through materials from focus group discussions with blacks residing in Gauteng[2] to identify key concerns in the lives of ordinary South Africans. The several hundred concerns identified initially were reduced to more manageable proportions in the pilot study conducted with samples drawn from the four official race groups under apartheid and, in the first round of research, conducted with a national sample.

Many of the domain-level concerns identified in this first phase turned out to be universal, such as concerns about the self, family, food, shelter, livelihoods and leisure. However, a number of criterion-level items put to respondents in the initial rounds of research did touch some of the raw nerves of South Africa's apartheid society. Examples included the *right* to vote, *treatment* in the work situation and *choice* in housing. There were also some blatant researcher biases in the initial selection of items. We had been preoccupied with studies of township housing to explore

[2] The province known as Gauteng since democracy is South Africa's economic centre that attracts people from all parts of the country. It could be assumed that the focus group materials would give insight into the views of a very broad cross-section of blacks representing diverse regions and cultural backgrounds.

the impact of living in 'matchbox'[3] houses on wellbeing (Møller and Schlemmer 1980). As a result of this research interest, housing issues received better coverage than other domains.

The final set of indicators included thirty-five items at the global, domain and criterion levels. The global items referred to satisfaction with life-as-a-whole, global happiness and perception of life getting better or worse. A number of statistical analyses assisted in making the choice of items in this final set. The selection criteria were cross-cultural relevance, reliability and validity, significant impact on overall perceived quality of life and policy relevance (Møller and Schlemmer 1989).

To aid comparison over time, the South African Quality of Life Trends Survey has used the same indicators in each of its national surveys that have been conducted by a single research organisation, MarkData, a reputable research organisation based in Pretoria. MarkData uses a carefully crafted sample design that covers the entire country and results are weighted to census figures. In line with best practice in South Africa, the sample surveys are administered by trained interviewers in the language of choice of respondents. In the first round of research, the questionnaires were translated into the major languages in use in the surveyed areas and back translated.

Critical research decisions

A number of critical research decisions taken at this stage of the research shaped the later course of the project.

Our research was driven by the idea that quality of life studies should lend a voice to the invisible people who were denied the rights of ordinary citizens in their own country. In what might be considered a renegade move at the time, we focused first on the needs and concerns of the socially excluded black or African sector of the population, which makes up the numerical majority. We also dismissed the conventional viewpoint that illiterate people cannot meaningfully participate in sample surveys.

The phrasing of probes used in our surveys represented a further considered decision. We wanted respondents to describe and evaluate their own lives, that is their personal quality of life, rather than passing judgement on society. We did not want respondents to give blanket evaluations of issues of little relevance to their own lives. Therefore all issues were personalised. Concerns were typically introduced as 'your'

---

[3] Brick and mortar housing units in townships reserved for blacks during the apartheid era that were built to a standard design.

or 'your family's' concern: the dwelling you live in here, the food you eat, your right to vote, etc. Respondents whose lives were not touched by the issue under consideration were not required to evaluate the concern. In the pilot phase, respondents first evaluated the importance of each concern before giving a satisfaction rating. In later stages, evaluations of items were only required if the concern was considered important, that is a salient issue, or if the concern applied to the respondent.

In hindsight, one might argue that there were serious flaws in this reasoning. First, we were restricting our study to personal quality of life regardless of the quality of society. As a more privileged member of South African society put it to us in a seminar held in the mid-1990s: 'How can I be happy when I know that many of my fellow country people are so badly off?'

Another shortcoming was the emphasis on the individual. In our strenuous efforts to avoid collecting superficial evaluations of life quality, we may have overlooked that South African society is largely collectivist. In line with the notion of African humanism, quality of life embraces whole families and households rather than mere individuals. Thus, many South Africans, like their counterparts in other collectivist societies, might consider it self-centred to reflect only on their personal wellbeing. Interestingly, we received echoes of collectivist perceptions of quality of life in the first survey returns. For instance, older individuals often refused to evaluate the education domain. 'Their' education was no longer a relevant issue in their lives, they maintained. Their time for learning had passed and they were more concerned that their children and grandchildren should receive a better education than they had.

A further decision concerned the evaluation descriptors. We reasoned that domain-level items should be evaluated in terms of satisfaction rather than happiness, as the former is considered to be the more cognitive assessment (McKennel and Andrews 1980; Michalos 1980). If public report cards were based on cognitive evaluations, we thought they would carry more weight with policy makers, an assumption that proved to be correct.

Careful consideration was also given to the calibration of the evaluation scale to ensure it was accessible to all respondents. We experimented with a number of scales and for simplicity's sake opted for the five-point labelled satisfaction scale ranging from 'very satisfied' to 'very dissatisfied' over a neutral 'neither/nor' mid-point. The majority of South Africans come from an oral tradition. We found that if we read out the labels that calibrated the satisfaction scale, South Africans from all walks of life could meaningfully participate in our quality of life surveys.

A further conscious decision was taken when it came to the reporting format. We decided to report results in terms of percentages, which are generally well understood, rather than scores that would call for explanatory notes. In the apartheid era, we were strongly tempted to report the negative emphases of evaluations. Nevertheless, we decided optimism should prevail and it would be more appropriate to report on the percentage satisfied in the population. Moreover, statistical analyses of the results from the first rounds of research found that there was a major divide between the 'satisfied' responses versus all others.

Quality of life researchers have always been fascinated by the idea of developing a Quality of Life (QoL) index to match the powerful Gross Domestic Product. Nobel laureate Amartya Sen notes that the single index commands far more attention than disaggregated indicators. 'People would look at them [separate indicators] respectfully, but when it came to using a summary measure of social development, they would still go back to the unadorned GDP, because it was crude and convenient' (Anand and Sen 1997, cited in Vogel and Wolf 2004: 7). We were aware of the strong appeal of a single-figure index to convey whether circumstances lived up to the public ideal. Initially, we had played with the idea of a composite quality of life index. Some seven indicators, mainly the global items, were identified as candidates for such an index. Notwithstanding the attractiveness of a QoL index for South Africa, we came to the same conclusion reached by many others: 'most public policy interventions can be achieved merely by tracking the components of QoL' (Hagerty, Vogel and Møller 2002: 6). We reasoned that a profile of quality of life indicators would clearly pinpoint areas that fell short of citizens' expectations of the good life, and needed urgent remedial action on the part of policy makers.[4]

The first round of research included a set of objective quality of life indicators to match the domains covered by subjective satisfaction indicators. The information for the objective indicators was collected by self-report, the same method currently used by Statistics South Africa to produce the country's official statistics on living conditions and opportunities. Essentially, the development of objective indicators was informed by Maslow's (1970) hierarchy of needs and the basic needs approach that was popular at the time (Streeten 1977).

---

[4] It is noteworthy that other South African quality of life researchers have taken up the challenge of a QoL index (Higgs 2003; Kok, Ndlovu and O'Donovan 1997) and Statistics South Africa produces a Human Development Index that is disaggregated by geographical region.

The match between subjective assessments and objective living conditions was so strong in the first round of research that, from that time forward, we decided to concentrate on monitoring subjective wellbeing, the dimension of quality of life that has been neglected in South Africa (Møller 1995b) as elsewhere (Veenhoven 2002c). We discovered that we would never be short of objective indicators to compare with our subjective ones if we bought into syndicated surveys to measure happiness and life satisfaction. Most local syndicated surveys supply the commissioned data as well as a wealth of information on demographics, economic and cultural indicators and, in some instances, even political indicators such as voting preferences.

11.3 The consolidation phase confirming trends and exploring parts of the whole picture

The full set of thirty-five indicators of subjective wellbeing including global and domain indicators has been applied three times during the apartheid and post-apartheid periods (Møller 1998). Longer trendlines have been produced for the key global indicators of life satisfaction, happiness and perceptions of life getting better or worse.

The trendlines for the global indicators are striking. Citizen satisfaction peaked in 1994 in the month after the first open democratic elections (see Figure 11.1). Under apartheid, levels of life and domain

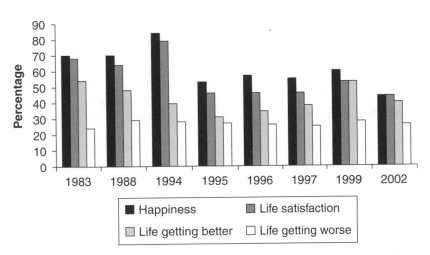

Figure 11.1 South African Quality of Life Trends: percentages of South Africans happy, satisfied with life, and seeing life as getting better or worse

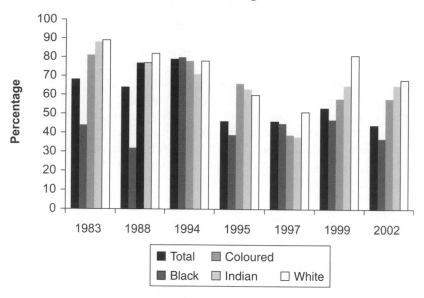

Figure 11.2 South African Quality of Life Trends: percentages satisfied with life-as-a-whole

satisfaction and happiness reflected the imposed racial hierarchy of power and privilege with whites mostly satisfied, blacks mostly dissatisfied and Indian and coloured people falling somewhere in between (Møller 1999b). In May 1994, a month after the first open elections, black and white and rich and poor were equally satisfied with life for the first time. South African levels of satisfaction reached ones generally found in western and democratic societies; approximately four in five South Africans stated they were satisfied with life overall and happy. It is noteworthy that, a year later, at the domain level, formerly dissatisfied non-voters now registered satisfaction with 'your right to vote' (Møller 1998).

Nonetheless, post-election euphoria was short-lived. Satisfaction levels have since returned to ones reminiscent of those under the former regime. For example, in the most recent survey undertaken for the South African Quality of Life Trends Study in mid-2002, only some 44 per cent of all South Africans stated they were satisfied with life. Some 68 per cent of whites were satisfied, 65 per cent of Indians, 58 per cent of coloureds, but only 37 per cent of blacks (see Figure 11.2) (Møller 2004). Levels of dissatisfaction are particularly pronounced in the domains of income, social security and access to jobs.

What would make ordinary South Africans happy? The 1999 round of questioning for the project posed this question. Poorer respondents thought they would be happier if their material living conditions improved and cited wants such as access to jobs and livelihoods, housing, infrastructure services – water, electricity, sanitation, and education. Essentially, poorer South Africans referred to the election promises and South Africa's ambitious post-1994 Reconstruction and Development Programme. In contrast, safety and security issues – 'less crime' and a strong economy featured more prominently in the wish lists of richer South Africans (Møller 1999a).

The conclusions to be drawn from these quality of life trends are clear. Once the majority of South Africans gained political freedom in 1994, 'bread and butter' issues eclipsed other life concerns among the black majority, which made up some 79 per cent of the country's population of 46 million in 2004.

On the basis of the trendlines for life satisfaction, happiness and projections into the future we were able to identify four key features of quality of life in South Africa.

1 There is a vast discrepancy between the levels of satisfaction of black and white and of rich and poor in society.
2 There is a close match between objective and subjective indicators, that is, between perceived wellbeing and actual standards of living.
3 Overall life satisfaction and domain satisfactions appear to be sensitive to changing circumstances in society. Importantly, satisfaction seems to increase with levels of living.
4 Optimism correlates negatively with current happiness and satisfaction. Black and poor South Africans expect to be more satisfied with life in future, albeit from a low satisfaction base, while more affluent whites and Indians tend to be more pessimistic and anxious about the future.

Case studies

During the consolidation phase of the project, a number of case studies were conducted to enquire in greater depth into the situation of specific categories of the population such as the unemployed (Møller 1993), migrant workers (Møller and Schlemmer 1981), return migrants (Møller 1988a), and polygamists (Møller and Welch 1990). Other studies focused on the quality of life of youth (Møller 1994a, 1996b, 2003; Møller, Richards and Mthembu 1991), the elderly (Møller 1992b) and social pensioners (Møller 1992d; Møller and Devey 2003; Møller and Ferreira 2003; Møller and Sotshongaye 1996). Studies of the quality of life of township dwellers were complemented with those of people living in the rural homelands. Enquiries into quality of life in unemployment were balanced by leisure studies to explore how coping skills and personal development opportunities enhanced wellbeing. Time-use studies among the youth (Møller 1992c) and the elderly (Møller 1996c) provided valuable insights into the manner in which South Africans achieved satisfaction in everyday life from their round of activities. Intergenerational studies enquired into the possibility of a transfer of perceived wellbeing from one generation to the next and the impact of period, cohort and age factors.

This series of case studies served two purposes. They lent support to results obtained in the trend study and they added depth to the trendlines by informing on the hopes and fears of South Africans and how such factors moderated wellbeing. We consistently found that groups higher up in the apartheid pecking order scored higher on life satisfaction than those lower down. The highest levels of dissatisfaction were found among the most disadvantaged and marginal groups in society who were dis-empowered by their lot in life. The unemployed typified the dissatisfied among the socially excluded. Extremely high levels of dissatisfaction were also observed among failed return migrants[5] who had little to show for a lifetime of labour. Typically, mineworkers with tuberculosis were sent back to their rural areas of origin in mid-career. It is a dubious distinction for South African quality of life studies that the level of satisfaction among marginal groups under apartheid was so low as to be discredited by international scholars. For instance, Cummins (2000) felt obliged to exclude the case of South African return migrants from his review of income and subjective wellbeing on the grounds that the scores were too low to be used for international comparison purposes.

Technical and cultural bias

We drew confidence from the case studies that confirmed the quality of life trendlines. Nevertheless, some reservations remained concerning technical and cultural factors that might interfere with a straightforward reading of the trendlines. Although we were careful to use the same

---

[5] Circulatory labour migration was a common feature of the apartheid economy. The system provided mainly male labour recruited in the former 'homelands' to work in the core economy and supplied cash income in the form of remittances to rural subsistence farmers. Migrants left their families behind and were housed in single-sex hostels on the mines and in urban areas. On reaching retirement age, labour migrants were forced to return to their rural homes. In the democratic era, circulatory migration is voluntary, hostels have been converted into family accommodation and many immigrants choose to remain in the urban areas permanently.

research company for repeat surveys, some *technical* inconsistencies had crept into surveys. Technicalities that might have influenced trends included minor changes in the wording of domain satisfaction items in successive surveys (Møller 1998), changes in the order in which response categories were presented and recorded (Møller 2001b), and the range of topics covered in successive omnibus surveys in addition to quality of life.

Regarding *cultural* bias, we were concerned that specific groups in society, say individualists or collectivists, might not be using the satisfaction scales in uniform manner. The literature has observed tendencies among certain non-western groups to avoid the poles or to 'play it safe' and use middle categories (Diener and Suh 2000). It is a known factor that the ideal of extraversion tends to exaggerate self-esteem and personal wellbeing in many western societies, whereas in Japanese and many other eastern societies, the ideal of modesty colours self-assessments of wellbeing.

Results from one of our early studies hinted that cultural factors might serve to exaggerate the differences in perceived subjective wellbeing among the South African elderly. In a study of the living circumstances of over sixties conducted in the early 1990s, we found that the black elderly tended to endorse most complaints covered in the survey, including illness, other minor disabilities, everyday activities of living and worries in life, whereas the white elderly appeared to deny experiencing many of these problems or to admit experiencing them only to a lesser degree. Differing attitudes to one's aches and pains and problems in life were also reflected in the extreme variations between black and white wellbeing scores. The white elderly were on average much more contented than the black elderly. Drawing on the anthropological literature in gerontology, we interpreted these divergent reactions by referring to contrasting norms prevailing in black and white communities (Møller and Ferreira 1992). The traditional ideal in African society is for older persons to be venerated. Respect for the older generation prescribes that the younger generation should care for the elderly and relieve them of duties and chores so they can sit back and be waited on. We reasoned that the 'complaining ethic' found in our survey might serve as a reminder to the general public of its duty to preserve the dignity of the older generation. In contrast, western society sets greater store by independence and self-reliance in seniors, which might have prompted the white elderly in our survey to respond in line with this social expectation. The case study illustrated how divergent cultural norms that reinforced discrepancies in living conditions and opportunities served to exaggerate the gulf between white and black wellbeing.

To a certain degree, suspicions that the happiness deficit of the black sector of South Africa's population might in part be due to cultural bias were laid to rest in 1994, the year of the first open elections in South Africa. A study conducted in the month following the elections to evaluate the success of voter education in the run-up to the elections opened up a unique opportunity to extend our quality of life trendlines. We inserted our standard life-satisfaction and happiness indicators into the study and to our amazement and delight, for the first time in South African survey history, the gap between black and white happiness and satisfaction vanished (Møller 1995c; Møller and Hanf 1995). The first open elections, which went off peacefully, were regarded as South Africa's miracle. For us, the fact that, under conditions of political freedom, first-time voters had no inhibitions in placing their mark on the top end of our happiness and satisfaction scales was no less of a miracle. This result boosted our faith enormously in the validity of the measures of wellbeing used in the South African Quality of Life Trends project.

A year later, confidence was boosted yet again, when the third round of research for the full set of thirty-five indicators showed that the election euphoria bubble had burst (Møller 1998). Happiness and life satisfaction scores among the materially less advantaged dropped closer to earlier levels. This result prompted us to speculate where the new set-level of South African happiness might come to rest in future, depending on whether the expectations of the newly enfranchised were met or frustrated (Møller 2001b).

The innovation phase: beyond the descriptive

In the course of the 1980s and 1990s, the global indicators of life satisfaction, happiness and life getting better or worse were included in all studies undertaken for the South African Quality of Life Trends Project. The global indicators proved to be convenient, inexpensive and powerful tools with which to monitor social change during South Africa's transition. While it was difficult to find financial support for regular rounds of research using the thirty-five indicators, it was possible to raise funds to continue the trendline for these three indicators.

To play it safe, if funds permitted, both global indicators of happiness and life satisfaction were used in these studies. For practical purposes, we assumed that the two highly correlated measures were interchangeable. If only one indicator could be applied, the choice of measure depended on the nature of the study. It seemed more fitting to apply a happiness rating in the context of a study on symbolic facets of quality of life. For example, happiness appeared to capture post-election euphoria better than life satisfaction. Similarly, when exploring the impact of the 'rainbow nation' as civil religion in the new democracy, it seemed more appropriate to use the measure of happiness (Dickow and Møller 2002; Møller, Dickow and Harris 1999). In contrast, when enquiring into the impact of service delivery on quality of life in the community setting, indicators of consumer satisfaction were considered most suitable (Møller 1996a, 1996d; Møller and Jackson 1997).

Focus on the material, relational and symbolic dimensions of quality of life

Research into development takes cognisance of material, relational and symbolic dimensions. Now that we were satisfied that our indicators were valid and sufficiently sensitive to detect shifts in the popular mood, we felt justified in extending our research interests. In the 1990s our research focus shifted from the descriptive to the analytic in an attempt to understand better the more subtle dimensions of life quality.

An obvious concern for the new democracy is the *material* aspect of quality of life. The post-1994 trendlines indicated that political freedom would not suffice to maintain the higher levels of happiness and satisfaction witnessed in the month following the first open elections. To address the material underpinnings of the new democracy, we shifted our attention to the delivery of basic services to the poor. We were informed by results from the Afrobarometer (2002) that citizens of Southern African countries were more likely to associate democracy with material benefits than with the basic tenets of democracy such as regular elections, freedom of association and communication and an independent press and judiciary. Findings from our own research suggested that material aspirations had been raised by the election promises. For example, low-income female householders in rural communities expected the new government to provide levels of services usually found in cities and at no cost to them (Sotshongaye and Møller 2000). An essay-writing competition among South African youth highlighted the new material concerns of the post-struggle generation that hoped to emulate the lifestyles of western age-peers (Leggett, Møller and Richards 1997).

In the mid-1990s, the implementation of the ambitious Reconstruction and Development Programme (RDP) experienced a setback when the new government discovered that its coffers were almost empty and it would first have to achieve economic stability before attempting to raise the living standards of the poor. Nevertheless, in spite of this setback, most of the new government's targets of building a million houses and providing access to clean water and electricity for the poor were achieved – as promised – within the first decade of democracy. One might expect habituation to set in with rising expectations – a factor to which economists attribute the lack of increase in happiness in spite of gains in affluence over time (Easterlin 2003). So far, habituation appears not to have occurred in South Africa according to studies connected to our project. Results from community surveys suggest that South Africans who have gained access to water and electricity and amenities in the home are appreciative of improvements to their living standards (Møller 1996a, 2000, 2001a). On the eve of democracy, at our insistence, Statistics South Africa (StatsSA) agreed to include a household-level satisfaction item ('how satisfied is this household with the way it lives these days') in its annual household surveys between 1995 and 1998. This item proved to be a useful tool for monitoring the perceived benefits of access to housing and service delivery among poorer households. Beneficiaries of basic services consistently indicated greater satisfaction with living conditions than non-beneficiaries in the lowest income brackets (Devey and Møller 2002; Møller and Devey 2003).

The *relational* facet of quality of life emerges as a powerful factor in our quality of life studies among the youth and the elderly. For example, a study of educational achievement in three-generation households suggested that self-confidence and life satisfaction might be passed on from one generation to the next (Møller 1995d). We found that if members of the older generation expressed high self-esteem, the younger generation was more likely to follow in their footsteps. The fact that government transfers to the poor are channelled through old-age pensions brings to the fore the power dynamics within households that impact on the material and subjective wellbeing of individual members. Respect relationships are particularly important in collectivist societies. According to qualitative survey evidence, the old-age pension increases the self-respect of the elderly, which in turn enhances their personal wellbeing (Møller and Sotshongaye 1996). However, the added responsibility of supporting a large number of dependents on their pension income detracts from happiness. In a time of rising costs of living, the vast majority of rural black pensioners surveyed in 2002 expressed dissatisfaction with life (Møller and Ferreira 2003).

The *symbolic* dimension of quality of life might be considered crucial in the phase of nation building following on South Africa's negotiated settlement. One of the rounds of research for the quality of life trends project took a closer look at achievements that inspired national pride. Achievements included the new civil religion of the 'rainbow nation' promoted by the country's first democratically elected president (Dickow and Møller 2002). The study found that South Africans who subscribed to the ideal of the rainbow nation tended to be more satisfied and optimistic for the future than others. This was particularly the case among Afrikaners, who are the losers under the new political dispensation. Interestingly, the study found that sporting achievements competed with the rainbow nation as the single most important national achievement that feeds South African self-esteem. One survey respondent remembered that he felt even more elated following South Africa's victory in the world rugby cup in 1995 than after the 1994 elections in which he voted for the first time (Møller and Dickow 2002). Sport not only influences personal wellbeing, it also plays an important role in South African politics. In 2004, South Africa was successful in its bid to host the 2010 soccer world soccer cup. It is significant that the South African delegation sent to secure the bid included the country's president, the former president and two Nobel peace prize-winners. If South Africa were to win the games in 2010, it is foreseeable that the country's aggregate happiness might soar to levels last recorded during the 1994 election euphoria.

South Africa's emergent black middle class

The case studies undertaken during the 1980s and early 1990s were mainly concerned with giving a voice to the ordinary person in the street. In the democratic era, it seemed equally important to enquire into the appreciation of life among South Africa's emergent black middle class. Since 1994, affirmative action and equity measures were put in place to speed up the process of black empowerment. Material gains under democracy acquired symbolic values associated with self-esteem and a sense of entitlement. Until recently, syndicated sample surveys produced too few cases of black respondents in the higher income groups to make meaningful comparisons between the satisfaction levels of black and white income elites. The 1999 survey for the quality of life trends study was the first to produce the required numbers. Results confirmed that levels of black and white satisfaction were equally high in the higher income brackets (Møller 1999a). Similar results were produced in a later round of research in 2002 that inquired into subjective wellbeing, optimism and attitudes to democracy. Black respondents with the highest material standards of living were compared with their less privileged black counterparts and with other income elites. The black elites scored above-average levels of life satisfaction and they were more optimistic than any other group in the survey. With regard to democratic attitudes, black elites exhibited greater tolerance towards other language and ethnic groups in society (Møller 2004).

International comparisons

Under apartheid, South Africa's closed society represented a unique case for quality of life studies. The research focus was inward-looking and concentrated on issues of racial discrimination and restrictions on social mobility that stunted the capabilities of oppressed individuals and communities and also depressed wellbeing. Quality of life researchers were preoccupied with within-society comparisons. When South Africa became a more open society under democracy it seemed appropriate to widen research horizons and to compare quality of life trends with those of other transition and middle-income countries.

An obvious choice for international comparison was with the states of the former Soviet Union. Several studies had attempted to understand better the impact on subjective wellbeing of rapidly changing economic fortunes in Russia's transition from a command to a liberal economy (Saris and Andreenkova 2001; Schyns 2001). This research thrust had found that income satisfaction tended to influence overall wellbeing in less developed countries, including transition Russia, while the effect was reversed or non-existent in more developed countries. The Dutch researchers who had teamed up with their Russian counterparts to test whether the top-down or bottom-up explanations of life satisfaction applied in the former Communist countries were invited to apply similar analyses to our South African quality of life trend data. Our South African trend study was conceived at a time when the bottom-up model was the dominant paradigm. The bottom-up model states that overall life satisfaction is the sum of satisfaction with all aspects of one's life. In the late 1980s, empirical research (Headey, Veenhoven and Wearing 1991; Lance, Mallard and Michalos 1995) started to cast doubts on the exclusive explanatory power of the bottom-up explanation versus the top-down explanation which states that overall life satisfaction spills over onto various aspects of life. This research indicated that causality might be in one or the other direction depending on the domain concerned. In the Russian case, the effect of income satisfaction tended to be bottom-up. In South Africa, the 'Mandela factor' and the extreme loyalty to the ruling party intimated that a 'feel good' factor might colour evaluations of specific domains in the afterglow of independence, especially for the black majority. Indeed the special analysis applied to the data on income, housing and social relations from the 1995 round of research suggested that the top-down model might have greater explanatory power in some instances. Among blacks and whites, the analysis found no bottom-up effects for these three domains and projections of future wellbeing influenced domain satisfactions in terms of the top-down effects (Møller and Saris 2001).

In the 1990s, South Africa regained a place in world society which opened up new opportunities for South African researchers to join international research efforts. With the backing of research partners in Europe, our project lobbied for the inclusion in Statistics South Africa's annual household survey of select items from the Euromodule. This household survey, together with the census, produces most of the country's official statistics on living conditions. A first for South Africa, the 2002 General Household Survey includes the Euromodule's eleven-point unlabelled satisfaction scale favoured by many contemporary quality of life researchers. A number of other items, including ones on anomia, also match the Euromodule. The aim of the Euromodule is to compare both quality of individual life and the quality of society in the older European Union countries and in the new members joining in May 2004 (Delhey 2001; Delhey, Böhnke, Habich and Zapf 2002). The addition of outliers, South Korea and South Africa, adds to the international flavour. In a further effort to compare South African appreciation of life with those of other countries, a trial run with an adapted version of the International Personal Wellbeing Index (Cummins, Eckersley, Pallant, van Vugt and Misajon 2003) was applied in a focused study on crime victims and their community and personal quality of life (Møller 2005).

11.4 The future quality of life research agenda

Which direction should quality of life studies for South Africa take in future? To a large degree, the challenges facing the young democracy will define the future research agenda (Schlemmer and Møller 1997). Expectations were raised by promises made to voters in the run-up to the national elections of 1994, 1999 and 2004. It is possible that higher living standards and the opening of new opportunities for the formerly disadvantaged in the population will not succeed in lifting levels of subjective wellbeing owing to habituation and a sense of entitlement. However, so far, the only evidence we have is that individuals and households that have made material gains under democracy are more satisfied with their lot than others. Nonetheless, the gap between rich and poor has increased since 1994. A task for future research will be to enquire more systematically into the reference standards used to appraise living conditions in the new era. A better understanding is needed of the manner in which relative deprivation and shifting reference standards affect personal wellbeing and perceptions of progress in achieving national development targets.

Certainly, one of the shortcomings of the South African Quality of Life Trends Project needs to be remedied. Launched some twenty-five years ago, the project was informed by the American rather than the European social indicators tradition. The result is a fairly narrow focus on the individual, an anomaly in a society that leans towards a collectivist worldview. To date, assessment of the quality of South African society has been applied mainly in community studies and opinion polls on controversial issues. In 2004, the government's ten-year review and the third democratic elections have focused South African minds on the quality of society, that is, on what needs to be achieved to ensure the good life for the masses. Interestingly, in a country where opinions tend to be polarised, there appears to be consensus on the major challenges facing South Africa in the next decade. There is agreement that solutions will have to be found to widespread poverty and inequality, crime and corruption, and the HIV/AIDS epidemic. These societal level issues will affect individual quality of life in future just as race relations cast a shadow on individual wellbeing in the past. Exploring the many factors still retarding human development in South Africa will occupy quality of life researchers for many years to come.

12 The complexity of wellbeing: a life-satisfaction conception and a domains-of-life approach

Mariano Rojas

> An economist who is nothing but an economist is a danger to his neighbours. Economics is not a thing in itself; it is a study of one aspect of the life of man in society.
>
> John R. Hicks 1941: 6–7, cited by Meier 1991: 352

12.1 Introduction

John Hicks's statement is important in many ways. First, it states that there are many aspects or domains in a person's life; thus, a person's wellbeing is expected to be related to her situation in all these aspects of life. Second, it recognises that economists usually deal with just one aspect of a person's life; hence, it is impossible to understand a person's wellbeing from an economic perspective alone. Third, it also recognises that economics, as a discipline, is an academic construct that studies only one aspect of a person's life. Hicks's comment refers to economics but it could also apply to any other of the social sciences. Fourth, it recognises that every person is in a society; hence, her wellbeing should be understood within her particular context and culture and in her relation to other persons. Consequently, a person is defined as such within her specific context, and there is no room for an out-of-any-context individual. Finally, it calls for an interdisciplinary study of human beings.

This investigation uses a life-satisfaction conception to study wellbeing. The investigation directly asks persons about their satisfaction with their lives, and this information is used as a proxy for a person's wellbeing. Hence, the investigation follows a subjective wellbeing approach to study wellbeing; it uses wellbeing as it is declared by the person herself. In addition, the investigation follows a domains-of-life approach to study life

The author is grateful to CONACYT for providing the financial support to run the survey which this study is based on.

satisfaction. The domains of life refer to concrete areas where a person is being human, and a person's wellbeing is studied on the basis of her situation in these areas. Furthermore, the investigation studies the existence of differences between overall satisfaction and satisfaction in domains of life across socioeconomic and demographic groups.

The empirical research is based on a relatively large survey applied in the central states of Mexico and the Federal District (Mexico City). The investigation shows that a subjective wellbeing approach provides useful information for the study of a person's wellbeing. Besides, the domains-of-life approach is a useful device to promote interdisciplinary research, because disciplines tend to concentrate on the study of specific domains, while the approach requires their concomitant study.

The chapter is structured as follows: first, it discusses the general approach; in particular, it deals with the subjective wellbeing approach, its life-satisfaction conception, and the relevant domains-of-life literature. Second, it explains the database and the construction of the domains-of-life and other relevant variables. Third, some descriptive statistics on life and domains-of-life satisfaction are presented. Fourth, it uses regression analysis to study the relationship between overall satisfaction and satisfaction in the particular domains of life. Fifth, differences in satisfaction across some socioeconomic and demographic groups are examined. Sixth, the relationship between domains-of-life satisfaction and socioeconomic and demographic variables is studied on the basis of regression analysis. Finally, some general conclusions and final considerations are made.

12.2   Methodological approach

What human wellbeing is and how to measure it constitute fundamental questions both in social sciences and in philosophy. The study of human wellbeing has been dominated by normative top-down approaches, which presume both what a good life is and how to attain it (Dohmen 2003; Veenhoven 2003) and take little feedback from human beings themselves. The Subjective Wellbeing approach (SWB) substantially differs from those approaches by following a bottom-up approach. On this ground it clearly constitutes a significant contribution to the understanding of human wellbeing.

The subjective wellbeing approach

The SWB approach has some particular characteristics (Rojas 2006b): *wholeness rather than partialness*. By directly asking people about their wellbeing, SWB studies the wellbeing of a person, rather than the wellbeing of an academically defined agent. Thus, it deals with a *human being of flesh and blood* (as in de Unamuno (2002)) and who is *in her circumstance* (as in Ortega y Gasset (2004)). By studying the wellbeing as declared by a person, in her circumstance, SWB deals with the person as she is. In this sense, a subjective wellbeing answer is connected to everything that makes a person what she is; including aspects such as her values, beliefs, aspirations, ambitions, joys, traumas, dependencies, worries, selective memories, intellectual and emotional capabilities, childhood and adolescence experiences, family upbringing, friends, cultural surrounding, education, social conditioning, and so on. Thus, it is the wellbeing of a person of *flesh and blood* and *in her circumstance* that must be studied, rather than the wellbeing of an academically constructed agent.

Inherently subjective   SWB states that a person's wellbeing is essentially subjective. It is the person herself who is living her life and experiencing her wellbeing. SWB accepts the inherent subjectivity of wellbeing. For example, Sumner (1996: 27) states that 'I believe there to be an interpretation of the subjective/objective distinction such that subjectivity turns out to be a necessary condition of success in a theory of welfare.'

The person as the authority   The person is the best authority to assess her wellbeing and to make an evaluation of her satisfaction with life. The approach accepts a person's judgement as a valid appraisal of her life satisfaction. It is neither the researcher nor the philosopher who judges a person's wellbeing, but the person herself, in her own terms and circumstance. The role of researchers is to understand the nature of a person's wellbeing assessment, rather than to assess it. The approach is positive because it deals with the wellbeing as it is appraised by a person as she currently is, given the personal and circumstantial factors that define her as she is. There is no person without circumstance; hence, there is no wellbeing judgement out of circumstance. A person's alternative is not to get rid of all her circumstances but to substitute them for different ones.

Inferential approach   SWB is based on an inferential, rather than normative, approach. SWB starts from a person's evaluation of her wellbeing and then follows an inferential approach to find its determinants. Normative approaches usually presume both the specific conception of human wellbeing and the factors that do explain it. SWB requires from a person just to be able to assess her life satisfaction or life happiness and to provide an answer that contains this information. The rest of the analysis, e.g. what are the determinants of wellbeing, is based on inferential techniques. In this way, the resources for wellbeing are inferred rather than presumed, and this bottom-up approach is flexible enough even to allow for heterogeneity across persons and across cultures.

Transdisciplinary approach   An SWB assessment is made by a person of flesh and blood; it incorporates all the complexity of what a person is. Therefore, the study of SWB is, in essence, transdisciplinary. It transcends the current organisation of knowledge and asks for approaching the issue as a human rather than as a disciplinary one. It is difficult to seize the complexity of an SWB assessment from any single discipline, since disciplines are based on an analytic-Cartesian paradigm of knowledge, which stresses the compartmentalisation of complex phenomena in as many parts as possible in order to study each part separately. In consequence, the current specialisation in knowledge implies that the understanding of a person's wellbeing assessment is clearly beyond any single discipline, and this becomes evident when it is realised that there is no single discipline which is framed to deal with happiness research.

Interdisciplinary research is a practical, but incomplete, solution to the problem of transdisciplinarity in wellbeing studies. It carries the limitations of a compartmentalised perspective of knowledge and professionals who decide to venture into interdisciplinary research must face such problems as the existence of different approaches, terminologies, methodologies and even interests and artificially set boundaries.

On the measurement of subjective wellbeing: life-satisfaction conception

SWB is commonly understood and measured either in its life-satisfaction or in its happiness conceptions (Cummins 1997, 1999; Ferrer-i-Carbonell 2002). The study of happiness and life satisfaction has a relatively long tradition in psychology (Argyle 2002; Diener 1984) and sociology (Michalos 1985; Veenhoven 1984, 1992). A few economists have recently recognised that there is useful information in a subjective wellbeing answer, and they have been using satisfaction variables as empirical proxies for their theoretical concept of utility. With the exception of the seminal work of Easterlin (1974), most research has taken place during the last decade. Having a proxy for utility opens enormous possibilities for economic research, and there has been a proliferation of studies in the last years (Clark and Oswald 1994; Di Tella, MacCulloch and Oswald 2001; Easterlin 1995, 2001; Frey and Stutzer 2000; McBride 2001; Oswald 1997; van Praag, Frijters and Ferrer-i-Carbonell 2003; van Praag and Ferrer-i-Carbonell 2004). It is noteworthy that most economists are not really concerned with the study of happiness and life satisfaction themselves; they are rather more interested in the use of satisfaction variables to study traditional economic issues (Rojas 2006a).

This chapter follows a life-satisfaction conception, which is expected to be less volatile and more cognitively oriented than happiness (Meadow, Mentzer, Rahtz and Sirgy 1992; Michalos 1980; Sirgy, Cole, Kosenko *et al.* 1995). Argyle states that

satisfaction is one of the main components of happiness. Joy is the emotional part, satisfaction is the cognitive part – a reflective appraisal, a judgment, of how well things are going, and have been going. In surveys we can ask either about satisfaction with 'life as a whole', or about specific domains, such as work, marriage, and health. (2002: 39)

The link between the cognitive and affective areas, and even the practice of approaching them as separate areas, is a matter of debate. Some authors have questioned the existence of this dichotomy, and many of them believe that the cognitive and the affective areas are not completely detached (Crooker and Near 1998; Lyubomirsky 2001).

Nevertheless, it is commonly accepted that people do have different things in mind when answering a happiness or a life-satisfaction question, and this reflects in less than perfect correlations when the two questions are asked of the same person.[1] Hence, life satisfaction is probably closer to the philosophers' conception of wellbeing as a happy life, which involves a person's judgement of her life (Tatarkiewicz 1976). This conception may be more relevant for public policy and development strategy than a wellbeing assessment based on transitory affective states.

Veenhoven (1984) states that SWB can only be measured on the basis of a person's answer to a direct question about her wellbeing; there is no room for speculation based on a person's possessions, facial expressions

---

[1] People in the survey were asked about their happiness and their life satisfaction. The correlation between the two variables is 0.49, which is high but not close to 1. Thus, it is clear that life satisfaction and happiness may share some information but they do not correspond to the same wellbeing appraisal.

or other extrinsic behaviour. However, Veenhoven states that it is not clear what kind of information an answer to a typical satisfaction question provides.

There has been some reluctance to accept a person's wellbeing statement. For example, economists have usually relied on so-called objective, directly observable, indicators of wellbeing, such as income and consumption expenditure. The dominance of these variables as proxies of wellbeing originates from two main characteristics of economic analysis: first, revealed preference theory implies reliance on people's actions rather than people's statements when judging what is in their interest; second, economic welfare analysis is based on the consumer, an academically constructed agent whose main role is, as her name says, to consume, and who is far away from a person of flesh and blood. In the psychological arena, Kahneman (1999) has used an 'objective-happiness' indicator which can be measured on the basis of observable variables such as smiling and other cheerful behaviours. He has a happiness conception that stresses hedonic experiences, and which privileges transitory affective states. However, whether this hedonic experience is what a human being of flesh and blood, and not an academically constructed psychological agent, has in mind when assessing her wellbeing is a matter for empirical research.

In any case, these so-called objective economic and psychological wellbeing indicators do need an external validation in order to be considered as indicators of a person's wellbeing. This external validation can only be based on a person's statement about her wellbeing. For example, Rojas (2006b) shows that income and consumption are not closely related to SWB. He studies three main reasons: First, there is much more in life than the standard of living, and a person's SWB depends not only on her consumption satisfaction but also on her situation in many other domains of life. Second, the same objective situation is perceived differently by different people, and for SWB what people perceive is more relevant than the objective situation itself. Third, there is heterogeneity in life purposes, and the factors that are relevant for a person's SWB may not be relevant for another person. In addition, Rojas (2005) shows that living a hedonic-oriented life is not everybody's idea of happiness.

The domains-of-life approach

The domains-of-life literature states that a person's life can be approached as a general construct of many specific domains, and that life satisfaction can be understood as the result of satisfaction in the domains of life (Cummins 1996; Headey, Holmström and Wearing 1984, 1985; Headey and Wearing 1992; Salvatore and Muñoz Sastre 2001; van Praag and Ferrer-i-Carbonell 2004; Veenhoven 1996).[2] The approach attempts to understand a general appraisal of life as a whole on the basis of a multidimensional vector of specific appraisals in more concrete spheres of being.

The enumeration and demarcation of the domains of life is arbitrary; it can go from a small number to an almost infinite recount of all imaginable human activities and spheres of being. Thus, there are many possible partitions of a human life, and the selected partition depends on the research's objectives. Nevertheless, any partition must value parsimony, meaning and usefulness.

On the basis of a meta-study of the literature, Cummins (1996) has argued for a seven-domain partition: material wellbeing, health, productivity, intimacy, safety, community and emotional wellbeing.

Van Praag et al. (2003) study the relationship of satisfaction in different domains of life (health, financial situation, job, housing, leisure and environment) and satisfaction with life as a whole. They state that 'satisfaction with life as a whole can be seen as an aggregate concept, which can be unfolded into its domain components' (van Praag et al. 2003: 3). Van Praag and Ferrer-i-Carbonell (2004) follow a domains-of-life approach in their book.

There has been some discussion on the causality of the relationship between satisfaction in domains of life and general satisfaction. Most researchers accept that satisfaction in domains of life contributes to the explanation of life satisfaction; however, some questions have been raised about the nature of the causality. It could be that satisfaction in domains of life explains life satisfaction but it could also be that global satisfaction explains a person's satisfaction in the domains of life (Argyle 2002; Diener 1984).[3] Because the issue of causality has not yet been settled, this investigation follows a bottom-up interpretation of the results; however, it recognises that a different interpretation is also possible.

[2] See also R. A. Cummins, 'A model for the measurement of subjective well-being through domains', draft, Deakin University, Australia, 2003.

[3] For a discussion on top-down versus bottom-up theories of life satisfaction see Headey, Veenhoven and Wearing (1991); Lance, Lautenschlager, Sloan and Varca (1989); Scherpenzeel and Saris (1996). Fox and Kahneman (1992) and Leonardi, Gagliardi, Marcellini and Spazzafumo (1999) propose a constructionist approach to the issue of causality.

12.3   The database

The survey and variables

A survey was conducted in five states of central and south Mexico,[4] as well as in the Federal District (Mexico City) during October and November of 2001. A stratified-random sample was balanced by household income, gender and urban-rural areas; 1,535 questionnaires were properly completed. However, only 579 observations are used in this investigation because of the need to work with who can report a satisfaction in all the domains of life under consideration.

The survey gathered information regarding the following quantitative and qualitative variables: demographic and socioeconomic variables, such as education, age, gender, civil status and current household income; a life-satisfaction variable associated with the following question: 'Taking everything in your life into consideration, how satisfied are you with your life?' A seven-option answering scale was used. The scale's answering options are: extremely unsatisfied, very unsatisfied, unsatisfied, neither satisfied nor unsatisfied, satisfied, very satisfied, extremely satisfied. Life Satisfaction was handled as a cardinal variable, with values between one and seven, where one was assigned to the lowest level of satisfaction and seven to the highest.[5] Variables about satisfaction with concrete areas of life were dealt with as follows: twenty-four questions were asked to enquire about satisfaction in many aspects of life, such as: housing conditions, job conditions, job responsibilities, working shifts, health, health services, financial solvency, income, neighbourhood relations, neighbourhood safety, rubbish collection in the neighbourhood, public transport, family relations, and so on. Domain satisfaction was measured with a similar scale to life satisfaction.

The construction of the domains of life and domain satisfaction variables

The following methodology was used to construct the domains of life: most of the 1,535 persons in the survey could not provide a satisfaction answer in some aspects of life under consideration. All these people had missing values in one or more aspects of life, not because they did not

---

[4] The states are: Oaxaca, Veracruz, Puebla, Tlaxcala and the State of Mexico.
[5] Ferrer-i-Carbonell and Frijters (2004) show that there are no substantial differences when satisfaction is treated either as a cardinal or as an ordinal variable. They state in their conclusions that: 'We found that assuming cardinality or ordinality of the answers to general satisfaction questions is relatively unimportant to results.'

want to provide an answer, but because that aspect of life was not pertinent for them. For example, some people were not employed and, as a result, could not state their satisfaction with their job, with their responsibilities, and so on. Many people did not have children or were not married. It is convenient to focus only on people who provide an answer in all aspects of life because the structural relationship between life satisfaction and satisfaction in domains of life is different for people who are absent from the domains. Thus, the investigation refers to those persons who provided an answer in all aspects of life under consideration; hence, only 579 persons out of the original 1,535 were considered.[6]

There were high correlations among satisfaction responses in many concrete areas of life. Hence, factor analysis was used to reduce the number of dimensions and to demarcate the domains of life. This technique permits the keeping of as much information as possible, while it avoids the problem of duplicating the use of information. Seven domains of life were identified on the basis of the factor analysis[7]: *health* domain – satisfaction with current health and with the availability and quality of medical services; *economic* domain – satisfaction with housing and living conditions, with income's purchasing power and with financial solvency; *job* domain – satisfaction with the job's activity and the job's responsibilities, with working shifts and with hierarchical working relations; *family* domain – satisfaction with spouse or stable-partner, with children and with rest-of-family; *friendship* domain – satisfaction with friends and with availability of time to spend with them; *personal* domain – satisfaction with availability of time to pursue personal hobbies and interests, with recreational activities, with personal growth and with education level; *community* domain – satisfaction with community services such as rubbish collection, public transport, road conditions, public lights, neighbourhood safety and trust in local authorities and neighbours.

It is obvious that the demarcation of the domains of life is somewhat determined by the original set of twenty-four questions. However, given the set of original questions, the factorial analysis allows not only for a reduction of the dimensions, but also for a good demarcation of the

---

[6] Most of the excluded people were unemployed (voluntarily or not), had no children or were not married.

[7] This classification is close to Cummins (1996). The health domain is considered by Cummins, while the family, job and economic domains closely resemble Cummins's intimacy, productivity and material domains. The community environment domain encompasses Cummins's safety and community domains. The friendship domain is not considered by Cummins as a separate domain. The personal domain is close to the leisure domain used by van Praag and Ferrer-i-Carbonell (2004).

Table 12.1 *Life satisfaction and satisfaction in domains of life: descriptive statistics*

	Mean	Standard deviation
	(scale 1 to 7)	
Life satisfaction	5.16	0.95
	(scale 1 to 100)	
Health	58.4	16.7
Economic	55.3	15.9
Job	62.0	16.8
Family	68.8	16.1
Friendship	54.6	15.8
Personal	54.4	16.3
Community	48.7	14.4

domains on the basis of clustering questions with similar information and setting apart questions with different information. Thus, factor analysis allows for a non-arbitrary demarcation of the domains of life.

Once the domains of life were defined, it was convenient to construct a single variable for satisfaction in each domain, rather than working with a vector of variables. A principal-components technique was used to create the new variable for satisfaction in each domain on the basis of the group of questions in the domain, and a regression method was used to calculate the factor score. The factor score was rescaled to a 1 to 100 basis to facilitate its manipulation and interpretation.

12.4   Satisfaction in domains of life and life satisfaction

Descriptive statistics

Table 12.1 shows the mean and standard deviation for life satisfaction, as well as for satisfaction in each domain of life. People report greater satisfaction in their family and job domains, while satisfaction is very low in the community domain. The mean value for life satisfaction is 5.16, which can be interpreted as people being, on average, a little above the satisfied category.

On the relationship: specification

A regression is run to study the nature of the relationship between life satisfaction and satisfaction in the domains of life. Most studies use a linear specification; however, it is a very restrictive one, because it implicitly assumes constant returns to any domain satisfaction, perfect substitutability between satisfaction in domains, and no synergies across domain satisfactions. This chapter uses a constant elasticity of substitution (CES) specification, which is a more flexible one and, in consequence, provides a better fit. The CES specification allows for flexible returns to domain satisfaction, for positive or negative synergies between domain satisfaction, for different degrees of substitution between domains, and for other commendable characteristics.[8]

The specification is expressed as:

$$LS_i = \left(\left(\alpha_1 Hea_i^\sigma \right) + \left(\alpha_2 Eco_i^\sigma \right) + \left(\alpha_3 Job_i^\sigma \right) + \left(\alpha_4 Fam_i^\sigma \right) \right. \\ \left. + \left(\alpha_5 Fri_i^\sigma \right) + \left(\alpha_6 Per_i^\sigma \right) + \left(\alpha_7 Com_i^\sigma \right) \right)^{\varepsilon/\sigma} + \mu_i \quad (12.1)$$

where:

LS_i: Life satisfaction of person i, in a 1 to 7 scale.
Hea_i: Health satisfaction of person i, in a 1 to 100 scale.
Eco_i: Economic satisfaction of person i, in a 1 to 100 scale.
Job_i: Job satisfaction of person i, in a 1 to 100 scale.
Fam_i: Family satisfaction of person i, in a 1 to 100 scale.
Fri_i: Friendship satisfaction of person i, in a 1 to 100 scale.
Per_i: Personal satisfaction of person i, in a 1 to 100 scale.
Com_i: Community services satisfaction of person i, in a 1 to 100 scale.
μ_i: error term for person i.
   ε, σ, α_j: parameters to be estimated, $j = 0, 1, 2, \ldots, 7$

On the relationship regression analysis

Equation 12.1 is estimated using Ordinary Least Squares (OLS) on the whole sample. There are good reasons to assume that the importance of domain satisfaction in overall satisfaction may differ across demographic groups. Thus, it could be appropriate to split the sample in order to estimate specific parameters for each demographic group. However, this chapter does not explore the issue and assumes that the parameters are identical for all groups in the sample. Table 12.2 presents the results from the analysis.

---

[8] An in-depth study of the relationship between life satisfaction and satisfaction in domains of life is found in Rojas (2006a).

Table 12.2 *Life satisfaction and domains of life satisfaction:
CES specification*

	Coeff.	Asymp.Prob>t
a-Health	0.074	0.07
a-Economic	0.044	0.12
a-Job	0.059	0.07
a-Family	0.107	0.09
a-Friendship	−0.014	0.25
a-Personal	0.067	0.07
a-Community	0.000	0.50
ϵ	0.525	0.00
σ	1.108	0.01
R-squared	0.334	

It is observed that life satisfaction is positively related to satisfaction in all domains except friendship. Satisfaction in the family domain is fundamental for a person's satisfaction with life; its coefficient is relatively large and statistically significant. It is important to remember that the family domain involves satisfaction with partner, children and the rest of the family. Satisfaction in the health, personal and job domains is also very important for a person's life satisfaction; their coefficients are statistically significant.

Satisfaction in the economic domain is less important but not negligible. It is important to remark that the CES specification implies that the impact on life satisfaction of any change in domain satisfaction is contingent on the initial satisfaction level in the domain. In other words, even if the coefficient is higher for family satisfaction than for economic satisfaction, it could be possible for a person who is highly satisfied with her family but fairly satisfied with her economy to benefit the most from an increase in economic rather than in family satisfaction.

It is surprising that satisfaction in the friendship and community domains is not related to life satisfaction. However, it is important to mention that the sample does not include single persons or couples with no children. It is expected that the friendship and community domains will be more relevant for such kinds of persons.

The goodness of fit of the regression is measured by the R-squared coefficient, which is 0.334. It is reasonably high, once it is recognised that there could be other domains of life not considered in the analysis, that the specification of the relationship could be different, that there may be some biases in a person's judgement about her life satisfaction and that there are many person-specific factors that play an important role in life satisfaction.

12.5   Life satisfaction and domains-of-life satisfaction by socio-demographic groups

A person's satisfaction in domains of life could depend on some socioeconomic and demographic characteristics. As stated by Cheung and Leung:

Conceivably, personal and societal conditions need not affect all citizens in the same way. A typical way to make sense of the heterogeneity of people is to pay attention to social stratification factors, usually including class, education, age, and gender. Accordingly, these factors not only determine the level of life satisfaction, but also shape the ways that personal and societal conditions affect one's life satisfaction. (2004: 26)

For example, it is reasonable to hypothesise that there are differences for women and men, given their physiological differences, their different roles in society and the differences in family upbringing (Eagly 1987). Role difference and family upbringing depend on a country's culture and traditions (Mallard, Lance and Michalos 1997), therefore this investigation's findings are valid only for Mexico and could substantially differ with respect to other countries. A similar reasoning could be used to argue for differences across age groups, education levels and economic status. Therefore, this section studies the differences between life satisfaction and satisfaction in the domains of life across variables such as gender, age, education, and income. The analysis is partial in the sense that it focuses on differences across one socioeconomic and demographic characteristic at a time. A joint consideration of all the socioeconomic and demographic characteristics is made in the following section.

Gender

Table 12.3 presents the mean satisfaction levels for women and men; these averages are calculated for life satisfaction and for satisfaction in each domain of life. Table 12.3 also shows a men to women ratio for these satisfactions.

It is observed that differences across gender are, on average, minimal. Men tend to be slightly more satisfied with their lives than women and they are also more satisfied in all domains except the economic one. Men are more satisfied in domains that have proven to be very important for life satisfaction, such as the family, job, health and personal

Table 12.3 *Differences in satisfaction across gender: mean values*

	Women	Men	Ratio men to women
Life satisfaction	5.10	5.20	1.02
Health	57.4	58.9	1.03
Economic	56.1	54.9	0.98
Job	61.3	62.4	1.02
Family	68.0	69.2	1.02
Friendship	54.0	54.9	1.02
Personal	52.8	55.2	1.05
Community	48.0	49.0	1.02

domains. This fact gives men an advantage with respects to their life satisfaction.

The greatest difference takes place in the *personal* domain, where men are 5 per cent more satisfied than women; it is important to remember that the personal domain refers to aspects of life such as education and personal growth, recreational activities and availability of time to pursue personal hobbies and interests.

Age

Three groups were formed according to a person's age: *younger*, between 18 and 30 years old, *middle*, between 31 and 50 years old and *elder* for people older than 50 years. Table 12.4 presents the mean values for life satisfaction and satisfaction in each domain of life across age groups.

It is observed that life satisfaction is, on average, almost the same for middle-aged and younger people. Elder people have a much lower satisfaction with life.

In reference to younger people, middle-aged persons have lower satisfaction in the health and family domains, which are very important for life satisfaction. But they have higher satisfaction in the economic, job and personal domains, which also contribute to life satisfaction. Middle-aged people also have higher satisfaction levels in the friendship and community domains of life.

In reference to younger people, elder persons have lower satisfaction in such important domains of life as family, job and health; as well as in the economic domain. They have higher satisfaction in the personal and community domains. Thus, it is not surprising that elder persons have lower life satisfaction than young and middle-aged persons.

Table 12.4 *Differences in satisfaction across age groups: mean values*

	Younger	Middle	Elder	Ratio middle/ younger	Ratio elder/ younger
Life satisfaction	5.16	5.19	5.08	1.01	0.98
Health	60.6	58.8	54.1	0.97	0.89
Economic	54.9	56.1	53.0	1.02	0.96
Job	60.8	63.8	57.6	1.05	0.95
Family	70.5	69.4	64.1	0.98	0.91
Friendship	53.1	55.6	53.1	1.05	1.00
Personal	52.3	55.2	54.6	1.05	1.04
Community	46.0	49.5	49.4	1.08	1.07

Education

For the following exercise, the original seven education groups are collapsed into the following three categories: The low-education category includes persons with an education level of secondary school at most. The mid-education category includes persons who have high school, technical, and semi-professional studies. The high-education category includes persons with university studies, at both the undergraduate and graduate levels.

Table 12.5 shows the mean values for life satisfaction and satisfaction in each domain of life across education groups. A clear and strong relationship between satisfaction and education is observed. Life satisfaction increases with a person's education level. A person in the mid-education group is, on average, 4 per cent more satisfied with her life than a person in the low-education group. This figure goes up to 6 per cent when the high- and the low-education groups are compared.

There are substantial increases in satisfaction in domains such as family, job, personal and health; which are fundamental for life satisfaction. There are also increases in economic satisfaction, which also makes a contribution to life satisfaction. In comparison to a low-educated person, a highly educated person is 28 per cent more satisfied with the economic aspects of her life, 22 per cent more satisfied in her personal domain, 16 per cent more satisfied with her health, 15 per cent more satisfied with her job activities and 11 per cent more satisfied in her family domain. Thus, results in Table 5 provide a hint about the importance of education for greater wellbeing; it seems that the benefits of education reach almost all domains of life and that further research on how these benefits take place would be valuable.

Table 12.5 *Differences in satisfaction across education groups: mean values*

	Low	Middle	High	Ratio middle/low	Ratio high/low
Life satisfaction	5.03	5.23	5.31	1.04	1.06
Health	54.8	59.5	63.8	1.09	1.16
Economic	50.1	56.5	64.0	1.13	1.28
Job	58.3	63.6	67.1	1.09	1.15
Family	65.6	70.3	73.0	1.07	1.11
Friendship	52.7	55.5	56.9	1.05	1.08
Personal	50.1	55.4	61.2	1.11	1.22
Community	48.5	47.0	51.0	0.97	1.05

Income

The sample was divided into two income categories: the first category includes people with a monthly household income of no more than 5,000 Mexican pesos[9]; these people can be considered as economically poor on the basis of the criteria set by the Mexican Social Development Secretariat. A second category includes people with a monthly household income above 6,000 Mexican pesos, and they can be considered as economically non-poor. A buffer zone was created for people with monthly household incomes of between 5,000 and 6,000 Mexican pesos. There are 250 people in the economically poor category, 249 in the non-poor category and 80 in the buffer zone.

Table 12.6 shows the mean values for life satisfaction, satisfaction in the domains of life and household income by income group.

The economically non-poor have, on average, a household income that is almost 300 per cent greater than that of the economically poor. There is a hint that being economically poor tends to hamper life satisfaction, as well as satisfaction in all domains of life. The economically non-poor are, on average, 6 per cent more satisfied with their lives. They are 25 per cent more satisfied in their economic domain, 16 per cent more satisfied in their job domain, 12 per cent more satisfied with their health, 10 per cent more satisfied in their personal domain and 8 per cent more satisfied in their family domain.

---

[9] The exchange rate at the time of the survey was approximately 9.30 Mexican pesos per US dollar.

Table 12.6 *Differences in satisfaction across income group: mean values*

	Economically poor	Economically non-poor	Ratio economically non-poor to poor
Life satisfaction	5.03	5.31	1.06
Health	55.1	61.7	1.12
Economic	49.4	61.6	1.25
Job	57.7	66.8	1.16
Family	66.4	71.7	1.08
Friendship	53.1	56.3	1.06
Personal	51.6	57.1	1.10
Community	48.8	48.6	1.00
Average monthly household income	3,160	12,570	3.97

12.6 Socioeconomic and demographic variables and satisfaction in the domains of life regression analysis

Socioeconomic and demographic factors do have an impact on life satisfaction through their relationship to a person's satisfaction in the domains of life. The previous section has provided some hints about the role of factors such as gender, age, education and income. However, it follows a partial analysis, that is, each factor is studied separately. It is convenient to study the role of all factors in a simultaneous way, especially because some factors are highly correlated. Thus, this section uses regression analysis to study the relationship between satisfaction in each domain of life and the group of socioeconomic and demographic variables.

A regression analysis was applied to the following general specification:

$$DS_{ik} = F(Y_i, G_i, A_i, E_i) \qquad k = 1, 2, \ldots, 7 \qquad (12.2)$$

where:

DS_{ik}:   person i's satisfaction in domain of life k, in a 1 to 100 scale, $k = $ *health, economic, job, family, friendship, personal* and *community* domains.

Y_i: person i's household income, in thousands of Mexican pesos.

G_i: person i's gender, 0 for woman and 1 for men.

A_i: person i's age, in years.

E_i: person i's education level, as an ordinal variable in a 1 to 7 scale.

Different specifications were tried with no substantial difference in the results; therefore, the results presented in this section refer to the following linear specification:

$$DS_{ik} = \beta_0 + \beta_1 Y_i + \beta_2 G_i + \beta_3 A_i + \beta_4 E_i + \mu_i \quad k = 1, 2, \ldots, 7 \quad (12.3)$$

Table 12.7 shows the results from the regression analysis for satisfaction in each one of the seven domains of life under consideration. The goodness of fit is very low for all but the economic domain of life. This finding indicates that the variables in the study are not main determinants of satisfaction in most domains of life and that there are many factors beyond the socioeconomic and demographic ones that play a role in domain satisfaction.

An analysis by domain of life indicates the following findings in the seven domains:

Health domain – age, gender and education are statistically related to satisfaction in the health domain. Health satisfaction strongly declines with age and men declare higher health satisfaction than women. Education is a very important explanatory variable of health satisfaction. The impact of income in health satisfaction is very weak. The goodness of fit (R-squared) is very low (0.084), hence, the socioeconomic and demographic variables explain only a small portion of the variability in health satisfaction.

Economic domain – satisfaction in this domain of life is strongly related to a person's income and education but it is affected by neither a person's gender nor her age. Keeping all other things constant, the difference in economic satisfaction between a highly educated person (category 7) and an uneducated person (category 1) is of about 14 points. On the other hand, an increase in monthly household income of 7,000 Mexican pesos, one standard deviation in the survey, would raise economic satisfaction by 4 points. The R-squared is relatively high (0.196) and thus the socioeconomic and demographic variables have their greater explanatory power in the economic domain.

Job domain – satisfaction in the job domain is greater for men than for women; it tends to decrease with age, and it is positively and strongly related to both education and income.

Family domain – this domain has proven to be strongly related to life satisfaction. It is found that family satisfaction is strongly related to a person's education level. Keeping all other things constant, the difference in family satisfaction between a highly educated person (category 7) and an uneducated person (category 1) is of about 11 points. Men are more

Table 12.7 *Satisfaction in domains of life and socioeconomic and demographic variables – linear specification: regression analysis*

	Health		Economic		Job		Family		Friendship		Personal		Community	
	coeff.	Prob. > t	coeff.	Prob. > t	coeff.	Prob. > t	coeff.	Prob. > t	coeff.	Prob. > t	coeff.	Prob. > t	coeff.	Prob. > t
Constant	55.92	0.00	43.60	0.00	55.86	0.00	66.30	0.00	46.81	0.00	36.93	0.00	44.12	0.00
Gender	2.846	0.05	−0.145	0.91	2.326	0.10	2.685	0.05	0.938	0.50	3.103	0.03	0.932	0.46
Age	−0.210	0.00	−0.054	0.32	−0.105	0.08	−0.169	0.00	0.028	0.64	0.063	0.29	0.067	0.22
Education	1.943	0.00	2.429	0.00	1.173	0.02	1.792	0.00	1.256	0.01	3.183	0.00	0.057	0.90
Income	0.151	0.15	0.565	0.00	0.554	0.00	0.074	0.46	0.149	0.15	0.040	0.70	0.139	0.14
R-squared	0.084		0.196		0.110		0.065		0.029		0.099		0.010	

satisfied in their family domain than women (2.7 points of difference), and family satisfaction tends to decline strongly with age. It is also found that a person's household income does not make a difference with respect to family satisfaction.

Friendship domain – satisfaction in this domain is positively related to a person's education. There is no relationship at all with a person's gender, age and household income.

Personal domain – satisfaction in this domain has also proven to be important for life satisfaction. It is found that satisfaction in this domain is strongly related to a person's education. Keeping all other things constant, the difference in personal satisfaction between a highly educated person (category 7) and an uneducated person (category 1) is of about 19 points. Personal satisfaction is also greater for men than for women. It is also found that income and age are not important explanatory variables of personal satisfaction.

Community domain – it is found that satisfaction in this domain of life is not related to any of the socioeconomic and demographic variables under consideration.

12.7   Final considerations

This investigation followed a subjective wellbeing approach to study a person's wellbeing. It was argued that life satisfaction, as declared by the person herself, provides information that is useful in the study of human wellbeing. The approach has many advantages, in particular because it deals with human beings as they are: human beings of *flesh and blood* and *in their circumstance*. In addition, according to the domains-of-life literature, a person's life satisfaction can be approached from a domains-of-life perspective, that is, life satisfaction is understood in its relation to satisfaction in concrete areas of being.

On the basis of information from a Mexican survey, the investigation used factor-analysis techniques to define seven domains of life (health, economic, job, family, friendship, personal and community) and to construct indicators of satisfaction in these domains. The empirical research confines itself to people who perform in all seven domains of life.

The relationship between life satisfaction and satisfaction in the domains of life was studied. It was found that satisfaction in the family domain is crucial for life satisfaction; this domain includes satisfaction with spouse, children and rest of family. Satisfaction in the health, job and personal domains is also very important for a person's satisfaction with her life. The economic domain, which refers to satisfaction in areas of life such as housing and living conditions, financial solvency and income, is relatively less important for life satisfaction; however, its importance becomes larger as economic satisfaction is lower. Hence, a person who is very unsatisfied in her family domain and satisfied in her economic domains may benefit the most from an increase in family rather than in economic satisfaction. However, a person who is satisfied in her family domain but very unsatisfied in her economic domain could attain an important increase in her life satisfaction by improving her economic satisfaction.

Socioeconomic and demographic variables affect life satisfaction through their influence in domains of life satisfaction. Hence, their importance depends on how strong their influence is in those domains that have proven to be important for life satisfaction. A variable is more important in explaining life satisfaction if it is strongly related to satisfaction in those domains that are more important in generating life satisfaction. Thus, SWB can be used to identify the relevant resources for a person's wellbeing; these resources do not have to be universal, they may be contingent on a person's own circumstance (see Rojas forthcoming).

The investigation found that the positive impact of more education spreads across almost all domains of life under consideration. Thus, education is a very important resource for increasing satisfaction in many domains of life and, especially, in those domains of life that are important for life satisfaction, such as family, health, personal, job and economic domains. The impact of education is relatively strong with respect to satisfaction in the personal, family and health domains. Hence, education could be a powerful resource in the social procurement of wellbeing, and future research should focus not only on the quantity of education but also on its quality.

The impact of more income on domain satisfaction is limited to the job and economic domains. Satisfaction in these domains has proven to make a contribution to life satisfaction and, in consequence, income can play a role in increasing life satisfaction. However, income is not a relevant resource for satisfaction in domains such as family and personal, which are also crucial for life satisfaction.

With respect to gender, it is found that men are more satisfied than women in the health, job, family and personal domains, which are important for life satisfaction. Similarly, it is found that satisfaction in the health, job and family domains declines with age. These gender and age differences in domain satisfaction could emerge from the interaction of physiological differences and social institutions that turn these differences into dissimilar satisfaction levels.

The low goodness of fit of the domains-of-life satisfaction regressions indicates that more research is needed to understand the main determinants of domains-of-life satisfaction. It is clear that satisfaction in the domains of life does not closely follow some objective economic indicators that are usually used as its proxy.

Wellbeing, understood as life satisfaction and approached from a domains-of-life perspective, is a complex phenomenon. As it is articulated in John Hicks's statement, it goes beyond the economics arena, to include other aspects of life. These domains of life are interrelated in intricate ways and their relationship to life satisfaction is non-linear. Concern for wellbeing improvement should focus not only on those domains that are very important, but also on those domains where satisfaction is relatively low and could easily be increased. In consequence, with respect to research and promotion of human wellbeing, it is better to keep a broad perspective and look at all those features that lead to a life which a person is satisfied with, rather than to concentrate in the promotion of satisfaction in just one domain, as economists do in the economic one. From an academic perspective, this implies that the study of wellbeing asks for an interdisciplinary, or a transdisciplinary, approach. In addition, the study of wellbeing cannot avoid subjectivity, since it is the person (subject) who, in the end, lives the condition of being well and has the authority to judge it.

Knowledge about which domains of life are important for a person being satisfied with her life is of value for the social procurement of wellbeing. It is necessary to identify those resources that contribute to a person's satisfaction in each domain of life. It is also important to understand the role that social institutions and the organisation of society play in domains-of-life satisfaction. Life satisfaction must be a core element in any definition of development.

Conclusion: researching wellbeing

13 Researching wellbeing across the disciplines: some key intellectual problems and ways forward

Philippa Bevan

[It] is generally not possible to ask all the interesting questions about any really significant phenomenon within the same theory or even within a set of commensurable, logically integratable theories. Noting this was one of the breakthroughs of modern physics, linked to the theory of relativity.

Calhoun 1995: 8

13.1   Introduction

Social science research into poverty, inequality and wellbeing has usually been conducted on a mono-disciplinary basis. The little cross-disciplinary research there has been has tended to take place within policy-related fields of study such as social policy and development studies, although even here true collaborations are rare. Since the early 1990s I have been involved, as a sociologist, in the theoretical and empirical study of poverty and related issues in Ethiopia and Uganda, and Africa more broadly. During this time I made a number of attempts to work with economists on these issues, recognising the potential synergies which could result from an interaction of the expertises. My failure to achieve a cross-disciplinary relationship with development economists is not unique, and I became interested in the underlying reasons, in particular in understanding the extent to which these are intellectual, rather than institutional, political and historical. This extended into a more general interest in cross-disciplinary collaboration, and, given the power of Sayer's argument for post-disciplinary approaches to 'concrete' issues, I was driven to

I am particularly grateful to Ian Gough and Allister McGregor for helpful comments on an earlier draft.

enquire why there has been so little cross-disciplinary collaboration in researching poverty in developing countries:

> While all disciplines ask distinctive and worthwhile abstract (i.e. one-sided) questions, understanding concrete (i.e. many-sided) situations requires an inter-disciplinary, or better, postdisciplinary approach, which follows arguments and processes wherever they lead, instead of stopping at conventional disciplinary boundaries, subordinating intellectual exploration to parochial institutional demands. (Sayer 1999: abstract)

Five sets of barriers to multi-disciplinary collaboration in poverty research can be identified, four of which are not considered here in any detail: disciplinary cultures, disciplinary habituses, and the histories and political economies of firstly the social sciences disciplines and secondly donor-related poverty research and policy. The fifth set of barriers explored here, the potentially conflicting intellectual assumptions which underpin different social science 'paradigms' or research models, seemed the most interesting and change-relevant, and in October 2002 I obtained a small ESRC grant[1] to finance a study entitled 'Towards a post-disciplinary understanding of global poverty'. The aim of the project was:

> to explore the *intellectual* reasons why it is so difficult in practice to conduct 'poverty' research which integrates useful perspectives and methods from the disciplines of economics, sociology, social anthropology, political science and psychology. The analysis will generate practical ideas for improving inter-disciplinary dialogues in academic and practitioner contexts, producing a deeper understanding of global poverty in the process. The research will follow two interacting paths: comparative discourse analyses of key academic and policy publications, and an action research study with members of a multi-disciplinary team based at Bath University and in Thailand, Peru, Bangladesh and Ethiopia, as they launch an ESRC research programme on poverty, inequality and the quality of life in October 2002.[2]

The methodology involved refining a conceptual framework for the analysis of key intellectual aspects of social science disciplines, through a process of iteration between framework and research objects. The project had two aspects: production of the framework and its use in the two contexts described in the proposal. As part of the analysis of policy-related academic approaches to global poverty the framework was used in a critical analysis of the 'Q-Squared' or 'Qual-Quant' approach to multi-disciplinarity launched by Kanbur in 2002 (Kanbur 2003) and to describe an alternative 'Q-Integrated' approach (Bevan, forthcoming). It was also used to inform an action research process with WeD

---

[1] ESRC Award number R000223987. It comprised eight months' research time between October 2002 and January 2003.
[2] Bevan Research Proposal to ESRC, 2002.

researchers to enable those who participated first to reflect privately[3] on the knowledge foundations underpinning their particular approach to poverty and subjective quality of life and secondly to engage in dialogue about such foundations with colleagues from other disciplines.

This chapter is informed by the WeD research project.[4] The framework is put to use to analyse intellectual assumptions within the different niche approaches to wellbeing which have been brought to the multi-disciplinary programme. The aim is to identify which intellectual barriers are spurious and which must be negotiated or circumvented for multi-disciplinarity to bring added value. Section 13.2 describes the Foundations of Knowledge Framework (FoKF): a conceptual framework which identifies nine types of knowledge assumption which empirical researchers with a policy focus must make, either explicitly or implicitly. In section 13.3 the framework is used to compare the wellbeing research models with which WeD is negotiating from social anthropology, sociology, political theory, psychology and economics across each type of knowledge assumption. In the process of these comparisons some key intellectual issues are identified and suggestions made of ways forward for the WeD programme. Section 13.4 presents the main conclusions.

13.2   A conceptual framework for exploring the disciplines: the Foundations of Knowledge Framework

While the framework described here was developed out of a wider reading programme, it draws particularly on four sources. The first is Andrew Sayer who, in two major works on social science methodology (1992, 2000), provided arguments to support a move to 'post-disciplinary studies' and tools to assist in the analysis of disciplinary ontologies, epistemologies, research methods and normative theories. The question at issue here is *how* you know what you think you know. Self-reflexivity in relation to this question can lead to a greater humility about one's own 'knowledge'. Applied to the knowledge of others it provides a transparent basis for both appreciation and criticism.

The second is Wallerstein (1999) who argued that within the social sciences lie a number of persistent challenges. The most important are Freud's challenge to the operationality of the concept of formal rationality; challenges to Eurocentrism; problems associated with our

---

[3] Either through written responses to a questionnaire (see Appendix 13A) or through an interview based on the questionnaire.
[4] This chapter is imbued with ideas I have picked up from the writings and talkings of WeD members over some years and non-WeD participants in the Hanse workshop.

dominant conceptions of time as nomothetic ('eternal time') and ideographic ('episodic time'); the challenges presented by complexity studies and their refutation of the most fundamental assumptions of Newtonian mechanics; the challenge of feminism; and the challenge of the idea that we have never really been modern.

Thirdly, post-modernism has encouraged more critical views of key categories of social thought, especially binary distinctions. However, much social science is based on binary oppositions; social phenomena are seen as either belonging to category A or category not-A. Some important examples of relevance to the analysis of global poverty are universal/relative, universal/local, universal/particular, global/local, objective/subjective, macro/micro, structure/action, qualitative/quantitative. 'Deconstructions' of concepts, sociological approaches developing 'complexity' and 'chaos' metaphors, and 'the new science of fuzzy logic' which recognises that sometimes phenomena are both A and not-A, all offer ways of thinking around and through oppositions which may no longer seem to be helpful.[5] Finally Myerson (1994) proposed and elaborated a definition of rationality as 'dialogue' which offers both theoretical and practical supports for FoKF approaches.

The FoKF identifies the following nine types of knowledge assumptions: research domain and questions; values/normative theory; ontology; epistemology; theories; methodological framework; types of empirical conclusion; rhetoric; and praxis. In going through these aspects, I use examples from development-related poverty studies; this will help to clarify what each of the elements of the framework involves while simultaneously providing information about the wider context of the WeD research.

Domain and problematic

Within each (sub)discipline, the focus has usually been on a domain conceptualised as univocal; as having one meaning. In recent development-related empirical poverty research, identification of the domain, problematic and research questions has been strongly driven by political values and standpoints. Thus, for example, in the policy-dominant neo-classical economics approach 'poverty' has usually meant household-level income/consumption poverty and its reduction related to modernisation via market forces (e.g. Meier 1995), while in the post-structuralist tradition, it is a concept invented by modernising Westerners to 'label' in order to facilitate a 'development' agenda which will destroy local cultures and

[5] On 'deconstructions' see Sayer, 2000; on 'complexity' and 'chaos' metaphors see Abbott 2001, Byrne 1998 and Eve *et al.* 1997; on 'fuzzy logic' see Kosko 1994 and Ragin 2000.

only benefit the developers (e.g. Escobar 1995). Other poverty discourses identifiable in the broader social science literature include the much-maligned culture of poverty discourse (e.g. O. Lewis 1967), the marxist focus on the power of capital (e.g. Hoogvelt 1997; Duffield 2001), populist 'participatory' approaches (e.g. Chambers 1983), social exclusion discourses (e.g. Rodgers *et al.* 1995), and welfarist modernisation approaches focusing on human poverty and wellbeing (e.g. Sen 1999).

Values/standpoints/normative theories

Each of the empirical research approaches described above is based on a normative theory about the 'good life', and how it might be obtained, which is more or less coherent and explicit. In this area there also exist a range of explicit and coherent normative theories based on philosophical argumentation few of which have engaged directly with empirical evidence. Some examples include: democratic liberalism (e.g. Sen 1999; Alkire, this volume), human need theories (e.g. Doyal and Gough 1991; Gasper, this volume), communitarianism (e.g. Lehman 2000), feminism (e.g. Gilligan 1983), marxism (e.g. Sutcliffe 2001), post-colonialism (e.g. Escobar 1995).

Ontology: what is the world assumed to be like?

This is an area of much more interest to some disciplines than others, and goes with a recognition of the importance of conceptualisation as both a theoretical and a methodological exercise. The key bifurcation here has been between those who claim that reality equates with empirical reality (positivism) and those battling with the various problems for such a belief raised by scientific developments early in the last century and later post-modern understandings of relativism. Poverty research in poor countries has been dominated by neo-classical economists, some of whom, while having little to say about ontology, have claimed a rigour resulting from their positivist research methods, mathematical modelling and statistical techniques, which are imagined as providing a scientific view of objective reality.[6] Extreme post-modernists claim there is no reality independent of people's ideas about it.

In recent years the positivist/relativist bifurcation has been challenged by the growing school of 'critical realism' (e.g. Sayer 2000) for whom ontology is very important. It is assumed that there is a reality which

---

[6] See, for example, the contributions from economists to the first Q-Squared workshop (Kanbur 2003).

exists independently of what any researcher might think about it, and further that what the researcher thinks is a small part of reality.[7] Critical realists draw a distinction between 'the real', 'the actual' and 'the empirical'. The real consists of the structures and powers of objects deriving from their nature, which, depending on circumstances, may or may not be actualised. The actual describes what happens if and when the powers of an object are activated, while the empirical is the domain of experience or what is observed.

Epistemology: how can the world be known about?

For positivists, reality is only accessible through direct sensory experience; the empirical is the real. Accordingly, the research objects they 'measure exist and measurements of them describe them as they are regardless of the context or character of the measurement process' (Byrne 2002: 15). At the other extreme, purist post-modernists assert 'a relativism based on unique interpretation – meaning alone and meaning which may be different for every interpreter' (ibid: 2). The critical realist approach to epistemology is one of 'fallibilism'; it is impossible to establish 'the truth' about what is real. The important questions for a piece of knowledge are: 'is it practically adequate at this point in time?' and 'what research might be done that would increase adequacy?' Such an approach enjoins a relaxed approach to epistemology, in the process removing one intellectual barrier to multi-disciplinary research. For example, it obviates any need to have abstract arguments about the relative merits of 'causal' and 'interpretive' approaches and opens a space for using them together in synergistic ways.

Four epistemological strategies have been identified by Blaikie. 'An inductive argument begins with singular or particular statements and concludes with a general or universal statement' (Blaikie 1993: 132). In relation to deduction '(r)ather than scientists waiting for nature to reveal its regularities, they must impose regularities (deductive theories) on the world and, by a process of trial and error, use observation to try to reject false theories' (ibid: 95). The abductive strategy 'is based on the Hermeneutic tradition... Abduction is the process used to produce social scientific accounts of social life by drawing on the concepts and meanings used by social actors, and the activities in which they engage' (ibid: 176). Retroduction is 'the process of building models of structures and mechanisms' (ibid: 168). These strategies are discussed further below

---

[7] The world is socially constructed, and, while each individual plays a tiny part in this, can be assumed to exist apart from any one individual's consciousness of it.

when I argue that an 'interductive'[8] strategy involving a mix of the four sub-strategies is particularly appropriate to the research questions and disciplinary niches of the researchers of poverty, such as those in WeD.

Theories, conceptual frameworks and models:: understanding and explanation

What constitutes a 'theory' and 'theoretical work' varies between, and within, disciplines often in ways which link to particular epistemologies. Mouzelis (1995) usefully identified three types of sociological theory: analysis of the theories of other scholars to provide raw material for further theoretical development (identified here as Theorising); conceptual frameworks to guide exploratory empirical research when not much is known about the particular topic (identified here as Conceptual Frameworks[9]); and sets of substantive propositions (Theories) sometimes formulated as models.

Frameworks are used to design research instruments which produce empirical findings that can be used in two ways. The first is to draw empirical conclusions about the case(s) that has(ve) been explored, while the second is as a basis for the development or testing of theoretical propositions. Theories are to do with understanding and explanation and may relate to structures, mechanisms, variables or cases. Different types of theoretical proposition require different methodological strategies. For example, the quantitative 'causal' tradition identifies dependent and independent variables and usually relies on theories/models which are synchronic or abstracted from time and survey data collected at one point in time. In a different research space, grounded theory starts with cases involving historically located people whose actions, interactions and structured relationships in time are interpreted and interrogated for regularities and differences.

Methodological frameworks: research objects, research instruments and modes of analysis

The research objects or cases in development-related poverty studies currently include: (1) a set of open social systems such as people,

---

[8] A concept coined by me.

[9] 'The purpose of [the WeD] research is to develop a conceptual and methodological framework for understanding the social and cultural construction of wellbeing in specific societies.' WeD Research Proposal to the ESRC, ('Communicating between the universal and the local: Conceptualising the relationships between poverty, inequality and the quality of life', 2006), funded under ESRC Award Reference M569 25 5001.

households, communities, regions, countries; (2) depending on discipline a variety of variables, for example poverty, inequality, capabilities, resources, identity, subjective quality of life, and so on; (3) a set of relationships, mechanisms and processes such as social exclusion, exploitation, reciprocity, communal sharing, status inconsistency, adverse incorporation, vicious and virtuous spirals; and (4) a set of issues such as economic growth, development, famine, HIV/AIDS, government–people relations, racism, violence. To engage with these research objects there is a range of data collection methods such as questionnaires, document archiving, interviews, and observation and participation, and a matching range of modes of analysis including thick description, discourse analysis and various qualitative and quantitative modes of comparison.

In recent years most policy-relevant social science research on developing-country poverty has been done by economists driven by a particular set of research methods. The key research objects have been, under (1), the household, under (2) income/consumption poverty, and under (4) economic growth and 'structural adjustment'. Data are collected through household surveys and analysed using statistical methods, predominantly regression analysis. The focus and excitement at 'the cutting edge' comes in the analysis phase from technical advances in mathematical modelling or econometrics expertise rather than substantive knowledge about poverty. Away from the cutting edge, research 'bureaucracies' in academia and policy organisations such as the World Bank have produced a huge number of studies based on this research approach. Since the mid-1990s, household and demographic survey-based Poverty Analyses have been supplemented with 'Participatory Poverty Assessments' (PPAs) conducted in a few 'communities' using a suite of 'participatory methods' such as ranking, mapping, Venn diagrams, etc.[10] These studies have helped to widen the definition of poverty since respondents have identified deprivation in a number of non-economic aspects of life as important.

Conclusions: types of conclusion and substantive findings

Researchers may be motivated to undertake research in this area in order to make empirical generalisations and distinctions and explain them, to increase understanding of a particular case, and/or to draw theoretical conclusions. Researchers employ various modes of comparison to establish regularities, diversities, structural location or internal

---

[10] Under the influence of economists these are becoming more formalised and linked to national-level data, for example the 2005 Ethiopia PPA conducted by Frank Ellis.

dynamics. Tilly (1984: 83) described four polar ideal-types for making comparisons, which can be used in combination. A purely individualising comparison treats each case as unique, while a purely universalising comparison identifies common properties among all instances of a phenomenon. Variation-finding comparisons examine systematic differences among instances, while the encompassing approach 'places different instances at various locations within the same system, on the way to explaining their characteristics as a function of their varying relationships to the whole system'. Case-focused empirical conclusions relate to a particular case, identify different types of case, or locate the case in wider structures. Variable-focused empirical approaches usually draw general conclusions on the basis of identifying commonalities. In a post-disciplinary approach to poverty, all four modes of comparison and conclusion-drawing would be used interactively according to the problem in hand.

Rhetoric: words, symbols and styles used to persuade others

Academic scholarship depends on the development and use of special 'languages'. Such languages serve functions beyond the intellectual. They mark status-related lines of exclusion and inclusion and, depending on the context, contribute to the power of the propositions being made. Equations, diagrams and reports of regression coefficients come with the message 'this is science'. Analytic pieces written in English[11] are often full of 'development tropes': words or phrases with an aura of broader meanings and assumptions. Ethnographic accounts involve the creative use of language in ways that parallel literary endeavours. During multi-disciplinary collaborations, the meanings of words and symbols become exceedingly important and there is a need for people from each discipline to struggle to be clear about what they mean, and to try to understand what people from other disciplines mean. This might involve negotiating over a set of key concepts to produce multi-vocal definitions which everyone can sign up to, or working on 'translating' technical terms into shareable English. The reflexivity which proper cross-disciplinary dialogue and negotiation can engender is a precious research resource.

Rhetoric is also involved when researchers enter the policy arena and is particularly relevant when the main research goal is linked to normative theories. Successful development tropes, such as 'economic

---

[11] In the world of cross-cultural research, matters are complicated by having to work in different languages. Some implications for the WeD programme are discussed below.

'growth', 'participation' and 'good governance', mobilise donor resources for research and action.

Implications for action and practice

Between and within disciplines there is considerable variation with respect to the meaning of 'praxis', or what is (to be) done and by whom. For example, development economists equate it with 'policy', interpreted by some as what the World Bank should tell recipient governments to do. Current recommendations are that economic growth depends on macroeconomic management of balances and restructuring through opening to the 'market', that governments should target 'safety nets' to the poorest, and that resources should be invested in good governance, civil society, building 'social capital' and 'empowering citizens'. At the opposite extreme, post-structuralists equate it with helping 'poor people' to refuse 'development' through participating in 'New Social Movements'. Those with a 'social policy' approach to anti-poverty action are linked with international and national donors who support the MDGs, especially the education and health goals, and are concerned with building partnerships with poor country governments, state support for markets and sustainable livelihoods. Marxists argued for raising the consciousness of poor people so that they understand that capitalism is the cause of their common plight and working with them to challenge the relevant owners and controllers of capital. Development practitioners working with NGOs committed to 'participatory' approaches have the 'empowerment of the poor' as a goal, while those convinced by culture of poverty arguments are most concerned to work on the next generation through family planning programmes and education.

Relations between the elements

Poverty researchers from different disciplinary specialisations pay more or less attention to these nine knowledge elements. For some, methods and techniques dominate, while for others, moral philosophy or epistemological arguments are key. Some highlight the importance of ontology, while others pursue empirical conclusions. However, wherever the focus, the policy-relevant empirical researcher is bound to make consequential assumptions, often implicit and unexamined, about all nine knowledge elements. There are also unexamined assumptions about the necessity of links between the elements, for example that statistical analysis goes with positivism, and that thick description goes with relativism.

The disciplinary structure and dynamics of social science are a result of a regularly renegotiated division of labour which to date has not been well coordinated.

> the larger, universal framework for social science is by no means the standard, often-parodied axiomatic structure. Rather it resembles what the Romans called the law of peoples (*ius gentium*), a law that applied to diverse groups at the edges of the empire and that they distinguished from the formalised law (*ius civile*). There is no universal social scientific knowledge of the latter kind – systematic, axiomatic, universal in a contentless sense. There is only universal knowledge of the former kind, a universal knowledge emerging from accommodation and conflict rather than from axioms, a universal knowledge that provides tentative bridges between local knowledges rather than systematic maps that deny them, a universal knowledge that aims, like the *ius gentium*, at allowing interchange among people who differ fundamentally. (Abbott 2001: 5)

Currently knowledge about poverty in poor countries exists as a set of local knowledges with few bridges among them. Policy makers looking for research to assist in tackling poverty rely mainly on knowledge produced by economists using mathematical models to guide household survey research analysed using regression techniques. NGOs are more likely to turn to development anthropologists and 'participatory' researchers. Other research by 'non-economists' tends not to travel far out of the academic domain. The growing cross-disciplinary research interest and parallel policy interest in 'wellbeing', with its focus on people and communities as well as households, offers an opportunity for a much greater understanding of the mechanisms and processes involved in the production and reproduction of poverty. This is more likely to be achieved if there is reflexivity and debate about intellectual assumptions 'among people who differ fundamentally'.

13.3 Researching 'wellbeing' across the disciplines: some ways forward

In this section I use the FoK framework to analyse the main disciplinary approaches that have been brought to the WeD programme, to identify what I see as the most important intellectual cross-disciplinary disjunctures and challenges, and to suggest some ways forward for WeD and other interdisciplinary researchers. As a guide to the discussion in this section Table 13.1 presents an *ideal-typical* representation of the research models identified as being most important to WeD so far. They come from social anthropology, sociology, political theory, psychology and economics.

Table 13.1 *An ideal-type depiction of some of the research models with which the WeD team is negotiating*

Questions	From social anthropology	From sociology	From political theory	From psychology	From economics
Focus: What are we interested in?	Local cultures and meanings; use of resources Local cultural repertoires	Unequal social structures, power, actors, and dynamics; access to resources Social mechanisms and processes	Universal human needs and intermediate needs-satisfiers Country poverty	Values, goals, resources to meet goals, satisfaction with resources and with life in general	Household poverty; individual functionings; global happiness/ satisfaction
Values: Why?	The agency of poor people should be recognised and respected	Social and human suffering should be eradicated	Human needs ought to be met and capabilities expanded	Subjective evaluations of wellbeing ought to be respected	Household poverty should be eradicated and human resources improved
Ontology: What is the 'reality' of what we are interested in?	There are different realities associated with different standpoints or habituses	Reality exists independent of our thoughts, is complexly constituted of things, people, relationships, structures, energy, and time, and much of it is unobservable	One observable reality exists independent of our thoughts	One reality exists independent of our thoughts and only what is observable is real	One reality exists independent of our thoughts and only what is observable is real
Epistemology: How can we know about reality?	Through the interpretation of local meanings in an *abductive* research approach	Truth should be understood as practical adequacy. Develop models of mechanisms/ processes (*retroduction*) through an iterative process of conceptualising and fieldwork.	We can observe it using scientific methods (*deduction/induction*) and we can establish truths/generalisations about human beings	We can observe it using scientific methods (*deduction/ induction*) and we can establish generalisations about human beings	Think about it using mathematical logic – *deductive*; observe it using surveys – *inductive*

Theorising:	Hermeneutic interpretations and reflexive theorising	Conceptual frameworks to guide exploratory research; explanatory middle range theories out of research results	Normative theories/critical theories Conceptual frameworks for taxonomising cases	Causal theorising through statistical techniques.	Causal theorising via mathematical modelling and statistical techniques
Research strategies: How can we establish what is really happening?	*Data:* Ethnography: a range of research instruments *Analysis:* interpretation and comparison	*Data:* Integrated use of surveys, participant observation, and protocols *Analysis:* retroductive; four strategies of comparison Also discourse analysis of key documents	*Data:* Secondary sources or 'codified knowledge' and 'experiential knowledge' *Analysis:* inductive	A psychological instrument for country cultures *Data:* exploratory, validation, use phases *Analysis:* statistical	*Data:* household surveys *Analysis:* econometric analysis of household survey data
Theoretical and empirical conclusions: What (kind of) conclusions can we draw?	Understanding of people's actions, and relationships in cultural context *Focus:* community	Identify universal mechanisms/processes and show how they work in different local contexts *Focus:* (interactive) person, household, community, country	Mapping objective wellbeing and analysing the contribution of different structures and institutions to it *Focus:* country and person	Descriptions of subjective quality of lives in the research countries Regularities with other non-psychological variables. *Focus:* person	Descriptive statistics using economic variables Explanatory: identification of regularities through regression analyses *Focus:* household
Rhetoric: How can we inform others about these?	Interpret local cultures in academic writings; advise practitioners; feedback to research communities	Academic papers and books; research and briefing papers for donors and other practitioners	Academic papers and books and networking through conferences etc with people influential in policy making	Academic papers; networking with relevant practitioners	Academic papers; policy advice to donors; inputs to PRSPs

Table 13.1 (*cont.*)

Questions	From social anthropology	From sociology	From political theory	From psychology	From economics
Praxis: What to do?	Constructive criticism of development approaches which are oblivious to local culture; suggestions of better ways of doing things	Constructive criticism of development approaches which are oblivious to local power structures and how things actually work in local contexts; suggestions of better ways of doing things	Good research helps combine top-down and bottom-up knowledges	Understanding of subjective QoL has implications for policy and practice	Identify the causes of household poverty in particular contexts and the contributing variables. Draw out policy implications
Who to do it?	Local inhabitants, NGOs, donors, government	Sympathetic national mega and meso actors, local inhabitants, government, donors, NGOs	International and national donors, governments		International and national donors, governments

The title of each column locates the research model within a particular discipline, though it is important to recognise that within each social science discipline there are a number of competing research models, that these change as time passes, and that researchers rarely spend a lifetime operating within just one of them. Furthermore some researchers are much less 'discipline-bound' than others. The table depicts my interpretation of the research models which have been most influential in WeD so far, rather than being a description of contributions from particular WeD members.

In discussing each element of the framework I present potential contributions from each of the research models and discuss contradictions and how they might be handled. I refer to other chapters in this book and also draw on the contributors to the Hanse[12] workshop which preceded it.

Mapping the domain and problematics

The WeD domain is defined by the 'umbrella concept' of 'wellbeing', embracing objective wellbeing, subjective wellbeing, and access to the resources through which livelihood and wellbeing outcomes are pursued (Chapter 1). With regard to the domain and problematics the first row of Table 13.1 shows what each discipline brings to the research design.

Political theory provides reasoned arguments as to the constituents of objective wellbeing, based on the concept of human need, and describes the types of resources necessary to meet needs, recognising that the instantiations of these will vary across livelihood systems and cultures. The social anthropology focus on local meanings introduces local constructions or models of 'objective wellbeing'. The concept of cultural 'repertoires' opens a space for considering local contestations about what 'the good life' might be for different kinds of person (Dean 2003). Since individuals interpret and evaluate their experiences in their own way the relation between local models of wellbeing and subjective wellbeing is complex. Psychology brings an approach to the subjective wellbeing of individuals which explores their values, their goals, the resources they think they need to meet their goals, and reported levels of satisfaction with those resources and with life in general.

The sociological perspective adds a focus on power and the unequal structures and dynamics to be found within communities and households.

---

[12] WeD-WIDER International Workshop on 'Researching Wellbeing in Developing Countries' at the Hanse Institute for Advanced Study in Delmenhorst, Germany in July 2004.

Unequal distributions of objective wellbeing, subjective wellbeing, and resources arise from institutionalised unequal power relationships between people in different roles which may involve exploitation, exclusion, domination, and/or violence against person and property (destruction). In the economics approach links between household human resources, assets and income and the objective and subjective wellbeing of household members are emphasised. From social anthropology comes the important insistence that all resources are culturally constructed.

Taken together these research models show how important interacting social, cultural and personal structures and dynamics are for personal outcomes in terms of survival and flourishing, and also the value of using the insights from all the models to inform study and analysis. Researchers working in each of the disciplinary niches can learn much from the rest. For example, the political theory definition of human needs has been enriched by readings in psychology. Sociologists can get a better handle on unequal power relations with the help of economists. Social anthropology teaches everyone else that life is lived in the round and in real time; it is meaningful action that is fundamental.

Our key research questions relate to the cultural and social construction of wellbeing in our country and community contexts. With regard to the *cultural* construction of wellbeing, we are interested in local and personal models of what it is desirable to have and to do, and explanations of why different kinds of people have what they have and experience what they do. We are also interested in comparing the meanings attached to wellbeing by social scientists, by policy makers, and the people under study and exploring related policy actions, reactions and outcomes (Chapters 1 and 7). Here we will need to make use of discourse analysis techniques as well as using hermeneutic approaches to interpret the values, beliefs and actions of our research subjects.

Identification of relevant social science, policy, local and personal models will also contribute to our analysis of the *social* construction of wellbeing. Our concern here is with *dynamic* distributions of wellbeing and its correlates and the underlying events, actions, relationships, structures, mechanisms and processes involved in the generation of those potentially unstable distributions. Since structures, mechanisms and processes are not directly observable, it is not possible to 'measure' them directly – we have to look for, describe and, where appropriate, measure observable 'traces' of their existence and operation. Such traces may be identified, for example, through the measurement of distributions of advantage and disadvantage at a point in time using survey methods, through observation and/or participants' accounts of events, through discourse analyses of documents describing established laws and other institutional forms, through descriptions of organisational structures and dynamics, through interpretation of the experiences of people occupying varying positions in local power structures. Establishing the distributions of resources, objective needs-satisfaction and subjective wellbeing and the connections between them requires a measurement approach; in this connection the contributions of Ryan, McGillivray, Møller, Bullinger and Rojas (see Chapters 3, 6, 10, 11 and 12 respectively) have given us some clues.

A major challenge is to make links with approaches which identify domains and problematics using other 'umbrella' concepts; importantly sustainable livelihoods (see Bebbington *et al.*, Chapter 8), social exclusion (Copestake, Chapter 9), security (Wood, Chapter 5) and capabilities (Alkire, Chapter 4).

Towards a simple normative framework

Row two of Table 13.1 shows that the commitment of WeD researchers to poverty and inequality reduction comes from a number of angles, mostly focused on improving human wellbeing in terms of the meeting of objective needs, subjective quality of life, and access to economic and other resources. In addition sociology provides the idea of '*social* suffering', which is socially structured and collectively shared (Kleinman *et al.* 1997), and, while the Hanse workshop was focused on human wellbeing, there were a number of voices which enjoined us not to forget that collective wellbeing is also important (Ryan, Møller[13]). Given that in our research countries we find local cultural constructions of wellbeing which privilege the collective above the individual, this will emerge at least in our local models of wellbeing.

In relation to individual wellbeing, the WeD normative framework is concerned with the optimisation of human potentials (Doyal and Gough 1991) and currently, partly as a result of our encounter with Self-Determination Theory (Ryan), we are considering four domains of experience as vital for such optimisation. The 'objective-need' candidates are context-relevant *competence*, which can include physical and mental health as well an appropriate set of skills, *autonomy* or the personal ownership of decisions affecting the self, and *relation*, both intimate and more widely social. People also have a need for *meaning* which is the foundation of subjective wellbeing.

---

[13] And Hetan Shah of the New Economics Foundation who participated in the Hanse workshop as a commentator.

The normative theories discussed at Hanse have been constructed in developed country contexts and it is important that WeD develops a simple but striking normative framework that negotiates between the case for a scientifically based universalist understanding and appreciation of all people's capabilities and needs and the case for respect for people's values and knowledge (see Sen 1999 and Gough 2003). There are resonances here with long-running arguments about 'development' and there are relevant development studies sources that have not yet been brought into collective WeD discussions (e.g. among many others Nederveen Pieterse 2001).

The importance of ontology

The first ontological issue relates to whether one 'reality' exists or not. The question is: how does what goes on in our heads relate to what goes on 'out there'? Row 3 in Table 13.1 suggests that WeD has access to three main answers. The first privileges cultural habitus; variation in understandings of 'reality' mean that there are many realities. The second accepts there is one reality out there and it consists of what is accessible to our senses.[14] The third is the critical realist approach described in section 13.2. This approach compromises between the other two. The only reality we can in some way be sure of is what we access 'through our senses', but first there are hidden and unobservable realities related to the structuration of the world and secondly depending on social location, habitus and standpoint we access different bits of reality through our senses. One advantage of the critical realist approach is that it can happily accommodate empirical findings produced by 'relativists' and 'positivists' without accepting their ontological assumptions about reality.

A more important set of ontological questions concerns how to describe what exists. The question of what the objects of our study are *really* like is not the same as the question of how it might be sensible to conceptualise them for a particular theoretical purpose. How are our research objects structured and what are their causal powers and liabilities? This is an important issue since social scientists are regularly tempted to believe that people are really like the models built of them for particular analytical purposes. So, for example, we find arguments over whether people 'really are' rational, when the question should be which types of behaviour and context can be usefully analysed using particular rational action models, and which cannot.

---

[14] For social scientists in this mode this translates into data collected by experimenting or questioning people.

The WeD approach is based on an agency/structure ontology, aspects of which are described in Chapters 1 and 14. Some of the implications of such an ontology are described more fully in Bevan,[15] the basic argument being that the material, peopled and historically evolving earth is a planet located in a space and time niche in the cosmos which determines concurrent environmental powers and liabilities to change. Key entities are people, social relationships and structures (societies), meanings, other forms of life, inanimate material things, time and energy.

While the Hanse workshop contributors used a number of conceptual frameworks useful for approaching the study of human wellbeing, none of them related the framework to a human ontology. This would recognise that babies take nine months to develop in the womb before they are born, that they are born male or female, that they are dependent on adults for care and socialisation for many years, that they are bio-logically constituted according to genetic inheritance, that they have complicated brains and minds which develop through continuous interaction with their environment, that they have some basic drives related to their physical construction, that their personal and social being – personalities, consciences, memories, skills, habits, beliefs, values, attitudes, etc. – involve ongoing culturally grounded learning, that they have a potential lifespan of no more than slightly over 100 years, and that in that lifespan, they face a number of key physical, social and moral challenges as they develop, mature and decline. Lives are conducted in interaction with other people and individual actions and choices have consequences for them. An ontologically grounded approach to human 'being' has many implications for the understanding and study of objective human needs, 'needs-satisfiers' and subjective experiences, as we recognise, for example, that the concept of the 'individual' applies to tiny babies, old women and male adolescents as well as 'economic man'.

We also have to develop ontologies which identify the causal powers and liabilities inherent in the social structures of societies and the pas-sage of time.

Epistemological diversity: many routes to knowledge

Earlier I argued for an acceptance of epistemological diversity; there are different routes to knowledge which need not be contradictory and can

---

[15] P. Bevan, 'Studying poverty and inequality in poor countries: Getting to grips with structure', unpublished paper, University of Bath, 2004.

be brought into dialogue with each other.[16] Row 4 in Table 13.1 shows that WeD has access to the four epistemological strategies based on contrasting forms of reasoning for generating new scientific knowledge described in section 13.2. From political theory, economics and psychology we have access to inductive and deductive reasoning based on linear logic. Inductive strategies start from observations on the basis of which empirical generalisations are made. These generalisations are used in a theorising process to form concepts and develop propositions as the basis for theorising. Theories are the starting point for deductive methods; consequences are deduced and predictions made as a basis for constructing hypotheses for testing through empirical observation.

Social anthropology and sociology provide access to strategies less familiar to the other three disciplines. Abduction and retroduction 'are based on cylic or spiral processes' (Blaikie, 1993: 162). From social anthropology comes an abductive strategy involving hermeneutic interpretations and reflexive theorising. 'Abduction is the process used to produce social scientific accounts of social life drawing on the concepts and meanings used by social actors, and the activities in which they engage' (*ibid*: 176). It is a relatively unknown strategy 'proposed as a method for generating hypotheses in the natural sciences, but is now advocated as the appropriate method of theory construction in Interpretive social science' (*ibid*: 162). While the retroductive strategy has been discussed by philosophers for many years and practised by scientists from various disciplines it has only recently been articulated as a philosophy of science (Bhaskar, 1979). This strategy involves the 'construction of hypothetical models as a way of uncovering the real structures and mechanisms which are assumed to produce empirical phenomena' (Blaikie, 1993: 168). Examples from science include 'atoms', 'viruses' and 'genes', all of which were hypothetical entities for some while before scientific technologies were advanced enough to observe them.

Given that expertises related to these four epistemological strategies are differentially distributed amongst the disciplines, our multi-disciplinary team is well placed to use them all. The challenge of developing an interductive strategy is to negotiate and coordinate among and between them at the levels of analysis and the reaching of empirical conclusions. The risk is that the four strategies will be pursued separately within the disciplinary barriers earlier described.

---

[16] Few of the contributors to this book embody clear epistemological positions. One is Rojas in Chapter 12 who uses an 'analytic-Cartesian paradigm' associated with *deductive* theories which resonates with the WeD microeconomics approach.

Theorising, frameworks and theories: the relation between ideas and evidence

In section 13.2 a distinction was made between Theorising, Conceptual Frameworks and Theories. The Hanse workshop was predicated on the assumption that Theorising, analysis of the theories of other scholars, is extremely valuable in providing raw material for further theoretical development and thus it has proved to be. Conceptual clarification and argumentation relating to existing literatures is important for being clear about the ideas one wishes to confront with empirical evidence. Conceptual analysis is a process which should continue through the field-work, analysis and writing-up stages as encounters with the evidence change and enrich our ideas.

A number of conceptual frameworks underpinning the study of the 'being' of people and its structural and cultural generation in society were hinted at during the workshop. In the WeD framework, people are conceived of as 'active agents' with material, social and cultural dimensions (see Chapters 7, 9 and 14). An important argument put by Ryan and by Bevan and Pankhurst, in a paper presented to the work-shop but not included here[17] recognised that there are lifespan changes in wellbeing so that the components vary with age. Gender differences must also be taken into account. As argued above, we need to develop a more adequate human ontology to underpin frameworks designed for particular purposes, which, in our multi-disciplinary context, may vary from the modelling of market relationships, to the measurement of people's values, goals, and resources, to an interpretation of a child's story about her situation.

In the WeD framework, the wellbeing-relevant activities of an agent are seen as enabled and constrained by his/her location in local political economy and socio-cultural structures. In *dynamic* terms, livelihoods and attempts to secure wellbeing are forms of social practice in which inter-actions are constructed through power relations embedded in social and cultural structures (White and Ellison, this volume). This perspective informs the welfare/insecurity regime framework (Gough and Wood *et al.* 2004) and the livelihoods framework described by Bebbington. To date these frameworks have contained little about the cultural construction of insecurity/wellbeing and this is something the WeD group is addressing. The structural/cultural arenas identified as important in the WeD

---

[17] P. Bevan and A. Pankhurst, 'Gendering' and 'ageing' human needs and human harm: some evidence from rural Ethiopia', WeD-WIDER International Workshop on 'Researching Wellbeing in Developing Countries' at the Hanse Institute for Advanced Study in Delmenhorst, Germany, July 2004.

framework are 'households', 'communities' and 'countries' with the recognition that these will be constructed differently in the different countries and communities and that in some cases establishing the boundaries of the 'case' are likely to be problematic.

The main purpose of the WeD programme is to develop a conceptual and methodological framework for understanding the social and cultural construction of wellbeing in specific societies and this Conceptual Framework will be shared across the disciplines. The process of iteration of ideas and evidence involved in the empirical programme will both contribute to the development of the final Conceptual Framework and produce contributions to Theory development. Such contributions will vary according to epistemological strategy and disciplinary niche and here we may find ourselves faced with some contradictions to negotiate.

Towards a methodological framework de-linking epistemology and research methods and de-linking data collection and analysis

Row 6 of Table 13.1 contains a range of empirical research strategies involving different assumptions and research skills which are usually not used together. They include ethnography, surveys, protocol-guided research, analysis of secondary sources, psychological measurement, and exploratory and confirmatory statistical analysis and interpretive analysis of survey data. Using such multi-level and multi-method data together successfully is a huge challenge; one which has rarely been taken on in development research. While multi-method approaches are becoming more popular in theory, they face many problems (Kanbur, 2003). Dialogue can be assisted if a conscious decision is made to de-link epistemology and research methods. For example, there are no good reasons why those with hermeneutic skills should not use them in relation to the design and administration of household surveys, or analysis and interpretation of the ensuing information (Byrne 2002), and this has already been part of the WeD process.

There is also a case for de-linking data collection and analysis. For example, given current computing power, appropriate statistical techniques can be brought to bear on hermeneutic data in a search for causes (Ragin 2000), while survey households can be purposively selected for in-depth 'narrative analysis' using all the survey datapoints together. The information being collected during the WeD programme includes: (1) country-level statistical data and qualitative discourses and secondary analyses from a range of disciplines; and (2) for four rural and two urban research sites, community profiles and a household survey administered to up to 1,500 households, followed by a fieldwork period of over a year during which studies of institutions, organisations, events, activities, and personal experiences and evaluations are being made. This will produce an integrated data set open to analysis in a range of ways. The household survey material can, for example, be used to analyse cases and produce household typologies as well as establish statistical relationships between variables. Life-histories can be interpreted and also submitted to qualitative comparative analysis across household types, research sites, and countries. To grasp and use this opportunity fully it is important to de-link as far as possible the data collection and analysis processes and to develop dialogues across expertise.

Theoretical and empirical conclusions

In relation to our research objects we will be able to draw country-relevant and more general empirical and theoretical conclusions relating to: (1) the open systems we have studied, namely people, households, communities, and countries and their global connections; (2) the key variables identified as important; (3) the key relationships, mechanisms and processes identified as important; and (4) the key issues facing each of our countries.

More broadly our conclusions will be threefold. First, our conceptual and methodological framework for studying the social and cultural construction of wellbeing in any society will contribute to theory in terms of Conceptual Frameworks. Secondly, we will produce a set of empirical conclusions through the use of the framework to produce four country studies mapping and explaining the social and cultural construction of wellbeing in Bangladesh, Ethiopia, Peru and Thailand at the beginning of the third millennium. Finally, we will be in a position to contribute to substantive theory development in, and perhaps across, the five disciplines, remembering Calhoun's injunction that it is generally not possible to ask all the interesting questions about any really significant phenomenon within a set of commensurable, logically integratable theories.

Dealing with rhetorical diversity

Under this heading, there are three important issues: communication across the academic disciplines; communication across the five WeD sub-cultures (Bath, Bangladesh, Ethiopia, Peru and Thailand); and communications with practitioners of various kinds.

Historically, WeD Bath outputs have been designed with our disciplines and RAE[18] criteria in mind making cross-disciplinary communication difficult. Some of us have difficulty with equations and regression coefficient tables, while others cannot grasp the subtleties of arguments couched using carefully defined concepts and argumentation. It must be good for us to try to explain the importance and relevance of our ideas and empirical conclusions in comprehensible English.

There is a more serious problem when it comes to historic cross-disciplinary disagreements and conflicts. For example, in the development studies area there are some historic tensions between economists and 'non-economists'. The latter have spent much time and energy in critiquing the intellectual assumptions, styles and conclusions of the former, while many economists not seeing themselves as being part of 'development studies' at all, have found no need to respond to these criticisms nor to familiarise themselves with contributions from other disciplines. Cross-disciplinary research requires mutual respect of skills and interests which will have to be worked for. One element of this relates to disciplinary claims implicit in the rhetoric. So, if a *theoretical* model, for example associated with assumptions about rational man, or about 'difference', or about 'universal needs', is presented as an *ontological* model about how the world really is, arguments are likely to ensue. This is also likely if findings produced from a cross-sectional survey conducted in a particular population at a point in time, or from one or two case studies, are used to make universal generalisations. There is a need for modesty in the rhetorical presentation of conclusions.

This chapter has focused on research models easily accessible in Bath. Their accessibility to country teams varies according to the disciplinary mix within the team. Country team members, working within particular local research and policy cultures, face the additional task of negotiating between WeD research models and those of salience at home. There is a further set of serious issues that WeD faces as a result of working in six other languages. The first is illustrated by experiences in Ethiopia where we have come up against the non-translatability of a number of English social science concepts and ideas into Amharic and Oromiffa and vice versa for local concepts. Secondly, in Thailand and Peru local academic and policy networks work in their home language and have no need for English,[19] creating tensions between the needs of the centre and the needs of local WeD teams.

[18] The British Research Assessment Exercise is key for the allocation of funds to university departments. To date the attitude to cross-disciplinary research has been unfriendly.
[19] In both Bangladesh and Ethiopia, English is well understood and often used in these circles.

One of our goals is to establish the WeD framework as an important resource for international donors, NGOs and developing country governments. Here we have to challenge and negotiate with entrenched poverty research frameworks. In this context is 'wellbeing' a potentially effective development trope?[20] How do we package and present our 'products'? This leads into the final knowledge element.

Mapping and linking approaches to praxis: what to do and who to do it?

The final row in Table 13.1 suggests that an important WeD policy message is that development policy and practice interventions by governments, donors and NGOs in any country or community context are unlikely to be effective unless based on a sophisticated understanding of local cultures and local power structures and dynamics, and that such an understanding requires social science knowledge which is both etic and emic, and variable-based and case-based. As described in section 13.2, economists have been providing direct advice to donors for many years, while in the past those working in the other disciplines have either (in the case of psychology) done little in the development field, or have adopted a critical stance to donors and governments identifying the 'grass roots' or collective action organisations as key praxis actors with whom to try to communicate. However, there are signs of a growing donor interest in 'non-economics' research, reflected in the way that the WeD political theory research model is currently being used by the World Bank to incorporate ideas from western social policy and the sociology research model to produce more realistic approaches to 'empowerment' (Bevan, Holland and Pankhurst forthcoming).

The advantage of being multi-disciplinary is that our approach to praxis need not be an 'either/or' one. With appropriate strategies our writings can reach international and government policy makers, international and national NGOs, civil societies at home and in our research countries, the people we have been researching as well as academics all over the world. Networking in all these arenas will improve the efficacy of our praxis strategies as will developing a WeD strategy in relation to ongoing events and trends at global levels.

13.4   Conclusions

In conclusion I first document a continuing concern that the focus on 'wellbeing' might lead us to ignore some important instances and causes

---

[20] A question raised by Gasper at the Hanse Conference.

of harm and suffering. I then identify the most important intellectual barriers to cross-disciplinary collaboration in the study of wellbeing in poor countries and make some suggestions of ways forward for WeD. Finally I briefly comment on the four other barriers to cross-disciplinary collaboration which were described at the beginning of the chapter.

Flourishing, surviving, suffering and dying

In Chapter 1, in justifying a research approach to poor people guided by the concept of wellbeing, it is argued that 'even alongside deprivations, poor people are able to achieve some elements of what they conceive of as wellbeing ... without this, we would argue, their lives would be unbearable'. While agreeing that the 'fully rounded humanity of poor men, women and children in developing countries' should be acknowledged, it is also important to acknowledge that for many poor people life *is* unbearable and often ends in a painful early death. The suffering and the lost years must not be ignored as they are in most poverty studies.[21]

'Every man who lives is born to die,' wrote John Dryden, some three hundred years ago. That recognition is tragic enough, but the reality is sadder still. We try to pack in a few worthwhile things between birth and death, and quite often succeed. It is, however, harder to achieve anything significant if, as in sub-Saharan Africa the median age of death is less than five years. (Sen 2005: xi)

Sen's quote comes from the preface to a book about the 'pathologies of power', in which Farmer argues that the nature and distribution of extreme suffering is associated with 'structural violence' arising from power disparities.

The capacity to suffer is, clearly, a part of being human. But not all suffering is equivalent ... Physicians practise triage and referral daily. What suffering needs to be taken care of first and with what resources? It *is* possible to speak of extreme human suffering, and an inordinate share of this sort of pain is currently endured by those living in poverty. (Farmer 2005: 50)

Structural violence involves harmful social action not only by rich and powerful social actors but also by the not so rich and powerful, including some who are poor themselves. 'Human beings do the most appalling things to each other, often in pursuit of lamentable ends. Cruelty and prejudice are far more widespread than benevolence and kindness' (Harré 1979: 31).

---

[21] Because the conceptual frameworks behind household surveys and Participatory Poverty Assessments have little space in them for suffering and death, and because a certain degree of security is necessary for the administration of these research instruments.

If we do not have the concepts, research questions and methods to help us to understand the social and cultural construction of extreme suffering we will be doing neither scientific nor humanitarian justice to many of the poor people we are studying.

Negotiating intellectual barriers to cross-disciplinary collaboration

The intellectual barriers to cross-disciplinary collaboration in the study of poverty and wellbeing take the form of 'disconnects' between the disciplines. Some of these can be explained by empty or skimpy knowledge-element boxes in one or both disciplines. Some are a result of parallel but separate activities which are never bridged. Some erupt in regular skirmishes. At issue is the importance of the different barriers: which are spurious? which can be circumvented or ignored? and which must be negotiated and how?

In section 13.2 three resources for making bridges across disciplinary divisions were proposed: the 'deconstruction' of concepts; fuzzy logic; and open social system models. These resources are called on as I consider these barriers. Rather than go through each of the nine knowledge elements, I will focus on just three: values, ontology and rhetoric.

Values   There are two disconnects here. The first is between those with an individualistic approach to wellbeing and those with a relational approach. From my (sociological) perspective our (laudable) concern to prioritise the wellbeing of the person[22] rather than the economic poverty of the household risks downplaying the importance of the quality of social relations which is implicit in notions of collective wellbeing and suffering.

The second disconnect has already been raised: the disconnect between those whose language is hopeful, for example 'development', 'capabilities', 'wellbeing', and 'civil society', and those who call for a language of 'dismay, disappointment, bereavement and alarm' (Kleinman *et al.* 1997: xi), including recognition of starvation, disease, community violence, domestic violence, suicide, depression, post-traumatic stress disorder, sexually transmitted diseases, HIV/AIDS, and so on. Researchers in this mode focus on the poor quality of social relations. Personal problems are often related to political violence and community disintegration: 'social suffering ruins the collective and the intersubjective connections of experience and gravely damages subjectivity' (*ibid*: x). The bridging of both of these

---

[22] In terms of what they have, what they do, and how they experience and evaluate what they have and do.

disconnects should start with a 'both-and' approach: both human and collective wellbeing and suffering.

Ontology Table 13.1 includes the relativist 'ontology' postulating different realities associated with different habituses and standpoints since this is a position we have to deal with. However, this position has not been advanced within WeD and I have argued that relativism is a matter of epistemology rather than ontology. I would also argue that social scientists from different disciplines engaged in studying the same topic should come to some agreement as to the powers and liabilities of their research objects, which have been identified here as societies, people, time, energy, other forms of life, and inanimate material 'things', the first three being the most important for us. The powers and liabilities of these entities arise from their nature or internal structures, and can be modelled from the perspectives of 'anatomy', 'physiology', and dynamics. The ontological depth that can be achieved at any point in time depends on the concurrent social/scientific knowledge.

The disconnect here is between those who have not appreciated the importance of ontology in relation to empirical research, and those who have used a deeper understanding of the parameters of social and human life to inform theoretical and empirical approaches to the cultural and social construction of well and illbeing. For example, and following up on discussions above, we must study *everything* that human beings are capable of being and doing (powers), and actually do, including the 'appalling'.

We also need to pay serious ontological attention to the social structures involved in the construction of wellbeing, and explore how time is involved in the structuring of individual lives and the structuring of social life. Those whose ontology box is empty or skimpy should be asked to think about it individually and collectively with the rest of the WeD group.

Rhetoric Disconnects in terms of scientific rhetoric or style are a major problem, both when we are trying to understand what researchers from other disciplines are saying, and when we are trying to agree common statements. As we move into writing mode we will have to find ways of bridging these rhetorical disconnects; solutions are likely to vary according to which discipline is leading.

A second rhetorical aspect relates to the 'truth' claims made by different disciplines about their theoretical and empirical conclusions. This is an arena where skirmishes often occur. There are incentives for researchers in all the disciplines to use words that raise the relative status of their discipline and lower that of others. The economists who describe their own work as rigorous, scientific and universal and qualitative studies as 'anecdotal' and particular are matched by the social anthropologists and sociologists who claim a unique understanding of those they research, and dismiss variable analyses as 'reification'. Self-reflection and modesty would help to bridge this disconnect.

Finally, there is sometimes a fine line between reporting research results and 'policy messaging' (Kanbur 2001) particularly on the part of researchers committed to a particular normative theory or policy model. The relation between research outputs and praxis is discussed in the next section; here I note the potential disconnect between those whose primary commitment is to 'truth' and those whose primary commitment is to changing the world. Skirmishes are probably to be welcomed in this area.

Other barriers to cross-disciplinary research and its use

In the introduction to this chapter I identified four additional barriers to cross-disciplinary collaboration: disciplinary cultures, disciplinary habituses, the histories and political economies of the social science disciplines, and the histories and political economies of donor-related poverty research and policy structures. The WeD actor-structure model includes the assumption that, acting individually and collectively, social actors can make changes to structures and cultures. When a researcher's goal is involvement in a post- or multi-disciplinary approach to global poverty and wellbeing the first step is to be reflexive about personal disciplinary habitus with a view to making appropriate changes.

The FoK analysis suggests that many researchers of poverty in poor countries are 'boxed in'; not only are they confined within a disciplinary research model, but often their intellectual efforts are also confined within two or three of the nine knowledge element boxes, while the others are ignored or receive ritual and perfunctory attention. Progress towards a post-disciplinary approach to global poverty requires lateral thinking; which in relation to Table 13.1 means both vertically and horizontally. According to Myerson (1994) cross-disciplinary research requires personal commitment, self-reflexivity, personal development of 'communicative character' and a 'dialogic orientation', and group development of a 'culture of intellectual encouragement'. He suggests the following conditions are necessary for fostering a wide dialogue:

1 People being disposed to communicate ideas, and therefore contexts in which it is safe and easy to do so.

2 Ways of thinking which favour comparisons, which are relative in that sense, not necessarily relativistic.

3 Creative forms of negation, which present new possibilities, or which supplement previous propositions.

4 Active tolerance of difficult emotions involved in the exchange of ideas and opinions. (*ibid*: 151)

These remain the essential codes of good practice for post-disciplinary research.

Appendix 13A: Foundations of Knowledge Questionnaire

Name:

Would you like this to be kept confidential? [yes or no]:

Discipline or study area (as you would describe it):

Date:

I would be very grateful if you would answer the following questions at as much length as you like. You can complete the questions in any order.

I. Domain, focus, problematic

1 We are talking about the related areas of poverty, inequality, and personal experience of being (well and ill) or subjective quality of life. Within this space what have been, are, and will be your particular interests and focus?

2 What are the bigger research questions or goals which lie behind your interest (if any)?

II. Values

1 What values do you think are driving your interest in poverty, inequality, quality of life, and well/ill being?

2 Where do they come from? (e.g. a particular religious or ideological framework)

3 Are there any contradictions?

4 How do you envisage 'the good life'?

5 How do you envisage the 'good society'?

6 How do you envisage the relation between the search for 'truth' and the pursuit of 'the good'?

III. Ontology – theories of existence

1 Describe in as much detail as possible your response to the assumptions that there is/is not a reality 'out there' separate from people's thoughts about it?
2 Assuming a 'reality' what for you as a social scientist are the important features of the following?

> people
> social relations and structures
> material things
> social change
> other important aspect(s)

3 How do you conceptualise the reality of?

> poverty
> inequality
> being
> quality of life

IV. Epistemology – theories of knowledge

1 *How* do you know what you think you know?
2 What are the philosophical foundations of your knowledge about whatever kind of social reality/ies you recognise as existing?
3 Would you describe yourself as a positivist, empiricist, logician, hermeneuticist, critical theorist or something else?
4 Does your approach come from a well-established tradition of research? Describe.
5 How is social science knowledge generated and accumulated through time?
6 In what ways does power affect social science knowledge?
7 How does social science knowledge work as source of power?
8 What do you think you can learn about the WeD domain from other social science disciplines?

V. Theories and explanations

1 What theories or theoreticians have inspired or lie behind your work in this area?

2 How would you describe 'theorising' in your particular disciplinary approach?
3 How important is abstraction to your work and what form does it take?
4 What do you think an explanation consists of?
5 In what ways is it useful to think of 'causes'?
6 What do you make of the 'quantitative-qualitative' distinction?
7 In what ways are empirical generalisations useful?

VI. Research methods

1 Describe the research methods you have used in the past to collect data.
2 Describe the ways in which you have you analysed data you have collected or had access to.
3 What methods are you keen to use in the WeD programme?
4 What aspects of other WeD people's methods do you appreciate?
5 What aspects make you apprehensive?

VII. Rhetoric (persuasive discourse)

'the social sciences float in warm seas of unexamined rhetoric' (Nelson *et al.* 1987: 16)

1 How do you usually communicate and disseminate the conclusions of your research?
2 What particular special devices do you use?
3 What audiences do you write for?
4 What does it demand of the reader to understand what you write?
5 To what extent do you see the claims you make in your academic output as 'findings' and to what extent as arguments?
6 When should we 'change our minds'?

VIII. Empirical conclusions – re poverty, inequality, being, and quality of life.

1 What general form(s) do you think empirical conclusions in this area should take?
2 What empirical conclusions have you drawn from past research in your bit of this area?
3 What kinds of empirical conclusion should we able to reach as a result of the WeD programme?

IX. Praxis

1 In what ways do you think the WeD research should be used to generate advice about practice?
2 What do you mean by practice?
3 Who should act?
4 What should/do they do?
5 Why should/do they do it?
6 What do you think the real consequences of this action would be?

Comments

If you think there are other things of interest which you would like to say that are not covered by these questions please add them here – plus any other comments you might like to make.

14 Researching wellbeing: from concepts to methodology

J. Allister McGregor

14.1 From concepts to methodology

This volume began by recalling the urgent policy challenges to eliminate extreme poverty in developing countries. The research programme around which this volume has been organised rests on the proposition that the concept of wellbeing is not only academically promising but also can be of practical policy value in both developed and developing worlds. Des Gasper, however, argues in Chapter 2 that if this is the case then two basic challenges must be met. The first is to demonstrate that the label of 'wellbeing' can be conceptually useful, or as he puts it 'appealing', to both academia and policy. The second is to answer, 'When will it promote priority to the basic needs of the poorest and under what conditions?' To achieve this, we contend, requires (a) combining different disciplinary perspectives to advance our understanding of wellbeing and (b) translating this into an agenda for empirical research. These are the topics of sections 14.3 and 14.4 of this chapter.

The formal objective of the Wellbeing in Developing Countries Research Group at the University of Bath has been to develop a conceptual and methodological framework for understanding the social and cultural construction of wellbeing in developing countries. The proposal was stimulated by recognition of a growing gap between advances in development philosophy and progress in research methods which seek to build our 'on the ground' knowledge of poverty outcomes and processes. While advances in both have been influential in different arenas of policy thinking, there remains a basic incoherence between them and this manifests itself in weaknesses in current development policy thinking. A wide range of authors have drawn attention to different shortcomings in

The author is grateful to a number of WeD colleagues who have refereed this chapter, and wishes to particularly acknowledge the contribution of Ian Gough. Thanks also to Des Gasper for constructive comments on an earlier draft.

both the conceptualisation of poverty and its relationship to policy (see amongst others Booth 2005; Hickey and Bracking 2005; Nederveen Pieterse 2002; Robeyns 2005). There has been a lack of 'joined-upness' across academic and policy thinking about how poverty is produced or maintained and how it might be reduced or eliminated.

We argue here that the concept of wellbeing can represent a means of reconnecting different strands of development thinking and of drawing upon wider social science contributions to improve our understanding of the dynamics of poverty. Such a conception of wellbeing must combine the 'objective' circumstances of a person and their 'subjective' perception of their condition. Furthermore, wellbeing cannot be thought of only as an outcome, but also as a state of being that arises from the dynamic interplay of outcomes and processes. This interplay of outcomes and processes must be understood as firmly located in society and shaped by social, economic, political, cultural and psychological processes. In basic terms we conceive of wellbeing as arising from the combination of:

1 what a person has
2 what they can do with what they have, and
3 how they think about what they have and can do.

The WeD research programme is a purposive venture into wellbeing thinking.[1] We recognise of course that throughout time and in many different literatures (not least of which we must count all organised bodies of religious thought), there have been many different and more sophisticated ways to elaborate this basic formulation of wellbeing. We have also noted throughout this volume the connections to (and departures from) Sen's concepts of entitlements, functionings and capabilities.

Our starting point was the three frameworks of needs, resources and quality of life, which have provided the architecture of this volume. This enables us to reframe the above three components of wellbeing as follows. Wellbeing can be conceived in terms of the interplay between:

1 the resources that a person is able to command;
2 what they are able to achieve with those resources, and in particular what needs and goals they are able to meet; and
3 the meaning that they give to the goals they achieve and the processes in which they engage. A key element of this last dimension of meaning, and a basic driver of the future strategies and aspirations of the person, is the quality of life that they perceive themselves as achieving.

---

[1] It has adopted a wellbeing perspective as a means of better understanding the conditions under which poverty persists in developing countries.

Once again we emphasise that all of these take place in the context of society and social collectivity. Later in this chapter we focus on how this conception of human wellbeing might be operationalised within a unified social science research methodology. A key and distinctive element of the WeD research programme has been its remit to carry out extensive and coordinated empirical fieldwork alongside the development of its conceptual thinking. As Alkire notes in Chapter 4, the most fecund concepts are weakened if they lack a 'methodological sidecar'. Often, however, these two strands of intellectual development are carried out apart or are separated in time. In this respect the experience of developing the wellbeing methodology and its application in studies in four developing countries[2] are equally important means of exploring the value of the concept.

The next part of this chapter summarises the key points of convergence and of tension between the different contributions to this volume. It moves on to identify the *differentia specifica* of the wellbeing approach: five key ideas which when combined in a single conceptual framework mark it off as distinct from other approaches. These are then brought together in an overarching wellbeing conceptual framework. The chapter then introduces the ways in which this general framework has been operationalised in the six research elements of the WeD research programme. Finally, it returns to broader issues and briefly considers the benefits and challenges that are thrown up by this perspective for effective policy making.

14.2   Needs, resources and quality of life: links and tensions

In the preceding chapter Bevan proposes a framework for understanding the intellectual barriers to the trans-disciplinary study of poverty and wellbeing. The Foundations of Knowledge Framework (FoKF) identifies nine elements of assumption and presumption, either explicit or implicit, that require careful consideration if meaningful progress in trans-disciplinary communication is to be achieved. We can use her framework to identify the links and tensions between the three approaches used to organise this volume.

At first sight the 'knowledge foundations' of the Theory of Human Need approach and the Resource Profiles Framework are very different. Yet, there are at least three common features. First, both eschew a hard and fast distinction between goals and means: need satisfactions, achieved functionings or capability sets can, and usually do, form

---

[2] Bangladesh, Ethiopia, Peru and Thailand.

resources in the next time period. The commonplace dichotomy between ends and means disappears once the ontology of real people acting in time is adopted (Qizilbash 2002). Second, social relationships and 'culture' are important satisfiers of basic needs. This applies to 'culture' as both successful repertoire to meet recurrent environmental challenge, and 'culture' as a source of meaning and identity in the constitution of social life. Both aspects provide elements of security and immediate need satisfaction and enable people to do and to be, and in other words play a vital role in the constitution of a person's wellbeing. Third, higher levels of need satisfaction (or larger capability sets) will usually expand people's abilities successfully to meet new environmental challenges and thus enhance their autonomy and wellbeing. There is a potential positive feedback between need satisfaction and sustainable social forms of life.

There are also tensions between the two approaches that hinge around the place of culture in a wellbeing framework. Specific cultural practices can be both a form of moral bonding and source of meaning, and can block the critical autonomy of persons and groups. History and the current news are replete with cases where local cultural practices – in north and south – conflict with notions of universal human needs and recognised human rights (Gough 2004). As a result, people can be forced into relationships whereby their wellbeing is grossly compromised, or is only achievable at the cost of exploited dependence on more powerful others[3] (McGregor 1989b, 1994; Wood 2003). This in turn can reproduce poverty and exclusion over time, as in Figueroa's sigma society model described by Copestake in Chapter 9. Taking a different example, we know that the addiction to consumption fostered in late capitalist societies undermines happiness and threatens global sustainability. In both situations, new ways of fostering critical autonomy are urgently required; in the process it is unlikely that existing cultural values and practices will remain unquestioned.

What are the links and tensions between the Theory of Human Need and the QoL/SWB approaches? Despite quite different foundations of knowledge there is a considerable overlap in the empirical results. Cross-national studies of QoL find high cross-cultural validity suggesting a high degree of universality. A comparison of the list of common domains and indicators developed within the WHOQOL group with the basic and intermediate needs of THN finds a considerable overlap across items, except for critical autonomy. This is supported by many other studies of local values in developing country contexts.

---

[3] What Wood has aptly labelled a 'Faustian bargain' (2003).

Yet, despite this agreement between the human needs and subjective QoL approaches, their conceptual origins remain quite distinct and cannot be ignored. The universal presence of 'habitus', of the taken for granted, of adaptation and endogenous preference formation, continually throws up areas where wants clash with needs. Using Gasper's framework of need, some human drives are potentially non-functional or dangerous, while 'some ethical priority goals lack motivational force'. Humans possess two informational systems, genetics and culture, and there is no necessary reason for the two to generate corresponding patterns of behaviour (Durham 1991). On the other hand, certain functional dispositions, such as self-confidence and goal achievement, emerge as critical components of subjective wellbeing and happiness and hence presumably reflect both genetic and cultural evolution.

Finally, notwithstanding their very different foundations of knowledge, there are at least two, perhaps unexpected, links between the Resource Profiles Framework and the QoL/SWB frameworks. First, the research findings on variations in SWB across nations demonstrate that income contributes little to SWB above a moderate threshold. This provides new justifications for a more encompassing notion of resources with which to understand the construction of wellbeing. We also develop the idea of 'resourcefulness' in this final chapter, to help us better understand the resilience of people operating in extremely impoverished and challenging circumstances. Second, both approaches emphasise the study of local values and meanings. Several psychological theories interpret subjective quality of life in terms of the gap between a person's actual status and the local standards and status of their peers within their community or other relevant reference groups. Similarly the 'thinking-doing' branch of the RPF emphasises the cultural construction of wellbeing, the imbrications of local values and identities in any understanding of quality of life.

Sufficient bridges thereby exist between the needs, resources and QoL frameworks to venture an integrated conceptual model and to justify an integrated programme of research into wellbeing. As noted, this must draw on contributions from different disciplines. The chapters here suggest that Sayer's ambition of post-disciplinarity is still some way off. Yet many of the predispositions which Bevan argues are necessary for advancing cross-disciplinary research have been met by the contributors to this volume. Certainly they have been concerned to communicate ideas across disciplinary boundaries; to accept insights from other disciplines; and to move beyond their usual disciplinary domains. They have operated with an 'active tolerance of difficult emotions involved in the exchange of ideas and opinions'. Myerson's four conditions for the successful pursuit of trans-disciplinarity, with which Bevan concludes her chapter, recognise not only the intellectual, but also the personal and emotional dimensions of this challenge, and these too must be confronted in any wellbeing research agenda.

14.3   Researching wellbeing: five key ideas

We contend that five key sets of ideas provide the conceptual scaffolding for a new theory of human wellbeing. These are:

1 The centrality of the social human being
2 Harm and needs
3 Meaning, culture and identity
4 Time and processes
5 Resourcefulness, resilience and adaptation.

The centrality of the social human being

First, the concept of human wellbeing brings the 'human' back to the centre of the analysis. As Rojas puts it, the ultimate purpose of his study is to consider the condition of 'the human being of flesh and blood ... and in her circumstance'. Although the human is present in all social science investigations she does not always appear at centre-stage. Thus it is possible to study structures such as 'the market', 'the state' or 'culture', or forms of organisation such as 'the household', 'the firm', 'the village', in all of which the person is present but is not the main subject of analysis. We can also study 'components' of the human such as personality, intelligence, morality, or entrepreneurship, but, while these all contribute to the being of the person, they do not wholly define her, him or them. The distinctive proposition of the wellbeing perspective is to understand the role that they play in the production of wellbeing for different men, women, boys and girls.

This notion of the centrality of the human is nascent in the three analytical frameworks of this volume and represents one of the basic bridges joining them (see also White 2002). We can judge whether needs have been met only with reference to the condition of the human being; resources ultimately can be identified as such only by human beings; and the feelings of a person are best reported by that person. Emphatically, however, and anticipating mischievous interpretations of this as a statement of rampant individualism, we argue that placing the human being at the centre of analysis requires us to acknowledge the entirely social nature of that human being. We cannot understand the human being without reference to the collectivities, communities and societies within which they are located and live their lives. These different forms of collectivities bring with them the social structures and ideologies within which human beings interact. But human beings differ: they are men, women, boys, girls, Christian, Muslim, Buddhist, Hindu, married, divorced, black, white, *mestizo*, indigenous, migrant, elite, peasant, worker, destitute, and so on. Such difference ensures that human beings are differently placed in relation to social structures and as such are differently able to negotiate their notions of and strategies for wellbeing.

Bevan warns of the potential disconnect between individualistic and relational approaches to wellbeing. The polarisation of individualist and relational perspectives manifests itself in many guises throughout the disciplinary literatures: in psychology the debate over the existence of individualist and collectivist societies or cultures; in economics and sociology over the merits and efficiencies of individual and collective action; and in political science and philosophy the relationship between individual and collective rights, for example. These themes are of great importance to debates within disciplines, but they are usually cast in binary contrasts (see Nederveen Pieterse 2001). Yet the individualistic and relational ways of conceiving of wellbeing need not be fetishised as opposite poles; rather our conception of wellbeing must recognise the person, their volition, and the ineluctably social nature of each.

In a powerful critique of the contemporary social sciences, Douglas and Ney (1998) argue that many of the theories that dominate the analysis of poverty, welfare and wellbeing operate without a theory of the person. Such a theory, they propose, would require a conception of the person as a 'social being' and for them to be understood as a 'whole person'. The social being they argue is constituted through relationships with other persons and the prime need of the 'social being' is communication. Their plea suggests that relationships and communication are pivotal for the wellbeing research agenda.

Doyal and Gough's *Theory of Human Need* already recognises the significance of relationships and the heuristic by which it relates abstract basic needs to needs satisfiers encourages recognition that all needs are satisfied through relationships. Whether these are satisfied through interactions with close relatives and friends, through personal or impersonal contacts with representatives of the state, or intermediaries in the market, or other relationships is then a matter for empirical verification in particular community and societal contexts (see Gough and Wood *et al.* 2004; Wood and Gough 2006).

White and Ellison in Chapter 7 illustrate how resources only have meaning in the context of specific relationships. Their use and value depends on the intentions of the person seeking to realise them and how that person interacts with the perceptions and actions of those others. The intentions of the resource user in turn reflect the meanings, values and norms at play in wider social structures. Similarly, differences between people will shape what resources they are able to realise and what outcomes they are able to achieve with them.

Douglas and Ney (1998) overlook the debate in the Subjective Wellbeing literature between hedonic positive psychology and eudaimonic perspectives on wellbeing. Yet, eudaimonic conceptions of wellbeing, and particularly Ryan and Deci's Self-Determination Theory, are fundamentally built around a notion of relatedness. As Ryan and Sapp note in Chapter 3, 'Self-Determination Theory begins by explicitly positing that humans are inherently active, relational beings.'

The second part of the Douglas and Ney proposition for a minimal model of the person, integral to our proposition to place the social human being at the centre of our framework for analysis, is the call for social sciences to conceive of the 'whole person'. On the surface this is an argument against the type of analytical vivisection of the person that is so pervasive in contemporary disciplinarist forms of social sciences. But while much of their criticism is heaped on the model of *homo œconomicus*, their challenge is more profound and applies to the deep influence of this type of approach across all of the social sciences.

There are long historical processes here which have been extensively studied by the sociology and anthropology of science and knowledge (Tambiah 1990; Weber 1904) and these have entailed the analytical contrivance of reducing people's lives to a single dimension so that social scientists can apply ever more sophisticated techniques to explore their behaviour in relation to that.[4] In this reduction, other key parts of the person's life or being are either assumed or ignored. But, more importantly, Douglas and Ney (1998) argue, the process of assuming or ignoring other aspects of being results in elements of moral judgement being hidden and smuggled into these analytical frameworks. They then go on to argue that by making moral and then also subjective dimensions of our understanding of the human disappear, these elaborate academic practices serve to advance a notion of 'objectivity' in the social sciences. The problem, however, is what is lost. As Douglas and Ney put it, 'So we are left with the paradox that the social sciences description of

---

[4] For the case of economics, see Gudeman (1986, 2001).

the self does not refer to the social being. As the microcosm[5] requires, everything has to be sacrificed to generality, which is expected to protect objectivity, but the generality evacuates meaning' (1998: 89). The problem of the use of the term 'objective' in the contemporary social sciences, and particularly in its relationship to policy, is returned to below.

Placing the social human being at the centre of a wellbeing framework has many ramifications but perhaps most basic and profound for social science enquiry is the attention it draws to its foundational ontology. As Bevan argues in the preceding chapter, a human ontology recognises that people are whole persons with a biological, psychological and emotional constitution; that they are also social beings; that they are actively engaged in the reception, interpretation and construction of meaning; that persons are different from each other, both in their internal constitution and their social being; and that they live in time.

Harm and needs

Bevan also writes in Chapter 13: 'While agreeing that the 'fully rounded humanity of poor men, women and children in developing countries' should be acknowledged, it is also important to acknowledge that for many poor people life is unbearable and often ends in a painful early death. The suffering and the lost years must not be ignored as they are in most poverty studies.' The adoption of a human ontology highlights the ubiquity of potential harm to the person: the notion of human wellbeing requires a concept of harm.

The core of the Doyal and Gough Theory of Human Need is that where universal basic needs are not satisfied then serious *harm* of an 'objective' kind will result. THN defines serious harm as 'fundamental disablement in the pursuit of one's vision of the good'. In this view harm is understood as something that affects both the human body and the ability of the person to participate in society. In particular, the basic need of autonomy is a profoundly social concept. In Chapter 3, Ryan and Sapp also work with the notion of harm, but from the social psychological perspective. Building upon a biologically and psychologically grounded notion of human growth and development, they claim, '*a basic psychological need* denotes only those nutriments essential for psychological growth and integrity (Ryan 1995). This suggests that there are psychological supports that humans must experience to thrive, and that when deprived of these supports, empirically observable degradation

---

[5] For example, the device of *homo œconomicus*.

results (chapter 3: 74–75).' As with Doyal and Gough, this approach appeals to a notion of harm that can be objectively verified. The claim that needs are 'objectively' linked to harm provides the basis for the claim to 'universal' status for both theories.

Self-Determination Theory provides a psychological deepening of the Doyal and Gough Theory of Human Need. In the latter, autonomy (or rather its lack) was partly defined and operationalised as 'learned helplessness' (from Seligman 1975) and severe mental illness. There was little discussion, however, of the circumstances or conditions leading to mental ill-health. The SDT rectifies this by identifying three psychological needs whose denial results in degraded mental wellness, which in turn and without intervention will be manifest in physical decline. Establishing the relationships between Theory of Human Need and Self-Determination Theory begins to place the psychological needs of the latter in their broader social and political context, but this needs to be further strengthened.

We have argued above that wellbeing is both constructed and largely achieved through relationships. In the THN, 'significant primary relationships' are a universal need satisfier and in SDT 'relatedness' is a basic psychological need. Ryan and Sapp define the latter:

Relatedness ... concerns feeling socially connected. Typically, one feels most related when one feels cared for and significant to others, but relatedness also pertains to a general sense of being integral to a social organisation that lies beyond the individual or what Angyal (1941) labelled homonomy.

'Feeling' and 'significant' are the two important terms to highlight here. They force us to consider how we identify and understand who are 'significant' others and how we know how to feel about our relationships to them. While the social construction of 'meaning' is central here, both SDT and THN tend to underplay its importance at key points of their argument.

Drawing on a different tradition, Lukes's (1974, 2005) analysis of power encourages us to consider how 'meanings' come about; how agendas are set; and how persons operate with particular frames of meaning and are socialised in ways that challenge their ability to conceive of other frames of meaning. From this perspective the construction of meaning involves profoundly social and political processes and as such these mediate how we are able to 'feel' about experiences. These feelings shape how we experience 'harm'.

With this in mind the claim by both sets of theories to the status of 'objective' can be misunderstood. Both THN and SDT are concerned with needs which involve much more than the physical nurturing of the biological person. In both theories, harm arises as much from a consequence of cognitive and social processes as from direct action which damages the biological entity. They both depend upon an appreciation of the person in social relationships and particularly in the context of socially and culturally constructed meaning. In this respect they connect to grand traditions in the social sciences where processes of relationship and meaning and their social consequences are discussed in terms of 'alienation' and 'anomie' (Marx, Weber and Durkheim).[6] Since the relational and cognitive (subjective) processes that mediate the relationship between needs and harm in large part involve social constructs of what is 'normal', 'desirable', or 'acceptable', then to refer to either SDT or THN as just 'objective' theories of need is an oversimplification.

Traditional western liberalism conceived of harm as intentional acts by individuals, groups or the state preventing other persons from pursuing their fundamental goals. The policy response was to enshrine various 'forbearances' in common law and/or in the form of civil and political rights. Socialist and reformist thinking in the twentieth century challenged this by recognising egregious structural but unintentional obstacles to the pursuit of fundamental goals, such as Beveridge's 'Five Giants' of 'Want, Disease, Ignorance, Squalor and Idleness'. The policy response was to enshrine a range of social and economic rights to the wherewithal for human survival and thriving. This has marked an historic extension of thinking on harm and wellbeing, on which this volume builds. It recognises what some call 'structural violence': interactions with others, at close or distant remove, where simply following rules or norms inevitably but unintentionally results in harm to others.

However, as Bevan among others argues, it is important when analysing poverty and illbeing in many developing countries today to re-emphasise and reinstate the active infliction of harm. Since wellbeing is a product of relationships, we must recognise that some of these relationships can – and are intended to – result in harm to other persons. This can include situations where a person is actively denied some key resources (such as land or water) or components of need satisfaction (such as health or security) by other persons. Bevan's analysis of insecurity regimes in Africa and the work of others, such as Farmer on suffering, provide harrowing examples (Bevan 2004a; Farmer 2005).

---

[6] I am grateful to Geof Wood for drawing attention to this point.

Meaning, culture and identity

All of the discussion so far points to the importance of 'meaning' for a wellbeing research agenda. Meaning acts as a bridge joining the three organising ideas of needs, resources and quality of life. In Chapter 1 we argue that, "It is systems of meaning, negotiated through relationships within society, that shape what different people can and cannot do with what they have. And, by giving sense to a person's doing, meaning translates the 'having' and 'doing' into 'being' ". This complements the 'centrality of the social human being' by recognising the role of social organisation and culture in the generation and transmission of the meanings through which our relationships are conducted and constrained.

In proposing their minimal model of the person Douglas and Ney write, 'As a social being the person needs to be capable of reading messages from other persons, of responding to these and of composing intelligible messages to send out' (1998: 89). A theory of the person depends on having a conception of culture and they emphasise a particular and partial definition of culture. 'Culture is the result of people getting together; it is the result of mutual encouragement and coercion ... Culture is the selective screen through which the individual receives knowledge of how the world works and how people behave' (1998: 91).

To study wellbeing therefore requires a framework of analysis that is able to comprehend the cultural construction of meanings in particular contexts. The analysis of the construction of meaning has been the core business of social anthropology since its invention in the nineteenth century and a key element in its academic arsenal has been the concept of *culture*. However, its value is periodically contested, partly because of the multiplicity of definitions and meanings that are attached to the notion. It can seemingly mean everything and nothing and, as Olivier de Sardan notes (2005: 81–82), its overuse encourages unhelpful stereotyping. But this does not render the concept useless.

To avoid these problems we require a much more specified and differentiated use of the concept. Cultures are seen here as dynamic systems of norms, values and rules that are developed by particular communities, founded in their relationships to particular natural and social environments. They are to be identified at all different levels of social collectivity, both within the nation state and beyond it. As suggested by Douglas and Ney (1998), these systems of norms, values and rules provide the guidelines as to what meanings are to be attached to what the participants in 'the culture' perceive and do. Cultures guide our aspirations. They represent systems of meaning with which people perceive what it is they need or want, and also provide the measures against which we decide whether we have enough of what we want, or whether we are satisfied with what we are able to do and be.

Cultures as systems of meaning entail histories and as such are characterised by path dependence. They are dynamic social products, with internal processes of contestation and reproduction and external processes of adaptation to other cultures and systems of values. Societies and their cultures are constantly in flux; meanings are contested; and people in all societies frequently engage in the renegotiation of meaning in their efforts to address new challenges. This view of culture is a considerable and necessary advance on a conception of it as just 'normative consensus' (see Doyal and Gough, 1991: 79–80).

Cultural analysis is an important ingredient of a wellbeing methodology,[7] affirming a view of the person as both recipient of meaning and generator of it. From the perspective of the person as *recipient* of meaning this requires us to acknowledge the power of those forms of meaning that are neither 'objective' in scientific terms nor 'subjective' in personal terms, but are nevertheless highly significant in our social lives. These are those ideas, values and other elements of meaning that are accepted as 'fact' or 'reality', but which are products of interpersonal agreement, social consensus and are regarded as culturally 'given'. That they are social constructs need not necessarily make them less 'real' or less difficult to refute in the lives of men, women and children as they pursue wellbeing than if they were 'hard facts' or pieces of stone. And, as both SDT and THN elaborate, failure to meet needs that are underpinned by these social constructs can just as inevitably result in physical human harm as can the denial of food. The perspective of the person as *generator* of meaning reminds us that these social facts are not immutable and the possibility of social change depends entirely on the fact that these social constructs can and do change, but it is important not to underestimate the power that is often associated with them.

Ryan and Sapp argue in Chapter 3:

Indeed, it will be a fundamental tenet of SDT that the reason people have a readiness to adopt and internalise ambient cultural values, no matter what their content, is that by doing so, they satisfy needs. It is by assimilating the values of one's group that one becomes more connected and related, and more competent

---

[7] The definition of cultural analysis offered by Thompson is particularly appropriate: 'the study of symbolic forms – that is, meaningful actions, objects and expressions of various kinds – in relation to the historically specific and socially constructed contexts and processes within which, and by means of which, the symbolic forms are produced, transmitted and received' (1990: 136).

and effective. Furthermore, the general tendency to make ambient values one's own, and to feel them as central to identity, is an expression of the need for and developmental tendency towards autonomy. Put differently, needs supply the underlying processes that explain how cultures become part of individual personality. These essentials are thus apparent across historical, cultural, political or economic contexts.

Here they almost exclusively emphasise the person as recipient of meaning, but in doing so they shed further light on how we might understand the relationship between needs and 'objectivity'. They argue that their three basic psychological needs operate together in a way that is inextricably linked to the functioning of particular cultural contexts.

Looking at this from a different angle, Doyal and Gough (1991) argue that the meeting of human needs is dependent upon the organisation of the society in which people are participating and that a key element of social organisation is the ability of societies to reproduce themselves. To do this they must first have systems for the transmission of meanings and values that are deemed (consciously or unconsciously) important for the society, and second, systems of authority to maintain, promote and protect these meanings and values. Just as much as if it were a matter of objective fact, the transgression of norms and given values by a person will often result in that 'society' punishing (inflicting harm) on the transgressor.

Culture, as an evolving and dynamic system of norms, values and rules, provides guidelines for what meanings are to be attached to what men, women and children in a particular societal context observe and do, and as such it is an essential medium of both societal transmission processes and systems of social authority. It tells the social being what is to be considered 'a fact', what is 'normal', or 'expected', or what is simply 'a given' in any social context, regardless of whether it is scientifically or statistically proven to be objectively 'a fact' or not. This reaffirms the view implicit in the formally stated objective of the WeD research, that wellbeing cannot be adequately perceived in just objective and subjective terms, but that it is a concept that crucially depends upon social construction. That is, there are elements of meaning that are key to our conceptions and construction of wellbeing that are *inter-subjective* (Giddens 1976: 26–27; Habermas 1987).

The Ryan and Sapp argument about the internalisation of culture essentially addresses the issue of *identity*. It argues that a person's ability to establish identity is closely bound up with their feelings of relatedness and competence in respect of the culture of the group in which they are interacting. However, at this time, in all of the WeD study countries and in all of the communities studied, struggles over identity are very much evident. In arguing for the importance of cultural analysis in contemporary thinking about international development, John Clammer quotes Friedman's contention that, in today's world, culture is 'a complex negotiation of identity now irretrievably embedded in globalisation and linked also with consumption as the dominant cultural form of late capitalist society.' (from Clammer 2005: 104). More than ever before we are aware that people in all societies can operate with multiple identities and that some of these identities are not wholly grounded in the specific social context in which they are living. Depending on the specific context and reason for interaction, sometimes the identity may be a religious one; in other social contexts it may be an ethnic identity; and in still others it may be an identity associated with an internationally marketed football club.

The adoption of different identities or 'cultural repertoires' (see Dean 2003) has implications for researching wellbeing in developing countries. An empirical wellbeing research programme must be aware of not only those systems of meaning that are engaged day to day and in face-to-face relations in particular communities, but also those that involve relationships with people at other levels of our social systems, including those who are 'imagined' and whom we experience through our participation in and identification with different levels of collectivity; from village to globe. Benedict Anderson wrote of the profound influence of print and text in the emergence of the nation state in the middle ages (Anderson 1983), and in the twentieth and twenty-first centuries we now need to take account of the globalisation of broadcasting in its many forms and of the role of information technology, the mobile phone and the internet. All of the communities in the WeD research reveal remarkable relationships with actors in global arenas (through international migration from highland Peruvian communities, or via satellite television in rural Thai villages).

Researching wellbeing today cannot ignore the realisation and challenges of our increasingly global community. Systems of meaning which have their roots in societies other than one's own, but which are conveyed by globalised travel and communications, can affect conceptions, aspirations and experiences of wellbeing (see Graham forthcoming; Graham and Pettinato 2002). We contend that human beings are at the centre of our analytical framework, but they must be understood in relation to all the contexts in which they relate and communicate. Escaping from the tendency to focus on just one level or another,[8] a

---

[8] Whether it be the anthropological 'my village, my people' mentality, or the international relations focus on 'big systems' to the exclusion of all others.

contemporary, empirical wellbeing research agenda cannot focus on any one of these levels and entirely ignore the others. The conceptual framework must recognise that these contexts are many and multi-dimensional, ranging from the household, to community, to nation state, and to the global community.

Finally, and in order to illustrate the significance of these arguments about culture, meaning and identity for wellbeing research, it is worth returning to interrogate the idea of 'autonomy'. Not only is 'autonomy' a 'need' and word that is shared between THN and SDT, but it is a concept that is closely bound up with our sense of identity in whichever culture we operate. It is also the element of both theories which most excites and agitates researchers who come from a more anthropological tradition. The concept particularly evokes tension between 'universalist' and 'localist' perspectives. Cultural analysis of the term itself may clarify its meanings and potential uses such that it can be comprehensible to both.

Ryan and Sapp note in Chapter 3 that, 'Autonomy does not herein mean independence or separateness, but rather refers to the self-endorsement of one's own behaviour – that is, feeling personal value and interest with respect to what one does'. It is important to acknowledge that, as with Doyal and Gough, autonomy must be distinguished from dependence or interdependence. From the cultural perspective the notions of 'self-endorsement' and 'personal value' are of particular importance. Our argument recognises that these are constructs that arise out of particular frames of meaning and the processes of internalising particular cultural values. In different cultural settings they are likely to be different and as such the ability to 'personally value' particular types of action or behaviour and to 'self-endorse' them is likely to be different.

This indicates that while 'autonomy' may be a category fundamental to a universal and abstract conception of wellbeing, what constitutes 'autonomy' in particular social contexts is socially constructed 'locally', in those different societies and cultures. The standards by which we 'self-endorse' and achieve 'personal value' are socially communicated and the meaning of what it is to be autonomous in any social context is constructed within particular sets of relationships, values and cultural contexts. Thus what constitute norms of autonomy will be quite different in (what some observers label as) 'individualistic' societies and 'collectivist' societies (see Devine et al. 2006).[9] Nevertheless, although it may be manifested differently in different cultures, the concept of

[9] Indeed the logic of the argument suggests that the terms 'individualistic' and 'collectivist' when used to label particular societies may be unhelpful. What we are interested in as an empirical project is to identify which cultures (and even subcultures) define autonomy in similar ways. This is unlikely to break down into two such broad categories.

'autonomy' remains essential to understand wellbeing in all. It is a concept that refers to the boundaries of the relationship between the self and others. It refers to what is normal and acceptable in terms of our interdependence with others in that culture.

The same argument then applies to the two other psychological needs identified in Ryan and Deci's SDT. While we may argue that 'relatedness' 'competence' and 'autonomy' are basic psychological needs in all societies, they are so in an abstract sense. The specific meaning or form of these 'needs' in particular societies is socially constructed. This begins to indicate what the relationship between the 'universal' and the 'local' must be in a wellbeing research agenda: a 'universal' theory of wellbeing must deal with analytical concepts that are abstracts but can be recognised as present in some form or other in all human societies. It must posit relationships between these different analytical concepts in a general conception of wellbeing. But the role of the 'local' is to define more concretely the manifestations of these different analytical concepts in different social and cultural contexts. Iteration between the two should then confirm the validity or otherwise of the relationships being proposed and where necessary modify the universal conception.

Time and processes

The different approaches in this volume highlight the importance of time in our analysis. For the comprehensive analysis of wellbeing that is aimed for here it is inappropriate to separate wellbeing outcomes from wellbeing processes. To abstract a particular moment in time, a 'snapshot', in order either to compare different snapshots or manipulate them to explore causation and effect, is but an analytical device. We do not deny here that such snapshots can have important analytical and policy functions, for example in allowing governments to assess how many poor or illiterate people they must budget for or how effective some policy interventions have been. But outcomes are abstracts and it is important for the analysis of wellbeing that they are always understood to be non-discrete, ongoing moments that are a part of an interplay of complex societal and cognitive processes. We need to adopt a methodology which can accommodate both 'snapshot' and 'movie'.

This helps us understand better the ways in which wellbeing is in a permanent process of construction; and this fosters more effective policy thinking about how to eradicate poverty or promote wellbeing. Policy intervention is inevitably and unavoidably about changing processes in a particular society. Whether that consists of directly trying to affect the behaviours and interactions of different persons or of changing the rules or structures that shape the interactions, it is dependent upon a view of how those processes work.

Contributions to this volume highlight some of the different ways to take account of time. Ryan and Sapp argue that for psychological needs to be considered universal they must be cross-developmental – that is they must apply to humans across all ages. Wood's discussion of security and autonomy focuses heavily on the time trade-offs that poor people must engage in as they seek to establish security for themselves and those near to them. He also highlights the importance of a person's expectations of future wellbeing for their present state of wellbeing. Bebbington *et al.* in Chapter 8 highlight misunderstandings over time-based priorities as the source of a major disconnect between NGO interventions and the aspirations of the rural people they are intended to serve in the Andes of Peru and Bolivia. The emphasis by NGOs on present agricultural practices does not, they argue, connect with the concern amongst rural peoples for investment in the education of their children, precisely so that in the future they may escape from agricultural livelihoods. Møller's study in Chapter 11 of quality of life in South Africa over a quarter of a century situates wellbeing within processes of economic and social transformation and political upheaval. These examples embrace a huge range of wider processes, from the near relationships in the family and household, to the most distant and anonymous relationships in global markets. Some of these interactions with elements of social structure are fleeting while others are more persistent in people's lives.

Following the work of Abbott, Bevan (2004b) proposes three ways of conceiving of time in the analysis of poverty: calendars and clocks, rhythms, and histories. Calendars and clocks refer to the ways in which our societies formally organise, measure and record time using such notions as minutes, hours, days and years. Rhythms refer to the patterns over time associated with biological and social rhythms. These include the different biological rhythms of human life, but also the rhythms of, for example, agricultural, business and political cycles. Histories acknowledge that all human interactions take place in the context of both a past and a future and that both of these are important for relationships and interactions in the present.

All three of these conceptions of time are important in understanding the processes in which people pursue wellbeing and the persistence of poverty. As Bevan puts it:

individual and local episodes of long-lasting poverty are embedded in unequal structures and dynamics. They can produce long-lasting harm, at three levels: long-lasting harm to people's bodies, minds, relationships and subjective quality of life; long-lasting harm to local political economies, societies and cultural repertoires ...; and long-lasting harm to global relations, values and interactions. (2004b: 16)

Important in understanding poverty are the effects of events that happen unexpectedly or out of their anticipated time, as the literature on vulnerability has demonstrated. For example, in Bangladesh it is not so much the regular event of flooding that produces hardship or a spiral of decline, but when floods occur sooner than expected and before crops are ripened or harvested, or when they last too long and people are consequently unable to find work in agricultural labouring. The literature on poverty is replete with examples of the relationship between time and poverty: the often disastrous impact of the 'untimely' death of the family breadwinner; the duration of drought; the impacts of cyclical trends in global markets which affect the prices of goods that poor people produce and upon which they depend for a living.

Resourcefulness, resilience and adaptation

A final common feature across the contributions to this volume has been an emphasis on resourcefulness, resilience and adaptation. The Resource Profiles Framework was developed partly in response to the observable paradox of people living in material poverty, even what appears to be life-threatening poverty, but being able to adopt strategies which permit them to survive and also gain some satisfaction and enjoyment from their lives (Camfield and McGregor 2005). One explanation offered by our framework is that money and material assets comprise only part of the portfolio of resources of peoples: relationships with others, both intimate and at further removes, are and always have been crucial components of the total resource portfolio that people apply to their struggle for wellbeing. As a result even the poorest of people may have other resources to draw upon: in one meaning of the term they are 'resourceful'.

But we can go further. The work of Biswas-Diener and Diener (2001) on the lives of people living in Calcutta slums is striking in this respect. From the positive psychology perspective, they found that the poor people included in their study reported being only slightly less satisfied overall than middle-class comparison groups and that satisfaction in particular areas of life was uniformly positive. This was particularly the case for the domain of 'social relationships'. The authors conclude:

The participants in this study do not report the kind of suffering we expect. Rather, they believe they are good (moral) people, they are often religious ... and they have rewarding families. (Biswas-Diener and Diener 2001: 348)

There are analytical and moral hazards in this area of debate, reflected in Amartya Sen's concern that people's perceptions of how they are doing 'can be easily swayed by mental conditioning or adaptive expectations' (1999: 62), leading to the 'scandalous' situation where,

If a starving wreck, ravished by famine, buffeted by disease, is made happy through some mental conditioning (say, via the 'opium' of religion), the person will be seen as doing well on this mental states perspective. (1985b: 188)

In support of this he cites evidence from a post-famine health survey of widows in India, which suggested significant disparities between self-reports and external observations (1984: 309). He appeals to a form of the 'false consciousness' argument by stating that peoples' accounts are shaped by wider social, cultural and political structures and as such cannot always be taken as 'true' reflections of their experience or satisfaction with it. There have always been problems in the social sciences with the 'false consciousness' type of argument (see Lockwood 1981, and Scott 1985, amongst others), but these insights from psychology and other theorising (Elster 1983) offer constructive new ways of interpreting and understanding this old dilemma.

Processes of adaptation can play an important role in explaining how men, women and children cope with what to external observers appear to be the most unbearable of circumstances.[10] Kahneman and Tversky (1984) argue that all human judgements are relative to the 'frame' in which they are made and that this frame is established through social comparison. Included in this are comparisons with the performance of others, but also reference to internalised values of what is necessary to get by. Research into subjective wellbeing finds that people are 'resourceful' in the sense that they are able to adapt through the management of meanings and comparisons.

The weak links between income or material resources and happiness or subjective wellbeing, a constant of this research, are the starting points of a richer notion of quality of life. This entails a multi-dimensional or domain approach, recognising the contributions of health, family and friends, occupation and community, among other things, to our ongoing construction of wellbeing. Referring back to the eudaimonic dimension, feelings of competence and confidence, and progress in achieving significant personal goals, are critical to enhanced wellbeing. But these feelings and achievements cannot be separated from the social processes through which meanings are generated and

---

[10] For one of the most striking pieces of writing on this refer to Primo Levi's reflections in 'If this is a man' on life in a concentration/extermination camp during the Second World War (1959).

shared. From this constructivist perspective even the poorest can be resourceful, hopeful and resilient.

This matches well with the centrality of autonomy as a basic human need in THN; on agency freedom in Sen's capability theory; on human dignity and of people 'as somehow awe-inspiringly above the mechanical workings of nature' in Nussbaum's version of capability theory. People endlessly exhibit creativity in facing demanding, even squalid or abusive, situations.[11] This second, and more usual, meaning of 'resourcefulness' is emerging as a common feature of twenty-first-century understandings of wellbeing. It features, for example, in Cummins's observation that subjective wellbeing indicators like happiness and life satisfaction are maintained by a 'dispositional brain system' that keeps each person's wellbeing within a narrow, positive range (2002a). Rather than see the unresponsiveness of SWB to other factors as a problem, Cummins argues: 'the fact that it is generally predictable and stable enhances its usefulness ... because the values for subjective QoL can be referenced to a normative range [which] is homeostatically maintained' (2002a: 264). He goes on to ask: 'what are the conditions that produce homeostatic defeat?' and 'what are the personal and instrumental resources that defend against such defeat?'[12]

14.4   A conceptual framework for researching wellbeing

The purpose of the discussion so far has been to prepare the ground for the presentation of a wellbeing research methodology. There are two steps in this process: the first is to draw together the observations made in the chapter so far and to represent these in a general and overarching conceptual framework. The second is then to provide greater specificity by describing the operationalisation of the general principles into a methodology for the empirical study of the social and cultural construction of wellbeing in developing countries.

Figure 14.1 draws together these observations to present a new perspective on the study of wellbeing. The diagram offers a view which is trans-disciplinary and deliberately seeks to be comprehensive in its notion of wellbeing. As we shall see, it also helps design a suite of specific methodologies for wellbeing research. It is unlikely that any single empirical study of wellbeing will be able to deal equally with all

---

[11] Indeed, we can consider the possibility that a totally secure environment may undermine resourcefulness (Standing 2004).

[12] The work of Camfield, Ruta and Donaldson (2006) offers some insights into the potential relationships between the work of Cummins and that of Sen and others in the more social dimensions of wellbeing.

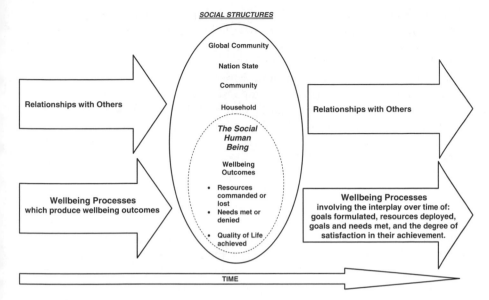

Figure 14.1 A wellbeing framework

aspects of the huge agenda that is implied by this diagram. Different empirical studies could choose to focus on some elements of the diagram to greater extent than others, but the argument here is that the perspective constitutes a package and even if not all parts are dealt with equally in any empirical study they must in some way be taken account of. The diagram helps ensure that specific studies remain consistent with the overarching wellbeing perspective.

Figure 14.1 adopts the human ontology and places the social human being at the centre of the analysis. These social humans then relate to others both in pursuit of their own wellbeing goals and also in the constitution of society (at all its levels of collectivity), in order to enable human goals to be better met. The diagram also acknowledges the inseparability of wellbeing outcomes and processes and emphasises their constant iteration through time, from processes to outcomes and then on to processes again, by envisaging time as flowing from left to right along the horizontal axis. The axis is given no scale since some of the relationships that are involved will take place over a short time span and others over much longer time scales.

The social person's wellbeing outcomes are represented in the central circle in the limited threefold sense discussed at the beginning of this chapter. They comprise the combination of needs met, resources commanded and quality of life achieved. The processes that generate these outcomes are seen as similarly involving the interplay of needs, resources and meanings. That is, we recognise that people formulate goals or objectives (which are likely to be a combination of needs and wants); they then deploy resources in seeking to meet these goals; and they adjust both their goals and their strategies for achieving them in relation to their perceived satisfaction in achieving their goals. This dynamic highlights the social and cognitive processes of adaptation that we discussed earlier. In the processes of goal formulation, in deciding on how to use resources and then in evaluating their own condition, social human beings are both resourceful and resilient.

Since the social human being exists in society then all utterances, actions and decisions are shaped by the frames of meaning at work in the context in which the person participates. Culture imbues all the levels of social structure that are identified in this diagram. However, we have argued for a view of culture that is neither monolithic nor static. In contemporary struggles over identity social human beings may engage in many different cultural contexts and may have open to them many different cultural repertoires. It is a matter of empirical study to identify what these different cultural repertoires may be for different people and then how these enable or constrain them in formulating and then pursuing wellbeing.

Harm to the social person primarily arises from the failure to meet needs (including where this is the direct and intended consequence of the action or actions of others), but we have expanded the definition of needs here to include social, affective and cognitive needs. The explanations as to why harm is generated can involve material, social, affective and cognitive processes or a combination of them. Thus, and as only limited examples, harm may arise from failing to have the necessary resources with which to meet material needs, but could also arise from aspiring to goals which cannot be then achieved, or aspiring to yet other goals which when achieved produce harm in themselves.[13]

The diagram conceives of human beings engaging in relationships with others, across a range of different levels of social structure, and over time. The terms household, community, nation state and global community are identified here and are used (ambiguously) to refer to both the location of the interaction and the types or domain of interaction. Thus, for example, we can envisage household relationships with family members who are not physically present in the household but who are to

[13] For a fuller discussion of these possibilities see Gaspers's discussion of the different usages of the term 'needs', in Chapter 2.

be found somewhere else in the world. The locations and types of interaction that are shown here are indicative and not exhaustive. Different analyses may require specification of alternative levels of social structure (for example, neighbourhood, workplace, or region).

The diagram does not imply that all relationships are necessarily 'real' or face-to-face, but as we have discussed earlier, it may be that certain wellbeing outcomes and processes depend on relationships which are essentially 'imagined' (for example, with other members of the nation state or with the global congregation of a particular faith group). Once again this raises the issue of identity and highlights the contemporary challenge of social beings physically located in particular societies nevertheless operating with multiple notions of identity, not all of which are rooted in that particular society.

14.5   A methodology for researching wellbeing

How can this broad framework be translated into a methodology for studying the ways in which different people attempt to construct their wellbeing? Here we summarise the approach adopted in the WeD research programme.

In order to study the social and cultural construction of wellbeing in developing countries the research group identified four countries in which to carry out the research: Bangladesh, Ethiopia, Peru and Thailand. These span three continents, four dominant religions, and include two middle-income and two low-income countries. Within each country six or seven research sites were selected to cover a spectrum of rural to urban communities. In each country case the country team selected communities on the grounds that they were neither representative nor exceptional, but that study of them would yield particular insights into the challenges to the achievement of wellbeing in the country at this time.

The composition and organisation of the WeD research group reflects the challenges of both the disciplinary scope of the wellbeing conceptual framework and the problematic of keeping both the 'local' and the 'universal' in focus. It is international, bringing together researchers from the five different countries involved, and it is multi-disciplinary (drawing upon anthropology, sociology, political theory, economics and psychology). Individual researchers in the group range in their emphasis and experience from those concerned more with revealing local ('emic') understanding and those whose interest is more fixed on universal ('etic') models. The group set out to reconcile these and other differences not only via the types of theoretical debate that have been reviewed here, but also by negotiating and implementing a joint programme of comparative and cross-national empirical research. As a microcosm of the tension between 'universalism' and 'localism' the process of constructing the WeD methodology involved considerable time in iteration between all parties, seeking agreement within the group over both the interpretation of the trans-disciplinary framework and the detail of fieldwork implementation.

The WeD research methodology comprises six distinct research components. Each of these generates data on key elements of the conceptual framework and they can be grouped into three categories: those that deal primarily with *outcomes*; those that deal mainly with *structures*; and those that deal with *processes*.

Outcomes

Two of the three dimensions of wellbeing outcome (see Figure 14.1) are addressed by one research instrument, the Resources and Needs Questionnaire (RANQ).

RANQ   The RANQ is a household survey that establishes both an outcomes benchmark and the basic population upon which other elements of the study can draw. The RANQ was specifically designed to map the distribution of resources and needs satisfactions within the communities being studied. The five categories of *resources* were derived from the Resource Profiles Framework: material, human, social, cultural and natural. The major categories of need satisfaction were derived from the Theory of Human Need (for example, health, education, food and housing). What marks the RANQ apart is that both needs and resources extend beyond those that are explored by the types of household survey conventionally used in international development research and policy. Thus resources extend to the social and cultural resources that a household and its members can command and the needs explored extend to relationships.

In each case the specific or 'local' form of the resources or needs had to be established by an extensive process of grounding and piloting. The result was a common set of questions but translated into each local language and with specific forms of resources and needs satisfiers where required. Thus the instrument does not ask about llamas in Bangladesh, or about *madrassa*[14] in rural Peru. Throughout, careful attention was paid to issues of cognitive and linguistic equivalence in order that results from the four countries could be analysed in relation to each other. Up to 250

---

[14] Islamic school for religion-based study.

households were included in the survey in each community studied, resulting in around 1,000 rural and 500 urban households surveyed in each country. Although a household survey, the RANQ gathers detailed information on every member of every household and in particular seeks to establish levels of needs satisfaction on an individual basis.

RANQ also gathers information on basic household demographics and on important instances of long-term shock and good fortune experienced by the households and their members over the previous five years. Having gathered the basic demographics for either the complete population of the community or a large sample of it, the RANQ then provides a basis for the sub-sampling of individuals and households for subsequent phases of fieldwork.

The third dimension of wellbeing outcome identified in the framework is Quality of Life, and this is investigated in our QoL research.

QoL   After an extensive review of available methodologies for measuring quality of life the research group concluded that none of these adequately met the needs of the wellbeing framework. Consequently the group adopted a three-phase strategy to study quality of life as both the outcomes experienced in the communities studied and the processes which generate them.

Phase 1: the approach to quality of life adopted has been 'bottom-up', recognising that no other QoL methodology has been developed through close engagement with people in relatively poor rural and urban communities in developing countries. In the first phase, exploratory and grounding work was carried out with community members, identifying what goals and resources were regarded by them as important to their QoL in their particular community. The first phase also explored the efficacy of a range of research methods for the study of QoL in these communities, where literacy rates can be low and where other aspects of community life and organisation limit the effectiveness of methods developed using highly educated participants from industrialised countries (see Schmidt and Bullinger, Chapter 13, here).

Phase 2: the substantive and methodological findings of the first phase were then used to define a workable definition of quality of life appropriate for such communities and a strategy for the implementation of a specific and unique instrument (WeDQoL). Adapting the WHO definition of Quality of Life, the WeD group has operated with a view of quality of life as emerging from 'the gap between people's goals and perceived resources, in the context of their environment, culture, values, and experiences' (Camfield, McGregor and Yamamoto 2006). The instrument that was developed gathers data on the key elements of this definition.

Phase 3: a common interview-administered instrument was developed and was then grounded in each country. The series of measures that it produces are then analysed in relation to each other and in relation to data generated by other parts of the WeD methodology. Importantly this approach permits the analysis of the relationship between subjective data and both quantitative and qualitative data that deal with the more objective dimensions of wellbeing and the frames of meaning with which people operate.

Structures

As illustrated in Figure 14.1, the social human being is embedded in society and this part of the research methodology is designed to comprehend those structures of society that are most relevant for the individuals and households studied. Again the WeD programme had to be selective, and we opted to study in depth just two of the hierarchy of social structures: the community and the nation state.

Community profiling   The community profile is a document which describes the salient demographic, social and physical characteristics of each of the communities included in the study. It is compiled using a variety of research approaches including the use of secondary data, key informant interviews and participatory methods. The community profiling also plays an important role in the sequence of the research. It has two interlinked purposes: it begins to build a relationship between the researchers and the people in the communities being studied and builds an appreciation of the meanings of wellbeing that are at play in each community. As the WeD methodology moves on it increasingly depends upon a growing level of trust between researchers and community members. Also the growing understanding of the community is important for subsequent elements of the methodology, where it allows a more attuned approach and more sharply focused work than otherwise might have been the case.

As a document the community profile can then be developed throughout the research, with more data being added as the results of further methods become available. In this sense it becomes an important resource document for the research team. Because the community profiles have been written broadly to the same format across the four countries, this also enables us to compare differences and similarities across the communities.

Structures research and welfare regimes   This component relates the wellbeing outcomes and processes observed to national systems and features (and to a certain extent regional and other sub-national features). The intent is to locate the research sites within national and global structures of power, exchange and information. It also seeks to draw attention to the way actors within the research sites mediate between the households and outside organisations and institutions, including government, business and civil society.

The approach we adopt draws particularly on the insecurity and welfare regimes framework developed to analyse developing countries by Gough *et al.* (2004). In conceptual terms this contributes to the developing critique of the 'Washington consensus' and the idea that there exists one linear path of economic development. Instead it posits distinct paths of development in different countries and regions, which constitute persistent and distinct welfare regimes. There is a close link here with the model of Sigma society and social exclusion developed by Figueroa, Altamirano and colleagues in the Peruvian WeD research team and discussed in Chapter 9 by Copestake. The data for this component of the research are mainly secondary and include both quantitative and qualitative data, but these are gathered in reference to the community profiles, 'the process research' and the identification of key community actors in the RANQ so that our understanding of structures is connected across the different levels.

Processes

Finally, the research framework in Figure 14.1 emphasises that wellbeing outcomes cannot be understood without reference to time and the processes that generate them. The research into the processes in which different individuals and households engage as they pursue their wellbeing provides us with insights into the relationships between wellbeing outcomes and structures. Two distinct research components were developed here. The first, obviously titled 'process research', entails largely qualitative engagement with a sub-sample of different individuals and households to discern the types of processes that they regard as most important in formulating their wellbeing goals and strategies. The second is the income and expenditure research.

Process research   This divides into two distinct strategies involving two different sets of research methods. The first of these is a 'thematic' approach, in which a series of prominent and contemporary 'wellbeing' issues are identified for particular attention. These 'themes' (for example, local collective action, livelihoods or migration) are identified by a combination of insights from the communities as well as cognisance of debates and discourses within each country. A sample of different individuals and households then are interviewed in relation to their process experiences in respect of these themes. The second approach is the 'core cases' approach, where a sub-sample of individuals and households undertake diary work and repeated interviews over an extended period. This data then can be used to identify and explore the range of different processes that are salient to their wellbeing. The purpose of both approaches, however, is the same: to illuminate a number of key relationships that these individuals and households engage in as they seek to achieve their desired state of wellbeing.

Income and expenditure research   This, a clear follow-on from the RANQ, provides information on how the portfolio of resources that a household commands is translated into incomes or other means by which needs or goals are satisfied, over a period of one year. The expenditures dimension of this work gives not only a view as to what goals or needs are actually met, but also an indication as to how these are distributed within the household. The research team have used two methods to collect this data. In Bangladesh and Peru a sample household survey has been conducted at three points through the year, providing a large sample of data[15] but with less information on periods between the surveys. The second method, monthly diaries applied in Ethiopia and Thailand, yields more qualitative information but for a smaller sample. In each case, however, because the data are gathered over a period of one year we gain some insight into the ways those seasonal fluctuations in both income and expenditure demands are dealt with by different kinds of household and individual.

Taken together these six elements of the wellbeing methodology are intended to provide a coherent set of data which are both quantitative and qualitative across a range of different households and individuals in the communities studied. Because all of the instruments have been designed with reference to the same basic framework there are important points of conceptual interconnection between them and the data from these different research components can be analysed in relation to each other. They are now all linked via an integrated database.

14.6   Conclusions and challenges

This final chapter has sought to show that wellbeing is a novel and potentially fruitful approach for both academic and policy thinking. We

---

[15] The surveys involve a sample of between 250 and 300 households, while the diaries cover around 75 households.

have offered a view as to how these different contributions can be brought together in a single conceptual framework and developed a methodology that seeks to operationalise that framework for empirical study in a selection of developing countries. These are yet early days for a wellbeing research agenda and there are many challenges both at conceptual and methodological levels which require much further work. However, having highlighted a number of the points of convergence evident in the different contributions to the volume, it is pertinent to conclude with some discussion of some of the more profound challenges that resurface throughout.

Multi-, inter-, and trans-disciplinarity

Inter-disciplinary research is both lauded and ignored across the social sciences, which exhibit their own languages, methodologies, and assumptions, and are organised in separate corporate structures comprising university departments, professional associations, journals, and library classifications. Cross-disciplinary fields of study do exist, of which development studies and social policy are two relevant examples; yet challenging the domination of disciplines is hard even at the multi-disciplinary level, let alone in a trans-disciplinary way.

The contributions to this book illustrate the degree of convergence at this time between authors writing from different disciplinary traditions as they engage with the concept of wellbeing. In the academic arena the concept of human wellbeing is one in which most if not all social science disciplines profess an interest. Most also have the humility to recognise that their own single disciplinary perspective and tools will be inadequate in comprehending the type of rounded conception of human wellbeing that we advance. As such the concept provides a timely and new opportunity for interchange between disciplines. Wellbeing has an important communicative function to fulfil within the global social science community at this time.

Each of the disciplines represented at the Hanse meeting and in the WeD research group has its own and different wellbeing discourses and its own traditions of dealing with the concept. It is therefore a challenge to understand the relations between these different histories and discourses, and then to find some acceptable common ground with which to take debate forward. The research agenda inevitably encounters what Bevan refers to as 'the political economy of disciplinarity'. These more basic barriers reflect how we currently organise our academic institutions and their relationship to policy, and are not to be underestimated either at a grand level of academic policy and funding allocation, or in the simple day-to-day attempts at communication between disciplinarians. But among the contributors to this volume there is evidence of positive willingness to recognise the validity and potential value of insights from other disciplines and research traditions.

Wellbeing and policy making

Apart from communications between social scientists, there is also the challenge of communication with policy makers. Des Gasper cautiously hopes that the concept of wellbeing can provide a new impetus for research and policy where he judges earlier theories of need to have failed. Injecting a note of realism he reminds us that in both the academic and policy dimensions, the potential of the concept is matched by real potential pitfalls arising from the confusion of discourses. Like 'need', 'wellbeing' can be used in diverse and loose ways. Such 'slipperiness' is, he argues, a profound obstacle to meaningful cross-disciplinary communication and a trans-disciplinary wellbeing agenda will require much clarification. Within WeD we have discovered that the review and harmonisation of terminology is an important undertaking not only for smooth inter-disciplinary communication but also to operationalise the research agenda within a workable methodology.

But Gasper, with a long-standing awareness of the 'needs of policy and policymakers' (Apthorpe and Gasper 1996; Schaffer 1985) then asks: 'How can these linked research programmes (needs and wellbeing) proceed effectively in political-intellectual-organisational space, aware not only of the precision, logic and empirical reference of discourse but also of its politics?' Here a major challenge confronts wellbeing researchers: the concept is inherently complex and yet we must reject some of our traditional social science ways of simplifying complex realities. How can such a holistic, woolly and intuitively appealing notion provide better political and policy leverage than the preceding discourses of needs?

The challenge is to advance a rigorous and well-disciplined academic debate around wellbeing; to do this in a way that permits the operationalisation of the concept in an empirical research agenda; and, at the same time, retain its simple intuitive appeal and rhetorical value. This will require compromises in two directions. The first is to ensure that amongst academics the conceptual debates are not elaborated *ad absurdum*, and that a balance is achieved between the inevitable disciplinary trade-offs and the necessary precision for research operationalisation. The second is to ensure that policy makers accept that wellbeing entails acceptance of a greater level of complexity than prior frameworks demand or than many are used to. It is not a concept that sits easily with the disciplinarist underpinnings that are prevalent in many contemporary bureaucratic divisions of labour.

Wellbeing, policy makers and politicians

While the relationship to policy makers is challenging enough, the wellbeing research agenda begins to highlight some broader and in some ways more profound challenges for our political systems. Indeed, the more that we engage with the concept the more we can wonder whether our current policy processes and political systems can cope with the implications of working with a concept of wellbeing that so profoundly incorporates both subjective dimensions and inter-subjective meaning.

The framework that is presented here implies that to formulate and implement an effective policy requires a good appreciation of the local realities that confront the human beings who are 'the objects' of that policy. A key dimension of these local realities is knowing what people think about what they conceive as wellbeing and how they are trying to achieve this (see McGregor 2004). This is what, in theory, systems of democracy are supposed to do. They are supposed to provide a means of communicating people's values to those who would seek to make policy on their behalf. It is well recognised, however, that even when working well our systems of democracy are often rather blunt instruments for this purpose (Pateman 1970, 1983) and need supplementing with more direct forms of participation.

Yet, if we are to accept that men, women and children have some kind of right to have their views of what goals they are trying to achieve and how they are trying to achieve them taken into account, then the challenges to our social and political systems are laid more open. At one level there is the basic challenge of how we organise political participation so as 'simply' to be able to hear different 'voices' at all levels of policy decision-making. Development policy makers and agencies have become increasingly aware of this through the work of pioneers such as Robert Chambers and also initiatives such as the World Bank's 'Voices of the Poor' exercises, but there remain tremendous obstacles to making this routinely effective in the politics and policy processes of many developing and developed societies. There is the deeper question of how to resolve conflicting and contested visions of what different people want for themselves and how we want our societies to be.

In this respect it is not just democracy but governance that matters. We have argued here that in order for people to achieve wellbeing then societies need to be organised in ways that enable them to meet their needs and achieve their goals. But alongside this comes a requirement for systems of authority that support such societal organisation, ensure that it is reproduced, enable it to evolve, but also to protect that social organisation from possible damage as a consequence of the actions of individuals. Earlier we noted that in the Doyal and Gough Theory of Human Need serious harm is defined as 'fundamental disablement in the pursuit of one's vision of the good'. But we argue here that not all 'visions of the good' are likely to be equally acceptable within societies if the values and organisation of that society are to remain intact in such a way as to better enable all in that society to pursue their wellbeing.[16]

As political science has long understood, authority rests on a balance between consent and coercion, but lessons from history and around the globe indicate that for societies to succeed then coercion has its limits and that authority has to be acceptable to the majority of people subject to it (Beetham 1991). The wellbeing agenda suggests that our ability to accept shared meanings and values requires that careful attention is paid to the mechanisms and processes whereby we reach consensus. This applies not just to overt policy decisions but also to debates over the very values upon which our societies depend.[17]

The global challenge of the social contract

Governance is a concept that applies to all levels of social collectivity from the household, through the village or town, to the nation state, and on to the global community. Recognising this returns us to what is perhaps the grandest challenge that the wellbeing agenda highlights. Stated in its most abstract form it requires us to consider what the relationship between the person and their society is to be.

Des Gaspers's deconstruction of the concepts of needs and wellbeing is important here. As he notes, the 'strongest' way in which the term 'need' is used refers to where 'it establishes a strong normative claim since the objective is a normative priority, and the requisite is indeed essential'. This normative prioritisation can then drive the allocation of resources. However, it prompts us to consider where such normative prioritisations come from. Hitherto, universal theories and then the policies that are founded in them, whether explicit, such those of Doyal and Gough, or covert, such as those of neo-classical economics, have

---

[16] As Des Gasper has noted in discussion, if one's 'vision of the good' entails actions that damage or eliminate particular sections of a society's population, then we have to ask whether that is an acceptable characteristic of a 'good' society.

[17] THN concludes that a 'dual strategy' is required to combine codified knowledge and experiential knowledge in a way that enhances human wellbeing: this returns us to the dilemma of devising locally legitimate and effective dual strategies.

sought to establish a superior claim to normative priority with reference to either the objectivity that their theoretical argument supports or to the evidence available that affirms their propositions. The argument presented here is that 'normative' statements in social theory and social policy tend to understate the social and cognitive processes that construct them. This is especially so when the argument depends strongly on a notion of objectivity. Rather 'universalist' statements, theories and policies must themselves be understood as global social and cultural constructs.

But this statement does not necessarily undermine their legitimacy. It is neither a collapse into post-modernism nor surrender to unfettered cultural relativism. Rather we must undertake cultural analysis at all levels of our global systems. We must consider how in any community and at any level, including at the global level, we reach our conclusions as to what is acceptable as a normative statement.

As we have argued throughout this volume, international development is fundamentally about competing visions of what wellbeing is or should be. It manifests itself in debates about what is meant by desirable and socially feasible. It is important for a future wellbeing research agenda to recognise and accept that both of these are and always will be matters of contestation. Subjective and inter-subjective dimensions are an integral part of our definition of wellbeing and this recognises that each vision of wellbeing is founded in sets of values and that those values are generated and maintained within particular societal contexts.

However, as Gough has noted elsewhere,

the two discourses – on the nature of wellbeing and on the institutions, processes and policies that affect wellbeing in developing countries – are disconnected. This disadvantages peoples – and notably the poor – in the developing world, for two reasons. First, they are deprived of influence over discourses and debates about universal and global goals. Second, they are deprived of influence over discourses and debates about local and place-specific means and policies. (2004: 276)

The challenge here then is how we are to take account of competing visions in our global deliberations on the universal and normative. This involves debating the political processes involved in establishing the universal normative. The purpose and promise of the wellbeing research agenda are that it represents a new analytical approach to these issues. It has the potential to generate, for example, a new perspective on debates over the roles of the state, market, community and individual in the creation of conditions to enable wellbeing. We have argued earlier for a definition of development as 'the creation of conditions where all people in the world are able to achieve wellbeing'. The incorporation of a subjective dimension in our conception of wellbeing implies that wellbeing cannot be wholly delivered by the state or market. Rather it is something that the person pursues and can seek to achieve. But they do not do so in a vacuum and the task of living together in society ensures that we must pay attention to our social structures and the systems of values with which we operate.

The US Declaration of Independence speaks of the 'right to pursue happiness' and in a similar sense our debates over the organisation of our societies and relations between them should be governed by judgements over whether the conditions are in place for people to pursue their notions of wellbeing. The concept of wellbeing has the potential to provide a basis for deliberations over what minimal standards of wellbeing would be and what societal conditions are necessary to make these possible. This is challenging at the level of the nation state, but it is equally important and necessary to consider the challenges in respect of our global community.

References

Aaronson, N. K., Acquadro, C., Alonso, J., Apolone, G., Bucquet, D., Bullinger, M., Bungay, K., Fukuhara, S., Gandek, B., Keller, S., Razavi, D., Sanson-Fisher, R., Sullivan, M., Wood-Dauphinee, S., Wagner, A. and Ware Jr, J. E. 1992. 'International Quality of Life Assessment (IQOLA) Project', *Quality of Life Research* 1: 349–351

Aaronson, N. K., Cull, A., Kaasa, S. and Sprangers, M. 1996. 'The European Organisation for Research and Treatment of Cancer (EORTC): Modular approach to quality of life assessment in oncology – an update', in Spilker, B. (ed.) *Quality of Life and Pharmacoeconomics in Clinical Trials*. 2nd edn. Philadelphia: Lippincott-Raven Publishers, pp. 179–189

Abbott, A. 2001. *Chaos of Disciplines*. London: University of Chicago Press

Abercrombie, N., Hill, S. and Turner, B. (eds.) 1994. *The Penguin Dictionary of Sociology*. London: Penguin

Acquadro, C., Jambon, B., Ellis, D. and Marquis, P. 1996. 'Language and translation issues', in Spilker, B. (ed.) *Quality of Life and Pharmacoeconomics in Clinical Trials*. 2nd edn. Philadelphia: Lippincott-Raven Publishers, pp. 575–587

Afrobarometer 2002. Afrobarometer Briefing Paper 1, www.afrobarometer.org

Alkire, S. 2002a. *Valuing Freedoms*. Oxford: Oxford University Press

Alkire, S. 2002b. 'Dimensions of human development', *World Development* 30: 181–205

Alkire, S. 2003. *A Conceptual Framework for Human Security*. CRISE Working Paper 2, Oxford: CRISE

Alkire, S. 2005. 'Subjective quantitative studies of human agency', *Social Indicators Research* 74 (1): 217–260

Alkire, S. 2006. 'Structural injustice and democratic practice: The trajectory in Sen's writing' in Deneulin, S., Nebel, M. and Sagovsky, N. (eds.) *Transforming Unjust Structures: The Capability Approach*. New York: Springer, ch. 3, pp. 47–62

Alloy, L. B. and Ackerman, L. Y. 1988. 'Depressive realism: Four theoretical perspectives', in Alloy, L. B. (ed.) *Cognitive Processes in Depression*. New York: Guilford Press, pp. 223–265

Alsop, R. and Heinsohn, N. 2005. *Measuring Empowerment in Practice: Structuring Analysis and Framing Indicators*. World Bank Policy Research Working Paper 3510 World Bank, Washington, DC: World Bank. Available at SSRN: http://ssrn.com/abstract=665062

Altamirano, T., Copestake, J., Figueroa, A. and Wright, K. 2003. *Poverty Studies in Peru: Towards a More Inclusive Study of Exclusion*. WeD Working Paper 5. Bath: Wellbeing in Developing Countries (WeD) Research Group, University of Bath

Altamirano, T., Copestake, J., Figueroa, A. and Wright, K. 2004. 'Universal and local understandings of poverty in Peru', *Global Social Policy* 4 (3): 312–336

Anand, S. and Sen, A. 1997. *Concepts of Human Development and Poverty: A Multidimensional Perspective*, Human Development Report 1997 Papers: Poverty and Human Development. New York: United Nations Development programme

Anderson, B. 1983. *Imagined Communities: Reflections on the Origins and Spread of Nationalism*. London: Verso

Anderson, R. T., Aaronson, N. K. and Wilkin, D. 1993. 'Critical review of the international assessment of health-related quality of life', *Quality of Life Research* 2 (6): 369–395

Andrews, F. M. and Withey, S. B. 1976. *Social Indicators of Well-Being*. New York: Plenum Press

Angyal, A. 1941. *Foundations for a Science of Personality*. New York: Commonwealth Fund

Appadurai, A. 2004. 'The capacity to aspire: Culture and the terms of recognition', in Rao, V. and Walton, M. (eds.) *Culture and Public Action: A Cross-Disciplinary Dialogue on Development Policy*. Stanford, CA: Stanford University Press

Apthorpe, R. and Gasper, D. 1996. 'Arguing development policy: Frames and discourse', *European Journal of Development Research* 8 (1)

Arefeen, H. K. 1982. 'Muslim stratification patterns in Bangladesh: An attempt to build a theory', *Journal of Social Studies* 16: 51–74

Argyle, M. 2002. *The Psychology of Happiness*. London: Routledge

Arneson, R. 1989. 'Equality and equal opportunity for welfare', *Philosophical Studies* 56: 77–93

Assor, A., Roth, G. and Deci, E. L. 2004. 'The emotional costs of parents' conditional regard: A self-determination theory analysis', *Journal of Personality* 72: 47–88

Baard, P. P., Deci, E. L. and Ryan, R. 2004. 'Intrinsic need satisfaction: A motivational basis of performance and well being in two work settings', *Journal of Applied Social Psychology* 34: 2045–2068

Bailey, F. G. 1966. 'Peasant view of the bad life', in Shanin, T. (ed.) 1971. *Peasants and Peasant Societies*. Harmondsworth: Penguin

Bandura, A. 1989. 'Human agency in social cognitive theory', *American Psychologist* 44: 1175–1184

Bandura, A. 1997. *Self-Efficacy: The Exercise of Control*. New York: Freeman

Bannock, G., Baxter, R. and Davis, E. (eds.) 1992. *The Penguin Dictionary of Economics*. 5th edn. London: Penguin

Bardhan, P. 2001. 'Distributive conflicts, collective action and institutional economics', in Meier, G. and Stiglitz, J. (eds.) *Frontiers of Development Economics: The Future in Perspective*. Oxford: Oxford University Press, pp. 269–298

Barrantes, R. and Iguiniz, J. M. 2004. *La investigación económica y social en el Perú: Balance 1999–2003 y prioridades para el futuro* [Economic and social research in Peru: Evaluation 1999–2003 and future priorities]. Lima: CIES

Barrientos, A. 2004. 'Latin America: Towards a liberal-informal welfare regime', in Gough, I., Wood, G., Barrientos, A., Bevan, P., Davis, P. and Room, G. (eds.) *Insecurity and Welfare Regimes*. Cambridge: Cambridge University Press, Ch. 4

Barry, B. 1990. *Political Argument*. 2nd edn. London: Harvester Wheatsheaf

Batterbury 2001. 'Landscapes of diversity: A local political ecology of livelihood diversification in south-western Niger', *Ecumene* 8 (4): 437–464

Baumeister, R. F. and Leary, M. R. 1995. 'The need to belong: Desire for interpersonal attachments as a fundamental motivation', *Psychological Bulletin* 117: 497–529

Bayliss-Smith, T. 1991. 'Food security and agricultural sustainability in the New Guinea Highlands: Vulnerable people, vulnerable places', *IDS Bulletin* 22 (3): 5–11

Bebbington, A. 1997. 'Social capital and rural intensification: Local organizations and islands of sustainability in the rural Andes', *Geographical Journal* 163 (2): 189–197

Bebbington, A. 1999. 'Capitals and capabilities: A framework for analyzing peasant viability, rural livelihoods and poverty', *World Development* 27 (12): 2021–2044

Bebbington, A. 2002. 'Sharp knives and blunt instruments: Social capital in development studies', *Antipode* 34 (4): 800–803

Bebbington, A. 2004a. 'Livelihood transitions, place transformations: grounding globalization and modernity', in Gwynne, R. and Kay, C. (eds.) *Latin America Transformed: Globalization and Modernity*. 2nd edn. London: Arnold, pp. 173–192

Bebbington, A. 2004b. 'NGOs and uneven development: Geographies of development intervention', *Progress in Human Geography* 28 (6): 725–745

Bebbington, A. 2005. 'Donor-NGO relations and representations of livelihood in nongovernmental aid chains', *World Development* 33 (6): 937–950

Bebbington, A., Hinojosa, L. and Rojas, R. 2002. *Contributions of the Dutch Co-financing Program to Rural Livelihoods and Rural Development in the Highlands of Peru and Bolivia*. Ede: Stuurgroep

Beck, S. and Preston, D. (eds.) 2001. *Historia, ambiente y sociedad en Tarija, Bolivia* [History, environment and society in Tarija, Bolivia]. La Paz: Editorial Instituto de Ecologa

Beck, T. 1994. *The Experience of Poverty: Fighting for Respect and Resources in Village India*. London: Intermediate Technology Publications

Beetham, D. 1991. *The Legitimation of Power*. Basingstoke: Macmillan Education

Bennett, F. and Roberts, M. 2004. *From Input to Influence: Participatory Approaches to Research and Inquiry into Poverty*. York: Joseph Rowntree Foundation

Bergner, M., Bobbit, R. A., Carter, W. B. and Gilson, B. S. 1981. 'The Sickness Impact Profile: Development and final revision of a health status measure', *Medical Care* 19: 780–805

Bergner, M., Bobbit, R.A., Pollard, W.E., Martin, D.K. and Gilson, D.S. 1976. 'The Sickness Impact Profile: validation of a health status measure', *Medical Care* 14: 57–67

Bernhard, J., Hürny, C.D.T., Coates, A. and Gelber, R. 1996. 'Applying quality of life principles in international cancer clinical trials', in Spilker, B. (ed.) *Quality of Life and Pharmacoeconomics in Clinical Trials*. 2nd edn. Philadelphia: Lippincott-Raven Publishers, pp. 693–707

Bernstein, H. 1979. 'African peasantries: A theoretical framework', *Journal of Peasant Studies* 6 (4): 420–444

Berzon, R., Hays, R.D. and Shumaker, S.A. 1993. 'International use, application and performance of health-related quality of life instruments', *Quality of Life Research* 2 (6): 367–368

Bevan, P. 2004a. 'Conceptualising in/security regimes', in Gough, I., Wood, G., Barrientos, A., Bevan, P., Davis, P. and Room, G. *Insecurity and Welfare Regimes in Asia, Africa and Latin America*. Cambridge: Cambridge University Press, Ch. 3

Bevan, P. 2004b. *Exploring the Structured Dynamics of Chronic Poverty: A Sociological Approach*. WeD Working Paper 6. Bath: Wellbeing in Developing Countries (WeD) Research Group, University of Bath

Bevan, P. 2005. *Studying Multi-dimensional Poverty in Ethiopia: Towards a Q-integrated Approach*. Q-Squared Working Paper Series www.q-squared.ca,

Bevan, P., Holland, J. and Pankhurst, A. forthcoming. *Power, Poverty and Subjective Quality of Life in Ethiopia: Four Rural Case Studies*. World Bank Poverty Reduction Group

Bhaskar, R. 1979. *The Possibility of Naturalism: A Philosophical Critique of the Contemporary Human Sciences*. Brighton: Harvester

Biswas-Diener, R. and Diener, E. 2001. 'Making the best of a bad situation: Satisfaction in the slums of Calcutta', *Social Indicators Research* 55: 329–352

Blaikie, N. 1993. *Approaches to Social Enquiry*. Cambridge: Polity Press

Boeke, J.H. 1942. *Economies and Economic Policy in Dual Societies*. Haarlem: Tjeenk Willnik

Booth, D. (ed.) 1994. *Rethinking Social Development Theory, Research and Practice*. Harlow: Longman

Booth, D. 2005. *Missing Links in the Politics of Development: Learning from the PRSP Experiment*. Overseas Development Institute (ODI) Working Paper 256 London: ODI

Bourdieu, P. 1977. *Outline of a Theory of Practice*. Cambridge: Cambridge University Press

Bourdieu, P. 1984. *Distinction*. London: Routledge and Kegan Paul

Bourdieu, P. 1990. *The Logic of Practice*. London: Polity Press

Bourdieu, P. 1998/2001. *Practical Reason*. Oxford: Polity Press

Bowden, A. and Fox-Rushby, J. 2003. 'A systematic and critical review of the process of translation and adaptation of generic health-related quality of life measures in Africa, Asia, Eastern Europe, the Middle East, South America', *Social Science and Medicine* 57 (7): 1289–1306

Bowlby, J. 1979. *The Making and Breaking of Affectional Bonds*. London: Tavistock

Bradburn, N. M. 1969. *The Structure of Psychological Well-Being*. Chicago: Aldine

Brass, T. 1996. 'Popular culture, populist fiction(s): The agrarian utopiates of A. V. Chayanov, Ignatius Donnelly and Frank Capra', *Journal of Peasant Studies* 24 (1): 153–190

Braybrooke, D. 1987. *Meeting Needs*. Princeton, NJ: Princeton University Press

Brazelton, T. B. and Greenspan, S. I. 2000. *The Irreducible Needs of Children*. Cambridge, MA: Perseus

Brickman, P., Coates, D. and Janoff-Bulman, R. 1978. 'Lottery winners and accident victims: Is happiness relative?', *Journal of Personality and Social Psychology* 36: 917–927

Brislin, R. W., Lonner, W. J. and Thorndike, R. M. 1973. *Cross-Cultural Research Methods*. New York: John Wiley

Brock, K. 1999. *It's Not Only Wealth that Matters – It's Peace of Mind Too: A Review of Participatory Work on Poverty and Ill-Being*. A study prepared for the World Development Report 2000/2001, Washington, DC: PREM, World Bank

Bromley, R. J. 1994. 'Informality, de Soto style: From concept to policy', in Rakowski, C. A. (ed.) *Contrapunto: The Informal Sector Debate in Latin America*. Albany: SUNY Press, pp. 131–152

Bromley, R. J. and Gerry, C. (eds.) 1979. *Casual Work and Poverty in Third World Cities*. New York: John Wiley

Brown, K. and Ryan, R. M. 2003. 'The benefits of being present: mindfulness and its role in psychological well-being', *Journal of Personality and Social Psychology* 84: 822–848

Bruton, H. 1997. *On the Search for Well-Being*. Ann Arbor: University of Michigan Press

Bullinger, M., Power, M. J., Aaronson, N. K., Cella, D. F. and Anderson, R. T. 1996. 'Creating and evaluating cross-cultural instruments', in Spilker, B. (ed.) *Quality of Life and Pharmacoeconomics in Clinical Trials*. 2nd edn. Philadelphia: Lippincott-Raven Publishers, pp. 659–669

Bullinger, M., Schmidt, S., Petersen, C. and the DISABKIDS-Group 2002. 'Assessing quality of life of children with chronic health conditions and disabilities: A European approach', *International Journal of Rehabilitation Research* 25 (3): 197–207

Buunk, B. P. and Gibbons, F. X. 2000. 'Towards an enlightenment in social comparison theory: Moving beyond classic and renaissance approaches', in Juls, J. and Wheeler, L. (eds.) *Handbook of Social Comparison: Theory and Research*. Plenum Dordrecht, Netherlands: Kluwer Academic Publishers, pp. 487–499

Byrne, D. 1998. *Complexity Theory and the Social Sciences: An Introduction*. London: Routledge

Byrne, D. 2002. *Interpreting Quantitative Data*. London: Sage

Cahill, M. 2005. 'Is the human development index redundant?', *Eastern Economic Journal* 31 (1): 1–6

Calhoun, C. 1995. *Critical Social Theory*. Oxford: Blackwells

Camfield, L. and McGregor, J. A. 2005. 'Resilience and wellbeing in developing countries', in Ungar, M. (ed.) *Handbook for Working with Children and Youth: Pathways to Resilence across Cultures and Contexts*. CA: Sage

Camfield, L., McGregor, J. A. and Yamamoto, J. 2006. *Quality of Life and its Relationship to Wellbeing*. Forthcoming Working Paper. Bath: Wellbeing in Developing Countries (WeD) Research Group, University of Bath

Camfield, L., Ruta, D. and Donaldson, C. 2006. *Sen and the Art of Quality of Life Maintenance: Towards a Working Definition of Quality of Life*. WeD Working Paper 12. Bath: Wellbeing in Developing Countries (WeD) Research Group, University of Bath

Campbell, A., Converse, P. E. and Rodgers, W. L. 1976. *The Quality of American Life: Perceptions, Evaluations and Satisfactions*. New York: Russell Sage Foundation

Cantril, H. 1965. *The Pattern of Human Concerns*. New Brunswick, NJ: Rutgers University Press

Carney, D. (ed.) 1998. *Sustainable Rural Livelihoods. What Contribution Can We Make?* London: Department for International Development

Carter, I. 1999. *A Measure of Freedom*. Oxford: Oxford University Press

Cella, D. F. and Bonomi, A. E. (1996). 'The Functional Assessment of Cancer Therapy (FACT) and Functional Assessment of HIV Infection (FAHI) quality of life measurement system', in Spilker, B. (ed.) *Quality of Life and Pharmacoeconomics in Clinical Trials*. 2nd edn. Philadelphia: Lippincott-Raven

Cella, D. F., Wiklund, I., Shumaker, S. A. and Aaronson, N. K. 1993. 'Integrating health-related quality of life into cross-national clinical trials', *Quality of Life Research* 2 (6): 433–440

Chakraverti, A. 2001. *Social Power and Everyday Class Relations: Agrarian Transformation in North Bihar*. New Delhi: Sage Publications

Chambers, R. 1983. *Rural Development: Putting the Last First*. Harlow: Longman

Chambers, R. 1987. *Sustainable Livelihoods, Environment and Development: Putting Poor Rural People First*. IDS Discussion Paper 240. Brighton: Institute of Development Studies

Chambers, R. 1989. 'Vulnerability, coping and policy', *IDS Bulletin* 20 (2): 1–7

Chambers, R. 1992. *Rural Appraisal: Rapid, Relaxed and Participatory*. IDS Discusssion Papers 311. Brighton: Institute of Development Studies

Chambers, R. 1997. 'Editorial: responsible well-being: A personal agenda for development', *World Development* 25 (11): 1743–1754

Chambers, R. and Conway, G. 1992. *Sustainable Rural Livelihoods: Practical Concepts for the 21st Century*. IDS Discussion Paper 296 Brighton: Institute of Development Studies

Chatterjee, P. 1993. *The Nation and Its Fragments: Colonial and Post-Colonial Histories*. Princeton, NJ: Princeton University Press

Cheung, C. K., and Leung, K. K. 2004. 'Forming life satisfaction among different social groups during the modernization of China', *Journal of Happiness Studies* 5: 23–56

Chirkov, V. I. and Ryan, R. 2001. 'Parent and teacher autonomy support in Russian and U.S. adolescents: Common effects on well-being and academic motivation', *Journal of Cross-Cultural Psychology* 32: 618–635

Chirkov, V. I., Ryan, R., Kim, Y. and Kaplan, U. 2003. 'Differentiating autonomy from individualism and independence: A self-determination theory perspective on internalization of cultural orientations and well-being', *Journal of Personality and Social Psychology* 84 (1): 97–110

Chirkov, V. I., Ryan, R. and Willnes, C. 2005. 'Cultural context and psychological needs in Canada and Brazil: Testing a self-determination approach to internalization of cultural practices, identity and well-being', *Journal of Cross-Cultural Psychology* 36: 423–443

Chong, K. 2003. 'Autonomy in the Analects', in Chong, K., Tan, S. and Ten, C. L. (eds.) *The Moral Circle of the Self: Chinese and Western Approaches.* Chicago, IL: Open Court, pp. 269–282

Chowdhury, A. 1978. *A Bangladesh Village: A Study in Social Stratification.* Dacca: Centre for Social Studies, Dacca University

Christopher, J. C. 1999. 'Situating psychological well-being: Exploring the cultural roots of its theory and research', *Journal of Counseling and Development* 77: 141–152

Chwalow, A. J. 1995. 'Cross-cultural validation of existing quality of life scales', *Patient Education and Counseling* 26 (1–3): 313–318

Clammer, J. 2005. 'Culture, development, and social theory: On cultural studies and the place of culture in development', *The Asia Pacific Journal of Anthropology* 6 (2): 100–119

Clark, A. E., Diener, E., Georgellis, Y. and Lucas, R. E. 2004. 'Unemployment alters the set-point for life satisfaction', *Psychological Sciences* 15: 8–13

Clark, A. E. and Oswald, A. J. 1994. 'Unhappiness and unemployment', *The Economic Journal* 104: 648–659

Clark, D. A. 2002. *Visions of Development: A Study of Human Values.* Cheltenham: Edward Elgar

Collard, D. A. 2003. *Research on Well-Being: Some Advice from Jeremy Bentham.* WeD Working Paper 2. Bath: Wellbeing in Developing Countries (WeD) Research Group, University of Bath

Cooke, B. and Kothari, U. (eds.) 2001. *Participation: The New Tyranny?* London: Zed Books

Copestake, J. 2005. 'Flexible standards for controlled empowerment? Microfinance as a case-study of aid management', in Folke, S. and Nielson, H. (eds.) *Aid Impact and Poverty Reduction.* Palgrave Macmillan

Cornwall, A. and Pratt, G. 2003. 'The trouble with PRA: Reflections on dilemmas of quality', *PLA Notes* (47)

Crooker, K. and Near, J. 1998. 'Happiness and satisfaction: Measures of affect and cognition', *Social Indicators Research* 44: 195–224

Cross, S. E. and Gore, J. S. 2003. 'Cultural models of the self', in Leary, M. R. and Tangney, J. P. (eds.) *Handbook of Self and Identity.* New York: Guilford Press, pp. 536–564

Csikszentmihalyi, M. 1990. *Flow: The Psychology of Optimal Experience.* New York: Harper and Row

Cummins, R. A. 1995. 'On the trail of a gold standard for subjective well-being', *Social Indicators Research* 35: 179–200

Cummins, R. A. 1996. 'The domains of life satisfaction: An attempt to order chaos', *Social Indicators Research* 38: 303–332

Cummins, R. A. 1997. *Comprehensive Quality of Life Scale – Adult.* 5th edn. Geelong, Australia: Deakin University

Cummins, R. A. 1999. *Directory of Instruments to Measure Quality of Life and Cognate Areas.* Geelong, Australia: Deakin University

Cummins, R. A. 2000. 'Personal income and subjective well-being: A review', *Journal of Happiness Studies* 1: 133–158

Cummins, R. A. 2002a. 'Normative life satisfaction: Measurement issues and a homeostatic model', *Social Indicators Research* 64: 225–256

Cummins, R. A. 2002b. 'The validity and utility of subjective quality of life: A reply to Hatton & Ager', *Journal of Applied Research in Intellectual Disabilities* 15: 261–268

Cummins, R. A., Eckersley, R., Pallant, J., van Vugt, J. and Misajon, R. 2003. 'Developing a national index of subjective wellbeing: The Australian Unity Wellbeing Index', *Social Indicators Research* 64 (2): 159–190

Cummins, R. A., Gullone, E. and Lau, A. 2002. 'A model of subjective wellbeing homeostasis: The role of personality', in Gullone, E. and Cummins, R. A. (eds.) *The Universality of Subjective Wellbeing Indicators.* Netherlands: Kluwer Academic Publishers Group, pp. 7–46

Cummins, R. A., Lau, A. L. D. and Stokes, M. 2004. 'HRQOL and subjective wellbeing: Non-complementary forms of outcome measurement', *Expert Reviews in Pharmacoeconomics Outcomes Research* 4: 413–420

Cummins, R. A. and Nistico, H. 2002. 'Maintaining life satisfaction: The role of positive cognitive bias', *Journal of Happiness Studies* 3 (1): 37–69

Darcy, J. and Hofmann, C. A. 2003. *According to Need? Needs Assessment and Decision-Making in the Humanitarian Sector.* Humanitarian Policy Group Report 15. London: Overseas Development Institute

Dasgupta, P. 1993. *An Inquiry into Well-Being and Destitution.* Oxford: Clarendon Press

Deacon, B., Hulse, M. and Stubbs, P. 1997. *Global Social Policy: International Organisations and the Future of Welfare.* London: Sage

Dean, H. 2003. *Discursive Repertoires and the Negotiation of Wellbeing: Reflections on the WeD Frameworks.* WeD Working Paper 4. Bath: Wellbeing in Developing Countries (WeD) ESRC Research Group, University of Bath

De Charms, R. 1968. *Personal Causation: The Internal Affective Determinants of Behaviour.* New York: Academic Press

Deci, E. L., Koestner, R. and Ryan, R. 1999. 'A meta-analytical review of experiments examining the effects of extrinsic rewards on intrinsic motivation', *Psychological Bulletin* 125: 627–668

Deci, E. L., Nezlek, J. and Sheinman, L. 1981. 'Characteristics of the rewarder and intrinsic motivation of the rewardee', *Journal of Personality and Social Psychology* 40: 1–10

Deci, E. L. and Ryan, R. 1985. *Intrinsic Motivation and Self-Determination in Human Behaviour.* New York: Plenum

Deci, E. L. and Ryan, R. 1980. 'The empirical exploration of intrinsic motivational processes', in Berkowitz, L. (ed.), *Advances in Experimental Social Psychology.* New York: Academic Press, pp. 39–80

Deci, E. L. and Ryan, R. 2000. 'The "what" and "why" of goal pursuits: Human needs and the self-determination of behavior', *Psychological Inquiry* 11: 227–268

Deci, E. L., Ryan, R., Gagné, M., Leone, D. R., Usunov, J. and Kornazheva, B. P. 2001. 'Need satisfaction, motivation, and well-being in the work organizations of a former Eastern Bloc country', *Personality and Social Psychology Bulletin* 27: 930–942

Degregori, C. I. (ed.) 2000. *No hay pas más diverso: Compendio de antropologa peruana* [There is not a more diverse country: Collection of works on Peruvian anthropology]. Lima: PUCP/UP/IEP

De Janvry, A. 1981. *The Agrarian Question and Reformism in Latin America.* Baltimore: Johns Hopkins University Press

Delhey, J. 2001. 'The prospects for catching up for new EU members: Lessons for the accession countries to the European Union from previous enlargements', *Social Indicators Research* 56 (2): 205–231

Delhey, J., Böhnke, P., Habich, R. and Zapf, W. 2002. 'Quality of life in a European perspective: The EUROMODULE as a new instrument for comparative welfare research', *Social Indicators Research* 58 (1–3): 163–176

De Sardan, O. 2005. *Anthropology and Development: Understanding Contemporary Social Change.* London: Zed Books

De Soto, H. 1989. *The Other Path: The Invisible Revolution in the Third World.* New York: Harper and Row

de Unamuno, M. 2002. *Del Sentimiento Trágico de la Vida.* [On the tragic feelings of life.] Barcelona: Ediciones Folio

Deneve, K. M. 1999. 'Happy as an extraverted clam? The role of personality for subjective well-being', *Current Directions in Psychological Science* 8 (5): 141–144

Devey, R. and Møller, V. 2002. 'Closing the gap between rich and poor in South Africa: Trends in objective and subjective indicators of quality of life in the October Household Survey', in Glatzer, W. (ed.) *Rich and Poor: Disparities, Perceptions, Concomitants.* Dordrecht, Netherlands: Kluwer Academic Publishers, pp. 105–122

Devine, J., Camfield, L. and Gough, I. 2006. *Autonomy or Dependence – or Both? Perspectives from Bangladesh.* WeD Working Paper 13. Bath: Wellbeing in Developing Countries (WeD) Research Group, University of Bath

de Waal, A. 1989. *Famine that Kills: Darfur, Sudan, 1984–1985.* Oxford: Clarendon

De Zeeuw, H., Baumeister, E., Kolmans, E. and Rens, M. 1994. *Promover la agricultura sostenible en la zona sur Andina: un estudio de los programas agropecuarios de siete contrpartes de Icco en la zona andina del Sur de Perú y el Norte de Bolivia* [Promoting sustainable agriculture in the south of the Andes: A study of the agricultural programmes of seven compartments of Icco in the south of the Peruvian Andes and the north of Bolivia]. Evaluaciòn Programática 49 La Haya: DGIS

DfID 2005. *Alliances against Poverty: DfID's Experience in Peru, 2000 to 2005.* London: Department for International Development

Di Tella, R., MacCulloch, R. J. and Oswald, A. J. 1997. *The Macroeconomics of Happiness.* CEP Working Paper 19. Oxford: Centre for Economic Performance and Institute of Economics, University of Oxford

Di Tella, R., MacCulloch, R. J. and Oswald, A. J. 2001. 'Preferences over inflation and unemployment: Evidence from surveys of happiness', *American Economic Review* 91: 355–341

Dickow, H. and Møller, V. 2002. 'South Africa's 'rainbow people', national pride and optimism: A trend study', *Social Indicators Research* 59 (2): 175–202

Diener, E. 1984. 'Subjective well-being', *Psychological Bulletin* 95: 542–575

Diener, E. 1994. 'Assessing subjective well-being: Progress and opportunities', *Social Indicators Research* 31: 103–157

Diener, E. and Biswas-Diener, R. 2002. 'Will money increase subjective well-being?', *Social Indicators Research* 57: 119–169

Diener, E. and Diener, M. 1995. 'Cross-cultural correlates of life satisfaction and self-esteem', *Journal of Personality and Social Psychology* 68: 653–663

Diener, E., Emmons, R. A., Larsen, R. J. and Griffin, S. 1985. 'The satisfaction with life scale', *Journal of Personality Assessement* 49 (1): 71–75

Diener, E. and Griffin, S. 1984. 'Happiness and life satisfaction: A bibliography', *Psychological Documents* 14 (11)

Diener, E., Oishi, S. and Lucas, R. E. 2003. 'Personality, culture, and subjective well-being: Emotional and cognitive evaluations of life', *Annual Review of Psychology* 54: 403–425

Diener, E., Scollon, C. K. N., Oishi, S., Dzokoto, V. and Suh, E. M. 2000. 'Positivity and the construction of life satisfaction judgements: Global happiness is not the sum of its parts', *Journal of Happiness Studies* 1: 159–176

Diener, E. and Suh, E. M. 1997. 'Measuring quality of life: Economic, social, and subjective indicators', *Social Indicators Research* 40: 189–216

Diener, E. and Suh, E. 1999. 'National differences in subjective well-being', in Kahneman, D., Diener, E. and Schwarz, N. (eds.) *The Foundations of Hedonic Psychology*. New York: Russell Sage Foundation, pp. 434–450

Diener, E. and Suh, E. M. (eds.) 2000. *Culture and Subjective Well-Being*. Cambridge, MA: MIT Press

Diener, E., Suh, E. M., Lucas, R. E. and Smith, H. L. 1999. 'Subjective well-being: Three decades of progress', *Psychological Bulletin* 125: 276–302

Dohmen, J. 2003. 'Philosophers on the "art-of-living"', *Journal of Happiness Studies* 4: 351–371

Douglas, M., Gasper, D., Ney, S. and Thompson, M. 1998. 'Human needs and wants', in Rayner, S. and Malone, E. L. (eds.) *Human Choice and Climate Change, Volume 1: The Societal Framework*. Colombus, OH: Batelle Press, Ch. 3, pp. 195–263

Douglas, M. and Ney, S. 1998. *Missing Persons: A Critique of Personhood in the Social Sciences*. Berkeley and Los Angeles: University of California Press

Doyal, L. and Gough, I. 1991. *A Theory of Human Need*. London: Macmillan

Doyal, L. and Gough, I. 1993. 'Need satisfaction as a measure of human welfare', in Glass, W. and Foster, J. (eds.) *Mixed Economies in Europe*. London: Edward Elgar

Drèze, J. and Sen, A. 1991. *Hunger and Public Action*. Oxford: Oxford University Press

Duffield, M. 2001. *Global Governance and the New Wars: The Merging of Development and Security*. London: Zed Books

Dupuy, H. J. 1984. 'The psychological general well-being (PGWB) index', in Wender, N. K., Mattson, M. E., Furberg, C. D. and Elinson, J. (eds.) *Assessment of Quality of Life in Clinical Trials of Cardiovascular Therapies* New York: Le Jacq, pp. 170–183

Durham, W. H. 1991. *Coevolution: Genes, Culture and Human Diversity*. Stanford: Stanford University Press

Dutt, A. 2001. 'Consumption, happiness and religion', in Dutt, A. and Jameson, K. P. (eds.) *Crossing the Mainstream*. Notre Dame, IN: University of Notre Dame Press, pp. 133–169

Eagly, A. H. 1987. *Sex Differences in Social Behaviour: A Social-Role Interpretation*. Hillsdale, NJ: Lawrence Erlbaum

Easterlin, R. A. 1974. 'Does economic growth improve the human lot? Some empirical evidence', in David, P. A. and Reder, M. W. (eds.) *Nations and Households in Economic Growth*. New York: Academic Press

Easterlin, R. A. 1995. 'Will raising the incomes of all increase the happiness of all?', *Journal of Economic Behaviour and Organization* 27 (1): 35–48

Easterlin, R. A. 2001. 'Income and happiness: Towards a unified theory', *The Economic Journal* 111: 465–484

Easterlin, R. A. 2003. 'Explaining happiness', *PNAS (National Academy of Sciences of the USA)* 100 (19): 11176–11183

Economist, The 2004. 'Indigenous people in South America: A political awakening', *The Economist* (21 February 2004), 53–55.

Eggers, A., Gaddy, C. and Graham, C. 2004. *Well Being and Unemployment in Russia in the 1990s: Can Society's Suffering Be Individuals' Solace?* Working Paper 35. Washington: Center on Social and Economic Dynamics

Ehrlich, P. R. 2000. *Human Natures: Genes, Cultures, and the Human Prospect*. New York: Penguin Books

Elliot, A. J., McGregor, H. A. and Thrash, T. M. 2002. 'The need for competence', in Deci, E. L. and Ryan, R. (eds.) *Handbook of Self-Determination Research*. Rochester, New York: University of Rochester Press, pp. 361–388

Elster, J. 1983. *Sour Grapes: Studies in the Subversion of Rationality*. Cambridge: Cambridge University Press

Emmons, R. A. 1989. 'The personal striving approach to personality', in Pervin, L. A. (ed.) *Goal Concepts in Personality and Social Psychology*. Hillsdale, NJ and UK: Lawrence Erlbaum Associates, Inc., pp. 87–126

Emmons, R. A. 1996. 'Striving and feeling: Personal goals and subjective well-being', in Gollwitzer, P. M. and Bargh, A. (eds.) *The Psychology of Action: Linking Cognition and Motivation to Behaviour*. New York: Guilford Publications, pp. 313–337

Escobál, J. 2001. 'The determinants of non-farm income diversification in rural Peru', *World Development* 29 (3): 497–508

Escobar, A. 1995. *Encountering Development: The Making and Unmaking of the Third World*. Princeton, NJ: Princeton University Press

Esping-Andersen, G. 1990. *Three Worlds of Welfare Capitalism*. Cambridge and Oxford: Polity Press

Esping-Andersen, G. 1999. *Social Foundations of Postindustrial Economies*. Oxford: Oxford University Press

European Group for Quality of Life and Health Measurement (EGQLHM) 1992. *European Guide to the Nottingham Health Profile*. Montpellier: ESCUBASE

Eve, R. A., Horsfall, S. and Lee, M. E. 1997. *Chaos, Complexity and Sociology*. London: Sage

Fafchamps, M. and Shilpi, F. 2004. *Isolation and Subjective Welfare*. Discussion Paper Series 216. Oxford: University of Oxford, Department of Economics

Farmer, P. 2005. *Pathologies of Power: Health, Human Rights, and the New War on the Poor*. London: University of California Press

Fernandez-Ballesteros, R., Diez-Nicolas, J. and Bandura, A. 2002. 'Determinants and structural relation of personal efficacy to collective efficacy', *Journal of Psychology: An International Review* 51 (1): 107–125

Ferrer-i-Carbonell, A. 2002. *Subjective Questions to Measure Welfare and Well-Being: A Survey*. Tinbergen, Netherlands: Tinbergen Institute Discussion Papers

Ferrer-i-Carbonell, A. and Frijters, P. 2004. 'How important is methodology for the estimates of the determinants of happiness?', *The Economic Journal* 114 (497): 641–659

Fields, G. 1980. *Poverty, Inequality and Development*. Cambridge: Cambridge University Press

Figueroa, A. 2000. 'La exclusiòn social como una teoría de la distribuciòn', in Gacitúa, E., Sojo, C. and Davis, S. (eds.) *Exclusiòn social y reducciòn de la pobreza en América Latina y el Caribe* [Social exclusion as a theory of distribution. In Social exclusion and reduction of poverty in Latin America and the Caribbean]. San Jose: FLACSO y Banco Mundial, pp. 25–50

Figueroa, A. 2001a. *Social Exclusion as Distribution Theory*. Washington, DC: World Bank

Figueroa, A. 2001b. *Reformas en sociedades desiguales. La experiencia peruana.* [Economic reform in unequal societies. The Peruvian experience.]. Fondo Editorial Lima: Pontificate Catholic University of Peru

Figueroa, A. 2003. *La sociedad sigma: una teoría del desarrollo econòmico.* [Sigma society: a theory of economic development.]. Fondo Editorial Lima: Pontificate Catholic University of Peru

Figueroa, A., Altamirano, T. and Sulmont, D. 2001. *Social Exclusion and Inequality in Peru*. Geneva: ILO

Finnis, J. 1980. *Natural Law and Natural Rights*. Oxford: Clarendon Press

Ford, M. E. 1992. *Motivating Humans: Goals, Emotions, and Personal Agency Beliefs*. Newbury Park, CA: Sage

Foster, J. and Sen, A. 1997. *On Economic Inequality: With a Substantial Annexe 'After a Quarter Century'*. 2nd edn. Oxford: Clarendon Press

Fox, C. R. and Kahneman, D. 1992. 'Correlation, causes and heuristics in survey of life satisfaction', *Social Indicators Research* 27: 221–234

Frank, R. H. 2004. 'How not to buy happiness', *Daedalus* 133 (2): 69–79

Franzblau, S. H. and Moore, M. 2000. 'Socialising efficacy: A reconstruction of self-efficacy theory within the context of inequality', *Journal of Community and Applied Social Psychology* 11: 83–96

Frederick, S. and Loewenstein, G. 1999. 'Hedonic adaptation', in Kahneman, D., Diener, E. and Schwarz, N. (eds.) *Well-Being: The Foundations of Hedonic Psychology*. New York: Russell Sage Foundation Press, pp. 302–329

Freire, P. 1970. *Pedagogy of the Oppressed*. New York: The Seabury Press

Freud, S. 1962. *The Ego and the Id*. New York: Norton

Frey, B. and Stutzer, A. 1999. 'Measuring preferences by subjective well-being', *Journal of Institutional and Theoretical Economics* 155: 755–778

Frey, B. and Stutzer, A. 2000. 'Happiness, economy and institutions', *The Economic Journal* 110: 918–938

Frey, B. and Stutzer, A. 2002. 'What can economists learn from happiness research?', *Journal of Economic Literature* 40: 402–435

Friedman, M. 2003. *Autonomy, Gender, Politics*. New York: Oxford University Press

Furnham, A. and Lewis, A. 1986. *The Economic Mind: The Social Psychology of Economic Behaviour*. Brighton: Harvester/Wheatsheaf

Galtung, J. 1994. *Human Rights in Another Key*. Cambridge: Polity Press

Gasper, D. 1996. 'Needs and basic needs: A clarification of foundational concepts for development ethics and policy', in Koehler, G., Gore, C., Reich, U. P. and Ziesemer, T. (eds.) *Questioning Development*. Marburg: Metropolis, pp. 71–101

Gasper, D. 2004. *The Ethics of Development: From Economism to Human Development*. Edinburgh: Edinburgh University Press

Gasper, D. 2005a. 'Securing humanity? Situating human security as concept and discourse', *Journal of Human Development* 6 (2): 221–245

Gasper, D. 2005b. 'Needs and human rights', in Smith, R. and van den Anker, C. *The Essentials of Human Rights*. London: Hodder Arnold, pp. 269–272

Gasper, D. 2005c. 'Human wellbeing: Concepts and conceptualisations', *World Economic Papers* 166 (3): 65–91

Geertz, C. 1973. *The Interpretation of Cultures: Selected Essays*. New York: Basic Books

Geertz, C. 1979. *Meaning and Order in Moroccan Society: Three Essays in Cultural Analysis*. New York: Cambridge University Press

Geertz, C. 1983. *Local Knowledge: Further Essays in Interpretive Anthropology*. New York: Basic Books

Giddens, A. 1976. *New Rules of Sociological Method: A Positive Critique of Interpretive Sociologies*. London: Hutchinson

Giddens, A. 1979. *Central Problems in Social Theory: Action, Structure and Contradiction in Social Analysis*. London: Macmillan

Giddens, A. 1984. *The Constitution of Society: Outline of the Theory of Structuration*. Cambridge: The Polity Press

Gilligan, C. 1983. *In a Different Voice: Psychological Theory and Women's Development*. Cambridge, MA: Harvard University Press

Glatzer, W. and Zapf, W. 1984. 'Anthropological perspectives: The importance of culture in the assessment of quality of life', in Spilker, B. (ed.) *Quality of Life and Pharmacoeconomics in Clinical Trials*. 2nd edn. Philadelphia: Lippincott-Raven Publishers, pp. 523–529

364 References

Goldberg, D. and Williams, P. 1988. *A User's Guide to the General Health Questionnaire.* Windsor: NFER-Nelson

Goldewjik, B. K. and de Gaay Fortman, B. 1999. *Where Needs Meet Rights.* Geneva: WCC Publications

Goldstein, K. 1939. *The Organism.* New York: American Book Co.

Goodwin, J. 1994. *The Price of Honour: Muslim Women Lift the Veil of Silence on the Islamic World.* New York: Penguin Books

Gough, I. 2003. *Lists and Thresholds: Comparing Our Theory of Human Needs with Nussbaum's Capabilities Approach.* WeD Working Paper 1. Bath: Wellbeing in Developing Countries (WeD) Research Group

Gough, I. 2004. 'Human well-being and social structures: Relating the universal and the local', *Global Social Policy* 4 (3): 289–311

Gough, I. and McGregor, J. A. 2004. 'Human well-being: Communicating between the universal and the local: Guest editors' contribution', *Global Social Policy* 4 (3): 275–276

Gough, I. and Wood, G. 2004. 'Introduction', in Gough, I., Wood, G., Barrientos, A., Bevan, P., Davis, P. and Room, G. (eds.) *Insecurity and Welfare Regimes in Asia, Africa and Latin America.* Cambridge: Cambridge University Press, pp. 1–11

Gough, I., Wood, G., Barrientos, A., Bevan, P., Davis, P. and Room, G. (eds.) 2004. *Insecurity and Welfare Regimes in Asia, Africa and Latin America.* Cambridge: Cambridge University Press

Graham, C. Forthcoming. 'The economics of happiness', in Durlauf, S. and Blume, L. (eds.) *The New Palgrave Dictionary of Economics.* 2nd edn. London: Palgrave Macmillan

Graham, C. and Pettinato, S. 2002. *Happiness and Hardship: Opportunity and Insecurity in New Market Economies.* Washington, DC: Brookings Institution Press

Gregg, P. M. and Salisbury, P. S. 2001. 'Confirming and expanding the usefulness of the extended satisfaction with life scale (ESWLS)', *Social Indicators Research* 54: 1–16

Grisez, G., Boyle, J. and Finnis, J. 1987. 'Practical principles, moral truth and ultimate ends', *American Journal of Jurisprudence* 32: 99–151

Grolnick, W. S., Deci, E. L. and Ryan, R. 1997. 'Internalization within the family: The self-determination theory perspective', in Grusec, J. E. and Kuczynski, L. (eds.) *Parenting and Children's Internalization of Values.* New York: Wiley, pp. 135–161

Grolnick, W. S. and Ryan, R. 1989. 'Parent styles associated with children's self-regulation and competence in school', *Journal of Educational Psychology* 81: 143–154

Guarnaccia, P. J. 1995. 'Anthropological perspectives: the importance of culture in the assessment of quality of life', in Spilker, B. (ed.) *Quality of Life and Pharmacoeconomics in Clinical Trials.* 2nd edn. New York: Lippincott-Raven Publishers, pp. 523–528

Guarnaccia, P. J., Rivera, M., Franco, F. and Neighbors, C. 1996. 'The experiences of ataques de nervios: Towards an anthropology of emotions in Puerto Rico', *Culture, Medicine and Psychiatry* 20: 343–367

Gudeman, S. 1986. *Economics as Culture*. London: Routledge and Kegan Paul

Gudeman, S. 2001. *The Anthropology of Economy: Community, Market and Culture*. Oxford: Blackwell

Guillemin, F., Bombardier, C. and Beaton, D. 1993. 'Cross-cultural adaption of health-related quality of life measures: Literature review and proposed guidelines', *Journal of Clinical Epidemiology* 46 (12): 1417–1432

Guillen-Royo, M. and Velazco, J. 2006. *Exploring the Relationship between Happiness, Objective and Subjective Wellbeing: Evidence from Rural Thailand*. WeD Working Paper 16. Bath: Wellbeing in Developing Countries (WeD) Research Group

Gullone, E. and Cummins, R. A. 1999. 'The Comprehensive Quality of Life Scale: A psychometric evaluation with an adolescent sample', *Behaviour Change* 16: 127–139

Guyatt, G. H. 1993. 'The philosophy of health-related quality of life translation', *Quality of Life Research* 2 (6): 461–465

Habermas, J. 1987. *The Theory of Communicative Action: Volume 2: Lifeworld and System*. Cambridge: Polity Press

Hagerty, M. R., Vogel, J. and Møller, V. (eds.) 2002. *Assessing Quality of Life and Living Conditions to Guide National Policy: The State of the Art*. Dordrecht: Kluwer Academic Publishers

Hamilton, L. 2003. *The Political Philosophy of Needs*. Cambridge: Cambridge University Press

Hampton, N. Z. and Marshall, A. 2000. 'Culture, gender, self-efficacy, and life satisfaction: A comparison between Americans and Chinese people with spinal cord injuries', *Journal of Rehabilitation* 66: 21–28

Harlow, H. F. 1958. 'The nature of love', *American Psychologist* 13: 673–685

Harré, R. 1979. *Social Being*. Oxford: Blackwell

Harriss, J. (ed.) 1982. *Rural Development: Theories of Peasant Economy*. London: Hutchinson

Hayamizu, T. 1997. 'Between the intrinsic and extrinsic motivation: Examination of reasons for academic study based on the theory of internalization', *Japanese Psychological Research* 39: 98–108

Hayo, B. and Seifert, W. 2003. 'Subjective economic well-being in Eastern Europe', *Journal of Economic Psychology* 24: 329–348

Headey, B., Holmström, E. and Wearing, A. J. 1984. 'The impact of life events and changes in domain satisfactions on well-being', *Social Indicators Research* 15: 203–227

Headey, B., Holmström, E. and Wearing, A. J. 1985. 'Models of well-being and ill-being', *Social Indicators Research* 17: 211–234

Headey, B., Veenhoven, R. and Wearing, A. J. 1991. 'Top-down versus bottom-up theories of subjective well-being', *Social Indicators Research* 24: 81–100

Headey, B. and Wearing, A. J. 1992. *Understanding Happiness: A Theory of Subjective Well-Being*. Melbourne, Australia: Longman Cheshire

Heckhausen, J. and Schulz, R. 1995. 'A life-span theory of control', *Psychological Review* 102: 284–304

Helliwell, J. F. 2003. 'How's life? Combining individual and national variables to explain subjective well-being', *Economic Modelling* 20: 331–360

Helm, D. T. 2000. 'The measurement of happiness', *American Journal on Mental Retardation* 105: 326–335

Helman, C. G. 2001. *Culture, Health and Illness*. 4th edn. London: Arnold

Herdman, M., Fox-Rushby, J. and Badia, X. 1998. 'A model of equivalence in the cultural adaptation of cultural HRQoL Instruments: The universalist approach', *Quality of Life Research* 7 (4): 323–335

Hermans, H. J. M. 1989. 'The meaning of life as an organized process', *Psychotherapy* 26: 11–22

Hickey, S. and Bracking, S. 2005. 'Exploring the politics of chronic poverty: From representation to the politics of justice', *World Development* 33 (6): 851–865

Hicks, J. R. 1941. *Education in Economics*. Manchester Statistical Society

Hicks, N. and Streeten, P. 1979. 'Indicators of development: The search for a basic needs yardstick', *World Development* 7: 567–580

Higgins, A. O. 1956. 'The dualistic theory of underdeveloped areas', *Economic Development and Cultural Change* January: 99–112

Higgs, N. T. 2003. '*EQLi^{tm}*: Understanding the Everyday Quality of Life model and its family of indices' (mimeographed). Johannesburg: Research Surveys

Hirschmann, A. O. 1970. *Exit, Voice and Loyalty*. Cambridge MA: Harvard University Press

Hirschmann, A. O. 1973. 'The changing tolerance for inequality in the course of economic development', *Quarterly Journal of Economics* 87 (4): 544–563

Holland, J. and Abeyasekera, S. (eds.) 2006 forthcoming. *Who Counts? Participation, Numbers and Power*. London: ITDG Publications

Honderich, T. (ed.) 2005. *The Oxford Companion to Philosophy*. 2nd edn. Oxford: Oxford University Press

Hoogvelt, A. 1997. *Globalisation and the Postcolonial World: The New Political Economy of Development*. London: Macmillan Press

hooks, b. 1984. *Feminist Theory: From Margin to Center*. Boston, MA: South End Press

Hu, L. and Bentler, P. M. 1999 'Cutoff criteria for fit indexes in covariance structure analysis: conventional criteria versus new alternatives', *Structural Equation Modelling* 6: 1–55

Hui, C. and Triandis, H. C. 1985. 'Measurement in cross-cultural psychology: A review and comparison of strategies', *Cross-Cultural Psychology* 16: 131–152

Hunt, S. M., McEwan, J., McKenna, S. P., Williams, J. and Papp, E. 1981. 'The Nottingham Health Profile: Subjective health status and medical consultations', *Social Science and Medicine* 19A: 221–229

Hunt, S. M. and McKenna, S. P. 1999. *Nottingham Health Profile (NHP)*. Manchester: American Thoracic Society

Hutchinson, J. E. 1996. 'Quality of life in ethnic groups', in Spilker, B. (ed.) *Quality of Life and Pharmacoeconomics in Clinical Trials*. 2nd edn. Philadelphia: Lippincott-Raven Publishers, pp. 587–595

Illich, I. 1978. *Towards a History of Needs*. New York: Pantheon

Illich, I. 1992. 'Needs', in Sachs, W. (ed.) *The Development Dictionary: A Guide to Knowledge as Power*. NJ: Atlantic Highlands

ILO 2004. *Economic Security for a Better World*. Geneva: ILO Socio-Economic Security Programme

Ingellheri, P. 1999. *From Subjective Experience to Cultural Change*. Cambridge: Cambridge University Press

Iyengar, S. S. and Lepper, M. R. 1999. 'Rethinking the value of choice: A cultural perspective on intrinsic motivation', *Journal of Personality and Social Psychology* 76: 349–366

Jack, J. C. 1927. *The Economic Life of a Bengal District*. London: Oxford University Press

Jackson, T., Jager, W. and Stagl, S. 2004. *Beyond Insatiability – Needs Theory, Consumption and Sustainability*. Working Papers 2004 2. ESRC Sustainable Technologies Programme, University of Surrey

Jacob, F. 1973. *The Logic of Life: A History of Heredity*. New York: Pantheon

Jahangir, B. K. 1982. *Rural Society, Power Structure and Class Practice*. Dacca: Centre for Social Studies, Dacca University

Jansen, E. G. 1986. *Rural Bangladesh: Competition for Scarce Resources*. Oslo: Norwegian University Press

Johnson, T. M. 1996. 'Cultural considerations', in Spilker, B. *Quality of Life and Pharmacoeconomics in Clinical Trials*. 2nd edn. Philadelphia: Lippincott-Raven Publishers, pp. 511–517

Kahneman, D. 1999. 'Objective happiness', in Kahneman, D., Diener, E. and Schwarz, N. (eds.) *Well-Being: The Foundations of Hedonic Psychology*. New York: Russell Sage Foundation

Kahneman, D., Diener, E. and Schwarz, N. (eds.) 1999. *Well-Being: The Foundations of Hedonic Psychology*. New York: Russell Sage Foundation

Kahneman, D. and Tversky, A. 1984. 'Choices, values and frames', *American Psychologist* 39: 341–350

Kanbur, R. 2001. 'Economic policy, distribution and poverty: The nature of disagreements', *World Development* 29 (6): 1083–1094

Kanbur, R. (ed.) 2003. *Qual-Quant: Qualitative and Quantitative Poverty Appraisal: Complementarities, Tensions and the Way Forward*. Delhi: Permanent Black

Kanbur, R. and McIntosh, J. 1989. 'Dual economies', in Eatwell, J., Milgate, M. and Newman, P. (eds.) *The New Palgrave: Economic Development*. London: Macmillan

Kasser, T. 2002. *The High Price of Materialism*. Cambridge, MA: MIT Press

Kasser, T. and Ryan, R. 1996. 'Further examining the American dream: Differential correlates of intrinsic and extrinsic goals', *Personality and Social Psychology Bulletin* 22: 80–87

Kasser, T., Ryan, R., Zax, M. and Sameroff, A. J. 1995. 'The relations of maternal and social environments to late adolescents' materialistic and prosocial values', *Developmental Psychology* 31: 907–971

Kaufmann, S. 2000. *Investigations*. Oxford: Oxford University Press

Khan, I. A. and Seeley, J. (eds.) 2005. *Making a Living: The Livelihoods of the Rural Poor in Bangladesh*. Dhaka: University Press Limited

Kind, P. 1996. 'The EuroQOL instrument: An index of health-related quality of life', in Spilker, B. (ed.) *Quality of Life and Pharmacoeconomics in Clinical Trials*. 2nd edn. Philadelphia: Lippincott-Raven, pp. 191–201

Klasen, S. 2000. 'Measuring poverty and deprivation in South Africa', *Review of Income and Wealth* 46 (1): 33–58

Kleinman, A. 1986. *Social Origins of Distress and Disease: Depression, Neurastenia and Pain in Modern China*. New Haven: Yale University Press

Kleinman, A., Das, V. and Lock, M. (eds.) 1997. *Social Suffering*. London: University of California Press

Kohlmann, T., Bullinger, M. and Kirchberger-Blumenstein, I. 1997. 'Die deutsche Version des Nottingham Health Profile: Übersetzungsmethodik und psychometrische Validierung' [German version of the Nottingham Health Profile: Translation and psychometric validation], *Sozial-und Präventivmedizin* 42 S: 175–185

Kok, P., Ndlovu, B. and O'Donovan, M. (eds.) 1997. *Development Indicators for Promoting Good Governance in KwaZulu-Natal*, vol. I. Pretoria, South Africa: Human Sciences Research Council Printers

Kosko, B. 1994. *Fuzzy Thinking: The New Science of Fuzzy Logic*. London: Flamingo

Kramsjo, B. and Wood, G. 1992. *Breaking the Chains*. London: IT Publications

Kuper, A. and Kuper, J. (eds.) 1994. *The Social Science Encyclopaedia*. 2nd edn. London: Routledge

Lai, D. 2000. 'Temporal analysis of human development indicators: Principal component approach', *Social Indicators Research* 51: 331–366

Lambert, H. and McKevitt, C. 2002. 'Anthropology in health research: From qualitative methods to multidisciplinarity', *BMJ* 325: 210–213

Lancaster, K. 1966. 'A new approach to consumer theory', *Journal of Political Economy* 74: 132–157

Lance, C. E., Lautenschlager, G. J., Sloan, C. E. and Varca, P. E. 1989. 'A comparison between bottom-up, top-down, and bidirectional models of relationships between global and life facet satisfaction', *Journal of Personality* 57: 601–624

Lance, C. E., Mallard, A. G. C. and Michalos, A. C. 1995. 'Tests of the causal directions of global-life facet satisfaction relationships', *Social Indicators Research* 34: 69–92

Larson, D. A. and Wilford, W. T. 1979. 'The Physical Quality of Life Index: A useful social indicator?', *World Development* 7: 581–584

Lawson, C. W., McGregor, J. A. and Saltmarshe, D. 2000. 'Surviving and thriving: Differentiation in a peri-urban community in Northern Albania', *World Development* 28 (8): 1499–1514

Layard, R. 2005. *Happiness: Lessons from a New Science*. London: Allen Lane

Lea, S., Tarpy, R. and Webley, P. 1987. *The Individual in the Economy*. Cambridge: Cambridge University Press

Leach, M., Mearns, R. and Scoones, I. 1999. 'Environmental entitlements: Dynamics and institutions in community-based natural resource management', *World Development* 27 (2): 225–247

Lederer, K. (ed.) 1980. *Human Needs*. Cambridge, MA: Oegelschlager, Gunn and Hain

Leggett, T., Møller, V. and Richards, R. 1997. *'My Life in the New South Africa': A Youth Perspective*. Pretoria, South Africa: Human Sciences Research Council Publishers

Le Grand, J. W. 1998a. 'Desarrollo fragmentado: discontinuidades en el ámbito de la intervención', in Zoomers, A. *Estrategias Campesinas en el Surandino de Bolivia: Intervenciones y desarrollo rural en el norte de Chuquisaca y Potos* ['Fragmented Development: Discontinuities in the intervention sphere', in Zoomers, A. (ed.) Peasant strategies in the Bolivian Andes: Interventions and rural development in the north of Chuquisaca and Potosí]. La Paz: CEDLA/CID/PLURAL

Le Grand, J. W. 1998b. 'Buscando resultados: estrategias campesinas impactos colaterales', in Zoomers, A. (ed.) *Estrategias Campesinas en el Surandino de Bolivia: Intervenciones y desarrollo rural en el norte de Chuqusaca y Potos* ['Looking for results: Peasant strategies, collateral impacts', in Zoomers, A. (ed.) Peasant strategies in the Bolivian Andes: Interventions and rural development in the north of Chuquisaca and Potosí]. La Paz: CEDLA/CID/PLURAL, pp. 397–422

Lehmann, A. D. 1986. 'The paths of agrarian capitalism, or a critique of Chayanovian Marxism', *Comparative Studies in Society and History* 28 (4): 601–627

Lehmann, A. D. 1990. *Democracy and Development in Latin America: Economics, Politics and Religion in the Post-war Period.* Cambridge: The Polity Press

Lehmann, E. W. (ed.) 2000. *Autonomy and Order: A Communitarian Anthology.* Lanham, MD: Rowman and Littlefield

Leonardi, F., Gagliardi, C., Marcellini, F. and Spazzafumo, L. 1999. 'The top-down/bottom-up controversy from a constructivist approach: A method for measuring top-down effects applied to sample of older people', *Social Indicators Research* 48: 187–216

Levi, P. 1959 (translation of 1947 work 'Se questo e un uomo'). *If this Is a Man.* New York: Orion Press

Lewis, D., Glaser, M., McGregor, J. A., White, S. and Wood, G. 1991. *Going it Alone: Female Headed Households in Bangladesh.* CDS Occasional Paper. Bath: Centre for Development Studies, University of Bath

Lewis, D. and McGregor, J. A. 1992. *Vulnerability and Impoverishment in Northern Albania.* CDS Occasional Paper. Bath: Centre for Development Studies, University of Bath

Lewis, O. 1967. *La Vida: A Puerto Rican Family in the Culture of poverty.* San Juan and New York: Secker and Warburg

Lewis, W. A. 1985. 'Racial conflict and economic development', in *The 1982 Du Bois Lectures* Cambridge, MA: Harvard University Press

Lichbach, M. I. 1998. *The Rebel's Dilemma.* Ann Arbor: Michigan University Press

Little, T. D. 1997. 'Means and covariance structure (MACS) analysis of cross-cultural data: Practical and theoretical issues', *Multivariate Behavioural Research* 32: 53–76

Llambi, L. 1989. 'Emergence of capitalized family farms in Latin America', *Comparative Studies in Society and History* 31 (4): 745–774

Lo, Y. K. 2003. 'Finding the self in the Analects: A philosophical approach', in Chong, K., Tan, S. and Ten, C. L. (eds.) *The Moral Circle of the Self: Chinese and Western Approaches.* Chicago, IL: Open Court, pp. 249–267

Lockwood, D. 1981. 'The weakest link in the chain? Some comments on the Marxist theory of action', in Simpson, R. and Simpson, I. (eds.) *Research on the Sociology of Work (Volume 1)*. Greenwich, Connecticut: JAI Press, pp. 435–481

Loevinger, J. 1976. *Ego Development*. San Francisco: Jossey-Bass

Long, N. 1989. 'Encounters at the interface: A perspective on social discontinuities in rural development', *Wageningen Studies in Sociology* 27: 13–19

Long, N. and Long, A. 1992. *Battlefields of Knowledge: The Interlocking of Theory and Practice in Social Research and Development*. London: Routledge

Losier, G. F. and Koestner, R. 1999. 'Intrinsic versus identified regulation in distinct political campaigns: The consequences of following politics for pleasure versus personal meaningfulness', *Personality and Social Psychology Bulletin* 25: 287–298

Loughhead, S., Mittal, O. and Wood, G. 2001. *Urban Poverty and Vulnerability in India: DfID's Experiences from a Social Policy Perspective*. London: Department for International Development

López, R. 1995. *Determinants of Rural Poverty: A Quantitative Anaylsis for Chile*. Washington, DC: World Bank

Lucas, R. E., Clark, A. E., Georgellis, Y. and Diener, E. 2003. 'Re-examining adaptation and the set point model of happiness: reactions to changes in marital status', *Journal of Personality and Social Psychology* 84 (3): 527–539

Lukes, S. 1974. *Power: A Radical View*. London: Macmillan

Lukes, S. 2005. *Power: A Radical View*. 2nd edn. London: Palgrave

Lyubomirsky, S. 2001. 'Why are some people happier than others? The role of cognitive and motivational processes in well-being', *American Psychologist* 56 (3): 239–249

Lyubomirsky, S., King, L. A. and Diener, E. 2005. 'The benefits of frequent positive affect: Does happiness lead to success?', *Psychological Bulletin* 131: 803–855

McBride, M. 2001. 'Relative-income effects on subjective well-being in the cross section', *Journal of Economic Behaviour and Organization* 45: 251–278

McGillivray, M. 1991. 'The Human Development Index: Yet another redundant composite development indicator?', *World Development* 19: 1461–1468

McGillivray, M. 2005. 'Measuring non-economic wellbeing achievement', *Review of Income and Wealth* 51 (2): 337–364

McGillivray, M. and White, H. 1993. 'Measuring development? The UNDP's Human Development Index', *Journal of International Development* 5: 183–192

McGregor, J. A. 1989a. 'Boro Gafur and Choto Gafur: Development interventions and idigenous institutions', *Journal of Social Studies* 43: 39–51

McGregor, J. A. 1989b. 'Towards a better understanding of credit in rural development: The case of Bangladesh: the patron state', *Journal of International Development* 1 (4): 467–486

McGregor, J. A. 1994. 'Village credit and the reproduction of poverty in rural Bangladesh', in Acheson, J. M. (ed.) *Anthropology and New Institutional Economics*. Washington, DC: University Press of America, pp. 261–281

McGregor, J. A. 2004. 'Researching well-being: Communicating between the needs of policy makers and the needs of the people', *Global Social Policy* 4 (3): 337–358

McKennel, A. C. and Andrews, F. M. 1980. 'Models of cognition and affect in perceptions of well-being', *Social Indicators Research* 8: 257–298

McLean, I. and McMillan, A. (eds.) 2003. *The Oxford Dictionary of Politics*. 2nd edn. Oxford: Oxford University Press

Malhotra, A., Schuler, S. and Boender, C. 2002. 'Measuring Women's Empowerment as a Variable in International Development'. Background paper prepared for the World Bank workshop on Poverty and Gender, New perspectives, 28 June

Mallard, A. G. C., Lance, C. E. and Michalos, A. C. 1997. 'Culture as a moderator of overall life satisfaction-life facet satisfaction relationship', *Social Indicators Research* 40: 259–284

Markus, H. R., Kitayama, S. and Heiman, R. J. 1996. 'Culture and basic psychological principles', in Higgins, E. T. and Kruglanski, A. W. (eds.) *Social Psychology: Handbook of Basic Principles*. New York: Guilford Press, pp. 857–913

Marshall, P. 1969/84. *The Chosen Place, The Timeless People*. New York: Random House

Maslow, A. H. 1954/1970. *Motivation and Personality*. 2nd edn. New York: Harper and Row

Mathias, S. D., Fifer, S. K. and Patrick, D. L. 1994. 'Rapid translation of quality of life measures for international clinical trials: Avoiding errors in the minimalist approach', *Quality of Life Research* 3 (6): 403–412

Maturana, H. R. and Varela, F. 1992. *The Tree of Knowledge: The Biological Roots of Human Understanding*. Boston, MA: Shambala

Max-Neef, M. 1989. 'Human scale development: An option for the future', *Development Dialogue* 1: 5–81

Max-Neef, M. 1991. *Human-Scale Development: Conception, Application and Further Reflections*. New York and London: Apex Press

Mayr, E. 1997. *This Is Biology*. London: Belknap Press

Meadow, H. L., Mentzer, I. T., Rahtz, D. R. and Sirgy, M. J. 1992. 'A life satisfaction measure based on judgement theory', *Social Indicators Research* 26: 23–59

Meehan, E. 1978. *In Partnership with People: An Alternative Development Strategy*. Arlington: Inter-American Foundation

Mehta, U. 1997. 'Liberal strategies of exclusion', in Cooper, F. and Stoler, A. L. (eds.) *Tensions of Empire: Colonial Cultures in a Bourgeois World*. Berkeley, CA and London: University of California Press, pp. 59–86

Meier, G. 1991. 'Pareto, Edgeworth and Hicks: The education of an economist', *Review of Political Economy* 3: 349–353

Meier, G. (ed.) 1995. *Leading Issues in Economic Development*. 6th edn. Oxford: Oxford University Press

Menon, N. 2002. 'Universalism without foundations? Review of Nussbaum', *Economy and Society* 31 (1): 152–169

Mesquita, B. and Frijda, N. H. 1992. 'Cultural variations in emotions: A review', *Psychological Bulletin* 112: 179–204

Michalos, A. C. 1980. 'Satisfaction and happiness', *Social Indicators Research* 8: 385–422

Michalos, A. C. 1985. 'Multiple discrepancy theory', *Social Indicators Research* 16: 347–413

Michalos, A. C. 1991. *Global Report on Student Well-Being: Volume 1 Life Satisfaction and Happiness*. New York: Springer

Michalos, A. C. 2003. 'Observations on Key National Performance Indicators' (mimeograph). Prince George, Canada: University of Northern British Columbia

Michalos, A. C. 2004. 'Social indicators research and health related quality of life research', *Social Indicators Research* 65 (1): 27–72

Miller, J. G. 1997. 'Cultural conceptions of duty: Implications for motivation and morality', in Munro, D., Schumaker, J. F. and Carr, A. C. (eds.) *Motivation and Culture*. New York: Routledge, pp. 178–192

Møller, V. 1988a. 'Quality of life in retirement: A case study of Zulu return migrants', *Social Indicators Research* 20 (6): 621–658

Møller, V. 1988b. 'The relevance of personal domain satisfaction for the quality of life in South Africa', *South African Journal of Psychology* 18 (3): 69–75

Møller, V. 1989. ''Can't Get No Satisfaction': Quality of life in the 1980s', *Indicator South Africa* 7 (1): 43–46

Møller, V. 1992a. 'A place in the sun: Quality of life in South Africa', *Indicator South Africa* 9 (4): 101–108

Møller, V. 1992b. 'Black South African women on excursions: A reflection on the quality of township life for seniors', *Journal of Cross-Cultural Gerontology* 7 (4): 399–428

Møller, V. 1992c. 'Spare time use and perceived well-being among black South African Youth', *Social Indicators Research* 26 (4): 309–351

Møller, V. 1992d. 'Living arrangements and subjective wellbeing: The South African Case', in Ferreira, M. (ed.) *Comparative Ageing in South Africa and Taiwan*. Cape Town: HSRC/UCT Centre for Gerontology, pp. 27–30

Møller, V. 1993. *Quality of Life in Unemployment: A Survey Evaluation of Black Township Dwellers*. Pretoria, South Africa: Human Sciences Research Council Publishers

Møller, V. 1994a. *Township Youth and their Homework*. Pretoria, South Africa: Human Sciences Research Council Publishers

Møller, V. 1994b. 'Post-election euphoria', *Indicator South Africa* 12 (1): 27–32

Møller, V. 1995a. 'Waiting for utopia: Quality of life in the 1990s', *Indicator South Africa* 13 (1): 47–54

Møller, V. 1995b. 'Indicators for Africa: The October Household Survey', *Indicator South Africa* 12 (3): 86–90

Møller, V. 1995c. 'Voter education and older African first-time voters in South Africa's 1994 elections', *South African Journal of Gerontology* 4 (1): 3–10

Møller, V. 1995d. 'Home environment and educational achievement among high-school pupils living in three generation urban black households', *South African Journal of Sociology* 26 (3): 87–97

Møller, V. 1996a. 'Household satisfaction: Past present and future perspectives', *Development Southern Africa* 13 (2): 237–254

Møller, V. 1996b. 'Life satisfaction and expectations of the future in a sample of university students: A research note', *South African Journal of Sociology* 27 (1): 16–26

Møller, V. 1996c. 'Intergenerational relations and time use in urban black South African households', *Social Indicators Research* 37 (3): 303–332

Møller, V. 1996d. *Perceptions of Development in KwaZulu-Natal: A Subjective Indicator Study*. University of Natal, Durban, South Africa: Indicator Press

Møller, V. 1998. 'Quality of life in South Africa: Post-apartheid trends', *Social Indicators Research* 43 (1–2): 27–68

Møller, V. 1999a. 'South African quality of life trends in the late 1990s: major divides in perceptions', *Society in Transition* 30 (2): 93–105

Møller, V. 1999b. 'Happiness and the ethnic marker: The South African case', in Hanf, T. (ed.) *Dealing with Difference. Religion, Ethnicity and Politics: Comparing Cases and Concepts*. Baden-Baden, Germany: Nomos Verlagsgesellschaft, pp. 283–303

Møller, V. 2000. 'Monitoring quality of life in Durban, South Africa', in Seik, F. T., Yuan, L. L. and Mie, G. W. K. (eds.) *Planning for a Better Quality of Life in Cities*. Singapore: School of Building and Real Estate, National University of Singapore, pp. 313–329

Møller, V. 2001a. 'Monitoring quality of life in cities: The Durban case', *Development Southern Africa* 18 (2): 217–238

Møller, V. 2001b. 'Happiness trends under democracy: Where will the new South African set-level come to rest?', *Journal of Happiness Studies* 2 (1): 33–53

Møller, V. 2003. 'Quality of life and positive youth development in Grahamstown East, South Africa', in Sirgy, M. J., Rahtz, D. R. and Samli, A. C. *Advances in Quality-of-Life Theory and Research*. Dordrecht: Kluwer Academic Publishers, pp. 53–80

Møller, V. 2004. *Peaceful Co-existence in South Africa in the Millennium: A Review of Social Indicators in the 2002 Democracy Study*. Letters From Byblos No. 4. Lebanon: International Centre for Human Sciences

Møller, V. 2005. 'Resilient or resigned? Criminal victimisation and quality of life in South Africa', *Social Indicators Research* 72 (3): 262–317

Møller, V. and Devey, R. 2003. 'Trends in living conditions and satisfaction among poorer older South Africans: Objective and subjective indicators of quality of life in the October Household Survey', *Development Southern Africa* 20 (4): 457–476

Møller, V. and Dickow, H. 2002. 'The role of quality of life surveys in managing change in democratic transitions: the South African case', *Social Indicators Research* 58 (1–3): 267–292

Møller, V., Dickow, H. and Harris, M. 1999. 'South Africa's 'rainbow people', national pride and happiness', *Social Indicators Research* 47 (3): 245–280

Møller, V. and Ferreira, M. 1992. 'Successful ageing in South Africa: opportunity structures and subjective well-being', *South African Journal of Gerontology* 1 (1): 5–8

Møller, V. and Ferreira, M. 2003. *Getting By: Benefits of Non-contributory Pension Income for Older South African Households.* Grahamstown and Cape Town: Institute of Social and Economic Research, Rhodes University and The Albertina and Walter Sisulu Institute of Ageing in Africa, University of Cape Town

Møller, V. and Hanf, T. 1995. *Learning to Vote: Voter Education in the 1994 South African Elections.* Durban: Indicator Press, University of Natal

Møller, V. and Jackson, A. 1997. 'Perceptions of service delivery and happiness', *Development Southern Africa* 14 (2): 169–184

Møller, V., Richards, R. and Mthembu, T. 1991. 'Lost generation found: Black youth at leisure', *Indicator South Africa* (Special Issue),

Møller, V. and Saris, W. E. 2001. 'The relationship between subjective well-being and domain satisfactions in South Africa', *Social Indicators Research* 55 (1): 97–114

Møller, V. and Schlemmer, L. 1980. *Quantity or Quality? A Survey Evaluation of Housing in Relation to the Quality of South African Black Township Life.* Durban: Centre for Applied Social Sciences, University of Natal

Møller, V. and Schlemmer, L. 1981. *Contract Workers and Job Satisfaction: A Study of Job Aspirations, Motivations and Preferences among Migrants in Durban.* Durban: Centre for Applied Social Sciences, University of Natal

Møller, V. and Schlemmer, L. 1983. 'Quality of life in South Africa: Towards an instrument for the assessment of quality of life and basic needs', *Social Indicators Research* 12: 225–279

Møller, V. and Schlemmer, L. 1989. 'South African quality of life: A research note', *Social Indicators Research* 21 (3): 279–291

Møller, V. and Sotshongaye, A. 1996. ' "My family eat this money too": Pension sharing and self-respect among Zulu grandmothers', *South African Journal of Gerontology* 5 (2): 9–19

Møller, V. and Welch, G. J. 1990. 'Polygamy, economic security and well-being of retired Zulu migrant workers', *Journal of Cross-Cultural Gerontology* 5: 205–216

Molyneux, M. 2002. 'Gender and the silences of social capital: Lessons from Latin America', *Development and Change* 33 (2): 167–188

Moser, C. 1998. 'The asset vulnerability framework: Reassessing urban poverty reduction strategies', *World Development* 26 (1): 1–19

Mouzelis, N. 1995. *Sociological Theory: What Went Wrong?* London: Routledge

Mudimbe, V. Y. 1988. *The Invention of Africa: Gnosis, Philosophy and the Order of Knowledge.* Bloomington, IN: Indiana University Press

Murray, H. A. 1938. *Explorations in Personality.* New York: Oxford University Press

Myers, D. G. 1999. 'Close relationships and quality of life', in Kahneman, D. and Diener, E. (eds.) *Well-being: The Foundations of Hedonic Psychology.* New York: Russell Sage Foundation, pp. 434–450

Myerson, G. 1994. *Rhetoric, Reason and Society: Rationality as Dialogue.* London: Sage

Narayan, D. (ed.) 2000. *Can Anyone Hear Us?* Voices of the Poor study, vol. 1. New York: Oxford University Press for the World Bank

Narayan, D. (ed.) 2005. *Measuring Empowerment: Cross-Disciplinary Perspectives*. Washington, DC: World Bank

Narayan, D. and Petsch, P. (eds.) 2002. *From Many Lands*. Voices of the Poor study, vol. III. New York: Oxford University Press for the World Bank

Narayan, D., and Chambers, R., Shah, M. K. and Petsch, P. 2000. *Crying Out for Change*. Voices of the Poor study, vol. II. New York: Oxford University Press for the World Bank

Nederveen Pieterse, J. 2001. *Development Theory: Deconstructions/Reconstructions*. London: Sage

Nederveen Pieterse, J. 2002. 'Global inequality: Bringing politics back in', *Third World Quarterly* 23 (6): 1023–1046

Nelson, J. S., Megill, A. and McColskey, D. N. 1987. 'Rhetoric of inquiry', in Nelson, J. S., Megill, A. and McColskey, D. N. *The Rhetoric of the Human Sciences*. London: University of Wisconsin Press

Ng, Y. K. 2003. 'From preferences to happiness: Towards a more complete welfare economics', *Social Indicators Research* 20: 307–350

Noorbakhsh, F. 1998. 'The Human Development Index: Some technical issues and alternative indices', *Journal of International Development* 10: 589–605

Nord, E., Arnesen, T., Menzel, P. and Pinto, J. 2001. 'Towards a more restricted use of the term 'Quality of life'', *Quality of Life Newsletter* (26): 1–28

North, D. 1990. *Institutions, Institutional Change and Economic Performance*. Cambridge: Cambridge University Press

Nussbaum, M. 1988. *Nature, Function and Capability: Aristotle on Political Distribution*. Oxford Studies in Ancient Philosophy vol. VI. Oxford: Clarendon Press

Nussbaum, M. 2000. *Women and Human Development: The Capabilities Approach*. Cambridge: Cambridge University Press

Nussbaum, M. 2006. *Frontiers of Justice: Disability, Nationality and Species Membership*. Cambridge, MA: Harvard University Press

O'Boyle, C. A., Browne, J., Hickey, A., McGee, H. M. and Joyce, C. R. B. 1996. *Schedule for the Evaluation of Individual Quality of Life (SEIQoL): A Direct Weighting Procedure for Quality of Life domains (SEIQoL-DW). Administration Manual*. Dublin: Royal College of Surgeons in Ireland

Ogata-Sen Commission 2003. *Human Security Now*. New York: Commission for Human Security, UNDP

Ogwang, T. 1994. 'The choice of principal variables for computing the Human Development Index', *World Development* 19: 2011–2014

Oishi, S. 2000. 'Goals as cornerstones of subjective well-being: Linking individuals and cultures', in Diener, E. and Suh, E. M. (eds.) *Culture and Subjective Well-Being*. Cambridge, MA: Bradford, pp. 87–112

Okun, A. 1975. *Equality and Efficiency: The Big Trade-off*. Washington, DC: The Brookings Institution

Olson, M. 1965. *The Logic of Collective Action: Public Goods and the Theory of Groups*. Cambridge, MA: Harvard University Press

Orley, J. and Kuyken, W. 1993. *Quality of Life Assessment: International Perspectives*. Berlin: Springer

Ortega y Gasset, J. 2004. *Meditaciones del Quijote* [Meditations of Quixote]. Madrid, Spain: Editorial Biblioteca Nueva

Oswald, A. J. 1997. 'Subjective well-being and economic performance', *The Economic Journal* 197: 1815–1831

Oyserman, D., Coon, H. and Kemmelmeier, M. 2002. 'Rethinking individualism and collectivism: Evaluation of theoretical assumptions and meta-analyses', *Psychological Bulletin* 128 (1): 3–72

Parducci, A. 1995. *Happiness, Pleasure, and Judgment: The Contextual Theory and its Applications*. Hillsdale, NJ: Erlbaum

Parekh, B. 1995. 'Liberalism and colonialism: A critique of Locke and Mill', in Nederveen, J. and Parekh, B. (eds.) *The Decolonization of the Imagination: Culture, Knowledge and Power*. London: Zed Books

Parfit, D. 1984. *Reasons and Persons*. Oxford: Oxford University Press

Pateman, C. 1970. *Participation and Democratic Theory*. Cambridge: Cambridge University Press

Pateman, C. 1983. 'Some reflections on participation and democratic theory', in Crouch, C. and Heller, F. A. (eds.) *International Yearbook of Organizational Democracy for the Study of Participation, Co-operation and Power, Volume 1: Organizational Democracy and Political Processes*. Chichester: Wiley

Penz, P. 1986. *Consumer Sovereignty and Human Interests*. Cambridge: Cambridge University Press

Penz, P. 1991. 'The priority of basic needs', in *Ethical Principles for Development: Needs, Capacities or Rights*. Upper Montclair, NJ: Montclair State University, pp. 35–73

Perkins, N., Devlin, N. and Hansen, P. 2004. 'The validity and reliability of health state evaluations using EQ5 D in a survey of the Maori', *Quality of Life Research* 13 (1): 271–274

Peters, P. (ed.) 2000. *Development Encounters: Sites of Participation and Knowledge*. Cambridge, MA: Harvard Institute for International Development, Harvard University Press

Peterson, C. 1999. 'Personal control and well-being', in Kahneman, D., Diener, E. and Schwarz, N. (eds.) *Well-Being: The Foundations of Hedonic Psychology*. New York: Russell Sage Foundation

Piaget, J. 1971. *Biology and Knowledge*. Oxford: University of Chicago Press

Plant, R., Lesser, H. and Taylor-Gooby, P. 1980. *Political Philosophy and Social Welfare*. New York: Routledge

Powelson, J. P. 1997. *Centuries of Economic Endeavour: Parallel Paths in Japan and Europe and their Contrast with the Third World*. Ann Arbor: University of Michigan Press

Power, M., Bullinger, M. and Harper, A. 1999. 'The World Health Organisation WHOQOL-100 Tests of the Universality of Quality of Life in 15 different cultural groups worldwide', *Health Psychology* 18: 495–505

Power, M., Quinn, K., Schmidt, S. and the WHOQOL-Old Group 2005. 'Development of the WHOQOL-Old module', *Quality of Life Research* 14 (10): 2197–2214

Preston, D. 1998. 'Post-peasant capitalist graziers: The 21st century in southern Bolivia', *Mountain Research and Development* 18 (2): 151–158

Preston, D., Macklin, M. and Warburton, J. 1997. 'Fewer people, less erosion: The twentieth century in Southern Bolivia', *Geographical Journal* 163 (2): 198–205

Putnam, R. 1993. *Making Democracy Work*. Princeton, NJ: Princeton University Press

Putzel, J. 1997. 'Accounting for the 'dark side' of social capital: Reading Robert Putnam on democracy', *Journal of International Development* 9 (7): 939–949

Qizilbash, M. 1996. 'Capabilities, well-being and human development: A survey', *Journal of Development Studies* 33: 143–162

Qizilbash, M. 2002. 'Development, common foes and shared values', *Review of Political Economy* 14 (4): 463–480

Ragin, C. 2000. *Fuzzy-Set Social Science*. London: University of Chicago Press

Rakodi, C. 1999. 'A capital assets framework for analysing household livelihood strategies: Implications for policy', *Development Policy Review* 17: 315–342

Ram, R. 1982. 'Composite indices of physical quality of life, basic needs fulfilment and income: A 'principal component' representation', *Journal of Development Economics* 11: 227–247

Ranis, G., Stewart, F. and Ramirez, A. 2000. 'Economic growth and human development', *World Development* 28: 197–219

Ravallion, M. and Lokshin, M. 2002. 'Self-rated economic welfare in Russia', *European Economic Review* 46: 1453–1473

Ravens-Sieberer, U., Gosch, A., Abel, T., Auquier, P., Bellach, B. M., Bruil, J., Dür, W., Power, M., Rajmil, L. and European KIDSCREEN Group 2001. 'Quality of life in children and adolescents: A European public health perspective', *Sozial- und Präventivmedizin* 46: 294–302

Rawls, J. 1970. *Theory of Justice*. Cambridge: Cambridge University Press

Rayner, S. and Malone, E. L. (eds.) 1998. *Human Choice and Climate Change*, vols. 1–4. Colombus, OH: Battelle Press

Reardon, T., Berdegué, J. and Escobar, G. 2001. 'Rural non-farm employment and incomes in Latin America: Overview and policy implications', *World Development* 29 (3): 395–410

Reber, A. and Reber, E. (eds.) 2001. *The Penguin Dictionary of Psychology*. 3rd edn. London: Penguin

Redfield, R. 1969. 'Peasant view of the good life', in *Peasant Society and Culture*. London: University of Chicago Press

Roberts, B. 1978. *Cities of Peasants*. London: Edward Arnold

Robeyns, I. 2005. 'The capability approach: A theoretical survey', *Journal of Human Development* 6 (1): 93–114

Rodgers, C., Gore, C. and Figueiredo, J. B. 1995. *Social Exclusion: Rhetoric, Reality Responses*. Geneva: ILO

Rogers, C. 1963. 'The actualizing tendency in relation to "motives" and to consciousness', in Jones, M. R. (ed.) *Nebraska Symposium on Motivation*. Lincoln, NE: University of Nebraska Press, pp. 1–24

Rojas, M. 2005. 'A conceptual-referent theory of happiness: Heterogeneity and its consequences', *Social Indicators Research* 74 (2): 261–294

Rojas, M. 2006a. 'Life satisfaction and satisfaction in domains of life: Is it a simple relationship?', *Journal of Happiness Studies* 7: 467–497

Rojas, M. 2006b. 'Well-being and the complexity of poverty: A subjective well-being approach', in McGillivray, M. (ed.) *Perspectives on Human Wellbeing.* Tokyo, New York and Paris: United Nations University Press

Rojas, M. Forthcoming 'Heterogeneity in the relationship between income and happiness: A conceptual-referent-theory explanation', *Journal of Economic Psychology*

Rosen, L. 1984. *Bargaining for Reality: The Construction of Life in a Muslim Community.* London: University of Chicago

Roy, T. K. and Niranjan, S. 2004. 'Indicators of women's empowerment in India', *Asian Pacific Population Journal* September: 23–38

Ruta, D. A. 1998. 'Patient generated assessment: The next generation', *MAPI Quality of Life Newsletter* 20: 461–489

Ruta, D., Camfield, L. and Donaldson, C. Forthcoming 'Sen and the art of quality of life maintenance: Towards a general theory of quality of life and its causation', *Journal of Social Economics*

Ryan, R. 1995. 'Psychological needs and the facilitation of integrative processes', *Journal of Personality* 63: 397–427

Ryan, R. 2005. 'The developmental line of autonomy in the etiology, dynamics, and treatment of borderline personality disorders', *Development and Psychopathology* 17 (4): 987–1006

Ryan, R. and Brown, K. W. 2005. 'Legislating competence: The motivational impact of high stakes testing as an educational reform', in Dweck, C. and Elliot, A. E. (eds.) *Handbook of Competence.* New York: Guilford Press

Ryan, R., Chirkov, V. I., Little, T. D., Sheldon, K. M., Timoshina, E. and Deci, E. L. 1999. 'The American Dream in Russia: Extrinsic aspirations and well-being in two cultures', *Personality and Social Psychology Bulletin* 25: 1509–1524

Ryan, R. and Connell, J. P. 1989. 'Perceived locus of causality and internalization: Examining reasons for acting in two domains', *Journal of Personality and Social Psychology* 57: 749–761

Ryan, R. and Deci, E. L. 2000a. 'The darker and brighter sides of human existence: Basic psychological needs as a unifying concept', *Psychological Inquiry* 11: 319–338

Ryan, R. and Deci, E. L. 2000b. 'Self-determination theory and the facilitation of intrinsic motivation, social development, and well-being', *American Psychologist* 55: 68–78

Ryan, R. and Deci, E. L. 2001. 'On happiness and human potentials: A review of research on hedonic and eudaimonic well-being', *Annual Review of Psychology* 52: 141–166

Ryan, R. and Deci, E. L. 2004. 'Autonomy is no illusion: Self-determination theory and the empirical study of authenticity, awareness, and will', in Greenberg, J., Koole, S. L. and Pyszczynski, T. (eds.) *Handbook of Experimental Existential Psychology.* New York: Guilford Press, pp. 449–479

Ryan, R., Deci, E. L. and Grolnick, W. S. 1995. 'Autonomy, relatedness, and the self: Their relation to development and psychopathology', in Cicchetti, D. and Cohen, D. (eds.) *Developmental Psychopathology*. New York: John Wiley & Sons, pp. 618–655

Ryan, R. and Grolnick, W. S. 1986. 'Origins and pawns in the classroom: Self-report and projective assessments of individual differences in children's perceptions', *Journal of Personality and Social Psychology* 50: 550–558

Ryan, R., Grolnick, W. S., La Guardia, J. G. and Deci, E. L. Forthcoming. 'The significance of autonomy and autonomy support in psychological development and psychopathology', Cicchetti, D. and Cohen, D. (eds), *Handbook of Developmental Psychopathology*. Cambridge: Cambridge University Press

Ryan, R., La Guardia, J. G., Solky-Butzel, J., Chirkov, V. I. and Kim, Y. 2005. 'On interpersonal regulation of emotions: Emotional reliance across gender, relationships, and cultures', *Personal Relationships* 12: 145–163

Ryan, R. and Lynch, J. 1989. 'Emotional autonomy versus detachment: Revisiting the vicissitudes of adolescence and young adulthood', *Child Development* 60: 340–356

Ryan, R., Rigby, S. and King, K. 1993. 'Two types of religious internalization and their relations to religious orientations and mental health', *Journal of Personality and Social Psychology* 65: 586–596

Ryan, R., Sheldon, K. M., Kasser, T. and Deci, E. L. 1996. 'All goals are not created equal: An organismic perspective on the nature of goals and their regulation', in Gollwitzer, P. M. and Bargh, A. (eds.) *The Psychology of Action: Linking Cognition and Motivation to Behavior*. New York: Guilford, pp. 7–26

Sahlins, M. 1974. *Stone Age Economics*. 2nd edn. London: Tavistock Publications Ltd.

Said, E. 1985. *Orientalism*. Harmondsworth: Penguin

St.Clair, A. L. 2004. 'The role of ideas in the United Nations Development Programme', in Bøas, M. and McNeill, D. (eds.) *Global Institutions and Development: Framing the World?* London: Routledge

St.Clair, A. L. 2006. 'Global poverty: The co-production of knowledge and politics', *Global Social Policy* 6 (1): 57–77

Saltmarshe, D. 2001. *Identity in a Post-communist Balkan State: An Albanian Village Study*. Aldershot, UK: Ashgate Publishing

Saltmarshe, D. 2002. 'The resource profile approach: A Kosovo case study', *Public Administration and Development* 22 (2): 179–190

Salvatore, N. and Muñoz Sastre, M. T. 2001. 'Appraisal of life: "Area" versus "dimension" conceptualizations', *Social Indicators Research* 53: 229–255

Samuels, F. 1984. *Human Needs and Behavior*. Cambridge, MA: Schenkman Publishers

Saris, W. E. and Andreenkova, A. 2001. 'Happiness in Russia', *Journal of Happiness Studies* 2 (2): 95–109

Sartorius, N., Jablensky, A. and Shapiro, R. 1978. 'Cross-cultural differnences in the short-term prognosis of schizophrenic psychoses', *Schizophrenia Bulletin* 4: 102–113

Sartorius, N. and Kuyken, W. 1994. 'Translation of health status instruments', in Orley, J. and Kuyken, W. (eds.) *Quality of Life Assessment: International Perspectives*. Berlin and Heidelberg: Springer, pp. 3–19

Sayer, A. 1992. *Method in Social Science*. London: Routledge

Sayer, A. 1999. 'For postdisciplinary studies: Sociology and the curse of disciplinary parochialism/imperialism', in Eldridge, J., MacInnes, J., Scott, S., Warhurst, C. and Witz, A. (eds.) *Sociology: Legacies and Prospects*. Durham, UK: Sociology Press

Sayer, A. 2000. *Realism and Social Science*. London: Sage

Schaffer, B. 1985. 'Policy makers have their needs too: Irish itinerants and the culture of poverty', in Wood, G. (ed.) *Labelling in Development Policy*. London: Sage, pp. 33–66

Schaffer, B. and Huang, W. 1975. 'Distribution and the theory of access', *Development and Change* 6 (2): 13–36

Schaffer, B. and Lamb, G. 1974. 'Exit, voice and access', *Social Science Information* 13: 89–106

Scheper-Hughes, N. 2000. 'The global traffic in human organs', *Current Anthropology* 41 (2): 191–224

Scherpenzeel, A. C. and Saris, W. E. 1996. 'Causal direction in a model of life-satisfaction: The top-down/bottom-up controversy', *Social Indicators Research* 38: 161–180

Schipper, H., Olweny, C. L. M. and Clinch, J. J. 1996. 'A mini-handbook for conducting small-scale clinical trials in developing countries', in Spilker, B. (ed.) *Quality of Life and Pharmacoeconomics in Clinical Trials*. 2nd edn. Philadelphia: Lippincott-Raven Publishers, pp. 669–681

Schlemmer, L. and Møller, V. 1997. 'The shape of South African society and its challenges', *Social Indicators Research* 41 (1–3): 15–50

Schmidt, S. and Bullinger, M. 2003. 'Current issues in cross-cultural quality of life instrument development', *Archives of Physical Medicine and Rehabilitation* 84: 29–33

Schmidt, S., Debensasson, D., Mühlan, H., Petersen, C., Power, M., Simeoni, M. C., Bullinger, M. and the European DISABKIDS Group 2006a. 'The DISABKIDS generic quality of life instrument showed cross-cultural validity', *Journal of Clinical Epidemiology* 59 (6): 587–598

Schmidt, S., Mühlan, H. and Power, M. 2006b. 'The EUROHIS-QOL 8-item index: Psychometric results of a cross-cultural field study', *European Journal of Public Health* 16 (4): 420–428

Schmidt, S., Power, M., Bullinger, M. and Nosikov, A. 2004. 'Interrelationship between health indicators and quality of life: Results from the cross-cultural analysis of the EUROHIS field study', *Clinical Psychology and Psychotherapy* 12 (1): 28–50

Schmidt, S. and Power, M. 2006. 'Cross-cultural analyses of determinants of quality of life and mental health: Results from the EUROHIS study', *Social Indiators Research* 77 (1): 95–138

Schwartz, C. E. and Sprangers, M. A. 1999. 'Methodological approaches for assessing response shift in longitudinal health-related quality of life research', *Social Science and Medicine* 48 (11): 1531–1548

Schweder, R. 1991. *Thinking through Cultures: Expeditions in Cultural Psychology.*
  Cambridge, MA: Cambridge University Press
Schyns, P. 2001. 'Income and satisfaction in Russia', *Journal of Happiness
  Research* 2 (2): 173–204
Scoones, I. 1998. *Sustainable Rural Livelihoods: A Framework for Analysis.* IDS
  Working Paper 72. Brighton: Institute for Development Studies
Scott, J. C. 1985. *Weapons of the Weak: Everyday Forms of Peasant Resistance.*
  London: Yale University Press
Scott, J. C. 1990. *Domination and the Arts of Resistance: Hidden Transcripts.* New
  Haven: Yale University Press
Seligman, M. 1975. *Helplessness: On Depression, Development and Death.* San
  Francisco: Freeman
Sen, A. 1979a. 'Informational analysis of moral principles', in Harrison, R.
  (ed.) *Rational Action.* Cambridge: Cambridge University Press, pp. 115–127
Sen, A. 1979b. *Equality of What?* Tanner Lecture on Human Values, Stanford
  University. www.tannerlectures.utah.edu
Sen, A. 1981a. *Poverty and Famines: An Essay on Entitlement and Deprivation.*
  Oxford: Clarendon Press
Sen, A. 1981b. *Theory of Famines.* Oxford: Clarendon Press
Sen, A. 1982. 'Liberty as control: An appraisal', *Midwest Studies in Philosophy* 7:
  207–221
Sen, A. 1984. *Resources, Values and Development.* Oxford: Basil Blackwell
Sen, A. 1985a. *Commodities and Capabilities.* Oxford: Elsevier Science
  Publishers
Sen, A. 1985b. 'Well-being agency and freedom: The Dewey Lectures 1984',
  Journal of Philosophy 82 (4): 169–221
Sen, A. 1988. 'Freedom of choice', *European Economic Review* 32: 269–294
Sen, A. 1990. 'Development as capability expansion', in Griffin, K. and Knight, J.
  (eds.) *Human Development and the international development strategy for the
  1990s.* London: Macmillan
Sen, A. 1992. *Inequality Reexamined.* Cambridge, MA: Harvard University Press
Sen, A. 1993. 'Capability and well-being', in Sen, A. and Nussbaum, M. *The
  Quality of Life.* Oxford: Clarendon Press
Sen, A. 1997. 'Editorial: Human capital and human capability', *World
  Development* 25 (12): 1959–1961
Sen, A. 1999. *Development as Freedom.* New York: Knopf Press
Sen, A. 2002. *Rationality and Freedom.* Cambridge, MA: Belknap Press
Sen, A. 2004. 'Elements of a theory of human rights', *Philosophy and Public
  Affairs* 32 (4): 315
Sen, A. 2005. 'Foreword', in Farmer, P. *Pathologies of Power: Health, Human
  Rights, and the New War on the Poor.* London: University of California
  Press
Shapiro, C. and Stiglitz, J. 1984. 'Unemployment as a worker discipline device',
  American Economic Review 74: 433–444
Shapiro, D. 1981. *Autonomy and Rigid Character.* New York: Basic Books

Sharif, I. and Wood, G. (eds.) 2001. *Second Generation Microfinance: Regulation, Supervision and Resource Mobilisation.* Dhaka: University Press Ltd.

Sheldon, K. M., Elliot, A. J., Ryan, R., Chirkov, V. I., Kim, Y., Wu, C., Demir, M. and Sun, Z. 2004. 'Self-concordance and subjective well-being in four cultures', *Journal of Cross-Cultural Psychology* 35: 209–223

Sirgy, M. J., Cole, D., Kosenko, R., Meadow, H. L., Rahtz, D. R., Cicic, M., Xi Jin, G., Yarsuvat, D., Blenkhorn, D. L. and Nagpal, N. 1995. 'A life satisfaction measure: Additional validational data for the congruity life satisfaction measure', *Social Indicators Research* 34: 237–259

Skevington, S., Lotfy, M. and O'Connell, K. A. 2004. 'The World Health Organization's WHOQOL-BREF Quality of Life Assessment: Psychometric properties and results of the international field trial. A report from the WHOQOL Group', *Quality of Life Research* 13: 299–310

Skinner, E. A. 1995. *Perceived Control, Motivation, & Coping.* Thousand Oaks, CA: Sage Publications

Sotshongaye, A. and Møller, V. 2000. '"We want to live a better life like other people': Self-assessed development needs of rural women in Ndwedwe, KwaZulu-Natal', *Development Southern Africa* 17 (1): 117–134

Spilker, B. 1990. *Quality of Life Assessments in Clinical Trials.* New York: Lippincott Williams and Wilkins

Spilker, B. (ed.) 1996. *Quality of life and pharmacoeconomics in Clinical Trials.* 2nd edn. New York: Lippincott-Raven Publishers

Spivak, G. C. 1988. 'Can the subaltern speak?', in Nelson, C. and Grossberg, L. (eds.) *Marxism and the Interpretation of Culture.* London: Macmillan

Springborg, P. 1981. *The Problem of Human Needs and Critique of Civilization.* London: Allen & Unwin

Srinivasan, T. N. 1994. 'Human development: A new paradigm or reinvention of the wheel?', *American Economic Review* 84: 238–243

Standing, G. 1999. *Global Labour Flexibility: Seeking Distributive Justice.* London and Basingstoke: Macmillan

Standing, G. 2002. *Beyond the New Paternalism: Basic Security as Equality.* London: Verso

Standing, G. 2004. *Economic Security for a Better World.* Geneva: ILO

Stern, N. 1989. 'The economics of development: A survey', *Economic Journal* 99 (127): 597–685

Stewart, F. 1985. *Planning to Meet Basic Needs.* London: Macmillan

Stewart, F. 1996. 'Basic needs, capabilities and human development', in Offer, A. (ed.) *Pursuit of the Quality of Life.* Oxford: Oxford University Press

Strack, F., Schwarz, N., Chassein, B., Kern, D. and Wagner, D. 1990. 'Salience of comparison standards and the activation of social norms: consequences for judgements of happiness and their communication', *British Journal of Social Psychology* 29 (4): 303–314

Streeten, P. 1977. 'The distinctive features of a basic needs approach to development', *International Development Review* 19: 8–16

Streeten, P. 1984. 'Basic needs: Some unsettled questions', *World Development* 12 (9): 973–978

Stroebe, M., Gergen, M., Gergen, K. and Stroebe, S. 1996. 'Broken hearts or broken bonds', in Klass, D., Silverman, P. R. and Nickman, S. L. (eds.) *Continuing Bonds: New Understandings of Grief*. Philadelphia: Taylor and Francis, pp. 31–44

Sugden, R. 2003. 'Opportunity as a space for individuality: Its value and the impossibility of measuring it', *Ethics* 113: 783–809

Suh, E. M. 2002. 'Culture, identity consistency, and subjective well-being', *Journal of Personality and Social Psychology* 83: 1378–1391

Suh, E., Diener, E., Oishi, S. and Triandis, H. C. 1998. 'The shifting basis of life satisfaction judgements across cultures: Emotions versus norms', *Journal of Personality and Social Psychology* 74: 482–493

Sumner, L. W. 1996. *Welfare, Happiness and Ethics*. Oxford: Clarendon Press

Sutcliffe, B. 2001. *100 Ways of Seeing an Unequal World*. London: Zed Books

Swift, J. 1989. 'Why are rural people vulnerable to famine', *IDS Bulletin* 20 (2): 9–15

Tambiah, S. J. 1990. *Magic, Science, Religion, and the Scope of Rationality*. London: Cambridge University Press

Tanaka, K. and Yamauchi, H. 2000. 'Influence of autonomy on perceived control beliefs and self-regulated learning in Japanese undergraduate students', *North American Journal of Psychology* 2: 255–272

Tatarkiewicz, W. 1976. *Analysis of Happiness*. The Hague: Martinus Nijhoff

Taylor, P. 1959. ''Need' statements', *Analysis* 19 (5): 106–111

Taylor, S. E., Wood, J. V. and Lichtman, R. R. 1983. 'It could be worse: Selective evaluation as a response to victimisation', *Journal of Social Issues* 39: 19–40

Thomson, G. 1987. *Needs*. London: Routledge

Thompson, J. B. 1990. *Ideology and Modern Culture: Critical Social Theory in the Era of Mass Communications*. Cambridge: Polity Press

Tilly, C. 1984. *Big Structures, Large Processes, Huge Comparisons*. New York: Russell Sage Foundation

Triandis, H. C. 1995. *Individualism and Collectivism*. Boulder, CO: Westview Press

Triandis, H. C. and Gelfand, M. J. 1998. 'Converging measurement of horizontal and vertical individualism and collectivism', *Journal of Personality and Social Psychology* 74: 118–128

Turner, B. L. and Brush, S. (eds.) 1987. *Comparative Farming Systems*. New York: Guilford Press

United Nations Development Programme (UNDP) 1990. *Human Development Report*. New York: Oxford University Press

United Nations Development Programme (UNDP) 1993. *Human Development Report*. New York: Oxford University Press

United Nations Development Programme (UNDP) 1994. *Human Development Report*. New York: Oxford University Press

United Nations Development Programme (UNDP) 2002. *Human Development Report*. New York: Oxford University Press

United Nations Development Programme (UNDP) 2004. *Human Development Report*. New York: Oxford University Press van Praag, B. M. S. and Ferrer-i-Carbonell, A. 2004. *Happiness Quantified: A Satisfaction Calculus Approach*. Oxford: Oxford University Press

van Praag, B. M. S., Frijters, P. and Ferrer-i-Carbonell, A. 2003. 'The anatomy of subjective well-being', *Journal of Economic Behaviour and Organization* 51: 29–49

Van Schendel, W. 1981. *Peasant Mobility: The Odds of Life in Rural Bangladesh*. Assen: can Gorcum

Veenhoven, R. 1984. *Conditions of Happiness*. Dordrecht: Kluwer Academic

Veenhoven, R. 1992. *Happiness in Nations*. Rotterdam: Erasmus University

Veenhoven, R. 1996. 'Developments in satisfaction research', *Social Indicators Research* 37: 1–45

Veenhoven, R. 2002a. *Happy Life Years in 67 Nations in the 1990s*. World Database of Happiness, Rank Report 2002/2 http://www.eur.nl/fsw/research/happiness

Veenhoven, R. 2002b. *Equality of Happiness in 59 Nations in the 1990s*. World Database of Happiness, Rank Report 2002/3 http://www.eur.nl/fsw/research/happiness

Veenhoven, R. 2002c. 'Why social policy needs subjective indicators', in Hagerty, M. R., Vogel, J. and Møller, V. (eds.) *Assessing Quality of Life and Living Conditions to Guide National Policy: The State of the Art*. Dordrecht: Kluwer Academic Publishers, pp. 33–45

Veenhoven, R. 2003. 'Arts-of-living', *Journal of Happiness Studies* 4: 373–384

Veenhoven, R. 2006. 'Subjective Measures of Well Being.' in McGillivray, M. (ed.), *Human Well-being: Concept and Measurement*. Basingstoke: Palgrave, pp. 214–239

Vitterso, J. and Nilsen, F. 2002. 'The conceptual and relational structure of subjective wellbeing, neuroticism, and extraversion: once again neuroticism is the important predictor of happiness', *Social Indicators Research* 57: 89–118

VMPPFM Banco Mundial 1998. *Estudio de Productividad Rural y Manejo de Recursos Naturales: Informe Principal* [A study of rural productivity and natural resources management: Main Report]. La Paz, Bolivia: Vice-Ministerio de Participaciòn Popular y Fortalecimiento Municipal

Vogel, J. and Wolf, M. 2004. 'Index för internationella välfärdsjämförelser: Sverige i täten' [Index for international welfare comparisons: Sweden in the lead], *Välfärd* 1: 7–14

von Benda-Beckmann, F. and von Benda-Beckmann, K. 1994. 'Coping with insecurity: An "underall" perspective on social security in the Third World', *Focaal* 22–23: 7–31

Wallerstein, I. 1999. *The End of the World as We Know It: Social Science for the Twenty-First Century*. London: University of Minneapolis Press

Ware, J. E. Jr. 'Conceptualization and measurement of health related quality of life: Comments on an evolving field', *Archives of Physical Medicine and Rehabilitation* 84 (4) Supplement 2: S43–51

Ware Jr, J. E., Gandek, B. L., Keller, S. D. and IQOLA Project Group 1996. 'Evaluating instruments used cross-nationally: Methods from the IQOLA Project', in Spilker, B. (ed.) *Quality of Life and Pharmacoeconomics in Clinical Trials*. 2nd edn. Philadelphia: Lippincott-Raven Publishers, pp. 681–693

Ware, J. E. and Sherbourne, C. D. 1992. 'The MOS 36-item short form health survey (SF-36): Conceptual framework and item selection', *Medical Care* 30: 473–483

Watzlawick, P., Weakland, J. H. and Fisch, R. 1974. *Change: Principles of Problem Formation and Problem Resolution*. London: W. W. Norton and Co.

Weber, M. 1904 (1930 English translation by Talcott Parson). *The Protestant Ethic and the Spirit of Capitalism*. New York: Charles Scribner's Sons

Webster, N. and Engberg-Pedersen, L. (eds.) 2002. *In the Name of the Poor: Contesting Political Space for Poverty Reduction*. London: Zed

Werner, H. 1948. *Comparative Psychology of Mental Development*. New York: International Universities Press

Whistler, D., White, K. J., Wong, S. D. and Bates, D. 2001. *SHAZAM User's Reference Manual Version 9*. Vancouver: Northwest Econometrics

White, R. W. 1959. 'Motivation reconsidered: The concept of competence', *Psychological Review* 66: 297–333

White, S. 2002. 'Being, becoming and relationship: Conceptual challenges of a child rights approach in development', *Journal of International Development* 14: 1095–1104

White, S. and Pettit, J. 2004. *Participatory Approaches and the Measurement of Human Well-Being*. WeD Working Paper 8. Bath: Wellbeing in Developing Countries (WeD) Research Group

WHOQOL Group 1994. 'The development of the World Health Organisation Quality of Life Assessment Instrument (the WHOQOL)', in Orley, J. and Kuyken, W. (eds.) *Quality of Life Assessment: International Perspectives*. Berlin Heidelberg: Springer, pp. 41–61

WHOQOL Group 1995. 'The World Health Organization Quality of Life Assessment (WHOQOL): Position paper from the World Health Organization', *Social Science and Medicine* 41: 1403–1409

WHOQOL Group 1999. 'The World Health Organisation WHOQOL-100: Tests of the universality of quality of life in 15 different cultural groups world-wide', *Health Psychology* 18: 495–505

Wiggins, D. 1985. 'Claims of need', in Honderich, T. (ed.) *Morality and Objectivity*. London: Routledge

Williams, G. C., Deci, E. L. and Ryan, R. 1998. 'Building health-care partnerships by supporting autonomy', in Hinton-Walker, A. L., Suchman, A. L. and Botelho, R. (eds.) *Partnerships, Power and Process: Transforming Health Care Delivery*. Rochester, New York: University of Rochester Press, pp. 68–87

Williams, R. 1983. *Keywords: A Vocabulary of Culture and Society*. Rev. edn. London: Fontana

Wisner, B. 1988. *Power and Need in Africa*. London: Earthscan

Wissing, M. P. and van Eeden, C. 2002. 'Empirical clarification of the nature of psychological well-being', *South African Journal of Psychology* 32: 32–44

Witkin, B. R. and Altschuld, J. W. 1995. *Planning and Conducting Needs Assessments*. Thousand Oaks, CA: Sage

Wood, G. 1985. *Labelling in Development Policy*. London: Sage

Wood, G. 2000. 'Prisoners and escapees: Improving the institutional responsibility square in Bangladesh', *Public Administration and Development* 20: 221–237

Wood, G. 2003. 'Staying secure, staying poor: The Faustian bargain', *World Development* 31 (3): 455–471

Wood, G. 2004. 'Informal security regimes: The strength of relationships', in Gough, I., Wood, G., Barrientos, A., Bevan, P., Davis, P. and Room, G. (eds.) *Insecurity and Welfare Regimes in Asia, Africa and Latin America.* Cambridge: Cambridge University Press, Ch. 2, pp. 49–87

Wood, G. 2005. 'Poverty, capabilities and perverse social capital: The antidote to Sen and Putnam?', in Khan, I. A. and Seeley, J. (eds.) *Making a Living: The Livelihoods of the Rural Poor in Bangladesh.* Dhaka: The University Press Limited, pp. 1–18

Wood, G. and Gough, I. 2006. 'A comparative welfare regime approach to global social policy', *World Development* 34 (10): 1696–1712

Wood, G. and Salway, S. 2000. 'Introduction: Securing livelihoods in Dhaka slums', *Journal of International Development* 12 (5): 669–688

Wood, G. and Shakil, S. 2005. 'Collective action: The threatened imperative', in Wood, G., Malik, A. and Sagheer, S. (eds.) *Valleys in Transition: 20 Years of AKRSP's Experience in N. Pakistan.* Karachi and Oxford: Oxford University Press

Worcester, R. M. 1998. 'More than money', in Christie, I. and Nash, L. (eds.) *The Good Life.* London: Demos

World Bank 2001. *World Development Report 2000/2001.* Washington, DC: World Bank

Wright, G. 1997. 'Savings: Flexible financial services for the poor', in Wood, G. and Sharif, I. (eds.) *Who Needs Credit? Poverty and Finance in Bangladesh.* London: Zed Books

Yamauchi, H. and Tanaka, K. 1998. 'Relations of autonomy, self-referenced beliefs and self-regulated learning among Japanese children', *Psychological Reports* 82: 803–816

Zimmerer, K. 1996. *Changing Fortunes: Biodiversity and Peasant Livelihood in the Peruvian Andes.* Berkeley: University of California Press

Zoomers, A. 1998. *Estrategias Campesinas en el Surandino de Bolivia: Intervenciones y desarrollo rural en el norte de Chuquisaca y Potos* [Peasant strategies in the Bolivian Andes: Interventions and rural development in the north of Chuquisaca and Potosí]. La Paz: CEDLA/CID/PLURAL

Zoomers, A. 1999. *Linking Livelihood Strategies to Development: Experiences from the Bolivian Andes.* Amsterdam: Royal Tropical Institute/Centre for Latin American Research and Documentation

Index

Note: Page numbers in bold refer to Tables; those in italics refer to Figures

activity, and wellbeing 61
'actual lives' 17
adaptability/adaptation 11
  to circumstances 30, 334–6
adult literacy
  as measure of wellbeing 136, 139, 142,
    147
  as resource 163
Afghanistan, Badakhshan 124
Africa
  clientelism 126
  HIV/AIDS funerals 117
Afrobarometer 253
age, as life-satisfaction variable 272, **273**,
    279
agency
  and culture 166
  and definition of resources 158
  and empowerment 102–3
  and freedom 94
  and livelihood 22–3
  measurement of 104–8
  and money poverty 6–7
  and resources in livelihood frameworks
    160–3, 165
  and self-efficacy 104–5
  and social protection 121
  and structure 301
  and subjectivity 172
agriculture
  Andes 185
  dairy production systems (La Paz) 191,
    193
  desencuentros in NGO models 186
  food security 19
  Green Revolution 128
  intensification 186
  potato production (Ravelo) 191, 192
  risk in 116
  and vulnerability to poverty 18

aid chain interventions, by NGOs 177,
    178, 183–4
alienation
  as harm 326
  and human security 111–12
  and social protection 112
Anderson, Benedict 330
Andes
  encuentros and *desencuentros* in NGO
    interventions 196–8
  livelihood asset management strategies
    183–92
  perception of environment and climate
    change 186, 195
  research into NGO aid chains 183–4
  stagnant regional economies 193
anthropology, and health-related quality of
  life 221–2
aspirations 177, 178, 187
Asset Vulnerability Framework 19, 24, 160
assets
  claiming untitled 127
  economic 202
  and economic opportunities 190–2
  and improvement in wellbeing 188
  livelihood bases 179, 180
  management strategies in the Andes
    183–92
  and purpose assigned to 171
  social 202
  transformation of 181, 187
  see also capitals/assets; resources
associational membership 129
authority
  consent and coercion 348
  dominant notions of 182
autonomous security 110, 113, 121
autonomy 34, 104, 299
  as basic need 75, 82–3
  comparative studies 84–8

autonomy (*cont.*)
   degrees of 105–6
   dependence/independence definitions
      106–7
   and dignity 118
   as human need 14, 16, 32
   and individualism 84–6, 107, 331
   Japan and China 84
   and personal control over life 32
   in relationships 88–9
   and resilience 336
   SDT measurement of 105–8
   and security 115
   in self-determination theory 211
   and social context 331–2

Bandura, Albert 104
Bangladesh
   flooding 334
   and Resource Profiles Framework (RPF)
      20–1, 162
basic needs 9, 50, 111
   application of 76–8
   see also human needs; needs
basista approach, to development 176
Battelle Foundation programme 54
Beck, Tony 21
Bentham, Jeremy 30
Beveridge, Lord 326
Bihar, India, dowry costs 123
Bolivia, need for rural economic growth
   192
Bourdieu, Pierre 162, 164, 172
Brazil, needs satisfaction and autonomy 86
Bulgaria, autonomy 87

Canada, needs satisfaction and autonomy
   86
Cantrill Self-Anchoring Striving Scale 224
capabilities 9–16, 63, 64
   and attainments 51
   and freedoms 94–5
   measurement of 12
   and social resources 121
   universal 13
capital markets 205
   dualism in 205
capitalism
   and primacy of social relations 165
   see also economic development models
capitalists
   role in economic growth 206
   in *sigma* model 202, 203
capitals/assets 19, 23
   natural 180, 187

physical 202
produced 180
reification of 161, 162
as social or cultural 165
   see also assets; human capital
charitable institutions
   codes of practices 125
   local mosques (Pakistan) 125
children, socialisation of 75, 78
China, autonomy 84
choice, and preference 61, 95
civil society 126
   and elections 130
clientelism 118, 210
   measures to end 125–7
climate change, perception of 186, 195
cognitive skills, impaired 14
Cold War, end of 10
collectivism, and autonomy 84–6, 88, 106,
   331
commodities
   acquisition of 61
   and utility 11
communications 322
community 120
   domains-of-life variable 267, 270, 278
   profiles 342
community institutions 130
   membership and rules of 131
   role in resource management 197
   social differentiation in 197
   supra-communal 189
competence 299
   as basic need 76, 82, 91
Comprehensive Development Framework
   (World Bank) 213
comunero systems 38
conceptual frameworks 284, 285–93, 289,
   303
Confucius 83
contingency, and subjectivity 168–74
credit *see* loans
critical realism 287–9, 300
cross-cultural issues
   equivalence in translation of measures
      227, 231, **232**
   in health-related quality of life research
      223–35, 238–40, 240–1
   instrument development 232–3, 233–5
   in quality of life (QoL) research 220–3
   sequential translations 231–2
   and use of term 'international' 222
   see also cultural difference
cross-disciplinary research 283–5, 293,
   307–12, 345–6

barriers and good practice 311–12
conceptual framework 284, 285–93
Foundations of Knowledge
  questionnaire 312–15
ideal-type depiction of research models 294
intellectual barriers to 284, 309–11
knowledge assumptions 286
main approaches 293–307, 294
  see also knowledge assumptions
cultural analysis 328, 349
cultural capital 180, 202
of y-workers 205
cultural contexts 336
and autonomy 85–6
psychological needs 76–8, 91
cultural difference 31, 34
and health 27
and individualism 31
in life-satisfaction surveys 271
and studies of autonomy 84–8
and universality of psychological needs
  79–80, 81
  see also cross-cultural issues
cultural exclusion, Peru 200
cultural habitus 300
cultural stability, relationship to
  psychological needs 91–2
culture
and agency 166
as dynamic systems of norms 327
as external 166
and identity 329–30
meaning and identity 327–32
resources of 6–7, 20, 21
and social life 167
and social organisation 329
and wellbeing 319
Cummins, R. A. 30

de-clientelisation 125–7
democracy
and development policy making 347
expectations of in South Africa 253
dependency 9, 178
dependent security 36, 110, 113, 118
desencuentros 38, 176, 196–8
and misconception of role of community
  organisation 197
in NGOs subsidies for agriculture 186
as result of targeted NGO intervention
  191–2
desire theories of wellbeing 60
development
basista approach 176
changing concept of 4, 213, 349

and concept of human needs 9–10
definition of 349
economic measurement of (GDP) 9
functional dualism in 178
as 'good change' 5
resources and relationships debate
  199–201
and social capital 19
tropes 291
  see also human development
development agencies
aims and perceived aims 189, 212
and construction of identity 166
and inclusion/exclusion theory 213–15
  see also NGOs
development intervention 38, 39
divergence from rural household
  aspirations 177, 333
and empowerment 189–90
ill-informed 173
and processes 332
  see also desencuentros; NGOs
development policy 292, 293
challenges for 316
need for new model 175
sigma model and 212–15
and wellbeing research 346–7, 349
development research 293
from concepts to methodology 316–18
informed by dependency 178
need for greater rigour 174
quality of life 25–33
  see also cross-disciplinary research;
  quality of life (QoL) research;
  Wellbeing in Developing Countries
  (WeD)
Diener, Ed 28, 31
dignity, and security 112, 118
DISABKIDS measure of QoL 234, 235
disconnect see desencuentros
disease
culture-bound 221–2
epidemics 117
domains of life, in quality of life research
  41–2
domains-of-life approach, to life
  satisfaction 259, 264–5, 278–80
analysis 268–71
and causality 265
relationship regression analysis 269–71,
  275–8
by socio-demographic groups 271–4, 279
variables 266–8
  see also life-satisfaction approach
  (Mexican survey); subjective wellbeing

dowry
  costs 123
  as economic hazard 117
  institution of 21
Dryden, John 308–9
dynamic comparative advantage (Ricardian
  ladder) theory 209

economic development
  and social development 209
  'Washington consensus' 343
economic development models 200
  epsilon model 201
  omega 201
    see also sigma model
economic domain, domains-of-life variable
  267, 270, 276, 279
economic indicators, of wellbeing 134
Economic Journal, The, study of needs 49
economics
  of happiness 29
  and wellbeing 259
economy
  capitalist growth 206
  structural relations between modern and
    popular 178
education 34
  as human or cultural resource 161
  as life-satisfaction variable 273, 274,
    279
  livelihood strategies to enhance 185–6,
    190, 196
  use of 163
educational attainment, as measure of
  wellbeing 135
elections
  civil society and 130
  free voting 127
electricity supplies, Andes 194
emic–etic distinction 110, 115, 116, 131,
  232, 339
employee rights 126
employment
  delinked from credit markets 127
  diversification of 128
empowerment
  degrees of 100
  measurement of 35, 99, 100–3
  NGO interventions and 189–90, 292
entitlement 6
  concept of 17–18
    see also human needs
epistemology 288, 301–2
  abduction 288
  deduction 288

inductive argument 288
  retroduction 287
equity, principles of 120
ESRC Research Group on Wellbeing in
  Developing Countries (WeD) 8, 49, 284
Ethiopia, empowerment study 101–2
eudaimonic wellbeing 16, 32, 131, 323
    see also happiness
EUROHIS measure of QoL 234–5
Euromodule household survey 257
European Organisation for Research and
  Treatment of Cancer (EORTC),
    EORTC Quality of Life Questionnaire
    224, 225, 229
European Quality of Life Project Group
  (EUROQOL) 224
expectations 30, 335
  and aspirations 177, 178, 187
  of democracy (South Africa) 249, 253

family
  as clientelism 126
  domains-of-life variable 267, 270, 276,
    278
family size 123
  family planning 186
famines
  Bengal (1943) 17
  Ethiopia (1973) 17
fear, and security 114
Figueroa, Adolfo, social exclusion theory
  199
food security 169
    see also Marshall, Paule
formal rationality, concept of 285
Foundations of Knowledge Framework
  (FoKF) 42, 285–93, 318
  questionnaire 312–15
freedom
  and agency 94
  and capability approach 93, 94–5, 97
  measurement of 96–9
  and processes 95–6
  rights perspective 110–11
  role of (in Sen's writings) 94–6
  to achieve 94
friendship, domains-of-life variable 267,
  270, 278
Functional Assessment of Cancer Treatment
  Questionnaire (FACT) 224, 225, 228,
  229
functionings
  concept of 6, 10, 11, 12, 24
  freedom 97
  measurement of side-effects 99

GDP (Gross Domestic Product), as measurement of economic development 9
gender, as life-satisfaction variable 271, 272, 279
gender empowerment, as measure of wellbeing 135, 147
General Health Questionnaire (GHQ) 224
Germany, population norms 230
global capitalism 203
globalisation
    challenges of 348–50
    of media 330
goals, and needs 89–90, 317, 318–21
goods, as resources 163
governance
    and globalisation 348
    and wellbeing policy 347
    see also institutions

habituation, and material expectation 254
'habitus' (Bourdieu) 172
happiness
    as criterion of wellbeing 51, 262
    economics of 29
    right to 350
    and satisfaction 245, 263
harm(s)
    and alienation 326
    as fundamental disablement 13
    intentional 326
    and needs 324–6, 338
    serious 324, 348
hazards
    preparation for 124
    vulnerability to 117
health
    cultural differences 27
    domains-of-life variable 267, 270, 276, 279
    physical 14
    and quality of life 7, 26–8
health-related quality of life 26–8, 39–40, 220
    anthropology and 221–2
    approaches to developing cross-cultural measures 223–35
    and decision-making 240
    disease-specific measures 224
    equivalence testing 231, 232, 234
    ethical issues in research 241
    ethnocentrism in 240
    international instrument testing 230–5
    issues 223, 237–40
    item choice and development 226–7

parallel approach 225
population norms 229–30
sequential approach 225
SF-36 measure 223, 224, 225
simultaneous approach 225, 234
testing metric quality of measures 229
translation of measures across cultures 227–8, 238–40
universal and national measures 223, 233, 241
WHOQOL measure 223, 224, 225
hedonism 60
hedonic psychology 28
Hicks, John R. 259
Hochosterwitz castle, siege of 157–8
Honduras, empowerment study 101
hostile environments 32
household 120
household budgets 123
    short-term needs 119
human capital 180
    concept of 93
    and empowerment 190
    investment in 187
    skilled and unskilled 202
human development 35
    capability and functioning perspective 110
    measurement and methodology 36
    and money poverty 6
    see also human needs
Human Development and Capability Association 6
Human Development Index (HDI) 12, 33, 34, 52, 93
    as multidimensional indicator 133, 136
    and security 132
Human Development Reports 6, 135, 136
human needs 33–7, 301
    basic 14, 33, 50, 52, 69, 76–8
    and capabilities 9–16, 51
    conceptualisation 52–9
    and development 9–10
    indicators for 10
    and motivations 13
    priorities 51, 64
    project framework 51
    satisfiers for 14–15, 22, 50
    societal preconditions 15, 73
    specific satisfiers 15
    universal 13
    use of term 33
    see also needs; psychological needs; Theory of Human Need

human organs, as resource 164
human rights
  and economic development 200
  and needs theory 52
Human Security (HS) 110
  and 'freedom from' needs 111
  limits of comprehensiveness 111
  objective of 111
humanitarian intervention 52

identity
  and caste 20
  culture and meaning 327–32
  development bureaucracies and 166
  and internalisation of culture 329–30
  and respect 21–2
inclusion/exclusion framework 200
  see also social exclusion theory
income
  distribution 206
  as life-satisfaction variable 274, 275, 279
  and wellbeing 29, 320
  as wellbeing achievement indicator 134,
    146–7, 148
income and expenditure research 344
India
  community development 130
  health survey 11
individualism 106, 321
  and autonomy 84–6, 107, 331
  and subjective wellbeing 31
information technology 330
infrastructure, as barrier to improved rural
    livelihoods 193–4
institutional responsibility matrix 120, 130
institutions
  as barrier to improved rural livelihoods 193
  collective 130–1
  and entitlements 120
  improved performance 129–30
  inequality of control over 118
  and livelihood options 179
  see also governance
insurance
  against hazards 124
  market segmentation 205
integration, of self 77
inter-generational transfers 123
internalisation 77
  of cultural values 86
International Labour Organisation 199
  Declaration of Principles and
    Programme of Action for a Basic
    Needs Strategy of Development
    (1976) 9

International Personal Wellbeing Index
    257
International Quality of Life Assessment
    Project Group (IQOLA) 224, 228, 229,
    239
International Society for Quality of Life
    Studies (ISQOLS) 8
Interpretive social science 302
ISOQOL (international health-related QoL
    network) 220
ISQOLS (international quality of life
    network) 219

Japan, autonomy 84
jobs, domains-of-life variable 267, 270,
    276, 279
Journal of Happiness Studies 8
judicial process
  and formal rights 125
  local and informal 127
justice, access to 125, 130

KIDSCREEN study of QoL 234, 235
kinship ties 168
knowledge assumptions 286
  conclusions and findings 290–1, 305
  domain and problematic 286–7, 297–9
  epistemology 288, 301–2
  implications for action and practice 292,
    307
  methodological frameworks 289–90,
    304–5
  normative framework 299–300
  ontology 287–8, 300–1, 310
  relations between elements 292–3
  rhetoric 291–2, 305–7
  theoretical and empirical conclusions
    305
  theories, conceptual frameworks and
    models 289, 303–4
  values, standpoints and normative
    theories 287, 309

labour markets 203
  capitalism and 208
  de-segmentation 129
  dualism 208
  exclusion in 200
  mobility 210
land
  inheritance systems 186
  as livelihood resource 167
land reform, Latin America 207
language
  academic use of 291, 306, 309

back translations 228
and cross-cultural QoL research 222,
    225, 230
forward translation 227, 228
harmonisation of terminology 346
sequential translations 231–2
in social exclusion theory 210
translation of QoL measures 227–8
Latin America
development theory 199
employee rights 126
indigenous movements 211
nature of wellbeing in 39
NGO interventions 38, 39
libertarianism 96
life expectancy, as wellbeing achievement
    indicator 136
life-satisfaction approach (Mexican survey)
    259, 278–80
analysis 268–71
answering scale 266
database 266–8
measurement of subjective wellbeing
    262–4
methodological approach 260–5
relationship regression analysis 269–71
by socio-demographic groups 271–4
subjective wellbeing approach 260–2
variables 266
see also domains-of-life
livelihood frameworks 158
and diversity of household livelihoods
    159
livelihoods 18–22
and agency 22–3, 178–83
asset bases 179, 180
and asset management strategies in the
    Andes 183–92
complexity of 176
in development programmes 24
diversification 188
encuentros and desencuentros in NGO
    interventions 196–8
outcomes (Andes) 188–92
and political capacity 181
strategies in Andes 184–8
time preference behaviour 123–4, 182
urban survival strategies 179
loans
credit relationships 162
high interest 119
long-term 123
micro-credit 126
local, and universal 331–2, 340
Long, Norman 19, 23

MarkData research organisation (Pretoria)
    244
market failures 205–6
markets 9, 20, 120, 292
basic 203
capital 205
effect on economic opportunities 191
and empowerment 101
well-regulated 129
see also labour markets
Marshall, Paule, The Chosen Place, The
    Timeless People 169–74
materialism
as motivation 80
and QoL 253–4
meaning 37–8, 299
and culture and identity 327–32
and power 325
Medical Outcomes Trust (Boston) 231
mental illness 14
mental health needs 64
methodological frameworks 289–90, 304–5
life-satisfaction approach 260–5
for wellbeing research 37, 66–70, 339–44
Mexico (states and Mexico City)
empowerment study 101
quality of life research 41–2
see also life-satisfaction approach
micro-credit 126
migration 129
labour market 203
South Africa 249, 250
to break clientelism 127
Millenium Development Goals (MDGs)
    10, 213
and basic needs 50
modes of needs discourse 53–8
money poverty
and human development 6
and resources and agency 6–7
and subjective wellbeing 7–8
Morocco, market behaviour 20
motivation
intrinsic 77, 78
materialism as 80

natural capital 180
use of 187
needs 74, 177
conceptualisation of 48, 50
dictionary definitions 56–8
and goals 89–90, 317, 318–21
and harms 324–6, 338
hierarchy of 81
meanings of term 52–3

needs (*cont.*)
  modal analysis of 64–6
  modes discourse of 53–8
  as motivational force 54, 56
  normative discourse of 58–9, 348
  physical (biological) 72
  and resources 171
  thwarted 80
  and universal goals 54, 56, 64
  and wellbeing 64–6
    see also human needs; psychological
    needs
needs satisfiers 14–15, 22, 50, 177, 340
needs theory
  dynamics of transformation 68
  explanatory 66
  normative 66, 68
  rise and fall of 49–52
  for wellbeing research 66–7, 69–70
    see also Theory of Human Need (Doyal
    and Gough)
neo-liberalism 9
Nepal, empowerment study 101
'New Social Movements' 292
NGOs (non-governmental organisations)
  and access to resources 192
  agro-centric view of livelihoods 196
  aid chain interventions 177, 178
  aims and perceived aims 189
  audits 125
  encuentros and *desencuentros* in
    interventions 196–8
  interventions and empowerment 189–90
  interventions to create economic
    opportunities 190–2
  research into aid chains in Andes 183–4
  role for in political economic policy
    change 195, 197–8
  targeted assistance 186, 190, 191–2,
    194, 196
non-economic wellbeing achievement
  indicators 136–9
normative needs discourse 58–9
Nottingham Health Profile (NHP) 224, 225,
  228, 230
Nussbaum, Martha 6, 12
nutritional levels, measurement of 98, 103

objective list theories, of wellbeing 60, 63
objective wellbeing 59, **60**, 64, 297
  external validation 264
  and research 317
objective-happiness indicator 264
objectivity, in social sciences 323, 325
ontology 287–8, 300–1, 310, *336*

opportunities
  and freedoms 94–5, 97
  measurement of 97–8
organisation
  tendency towards 73
    see also social organisation
outcomes 340–2

Pakistan
  local philanthropy 125
  Rural Support Programme movement
    130
Parfit, Derek, wellbeing types 60
participation
  in local institutions 112
  participatory research 25, 292
Participatory Numbers Network 26
Participatory Poverty Assessments 290
Participatory Rural Appraisal (PRA) 26
patriarchy 182
Person Generated Index 26
personal domain, domains-of-life variable
  267, 270, 278, 279
personality, as factor in happiness 29
Peru
  inclusion and exclusion 39, 199
  need for rural economic growth 192
Physical Quality of Life Index 47
political capital 202
political economic forces
  as barrier to improved rural livelihoods
    192–3, 197–8
  effect on assets 188
  influence on rural household aspirations
    178, 182
political parties, pro-poor commitments
  130
politicians
  accountability to courts 130
  and policy making 347–8
  in *sigma* model 202
poor people
  problem of security for 116–22
  research approach to 308
population growth, in *sigma* model 209
population levels, Andes 186
Positive Psychology movement 32
positivism 208, 287, 292
post-modernism 286
poverty
  conceptualisation of 286
  definitions of, [relative and absolute] 3
  multidimensional 179
  and resourcefulness 17
  and vulnerability 18

wellbeing in spite of, people not defined
    by 3
  see also money poverty
Poverty Analyses 290
Poverty Reduction Strategy Papers 66
power
  asymmetric 278
  and meanings 325
praxis 292, 307
preference, and choice 61, 95
preference fulfilment 63
priorities 51
  normative 64
process research 343
processes 343–4
  and freedoms 95–6, 97
  measurement of 98–9
  and time 332–4
produced capital 180
Psychological General Wellbeing Index 224
psychological needs 71, 325
  autonomy as 84–8
  and cultural stability 91–2
  as innate 34, 78–9
  multiple 80–1
  Murray's definition 74
  research on 82–90
  and Self-Determination Theory 72–4,
    74–5
  social contexts of 76–8, 91
  as universal 79, 82–3
  see also human needs
psychology
  innate needs 34
  and quality of life assessment 28–9
  and resilience 334
psychometric testing, in health-related QoL
    229, 239
public goods, to insure against hazard 124
Purchasing Power Parity (PPP) GDP per
    capita, as measure of wellbeing 135,
    136

Q-squared (Qual-Quant) approach 284
quality of life (QoL) 7–8, 246, 318–21,
    341–2
  concept of 219–20, 237–8, 317
  measures 238–9
  objective indicators 220, 246
  psychological measurement of 28–9
  and public policy intervention 246
  subjective indicators 25–33, 220, 247
  see also health-related quality of life
quality of life (QoL) research 47
  components 223

cross-cultural issues 220–3
  and Resource Profiles Framework 320
  and Theory of Human Need 319–20

racisms 182, 208
Rapid Rural Appraisal (RRA) 25
reciprocal exchange 127
relatedness
  as basic need 76, 82, 91, 325
  in self-determination theory 211, 299,
    323
relationships
  autonomy in 88–9
  of credit 162
  and quality of life 254
  and resources 199–201, 323
  and wellbeing 322, 338
relativism 287
relief assistance 52
Resource Profiles Framework (RPF) 7, 19,
    160, 318, 334
  and Bangladesh 20–1
  and quality of life (QoL) research 320
  role of social and cultural resources 24,
    162, 167
resources 17–24, 199, 297, 317, 318–21
  access to 178, 182–3
  and agency in livelihood frameworks
    160–3
  classification of 163–6, 340
  and consequences 212
  deployment of 157–8, 292
  indeterminacy of definition 166–8
  and meaning 37–8
  new (human organs) 164
  objective existence of 164
  reification of 161, 162, 164, 174
  social and cultural 6–7, 20, 21, 165
  structural constraints on access to
    192–5
  symbolic 168
  use of 162
  see also assets; social resources
Resources and Needs Questionnaire
    (RANQ) 340–1, 344
revealed-preference theory 264
rhetoric 291–2, 305–7, 310
rights
  and development policy 213
  economic 326
  formalisation of 125
  human 52, 200
  and security 110
  universal 207
  and universalist social protection 111

risk
 co-variant 116
 enlargement of pool of 128–9
 use of term 53
  see also hazards; shocks
risk aversion, and dependent security 119
'risk averters' 109, 120
Romania, QoL research 235
Rosen, Laurence 20
rural households
 aspirations 177, 178, 187
 livelihood approaches 178
 resource accessing strategies 178
 structural barriers to improvement
  192–3, 193–4, 197–8
  see also livelihoods
Russia
 compared with South Africa 256
 life goals 89
 study of autonomy in 84–6
Ryan, Richard 35

satisfaction
 and happiness 245
  see also life-satisfaction approach
savings, non-local circulation of 128
*Schedule for the Evaluation of Individual
 Quality of Life* (SEIQOL) 225
school enrolments, as standard indicator
 of wellbeing 136
Scott, James C. 23
security 109–10
 autonomous 110, 113, 118, 121
 dependent 36, 110, 113, 118
 and fear 114
 importance of 36
 individual and societal 110–13
 informal regimes 125
 principles of improvement 122–31
 problem for poor people 116–22, 131–2
 and regime type **114**
 and wellbeing 114–15
security improvement, principles of 122–31
 alteration of time preference behaviour
  123–4
 de-clientelisation 125–7
 enlargement of risk pool 128–9
 formalising rights 125
 indicators 122–3
 institutional performance 129–30
 preparation for hazards 124
 well-functioning collective institutions
  130–1
Self-Determination Theory (SDT) 71,
 90–1, 299

and cultural values 328
 implications of 78–81
 and learned helplessness 325
 and measurement of autonomy 105–8
 and psychological needs 72–4, 74–5,
  325
 and relatedness 211, 323
 research projects 82–90
 view of autonomy 83, 91, 211, 325
self-efficacy 104–5
self-reflexivity 285
Sen, Amartya 5, 6, 10, 246
 and capabilities 35, 63, 93, 104
 and concept of entitlement 6, 17
 and concept of functionings 6, 10, 11,
  12, 24
 Development as Freedom 93
 role of freedom 94–6
 and wellbeing indicators 135
service providers 129
SF-36 Health Survey 225, 228, 229, 231
shocks, vulnerability to 117, 334
Sickness Impact Profile (SIP) 224
sigma society model of economic
 development 39, 200, *201*
 capitalists **202**
 critique of 200, 208–12
 description of 202–8
 and labour market dualism 208
 politicians 202
 relevance to development policy
  212–15
 y-workers 201, 203
 z-workers 201, 203
skills base, extension of 128
social anthropology 302
social capital 19, 23, 180
 and access to education 190
 and community organisations 189
 of households 168
 and social resources 120–1, 129
social contexts
 and autonomy 331–2
 of basic needs 76–8, 91
 and wellbeing 329
social development, and economic
 development 209
social exclusion
 black Africans in South Africa 244
 and coercive inclusion 210
 and complexity of actions 211
 and elites 210
 and nature of wellbeing 211
 and political action 211
 and social identity 210

social exclusion theory 199, 209
  reflexive role of development agencies
    213–15
  see also *sigma society* model
social human being
  centrality of 321–4, *336*
  as generator of meaning 328
social inclusion, coercive 210
Social Indicators movement 219
social insurance, access to 124, 125
social organisation
  and cultural needs 329
  structures 342–3
social practice 158, 172
  wellbeing as 175
social relationships 165, 199
  and population growth 209
social resources 120–1, 167–8
  and culture 167
social science
  interpretive 302
  and whole person 323
socialisation, importance of 75, 78, 90
society, and empowerment 101
South Africa 242
  challenges for 258
  collectivist society 245, 254
  emergent black middle class 255
  first open elections 248, 252
  quality of life research 40–1
  and 'rainbow nation' expectations 253, 254
  Reconstruction and Development
    Programme 249, 253
  sporting achievements 255
  under apartheid 243, 256
    see also South African Quality of Life
    Trends Project
South African Quality of Life Trends
  Project 242, 298
  aspirations and expectations 249
  black sector happiness deficit 252
  case studies 249–50
  cultural bias 251–3
  development of concepts and models
    243–7
  emphasis on individual 245
  flaws in 245, 257
  future agenda for 257–8
  global indicators 244, 247, 252–3
  habituation 254, 257
  housing 243
  identification of concepts 243
  intergenerational studies 250, 251, 254
  international comparisons 256–7
  MarkData research organisation 244

  material aspects of QoL 253–4
  migrant workers/return migrants 249, 250
  personalised survey issues 244
  and public policy intervention 246
  relations aspects of QoL 254
  reporting format 246
  research decisions 244–6
  satisfaction levels 245, 248
  symbolic dimension of QoL 254–5
  technical inconsistencies 250–1
  trends 247–9
South America see Andes; Latin America;
  Mexico
South Asia
  clientelism 126
  role of dowry in 21
Soviet Union, former, comparison with
  South Africa 256
state 120
  and empowerment 101
  as guarantor of basic needs 111
  influence on livelihoods 182
  and market failures 205–6
  regime type and security **113**
  and *sigma* model 205–8
  stakeholder analysis of economic
    exclusion 204, **205**
  welfare regimes 342–3
state budgets
  media 'pro-poor' critique of 129
  shift in priorities 130
static equilibrium, in *sigma* model 202, 203
Statistics South Africa 246
  and European comparisons 257
  household surveys 254
Stern, Nick 49
structure 342–3
  and agency 301
Sub-Saharan Africa 10
subjective wellbeing 25–33, 60, 77–8,
  158–9, 259
  extrinsic and intrinsic goals 89–90
  and happiness 323
  homeostatic theory of 30
  and money poverty 7–8
  research 48, 317
  and social comparison 31
subjective wellbeing approach 260–2, 297,
  299, 320
  characteristics 260, 280
  inferential approach 261
  inherent subjectiveness of 261
  measurement 262–4
  person as best authority 261
  transdisciplinary approach 262, 280

subjectivity
  agency and 172
  and contingency 168–74
  and human security 112
suffering 308
survival 308
sustainability 9
Sustainable Livelihoods Framework 160,
    166
  'asset pentagon' 161
Sustainable Rural Livelihoods framework 19

Theories 289, 304
Theorising 289, 303
Theory of Human Need (Doyal and
    Gough) 13–16, 22, 66–7, 318, 340
  and harms 324
  and psychological needs 325
  and QoL/SWB approach 319–20
  and relationships 322
time
  and process 332–4
  and rhythms 333
time preference behaviour 123–4, 182

uncertainty, and security 116
United Kingdom, Department for
    International Development (DfID) 24
United Nations
  Millennium Declaration 4, 10
  Summit on Social Development,
    Copenhagen (1995) 10
United Nations Development Programme
    (UNDP)
  Human Development Report office 52,
    135, 136
  Human Development school 48
  see also Human Development Index
    (HDI)
United States
  Declaration of Independence 350
  life goals 89
  needs satisfaction 87
  study of autonomy in 84–6
universal, and local 331–2, 340
urban poor, co-variant risk 117
utilitarianism 96
utility, and commodities 11

violence, structural 326
vulnerability, and poverty 18

wages 127
water supplies, Andes 194

wealth gap, South Africa 257
welfare
  GDP as measurement of 9
  options for personal 111
  origins of term 4
  regimes 342–3
wellbeing 33–7
  complexity of 280
  in concept of international development 3
  concepts of 4–5, 59–66, 71, 297, 317
  conceptualisation of 48
  cultural construction of 298
  and culture 319
  dynamic distributions of 298
  links between utility and commodity 11
  measurement and methodology 37,
    66–70
  and mental capacity 11
  and need fulfilment 68–9
  and needs 64–6
  outcomes 332
  and physical capacity 11
  plurality of 5
  and policy making 346–7, 347–8
  as research focus 47, 69–70
  research frameworks 42, 66–70
  and security 114–15
  seven concepts of 61–4
  and social context 329
  and social exclusion theory 211
  types 60
  use of term 34, 69
    see also subjective wellbeing; wellbeing
    research
wellbeing achievement indicators
  correlates with μ_1 140–6
  correlation coefficients 137, 138, 139
  hypothesis testing issues 150–3
  inter-country variations 134, 139, 140
  multidimensional 133
  non-economic 136–9
  non-standard variables 141, 142, 143
  null hypothesis 141, 142–6
  Pearson (zero-order) coefficients 136,
    140, 141
  Spearman (rank-order) coefficients 136,
    137, 141
  technical analysis 137, 138, 141,
    148–50
Wellbeing in Developing Countries (WeD)
  ESRC Research Group 8, 49, 284
  formal objective 316
  methodology 339–40
  outcomes 340–2
  processes 343–4

Wellbeing in Developing Countries (WeD)
    (*cont.*)
  and QoL studies 220
  structures 342–3
    see also cross-disciplinary research;
    development research; knowledge
    assumptions; Theory of Human Need
wellbeing research
  centrality of social human being 321–4
  challenges for 344–50
  conceptual framework for 336–9
  cultural analysis and 328, 349
  harms and needs 324–6
  key ideas 321–36
  meaning, culture and identity 327–32
  methodology for 339–44
  resourcefulness, resilience and
    adaptation 334–6
  time and processes 332–4
women
  empowerment 100, 101–2
  empowerment study in Ethiopia 101–2
World Bank
  Comprehensive Development
    Framework 213
  Integrated Questionnaire for the
    Measurement of Social Capital 102
  Living Standard Measurement Survey 102

political theory research model 307
Social Development Division 132
'Voices of the Poor' exercises 347
work on basic needs (1978) 9
World Development Report (2000/
    2001) 94
  see also Asset Vulnerability
    Framework
World Health Organisation (WHO)
    221
World Health Organisation (WHO)
    Quality of Life Group (WHOQOL)
    27, 40, 224, 225
  conceptual equivalence 231
  cross-cultural validation 233, 239
  instrument development 233–4
  psychometric testing 229
  and Theory of Human Need 319
  translations 228
  WHOQOL-Old study 233, 234, 235

y-workers (skilled) 201, 203
  and economic growth 206
youth literacy 147

z-workers (unskilled) 201, 203
  weak political resources 205